THE HARMONY
OF THE DIVINE ATTRIBUTES

WILLIAM BATES

SOLID GROUND CHRISTIAN BOOKS
BIRMINGHAM, ALABAMA USA

OTHER PURITAN TITLES
FROM SOLID GROUND CHRISTIAN BOOKS

In addition to *the Harmony of the Divine Attributes* by Bates, Solid Ground is delighted to offer the following Puritan titles:

A Body of Divinity by Archbishop James Ussher

The Christian Warfare by John Downame

Commentary on the Epistle to the Hebrews by William Gouge

Commentary on the New Testament by John Trapp

Commentary on the Second Epistle of Peter by Thomas Adams

Exposition of the Epistle of Jude by Thomas Jenkyn

Exposition of the Ten Commandments by Ezekiel Hopkins

*Gospel Sonnets by Ralph Erskine

Heaven Upon Earth by James Janeway

Marrow of True Justification by Benjamin Keach

**Practical Atheism* by Stephen Charnock

Redeemer's Tears Wept Over Lost Souls by John Howe

Scriptural Exposition of the Baptist Catechism by Benjamin Beddome

Short Explanation of the Epistle to the Hebrews by David Dickson

Travels of True Godliness by Benjamin Keach

Works of Thomas Manton (in 22 volumes)

*pre-publication titles as of January 2010

THE HARMONY

OF

THE DIVINE ATTRIBUTES

IN THE

CONTRIVANCE AND ACCOMPLISHMENT

OF

MAN'S REDEMPTION.

BY WILLIAM BATES, D. D.

PHILADELPHIA:
PRESBYTERIAN BOARD OF PUBLICATION.

Solid Ground Christian Books
715 Oak Grove Road
Homewood, Alabama 35209
205-443-0311
sgcb@charter.net
www.solid-ground-books.com

The Harmony of the Divine Attributes
in the Contrivance and Accomplishment of Man's Redemption
William Bates (1625-1699)

Taken from the 1853 edition by The Presbyterian Board of Publication, Philadelphia, PA

First Solid Ground edition in January 2010

Cover photo by Ric Ergenbright and used with permission.

Cover image and design by Borgo Design of Tuscaloosa, AL.
Contact them at borgogirl@bellsouth.net

ISBN: 978-159925-241-4

CONTENTS.

CHAP. I.—*The Introduction.*—A short view of man's primitive state. His conformity to God; natural, moral, and in happiness and dominion over the creatures. The moral resemblance, as it refers to all the faculties. The happiness of man, with respect to his sensitive and spiritual nature. Of all sublunary creatures he alone is capable of a law. What the law of nature contains. God entered into a covenant with man. The reasons of that dispensation. The terms of the covenant were becoming God and man. The special clause in the covenant concerning the tree of knowledge of good and evil. The reasons of the prohibition. - - - - - - - - - - 17

CHAP. II.—*The Fall of Man.*—Man's natural state was mutable. The devil, moved by hatred and envy, attempts to seduce him. The temptation was suitable to man's compounded nature. The woman being deceived, persuades her husband. I. The quality of the first sin; many were combined in it. II. It was perfectly voluntary. Man had power to stand. The devil could only allure, not compel him. His understanding and will the causes of his fall. III. The punishment was of the same date with his sin. He forfeited his righteousness and felicity. The loss of original righteousness, as it signifies the purity and liberty of the soul. The torment of conscience that was consequent to sin. A whole army of evils enters with it into the world. - - 32

CHAP. III.—*The Corruption of Human Nature.*—I. All mankind is involved in Adam's guilt, and is under the penal consequences that follow upon it. Adam, the natural and moral principle of mankind. An hereditary corruption is transmitted to all that are propagated from him. The account the scripture gives of the conveyance of it. It is an innate habit. It is universal. Corrupt nature contains the seeds of all sins, though they do not shoot forth together. It is voluntary and culpable. II. The permission of the fall is suitable to the wisdom, holiness, and goodness of God. The imputation of Adam's sin to his posterity is consistent with God's justice. - - - - - - 43

CHAP. IV.—*The Moral Impotence of Man.*—The impossibility of man's recovery by his natural power. I. Man cannot regain his primitive holiness. The understanding and will, the superior faculties, are depraved. The mind is ignorant and insensible of our corruption. The will is more depraved than the mind; it embraces only sensual good; carnal objects are wounding to the conscience and unsatisfying to the affections; yet the will eagerly pursues them. The moral impotence, that ariseth from a perverse disposition of the will, is culpable. Neither the beauty nor the reward of holiness can prevail upon the unrenewed will. II. Guilty man cannot recover the favour of God. He is unable to make satisfaction to justice. He is incapable of real repentance, which might qualify him for pardon, - - - - 53

CHAP. V.—*The Wisdom of God in Redemption.*—Of the divine wisdom in the contrivance of man's redemption. Understanding agents propound an end, and choose means for the obtaining of it. I. The end of God is of the highest consequence, his own glory and man's recovery. The difficulty of accomplishing it. II. The means are proportionable. The divine wisdom glorified in taking occasion from the sin and fall of man to bring glory to God, and to raise man to a more excellent state. It appears in ordaining such a Mediator, as was fit to reconcile God to man, and man to God. It is discovered in the designation of the second person to be our Saviour; and making the remedy to have a proportion to the cause of our ruin. It is visible in the manner whereby our redemption is accomplished; and in the ordaining of such contemptible means to produce such glorious effects; and laying the design of the gospel, so as to provide for the comfort and promote the holiness of man. - - - 72

CHAP. VI.—*Practical Inferences.*—I. A superlative degree of praise and thankfulness due to God for the revelation of the gospel. It is not discovered by the creation; it is above the reach of natural reason; the heathen world is entirely ignorant of it. It is pure grace that distinguishes one nation from another, in sending the gospel. II. Evangelical knowledge deserves our most serious study. The gospel exceeds all contemplative and practical sciences; contemplative, in the greatness of its object, and the certainty of its principle; practical, in the excellency of its end, and the efficacy of the means. - - - - - 95

CHAP. VII.—*The Causes and Unreasonableness of Unbelief.*—The simple speculation of the gospel not sufficient without a real belief, and cordial acceptance. I. The reasons why the Jews and Gentiles conspired in the contempt of it. II. How just it is to resign up the understanding to revelation. God knows his own nature and will, and cannot deceive us. We must believe the things that are clearly revealed, though we do not understand the manner of their existence; although they are attended with seeming contradictions. No article of faith is really repugnant to reason. We must distinguish between things incomprehensible and inconceivable, between corrupt and right reason. How reason is subservient to faith. Humility and holiness qualify for the belief of the gospel-mysteries. A naked belief of supernatural truths is unprofitable for salvation. An effectual assent that prevails upon the will and renders the whole man obsequious, is due to the quality of the gospel-revelation. - - 110

CHAP. VIII.—*The Freeness of the Divine Mercy in Redemption.*—The mercy of God is represented with peculiar advantages above the other attributes. It is eminently glorified in our redemption, in respect of its freenesss and greatness. The freeness of it amplified from the consideration, I. of the original, and, II. of the object of it. God is perfectly happy in himself, and needs not the creature to preserve or heighten his felicity. The glorious reward conferred upon our Saviour doth not prejudice the freeness of his love to man. There was no tie upon God to save man. The object of mercy is man in his lapsed state. It is illustrated by the consideration of what he is in himself. No motives of love are in him; he is a rebel impotent and obstinate. The freeness of mercy set forth by comparing him with the fallen angels who are left in perfect, irremediable misery. Their first state, fall, and punishment. The reasons why the wisdom of God made no provisions for their recovery. - - - 124

CHAP. IX.—*The Greatness of the Divine Mercy in Redemption.*— The greatness of redeeming love discovered by considering, I. The evils from which we are freed—the servitude of sin, the tyranny of Satan, the bondage of the law, the empire of death. The measure of love is proportionable to the degrees of our misery. No possible remedy for us in nature. Our deliverance is complete. II. The divine love is magnified in the means by which our redemption is accomplished; they are the incarnation and sufferings of the Son of God. Love is manifested in the incarnation, upon account of the essential condition of the nature assumed, and its servile state: Christ took our nature after it had lost its innocency. The most evident proof of God's love is in the sufferings of Christ. The description of them with respect to his soul and body. The sufferings of his soul set forth from the causes of his grief, the disposition of Christ, and the design of God in afflicting him. The sorrows of his forsaken state: all comforting influences were suspended, but without prejudice to the personal union, or the perfection of his grace, or the love of his Father towards him. The death of the cross considered, with respect to the ignominy and torment that concurred in it. The love of the Father and of Christ amplified upon the account of his enduring it. - - - - - 135

CHAP. X.—*Divine Mercy is Magnified in the Excellency of the State to which Man is advanced.* He is enriched with higher prerogatives, under a better covenant, entitled to a more glorious reward than Adam at first enjoyed. The human nature is personally united to the Son of God. Believers are spiritually united to Christ. The gospel is a better covenant than that of the law. It admits of repentance and reconciliation after sin. It accepts of sincerity instead of perfection. It affords supernatural assistance to believers, whereby they shall be victorious over all opposition in their way to heaven. The difference between the grace of the Creator and that of the Redeemer. The stability of the New-Covenant is built on the love of God which is unchangeable, and the operations of his Spirit that are effectual. The mutability and weakness of the human will, and the strength of temptations, shall not frustrate the merciful design of God in regard of his elect. The glorious reward of the gospel exceeds the primitive felicity of Adam, in the place of it, the highest heaven. Adam's life was attended with innocent infirmities, from which the glorified life is entirely exempt. The felicity of heaven exceeds the first, in the manner, degrees, and continuance of the fruition. - - - - - - 155

CHAP. XI.—*Practical Inferences.*—I. Redeeming love deserves our highest admiration and humble acknowledgments. The illustration of it by several considerations. God is infinitely amiable in himself, yet his love is transient to the creature. It is admirable in creating and preserving man, more in redeeming him and that by the death of his Son. II. The discovery of God's love in our redemption is the strongest persuasive to repentance. The law is ineffectual to produce real repentance. The common benefits of providence are insufficient to cause faith and repentance in the guilty creature. The clear discovery of pardoning mercy in the gospel alone can remove our fears, and induce us to return to God. III. The transcendent love of God should kindle in us a reciprocal love to him. His excellencies and ordinary bounty to mankind cannot prevail upon us to love him: his love to us in Christ alone conquers our hatred. Our love to him must be sincere and superlative. IV. The despising of saving mercy is the highest provocation: it makes the condemnation of men most just, certain, and heavy. - - - - - - 171

CHAP. XII.—*The Justice of God in Redemption.*—Divine justice concurs with mercy in the work of our redemption. I. The reasons why we are redeemed by the satisfaction of justice are specified; to declare God's hatred of sin, to vindicate the honour of the law, to prevent the secure commission of sin. These ends are obtained in the death of Christ. II. The reality of the satisfaction made to divine justice considered. The requisites in order to it. The appointment of God, who in this transaction is to be considered not as a judge, that is minister of the law, but as governor. His right of jurisdiction to relax the law as to the execution of it. His will declared to accept of the compensation made. The consent of our Redeemer was necessary. He must be perfectly holy. He must be God and man. - 183

CHAP. XIII.—*The Justice of God in Redemption.*—Divine justice is declared and glorified in the death of Christ. The threefold account the scripture gives of it, as a punishment inflicted for sin, as a price to redeem us from hell, as a sacrifice to reconcile us to God. Man was capitally guilty; Christ, with the allowance of God, interposes as his surety. His death was inflicted on him by the supreme Judge; the impulsive cause of it was sin. His sufferings were equivalent to the sentence of the law; the effect of them is our freedom. An answer to the objection, that it is a violation of justice to transfer the punishment from the guilty to the innocent. The death of Christ is the price that redeems from hell. This singular effect of his death distinguishes it from the death of the martyrs. An answer to the objections— how could God receive this price, since he gave his Son to that death which redeems us? and how our Redeemer, supposing him God, can make satisfaction to himself? The death of Christ represented as a sacrifice. The expiatory sacrifices under the law were substituted in the place of guilty men. The effects of them answerable to their threefold respect to God, sin and men; the atonement of anger, the expiation of sin, and freedom from punishment. All sorts of placatory sacrifices are referred to Christ, and the effects of them in a sublime and perfect manner. No prejudice to the freeness and greatness of God's love, that Christ by his death reconciled him to men. - - - 195

CHAP. XIV.—*The Justice of God in Redemption.*—III. The completeness of Christ's satisfaction proved from the causes and effects of it. The causes are the quality of his person and degrees of his sufferings. The effects are his resurrection, ascension, intercession at God's right hand, and his exercising the supreme power in heaven and earth. The excellent benefits which God reconciled bestows on men, are the effects and evidences of his complete satisfaction. They are pardon of sin, grace, and glory. That repentance and faith are required in order to the partaking of the benefits purchased by Christ's death, doth not lessen the merit of his sufferings; that afflictions and death are inflicted on believers doth not derogate from their all-sufficiency. - - - - - - - - 214

CHAP. XV.—*Practical Inferences.*—I. In the death of Christ there is the clearest discovery of the evil of sin. II. The strictness of divine justice is most visible in it. III. The consideration of the ends of Christ's death takes off the scandal of the cross, and changes the offence into admiration. IV. The satisfaction of justice by Christ's sufferings affords the strongest assurance that God is ready to pardon sinners. V. The absolute necessity of complying with the terms of the gospel for justification. There are but two ways of appearing before the supreme Judge; either in innocence, or by the righteousness of Christ. The causes why men reject Christ are, a legal temper that is natural to them, and the predominant love of sin. The unavoidable misery of all that will not submit to our Saviour. - - 235

CHAP. XVI.—*The Holiness of God in Redemption.*—Of all the divine perfections, holiness is peculiarly admirable. The honour of it is secured in our redemption. I. In the bitter sufferings of Christ, God declared himself unappeasable to sin, though appeasable to sinners. II. The privileges purchased by Christ, are conveyed upon terms honourable to holiness. Pardon of sin, adoption, the inheritance of glory, are annexed to special qualifications in those who receive them. III. The Redeemer is made a quickening principle to inspire us with new life. In order to our sanctification, he hath given us the most perfect rule of holiness, he exhibited a complete pattern of it, he purchased and conveys the Spirit of holiness to us, he presents the strongest motives to persuade us to be holy. The perfect laws of Christ are considered, as they enjoin an absolute separation from all evil, and command the practice of all substantial goodness. Some particular precepts, which the gospel especially enforces, with the reasons of them, are considered. - - 249

CHAP. XVII.—*The Perfection of the Laws of Christ.*—The perfection of Christ's laws appears by comparing them with the precepts of Moses. The temple service was managed with pomp suitable to the disposition of the Jews, and the dispensation of the law; the Christian service is pure and spiritual; the Levitical ceremonies and ornaments are excluded from it, not only as unnecessary, but inconsistent with its spirituality. The obligation to the rituals of Moses is abolished, to introduce real righteousness. The indulgences of polygamy and divorce is taken away by Christ, and marriage restored to its primitive purity. He cleared the law from the darkening glosses of the Pharisees, and enforced it by new obligations. The law of Christ exceeds the rules which the highest masters of morality in the school of nature ever prescribed. Philosophy is defective as to piety, and in several things contrary to it. Philosophers delivered unworthy conceptions of God. Philosophy doth not enjoin the love of God, which is the first and great command of the natural law. Philosophers lay down the servile maxim, to comply with the common idolatry. They arrogated to themselves the praise of their virtue and happiness. Philosophy doth not propound the glory of God for the supreme end of all human actions. Philosophy is defective as to the duties respecting ourselves and others. It allows the first sinful motions of the lower appetites. The Stoics renounce the passions. Philosophy insufficient to form the soul to patience and content under afflictions, and to support in the hour of death. A reflection upon some immoral maxims of the several sects of philosophers. - - - - - 266

CHAP. XVIII.—*The Example of Christ and the Gift of the Holy Spirit.*—Examples have a special efficacy above precepts to form us to holiness. The example of Christ is most proper to that end, being absolutely perfect, and accommodated to our present state. Some virtues are necessary to our condition as creatures, or to our condition in the world, of which the Deity is incapable; and these eminently appear in the life of Christ; they are humility, obedience, and love in suffering for us. His life contains all our duties, or motives to perform them. Jesus Christ purchased the Spirit of holiness by his sufferings, and confers it since his exaltation. The sanctifying Spirit is the concomitant of evangelical mercy. The supernatural declarations of the law on mount Sinai, and the natural discovery of the divine goodness in the works of creation and providence, were not accompanied with the renewing efficacy of the Spirit. The lower operations of the Spirit alone were in the heathens. The philosophical change differs from the spiritual and divine. Socrates and Seneca considered. Our Saviour presents the strongest inducements to persuade us to be holy. They are proper to work upon fear, hope, and love. The greatness of those objects, and their truth, are clearly manifest in the gospel. - - - - 287

CHAP. XIX.—*Practical Inferences.*—I. The completeness of our recovery by Jesus Christ; he frees us from the power as well as guilt of sin. Sin is the disease and wound of the soul; the mere pardon of it cannot make us happy. Sanctification equals, if not excels, justification; it qualifies us for the enjoyment of God. II. Saving grace doth not encourage the practice of sin. The promises of pardon and heaven are conditional. To abuse the mercy of the gospel is dishonourable to God and pernicious to man. III. The excellency of the Christian religion discovered from its design and effect. The design is to purge men from sin, and conform them to God's holiness according to their capacity; this gives it the most visible pre-eminence above other religions. The admirable effect of the gospel in the primitive

Christians. An earnest exhortation to live according to the purity of the gospel, and the great obligations our Saviour hath laid on us. - - - - - - - - 313

CHAP. XX.—*The Power of God in Redemption.*—The divine power is admirably glorified in the creation of the world, in respect of the greatness of the effect and the manner of its production. It is as evident in our redemption. The principal effects of it are considered. I. The incarnation of the Son of God is a work fully responsible to omnipotence. II. Our Redeemer's supernatural conception by the Holy Ghost. III. The divine power was eminently declared in the miracles Jesus Christ wrought in the course of his ministry. His miracles were the evidence of his celestial calling; they were necessary for the conviction of the world: their nature considered. IV. The divine power was glorified in making the death of Christ victorious over all our spiritual enemies. V. The resurrection of Christ the effect of glorious power. The reasons of it from the quality of his person, and the nature of his office, that he might dispense the blessings he had purchased for believers. His resurrection is the foundation of faith. It hath a threefold reference, to his person as the Son of God, to his death as an all-sufficient sacrifice, to his promise of raising believers at the last-day. - - 327

CHAP. XXI.—*The Power of God in Redemption.*—VI. The divine power was glorified in the conversion of the world to Christianity. Notwithstanding the imaginary infirmity in Christ crucified, yet to the called he was the power of God. The numerous and great difficulties that obstructed the receiving of the gospel. What the state of the world was at the first preaching it. Ignorance was universal, idolatry and the depravation of manners, were the consequences of it. Idolatry was fortified by custom, antiquity, and external pomp. The depravation of manners was extreme. The principal account of it from their disbelieving a future state, and their attributing to their gods those passions and vices that were pleasing to the flesh. The aversion of the vulgar heathens was strengthened by those in veneration among them. The philosophers, priests, and princes, vehemently opposed the gospel; an account of their enmity against it. The consideration of the means by which the gospel was conveyed, discovers that omnipotency alone made it successful. The persons employed were a few fishermen, without authority and power to force men to obedience, and without art or eloquence to insinuate the belief of their doctrine. The great, sudden, and lasting change in the world, by the preaching of the gospel, is a certain argument of the divine power that animated those weak appearances. Idolatry was abolished. A miraculous change followed in the lives of men. Christians gave a divorce to all the sinful delights of sense; and embraced, for the honour of Christ, those things that nature most abhors. A short view of the sufferings and courage of the martyrs; Their patience was inspired from heaven. Christianity was victorious over all opposition. VII. The divine power will be gloriously manifested in the complete salvation of the church at the last day. Our

Saviour shall then finish his mediatory office. Death, the last enemy, shall be destroyed. The bodies of the saints shall be raised and conformed to the glorious body of Christ. - - 339

CHAP. XXII.—*Practical Inference.*—The extraordinary working of the divine power is a convincing proof of the verity of the Christian religion. The internal excellencies of it are clear marks of its divinity, to the purified mind. The external operations of God's power were requisite to convince men in their corrupt state, that the doctrine of the gospel came from God. The miraculous owning of Christ by the whole Divinity from heaven. The resurrection of Christ the most important article of the gospel, and the demonstration of all the rest. How valuable the testimony of the apostles is concerning it; that it was impossible they should deceive or be deceived. The quality of the witnesses considered. There cannot be the least reasonable suspicion of them. It is utterly incredible, that any human, temporal respects moved them to feign the resurrection of Christ. The nature of the testimony considered. It was of a matter of fact, and verified to all their senses. The uniformity of it assures us there was no corruption in the witnesses, and that it was no illusion. They sealed the truth of it with their blood. The miracles the apostles did in the name of Christ, a strong demonstration that he was raised to a glorious life. That power was continued in the church for a time. The conclusion, how reasonable it is to give an entire assent to the truth of Christianity It is desperate infidelity not to believe it; and the highest madness to pretend to believe it; and to live in disobedience to it. 365

CHAP. XXIII.—*The Truth of God in Redemption.*—The honour of God's truth, with respect to the legal threatening, was preserved in the death of Christ. The divine truth, with respect to the promises and types of Christ under the law, was justified in his coming and the accomplishment of our redemption by him. I. Some special predictions considered, that respect the time of his coming. The particular circumstances that represent the Messiah, are verified in Jesus Christ. The consequences of the Messiah's coming, foretold by the prophets, are all come to pass. II. The types of the law are complete in Christ. A particular consideration of the manna, the rock, and the brazen serpent, as they referred to him. The paschal lamb considered. A short parallel between Melchizedec and Christ. The divinity of the gospel proved, by comparing the ancient figures with the present truth, and predictions with the events. The happiness of Christians above the Jews, in a clear revelation of our Saviour to them. From the accomplishment of prophecies concerning the first coming of Christ, our faith should be confirmed in the promise of his second. - - - - - - 376

Introduction

William Bates (1625–1699)

Joel R. Beeke

William Bates was one of the most popular and esteemed preachers among the Nonconformists; a master of the Puritan plain style of preaching, his stress on piety earned him the name "silver-tongued." Born in November 1625, he was the son of William Bates, gentleman of St. Mary Magdalene parish, Bermondsey, Surrey. He graduated from Queen's College with a Bachelor of Arts degree in 1645 and a Master of Arts degree in 1648. The following year he became vicar of Tottenham, Middlesex, and a few years later succeeded William Strong as vicar of St. Dunstan-in-the West. Like other Puritans, Bates often lectured at the famous morning exercises at Cripplegate Church.

According to Richard Baxter, Bates played a major role in negotiating for the restoration of Charles II. As a reward, he was appointed royal chaplain in 1660. That same year he was appointed as a commissioner for the approbation of ministers by the Rump Parliament and was given a doctorate in divinity from Cambridge University by royal mandate. The following year he represented the Presbyterians as a commissioner at the Savoy Conference, of which one purpose was to review public liturgy. That included pointing out weaknesses in the *Book of Common Prayer*.

Bates's first wife died young, as did his first daughter. At age thirty-six, he married Margaret, 21-year-old daughter of Edward Gravenor, gentleman of St. Giles Cripplegate. She outlived him by a generation.

In 1662, Bates was one of 2,000 ministers ejected by the Act of Uniformity. Yet he did not take offense. In his farewell sermon to the St. Dunstan's church, he made no mention of the coming ejections, other than to say rather mildly in his conclusion that his Nonconformity was motivated only by his fear of offending God. He then added, "If it be my unhappiness to be in an error, surely men will have no reason to be angry with me in this world, and I hope God will pardon me in the next" (*Oxford DNB*, 4:327).

Bates labored for the next ten years in a variety of ways, often with men like Thomas Manton, Edmund Calamy, Richard Baxter, for the inclusion of Nonconformists within the Anglican church and for toleration of other churches. On two occasions, he addressed William III and Mary on behalf of his fellow Nonconformists. All of these efforts remained largely fruitless, however, for Charles never fulfilled his promises to work toward nonconformist inclusion.

After his ejection, Bates often preached in the vicinity of St. Dunstan's, most commonly at the house of the countess of Exeter and in a room over Temple Bar Gate, beside his old church. From 1669 onward he apparently served as one of the lecturers at a dissenting congregation at Hackney. In 1672, he was licensed as a Presbyterian teacher and was appointed to lecture at Pinner's Hall (later called the Ancient Merchants lecture). When Daniel

Williams was expelled from this lectureship in 1694, Bates surrendered his lectureship as well and founded the Salters Hall lecture, where he drew large crowds.

Throughout the last decades of his life, Bates had several brushes with the authorities, including at least three fines for holding conventicles, notwithstanding his irenical character, mild manner of preaching, growing reputation as a respectable scholar, and friendships with leading Anglican authorities, such as Archbishop Tillotson. Bates remained a leading Puritan until the end of his life, often being invited to preach at the funerals of close Puritan friends, including Richard Baxter, Thomas Manton, Thomas Jacomb, and David Clarkson.

Bates died in Hackney on July 21, 1699. His funeral sermon, preached by John Howe, a close friend of more than forty years, was a rich testimony to his godly life and diligent study. His excellent library, purchased by Daniel Williams, helped establish the Dr. Williams's Library, now situated at Gordon Square, London.

Bates's writings were first collected in a 1700 folio edition; in 1815, they were printed in four volumes as *The Complete Works of William Bates*. Sprinkle Publications reprinted them in 1990.

All of Bates's writings convey good scholarship, wide reading, and careful writing. John Howe called Bates a "devourer of books," and one who yearned to study about God and set forth His love and mercy: "Into what transports of admiration and love of God, have I seen him break forth," Howe said (*Works of Bates*, 1:xviii). That comes to the fore in Bates's most frequently reprinted book, *The Harmony of the Attributes of God* (1674). His chapters on the mercy of God are some of the finest ever written on this precious subject. Here are four practical inferences Bates draws from reveling in the infinity of divine love: "(1) Redeeming love deserves our highest admiration and most humble acknowledgments. (2) The love of God discovered in our redemption, is the most powerful persuasive to repentance. (3) The transcendent love that God hath expressed in our redemption by Christ, should kindle in us a reciprocal affection to him. (4) What an high provocation is it to despise redeeming mercy, and to defeat that infinite goodness which hath been at such expense for our recovery?" (1:329–40).

Some consider Bates's greatest work to be *The Four Last Things* (1691), a short, poignant treatment on death, judgment, heaven, and hell. His 50-page treatise *On Divine Meditation* is typically Puritan and one of the best in its field, covering the basics of its nature, necessity, time, advantages, rules, and applications—no word wastage here! His other major publications include *The Select Lives of Illustrious and Pious Persons*, *Discourses on the Existence of God*, *The Immortality of the Soul*, *The Great Duty of Resignation*, *The Danger of Prosperity*, *Sermons on the Forgiveness of Sins*, and *The Sure Trial of Uprightness*. Complete Works includes numerous sermons and several treatises on Christian living, all of which are succinctly written and packed with edifying material. If you are looking for a Puritan who always writes well, is both practical and heavenly, and is never tedious, read William Bates.

AUTHOR'S PREFACE.

The subject of the ensuing discourses is of that inestimable excellency and importance, that it deserves our deepest reflections and care to consider and apply it; it is the great mystery of godliness, the design of eternal wisdom, the chiefest of all God's works, that contains the glorious wonders of his mercy and power, wherein he renders himself most worthy of our supreme veneration and affection. Our most raised thoughts are infinitely beneath its dignity. Though the light of the gospel hath clearly revealed so much of it, as is requisite to be known in our earthly state, yet the sublimer parts are still secret, and reserved for a full discovery, by the brightness of our Saviour's appearance. Now if the excellency of things excites our spirits to be attentive in searching into their nature, this divine object should awaken all our powers and arrest our minds, in the serious, steady contemplation of it, being alone capable to satisfy their immortal appetite.

The importance of it is correspondent to its excellency; for it is no less than the recovery of us from extreme and eternal misery, and the restoring of us to the enjoyment of the blessed God; a felicity without comparison or end. If we have any regard to salvation, (and who would be so unhappy as to neglect it for unconcerning, frivolous vanity?) it will be delightful to know the means by which we may obtain it, and to employ the flying moments of our short time in those things that are profitable for our last end, that we may not lose temporal and eternal life together.

Many of the ancient and modern divines have written of this noble argument, from whom I have received benefit in the following composure; but none, as I know, hath considered all the parts together, and presented them in one view. There still remains a rich abundance for the perpetual exercise of our spirits. The eternal word alone was able to perfect all things by once speaking. Human words are but an echo that answers the voice of God, and cannot fully express its power, nor pass so immediately through the sense to the heart, but they must be repeated. Should these discourses be effectual to inflame us with the most ardent love to our Saviour, who ransomed us with the invaluable price of his own blood, and to persuade us to live for heaven, the purchase of that sacred treasure; I shall for ever acknowledge the divine grace, and obtain my utmost aim.

THE HARMONY

OF

THE DIVINE ATTRIBUTES.

CHAPTER I.

THE PRIMITIVE STATE OF MAN.

THE felicity which the Lord Jesus procured for believers, includes a perfect freedom from sin, and all afflictive evils, the just consequences of it; and the fruition of righteousness, peace and joy, wherein the kingdom of God consists. In this the evangelical covenant excels the natural. The law supposes a man upright, and the happiness it promises to exact obedience, is called *life;* it rewards innocence with immortality. But the blessedness of the gospel is styled *salvation*, which signifies the rescuing of lapsed man from a state of misery, and the investing of him with unperishing glory.

In order to the discovering of the excellency of this benefit, and the endearing obligations laid on us by our Redeemer, it is necessary to take a view of that dreadful and desperate calamity which seized upon mankind. The wretchedness of our captivity illustrates the glory of our redemption. And since the misery of man was not the original condition of his nature, but the effect of his guilty choice, it is necessary to make some reflection upon his first state, as he came out of the pure hands of God; that comparing our present misery with our lost happiness, we may revive in our breasts the affections of sorrow, shame, and indignation against ourselves; and considering that the heavenly Adam hath purchased for us a title to a better inheritance than was forfeited by the earthly one, we may, with the more affectionate gratitude, extol the favour and power of our Redeemer.

God who is the living fountain of all perfections, spent eternity in the contemplation of his own excellencies, before any creature was made. In the moment appointed by his wisdom, he gave the first being to the world. Three distinct orders of natures he formed, the one purely spiritual, the other purely material, and between both one mixed, which unites the extremes in itself. This is man, the abridgment of the universe, allied to the angels in his soul, and to material things in his body, and capable of the happiness of both; by his internal faculties enjoying the felicity of the intellectual, and by his external, tasting the pleasures of the sensitive, world. Man's greatest excellency was a perfect conformity to the divine pattern. " God created man in his own likeness, in the image of God created he him." This includes the natural similitude of God in the substance of the soul, as it is an intelligent, free, spiritual, and immortal being; this is assigned to be the reason of the law, that " whoso sheddeth man's blood, by man shall his blood be shed; for in the image of God made he man," Gen. ix. 6 ;—a moral resemblance in its qualities and perfections; that happiness and dignity of man's state, which was the consequent of and accession to his holiness.

The natural resemblance I shall not insist on. For the distinct illustration of the other, we must consider God in a threefold respect: 1. in respect of his absolute holiness, unspotted purity, infinite goodness, incorruptible justice, and whatever we conceive under the notion of moral perfections: 2. with respect to his complete blessedness, the result of his infinite excellencies; as he is perfectly exempt from all evils which might alloy and lessen his felicity, and enjoys those pleasures which are worthy of his pure nature and glorious state: 3. in regard of his supreme dominion, which extends itself to all things in heaven and earth. Now in the participation of these the image of God did principally consist. The holiness of man was the copy of the divine purity; his happiness a representation of the divine felicity; and his dominion over the lower world the resemblance of

God's sovereignty. I will take a particular survey of them.

I. Man was conformed to God in holiness. This appears by the expressions of the apostle concerning the sanctification of corrupt man, which he sets forth by the renewing of him in knowledge, righteousness, and holiness, after the image of his Creator. The renovation of things is the restoring of them to their primitive state, and is more or less perfect, by its proportion to or distance from the original. Holiness and righteousness are the comprehensive sum of the moral law, which not only represents the will, but the nature of God in his supreme excellency; and in conformity to it the divine likeness eminently appeared. Adam was created with the perfections of grace. The progress of the most excellent saints is incomparably short of his beginning; by this we may, in part, conjecture the beauty of holiness in him, of which one faint ray appearing in renewed persons is so amiable. The primitive beauty is expressed in Scripture by rectitude: "God made man upright." There was an universal, entire rectitude in his faculties, disposing them for their proper operations. This will more fully appear by considering the distinct powers of the soul, in their regular constitutions.

1. The understanding was enriched with knowledge. Nature was unveiled to Adam; he entered into its sanctuary, and discovered its mysterious operations. When the creatures came to pay their homage to him, "whatsoever he called them, that was the name thereof," Gen. ii. 19. And their names expressed their natures. His knowledge reached through the whole compass of the creation, from the sun, the glorious vessel of light, to the glow-worm that shines in the hedge. And this knowledge was not acquired by study, it was not the fruit of anxious inquiry, but as the illumination of the air is in an instant by the light of the morning, so his understanding was enlightened by a pure beam from the Father of lights.

Besides, he had such a knowledge of the Deity, as was sufficient for his duty and felicity. His mind did not stick in the material part of things, but ascended by the several ranks of beings to the universal cause. He discovered the glory of the divine essence and attributes by their wonderful effects.

(1.) Almighty power. When he first opened his eyes, the stupendous fabric of heaven and earth presented itself to his view, and in it the most express and clear characters of that glorious power which produced it. For what could overcome the infinite distance between not being and being, but infinite power? As there is no proportion between not being and being, so the cause which unites those terms, must be without limits. Now the divine world alone, which calls the things which are not, as if they were, caused the world to rise from the abyss of empty nothing. At God's command the heavens and all their host were created. And this led him to consider the immensity of the divine essence; for infinite power is incompatible with a finite essence, and by the consideration of the immensity, he might ascend to the eternity of God. To be eternal without beginning, and infinite without bounds, infer one another, and necessarily exist in the same subject; for it is impossible that any thing which is formed by another and hath a beginning, should not be limited in its nature by the cause that produced it. Therefore the apostle declares, Rom. i. 20, that "the eternal power" of God is set forth in the creation of the world; joining with the discovery of his power, that of his eternity.

(2.) Admirable wisdom appeared to man in the creation; for by considering the variety and union, the order and efficacy, the beauty and stability of the world, he clearly discerned that wisdom which so regularly disposed all. It is thus that Wisdom speaks, Prov. viii. 27—29: "When he prepared the heavens, I was there: when he set a compass upon the face of the depth; when he established the clouds above; when he strengthened the fountains of the deep; when he gave the sea his decree, that the waters should not pass his commandment; when he appointed the foundations of the earth; then I was with him," contriving all in the best manner for ornament and use. The knowledge of this filled his soul with wonder and delight. The Psalmist breaks forth with astonishment, as one in the midst of innumerable miracles; "O Lord, how manifold are thy works! in wisdom hast thou made them all," Psalm civ. 24. And if he discovered such wonderful and divine wisdom in the works of God, when the vigour of the human understanding was so much impaired by the fall, how much more did Adam, who perfectly understood universal nature, the offices of its parts, the harmony of the whole, and all the just laws of union by which God hath joined together such a multitude of beings so distant and disagreeing, and how the public peace is preserved by their private enmity! This discovery caused him to acknowledge, that "great is the Lord, and of great power; his understanding is infinite."

(3.) Infinite goodness shined forth in the creation. This is the leading attribute that called forth the rest to work. As there was no matter, so no motive to induce God to make the world, but what arose from his goodness; for he is an all-sufficient being, perfectly blessed in himself. His majesty is not increased by the adoration of angels, nor his greatness by the obedience of nature; neither was he less happy or content in that eternal duration before the existence of any creature, than he is since. His original felicity is equally incapable of accession, as of diminution. It is evident, therefore, that only free and unexcited goodness moved him to create all things, that he might impart being and happiness to the creature, not enrich his own.

And as by contemplating the other works of God, so especially by reflecting upon himself, Adam had a clear sight of the divine attributes which concurred in his creation. Whether he considered his lowest part, the body, it was formed of the earth, the most artificial and beautiful piece of the visible world. The contrivance of its parts was with that proportion and exactness, as most conduced to comeliness and service. Its stature was erect and raised, becoming the lord of the creatures, and an observer of the heavens. A divine beauty and majesty was shed upon it. And this was no vanishing ray, soon eclipsed by a disease, and extinguished by death, but shined in the countenance without any declination. The tongue was man's peculiar glory, being the interpreter of the mind, and capable to signify all the affections of the soul. In short, the body was so framed, as to make a visible discovery of the prerogatives of his creation. And when he reflected upon his soul that animated his dust, its excellent endowments wherein it is comparable to the angels, its capacity of enjoying God himself for ever, he had an internal and most clear testimony of the glorious perfections of his Creator; for man, who alone admires the works of God, is the most admirable of all.

2. The image of God was resplendent in man's conscience, the seat of practical knowledge, and treasury of moral principles. The directive faculty was sincere and uncorrupt, not infected with any disguising tincture: it was clear from all prejudices which might render it an incompetent judge of good and evil. It instructed man in all the parts of his relative obligations to God and the creatures. It was not fettered and confined, fearfully restraining from what is lawful; nor licentious and indulgent in what is forbidden. Briefly, conscience in Adam upright, was a subordinate God, that gave laws and exacted obedience to that glorious Being who is its superior.

3. There was a divine impression on the will. Spiritual reason kept the throne, and the inferior faculties observed an easy and regular subordination to its dictates. The affections were exercised with proportion to the quality of their objects. Reason was their inviolable rule. Love, the most noble and master affection, which gives being and goodness to all the rest, even to hatred itself; (for so much we hate an object, as it hinders our enjoyment of the good we love)—this precious incense was offered up to the excellent and supreme Being, who was the Author of his life. Adam fully obeyed the first and great command, of loving the Lord with all his heart, soul, and strength. His love to other things was regulated by his love to God. There was a perfect accord between flesh and spirit in him. They both joined in the service of God, and were naturally moved to their happiness. As the two eyes consent in their motion, so reason and sense agreed for the same

end. In short, the image of God in Adam, was a living, powerful principle, and had the same relation to the soul which the soul hath to the body, to animate and order all its faculties in their offices and operations, according to the will of his Creator.

II. The image of God consisted, though in an inferior degree, in the happy state of man. Herein he resembled that infinitely blessed Being.

This happiness had relation to the two natures which enter into man's composition:

1. To the animal and sensitive; and this consisted in two things:—in the excellent disposition of his organs;—in the enjoyment of convenient objects.

(1.) In the excellent disposition of the organs. His body was formed immediately by God, and so not liable to those defects which proceed from the weakness of second causes. No blemish or disease, which are the effects and footsteps of sin, were to be found in him. His health was not a frail, inconstant disposition, easily ruined by the jarring elements, but firm and stable. The humours were in a just temperament, to prevent any distemper which might tend to the dissolution of that excellent frame. Briefly, all the senses were quick and lively, able to perform with facility, vigour, and delight, their operations.

(2.) There were convenient objects to entertain his sensitive faculties. He enjoyed nature in its original purity, crowned with the benediction of God, before it was blasted with the curse. The world was all harmony and beauty, becoming the goodness of the Creator; and not, as it is since the fall, disordered and deformed in many parts, the effect of his justice. The earth was liberal to Adam of all its treasures, the heavens of their light and sweetest influences. He was seated in Eden, a place of so great beauty and delight, that it represented the celestial paradise which is refreshed with rivers of pleasure. And as the ultimate end of the creatures was to raise his mind, and inflame his heart with the love of his great Benefactor; so their first and natural use was the satisfaction of the senses, from whence the felicity of the animal life did proceed.

3. His supreme happiness consisted in the exercise of his most noble faculties on their proper objects. This will appear by considering, that as the spiritual faculties have objects which infinitely excel those of the sensitive; so their capacity is more enlarged, their union with objects is more intimate, and their perception is with more quickness and vivacity; and thereby are the greatest instruments of pleasure to the rational being. Now the highest faculties in man are the understanding and will; and their happiness consists in union with God by knowledge and love.

(1.) In the knowledge of God. As the desire of knowledge is the most natural to the human soul, so the obtaining of it produces the most noble and the sweetest pleasure. And proportionably to the degrees of excellency that are in objects, so much of rational perfection and satisfaction accrues to the mind by the knowledge of them. The discovery of the works of God greatly affected man, yet the excellencies scattered among them are but an imperfect and mutable shadow of God's infinite and unchangeable perfections. How much more delightful was it to his pure understanding, tracing the footsteps and impressions of God in natural things, to ascend to him who is the glorious original of all perfections! And though his finite understanding could not comprehend the divine excellencies, yet his knowledge was answerable to the degrees of revelation wherein God was manifested. He saw the admirable beauty of the Creator through the transparent veil of the creatures. And from hence there arose in the soul a pleasure pure, solid, and satisfying; a pleasure divine, for God takes infinite contentment in the contemplation of himself.

(2.) The happiness of man consisted in the love of God. It was not the naked speculation of the Deity that made him happy, but such a knowledge as ravished his affections; for happiness results from the fruitions of all the faculties. It is true, that by the mediation of the understanding the other faculties have access to an object; the will and affections cannot be inclined to any thing, but by virtue of an act of the mind which propounds it as worthy of them: it follows, therefore, that when by the discovery of the transcendent excellencies in God the soul is excited to love and to delight in him as its supreme good, it is then really and perfectly happy. Now as Adam had a perfect knowledge of God, so the height of his love was answerable to his knowledge, and the completeness of his enjoyment was according to his love. All the divine excellencies were amiable to him. The majesty, purity, justice, and power of God, which are the terror of guilty creatures, secured his happiness whilst he continued in his obedience. His conscience was clear and calm; no unquiet fears discomposed its tranquillity; it was the seat of innocence and peace. Briefly, his love to God was perfect, without any alloy of tormenting fear; and delight, its inseparable attendant, was pure, without the least mixture of sorrow.

III. There was in man's dominion and power over the creatures a shining part of God's image. He was appointed God's lieutenant in the world, and adorned with a flower of his crown. God gave him the solemn investiture of this dignity, when he brought the creatures to receive their names from him, which was a mark of their homage, and a token of his supreme empire to command them by their names, Psalm viii. 5, 6. As this dominion was established by the order of God, so it was exercised by the mediation of the body. In his face and words there was something so powerful, as commanded all the hosts of the lower world. And as their subjection was most easy, without constraint or resistance, so it was most equal, without violence and oppression.

Thus holy and blessed was Adam in his primitive state. And that he might continue so, he was obliged for ever to obey the will of God, who bestowed upon him life and happiness. By the first neglect of his duty he would most justly and inevitably incur the loss of both. This will appear by considering the design of God in the creation.

God did not make the world and man for the mere exercise of his power, and so left them; but as the production of all things was from his goodness, so their resolution and tendency are for his glory. He is as universally the final, as the efficient cause of all creatures; for that which receives its being from another, cannot be an end to itself; for the provision of the end in the mind of the Creator sets him a work, and is antecedent to the being of the creature. Therefore, the wise man tells us, Prov. xvi. 5, that "God made all things for himself;" and the apostle, Rom. xi. 36, that "of him, and through him are all things; to whom be glory for ever." The lower rank of creatures objectively glorify God, as there is a visible demonstration of his excellent attributes in them: man only is qualified to know and love the Creator. As the benefit of all redounds to him, it is his duty to pay the tribute for all. By his mouth the world makes its acknowledgment to God. He is the interpreter of the silent and uninterrupted praises, which the full choir of heaven and earth renders to him. "All thy works shall praise thee, O Lord," from the most noble to the least worthy, "and thy saints shall bless thee," Psalm cxlv. 10. Thankfulness is the homage due from understanding creatures.

And from hence it follows, that man only was in a state of moral dependence, and capable of a law. For a law being the declaration of the superior's will, requiring obedience and threatening punishment on the failure thereof, there must be a principle of reason and choice in that nature that is governed by it, to discover the authority that enjoins it—to discern the matter of the law—to determine itself, out of judgment and election, to obedience, as most excellent in itself and advantageous to the performer.

Now all inferior creatures are moved by the secret force of natural inclinations; they are insensible of moral engagements, and are not wrought on in an illuminative way by the foresight of rewards and punishments: but man who is a reasonable creature, owes "a reasonable service." And it is impossible that man should be exempt from a law; for as the notion of a God, that is, of a first supreme Being, excludes all possibility of obligation to another, "Who hath first given to him, and it shall be recompensed unto him again?" Rom. xi. 35;

and of subjection to a law, for supremacy and subjection are incompatible; so the quality of a creature includes the relation of dependence and natural subjection to the will of God. This is most evident from that common principle which governs the intelligent creation: it is a moral maxim to which the reasonable nature necessarily assents, that the dispensing of benefits acquires to the giver a right to command, and lays on the receiver an obligation to obey; and these rights and duties are measured by the nature of the benefits as their just rule. This is visible in that dominion which is amongst men.

If we ascend to the first springs of human laws, we shall find the original right of power to arise either from generation in nature, or preservation in war, or some public good accruing to the society by the prudent care of the governor. Now the being and blessedness of the creature are the greatest and most valuable benefits that can be received; and in the bestowing of them is laid the most real foundation of power and authority. Upon this account man, who derives his life and felicity from God, is under a natural and strong obligation to comply with his will. From this right of creation God asserts his universal dominion: "I have made the earth, and created man upon it; I, even my hands have stretched out the heavens, and all their host have I commanded," Isa. xlv. 12. And the Psalmist tells us, Psalm c. 3, "Know ye that the Lord he is God; it is he that hath made us, and not we ourselves; we are his people, and the sheep of his pasture." His jurisdiction is grounded on his propriety in man; and that arises from his giving being to him. "Remember, O Israel, for thou art my servant, I have formed thee," Isa. xliv. 21. From hence he hath a supreme right to impose any law, for the performance of which man had an original power. Universal obedience is the just consequent of our obligations to the divine goodness.

Suppose that man were not the work of God's hands, yet the infinite excellency of his nature gives him a better title to command us, than man hath upon the account of his reason to govern those creatures that are inferior to him. Or suppose that God had not created the matter of which the body is composed, but only inspired it with a living soul, yet his right over us had been unquestionable. The civil law determines, that when an artificer works on rich materials, and the engraving be not of extraordinary value, the whole belongs to him who is the owner of the materials; but if the matter be mean and the workmanship excellent, in which the price wholly lies; as if a painter should draw an admirable picture on a piece of canvass, the picture of right belongs to him that drew it; Instit. Justin. So if, according to the error of some philosophers, (Plato,) the matter of which the world was made had been eternal, yet God having infused a reasonable soul into a piece of clay, which is the principle of its life, and gives it a transcendent value above all other beings which were made of the same element, it is most just he should have a property in him and dominion over him.

The law of nature, to which man was subject upon his creation, contains those moral principles concerning good and evil, which have an essential equity in them, and are the measures of his duty to God, to himself, and to his fellow-creatures. This was published by the voice of reason, and is "holy, just, and good;"—holy, as it enjoins those things wherein there is a conformity to those attributes and actions of God, which are the pattern of our imitation: so the general rule is, "be ye holy," as God is holy, "in all manner of conversation," 1 Pet. i. 15: and this is most honourable to the human nature. It is just, that is exactly agreeable to the frame of man's faculties, and most suitable to his condition in the world. And good, that is beneficial to the observer of it; "in keeping of it, there is great reward," Psalm xix. 11. And the obligation to it is eternal; it being the unchangeable will of God, grounded on the natural and unvariable relations between God and man, and between man and the creatures.

Besides the particular directions of the law of nature, this general principle was planted in the reasonable soul, to obey God in any instance wherein he did prescribe his pleasure.

Moreover, God was pleased to enter into a covenant with Adam, and with all his posterity naturally descending from him. And this was the effect—of admirable goodness; for by his supremacy over man, he might have signified his will merely by the way of empire, and required obedience; but he was pleased to condescend so far as to deal with man in a sweeter manner, as with a creature capable of his love, and to work upon him by rewards and punishments, congruously to the reasonable nature.—Of wisdom, to secure man's obedience; for the covenant being a mutual engagement between God and man, as it gave him infallible assurance of the reward to strengthen his faith, so it was the surest bond to preserve his fidelity. It is true, the precept alone binds by virtue of the authority that imposes it, but the consent of the creature increases the obligation; it twists the cords of the law, and binds more strongly to obedience. Thus Adam was God's servant, as by the condition of his nature, so by his choice, accepting the covenant, from which he could not recede without the guilt and infamy of the worst perfidiousness.

The terms of the covenant were becoming the parties concerned, God and man; it established an inseparable connection between duty and felicity. This appears by the sanction, Gen. ii. 17; "In the day that thou eatest" of the forbidden fruit, "thou shalt surely die:" in that particular species of sin the whole genus is included; according to the apostle's exposition, Gal. iii. 10; " Cursed is every one that continueth not in all things which are written in the book of the law to do them." The threatening of death was expressed, it being more difficult to be conceived; the promise of life upon his obedience was implied, and easily suggested itself to the rational mind. These were the most proper and powerful motives to excite his reason and affect his will; for death primarily signifies the dissolution of the vital union between the soul and body, and consequently all the preparatory dispositions thereunto, diseases, pains, and all the affections of mortality which terminate in death as their centre. This is the extremest of temporal evils, which innocent nature shrunk from, it being a deprivation of that excellent state which man enjoyed. But principally it signified the separation of the soul from God's reviving presence, who is the only fountain of felicity. Thus the law is interpreted by the Lawgiver, "the soul that sinneth, it shall die," Ezek. xviii. 4. Briefly, death in the threatening is comprehensive of all kinds and degrees of evils, from the least pain to the completeness of damnation. Now it is an inviolable principle deeply set in the human nature, to preserve its being and blessedness; so that nothing could be a more powerful restraint from sin, than the fear of death, which is destructive to both.

This constitution of the covenant was founded not only in the will of God, but in the nature of things themselves; and this appears by considering,—that holiness is more excellent in itself and separately considered, than the reward that attends it. It is the peculiar glory of the Divine nature; "God is glorious in holiness." And as he prefers the infinite purity of his nature before the immortal felicity of his state; so he values in the reasonable creatures the virtues by which they represent his holiness, more than their perfect contentment by which they are like him in blessedness. Now God is the most just esteemer of things, his judgment is the infallible measure of their real worth; it is, therefore, according to natural order, that the happiness of man should depend upon his integrity, and the reward be the fruit of his obedience. And though it is impossible that a mere creature, in what state soever, should obtain any thing from God by any other title but his voluntary promise, the effect of his goodness, yet it was such goodness as God was invited to exercise by the consideration of man's obedience. And as the neglect of his duty had discharged the obligation on God's part, so the performance gave him a claim by right of the promise to everlasting life. As the first part of the alliance was most reasonable, so was the second, that death should be the wages of sin. It is not conceivable that God should continue his favour to man, if he turned rebel against him; for this were to disarm the law, and expose the authority of the Lawgiver to contempt, and would reflect upon the wisdom of God. Besides, if the reasonable creature violates the law, it necessarily contracts an obligation to punishment. So that if the sinner who deserves death, should enjoy life, without satisfaction for the offence, or repentance to qualify him for pardon, (both which were without the compass of the first covenant) this would infringe the unchangeable rights of justice, and disparage the divine purity.

In the first covenant there was a special clause, which respected man as the inhabitant of paradise, that he should "not eat of the tree of knowledge of good and evil" upon pain of death. And this prohibition was upon the most wise and just reasons:—to declare God's sovereign right in all things. In the quality of Creator he is supreme Lord. Man enjoyed nothing but by a derived title from his bounty and allowance, and with an obligation to render to him the homage of all. As princes, when they give estates to their subjects, still retain the royalty, and receive a small rent, which, though inconsiderable in its value, is an acknowledgment of dependence upon them; so when God placed Adam in paradise, he received this mark of his sovereignty, that in the free use of all other things, man should abstain from the forbidden tree; to make trial of man's obedience in a matter very congruous to discover it. If the prohibition had been grounded on any moral internal evil in the nature of the thing itself, there had not been so clear a testimony of God's dominion, nor of Adam's subjection to it. But when that which in itself was indifferent, became unlawful merely by the will of God, and when the command had no other excellency but to make his authority more sacred, this was a confining of man's liberty, and to abstain was pure obedience.

Besides, the restraint was from that which was very grateful, and alluring to both the parts of man's compounded nature. The sensitive appetite is strongly excited by the lust of the eye; and this fruit being beautiful to the sight, the forbearance was an excellent exercise of virtue in keeping the lower appetite in obedience. Again; the desire of knowledge is extremely quick and earnest, and, in appearance, most worthy of the rational nature. "*Nullus animo suavior cibus*," Lactantius. It is the most high and luscious food of the soul. Now the tree of knowledge was forbidden; so that the observance of the law was the most eminent, in keeping the intellectual appetite in mediocrity. In short, God required obedience as a sacrifice; for the prohibition being in a matter of natural pleasure, and a curb to curiosity, which is the lust and concupiscence of the mind after things concealed; by a reverent regard to it, man presented his soul and body to God as a living sacrifice, which was his reasonable service, Rom. xii. 1.

CHAPTER II.

THE FALL OF MAN.

MAN was created perfectly holy, but in a natural, therefore, mutable state. He was invested with power to prevent his falling, yet under a possibility of it. He was complete in his own order, but receptive of sinful impressions. An invincible perseverance in holiness belongs to a supernatural state; it is the privilege of grace, and exceeds the design of the first creation.

The rebellious spirits, who by a furious ambition had raised a war in heaven and were fallen from their obedience and glory, designed to corrupt man and to make him a companion with them in their revolt. The most subtle among them sets about this work, urged by two strong passions, hatred and envy. By hatred: for being under a final and irrevocable doom, he looked on God as an irreconcilable enemy; and not being able to injure his essence, he struck at his image; as the fury of some beasts discharges itself upon the picture of a man. He singled out Adam as the mark of his malice, and by seducing him from his duty, he might defeat God's design, which was to be honoured by man's free obedience; and to obscure his glory as if he had made man in vain. He was solicited by envy, the first native of hell; for having lost the favour of God, and being cast out of heaven, the region of joy and blessedness, the sight of Adam's felicity exasperated his grief. That man, who by the condition of his nature was below him, should be prince of the world, whilst he was a prisoner under those chains which restrained and tormented him, the power and wrath of God, this made his state more intolerable. His torment was incapable of allay, but by rendering man as miserable as himself. And as hatred excited his envy, so envy inflamed his hatred, and both joined in mischief. And thus pushed on, his subtilty being equal to his malice, he contrives a temptation, which might be most taking and dangerous to man in his raised and happy state. He tempts him with art, by propounding the lure of knowledge and pleasure, to inveigle the spiritual and sensitive appetites at once. And that he might the better succeed, he addresses the woman, the weakest and most liable to seduction. He hides himself in the body of a serpent, which before sin was not terrible to her; and by this instrument insinuates his temptation. He first allured with the hopes of impunity, "Ye shall not die;" then he promised a universal knowledge of good and evil. By these pretences he ruined innocence itself; for the woman, deceived by those specious allurements, swallowed the poison of the serpent, and having tasted death, she persuaded her husband, by the same motives, to despise the law of their Creator. Thus sin entered, and brought confusion into the world; for the moral harmony of the world consisting in the just subordination of the several ranks of beings to one another, and of all to God, when man who was placed next to God, broke the union, his fall brought a desperate disorder into God's government.

And though the matter of the offence seems small, yet the disobedience was infinitely great; it being the transgression of that command, which was given to be the instance and real proof of man's subjection to God. "*Totam legem violavit in illo legalis obedientiæ præcepto,*" Tertul. The honour and majesty of the whole law was violated in the breach of that symbolical precept. It was a direct and formal rebellion, a public renunciation of obedience, a universal apostasy from

God, and a change of the last end, that distinguished the habit of original righteousness.

I. Many sins were combined in that single act.

1. Infidelity. This was the first step to ruin. It appears by the order of the temptation. It was first said by the devil, "Ye shall not die," to weaken their faith; then, "Ye shall be like gods," to flatter their ambition. The fear of death would have controlled the efficacy of all his arguments; till that restraint was broke, he could fasten nothing upon them. This account the apostle gives of the fall, 1 Tim. ii. 14; "The woman being deceived, was in the transgression." As obedience is the effect of faith, so is disobedience of infidelity; and as faith comes by hearing the word of God, so infidelity, by listening to the words of the devil. From the deception of the mind proceeded the depravation of the will, the intemperance of the appetite, and the defection of the whole man. Thus as the natural, so the spiritual death made its first entrance by the eye. And this infidelity is extremely aggravated, as it implies an accusation of God both of envy and falsehood.—Of envy; as if he had denied them the perfections becoming the human nature, and they might ascend to a higher orb than that wherein they were placed, by eating the forbidden fruit. And what greater disparagement could there be of the divine goodness, than to suspect the Deity of such a low and base passion, which is the special character of the angels of darkness? It was equally injurious to the honour of God's truth; for it is not easy to conceive, that Adam, who was so lately the effect of God's omnipotence, should presently distrust it as unable to inflict the punishment threatened; but his assent was weakened as to the truth of the threatening; he did not believe the danger to be so great or certain upon his disobedience; and "he that believeth not God, hath made him a liar;" an impiety not to be thought on without horror. And that which heightens the affront, is, that when he distrusted the fountain of truth, he gave credit to the father of lies; as appears by his compliance, the real evidence of his his faith. Now what viler contumely could be offered to the Creator?

2. Prodigious pride. He was scarce out of the state of nothing, no sooner created, but he aspired to be as God. Not content with his image, he affected an equality, to be like him in his inimitable attributes. He would rob God of his eternity, to live without end ; of his sovereignty, to command without dependence ; of his wisdom, to know all things without reserve. The promise of the tempter that they should not die, encouraged him to believe that he should enjoy an immortality not depending on God's will, but absolute; which is proper to God alone. Infinite insolence, and worthy of the most fiery indignation! That man, the son of the earth, forgetful of his original, should usurp the prerogatives which are essential to the Deity, and set up himself a real idol, was a strain of that arrogancy which corrupted the angels.

3. Horrid ingratitude. He was appointed heir apparent of all things; yet undervaluing his present portion, he entertains a project of improving his happiness. The excellent state newly conferred upon him, was a strong obligation to pay so small an acknowledgment to his Lord. The use of all the garden was allowed to him, a tree only excepted. Now in the midst of such variety and plenty, to be inflamed with the intemperate appetite of the forbidden fruit, and to break a command so equal and easy, what was it but despising the rich goodness of his great Benefactor? Besides, man was endued with a diviner spirit than the inferior order of creatures: reason and liberty were the special privileges of his nature ; and to abuse them to rebellion, renders him, as more unreasonable, so more disingenuous than the creatures below him, who inflexibly obey the will of God.

4. The visible contempt of God's majesty, with a slighting of his justice ; for the prohibition was so express and terrible, that till he had cast off all respects to the Lawgiver, it was not possible he should venture to disobey him. The sin of Adam is, therefore, called by the apostle "disobedience," Rom. v. 19; as eminently such ; it being the first and highest instance of it, and virtually a breach of all the laws at once in that contempt of the Lawgiver. It was the profanation of para-

dise itself, the place of God's special presence: there he fell, and trampled on God's command before his face. What just cause of astonishment is it, that a reasonable creature should bid open defiance to the Author of its life! that a little breathing dust should contemn its Creator! that a man should prefer servile compliance to the will of the tempter, before free subjection to his Father and Sovereign! To depose God, and place the devil in his throne, was double treason, and provoked his infinite jealousy.

5. Unaccountable and amazing folly. What a despicable acquisition tempted him out of happiness! If there had been any possible comparison between them, the choice had been more excusable. But that the pleasures of taste and curiosity should outvie the favour of God which is better than life; that the most pernicious evil, gilded with the thin appearance of good, should be preferred before the substantial and supreme good, is the reproach of his reason, and makes the choice so criminal. And what less than voluntary madness could incline him to desire that, which he ought infinitely to have feared, that is, the knowledge of evil? for nothing could destroy his happiness but the experience of evil. What but a wilful distraction could induce him to believe, that by defacing God's image, he should become more like him? Thus "man being in honour," but without understanding, became "like the beasts that perish," Psalm xlix. 12.

6. A bloody cruelty to himself and all his posterity. When God had made him a depository, in a matter of infinite moment, that is, of his own happiness and all mankind's, this should have been a powerful motive to have kept him vigilant: but giving a ready ear to the tempter, he betrayed his trust, and at once breaks both the tables of the law, and becomes guilty of the highest impiety and cruelty. He was a murderer before he was a parent; he disinherited all his children before they were born, and made them slaves before they knew the price of liberty.

II. And that which increases the malignity of this sin, and adds an infinite emphasis to it, is, that it was perfectly voluntary; his will was the sole cause of his fall. And this is evident by considering:

1. That Adam innocent had a sufficient power to persevere in his holy state. There was no subtraction of any grace which was requisite to his standing; he left God before he was forsaken by him. Much less was there any internal impulsion from God. It is inconsistent with the divine purity to incline the creature to sin. As "God cannot be tempted with evil, neither tempteth he any man." It is injurious to his wisdom, to think that God would spoil that work which he had composed with so much design and counsel; and it is dishonourable to his goodness. He loved his creature, and love is an inclination to do good; it was impossible, therefore, for God to induce man to sin, or to withdraw that power which was necessary to resist the temptation, when the consequence must be his inevitable ruin.

2. The devil did only allure, he could not ravish his consent. Though his malice is infinite, yet his power is so restrained, that he cannot fasten an immediate, much less an irresistible impression on the will: he, therefore, made use of an external object to invite him. Now objects have no constraining force; they are but partial agents, and derive all their efficacy from the faculties to which they are agreeable. And although, since sin hath disordered the flesh, there is difficulty in resisting those objects which pleasantly insinuate themselves; yet such a universal rectitude was in Adam, and so entire a subjection of the sensual appetite to the superior power of reason, that he might have obtained an easy conquest. A resolute negative had made him victorious; by a strong denial he had baffled that proud spirit: as the heavenly Adam, when he who is rich in promises only, offered to him the monarchy of the world with all its glory, disdained the offer, and cast off Satan with contempt. The true Rock was unmoved, and broke all the proud waves that dashed against it.

3. It will fully appear that the disobedience was voluntary, by considering what denominates an action to be so. The two springs of human actions are the understanding and will; and as there is no particular good

but may have the appearance of some difficult, unpleasant quality annexed, upon which account the will may reject it; so any particular evil may be so disguised by the false lustre of goodness, as to incline the will to receive it. This is clearly verified in Adam's fall; for a specious object was conveyed through the unguarded sense to his fancy, and from that to his understanding, which, by a vicious carelessness, neglecting to consider the danger, or judging that the excellency of the end did outweigh the evil of the means, commended it to the will, and that resolved to embrace it. It is evident, therefore, that the action which resulted from the direction of the mind and the choice of the will, was absolutely free.

Besides, as the regret that is mixed with an action, is a certain character that the person is under constraint; so the delight that attends it, is a clear evidence that he is free. When the appetite is drawn by the lure of pleasure, the more violent, the more voluntary is its motion. Now the representations of the forbidden fruit were under the notion of pleasure. The woman saw the " fruit was good for food," that is, pleasurable to the palate, and " pleasant to the eyes, and to be desired to make one wise," that is, to increase knowledge, which is the pleasure of the mind; and these allurements draw her into the snare. Adam with complacency received the temptation, and by the enticement of Satan, committed adultery with the creature, from whence the cursed race of sin and miseries proceed.

Suppose the devil had so disguised the temptation, that notwithstanding all circumspection and care, Adam could not have discovered its evil; his invincible ignorance had rendered the action involuntary: but Adam was conscious of his own action; there was light in his mind to discern the evil, and strength in his will to decline it. For the manner of the defection, whether it was from affected ignorance, or secure neglect, or transport of passion, it doth not excuse: the action itself was of that moment, and the supreme Lawgiver so worthy of reverence, that it should have awakened all the powers of his soul to beware of that which was rebellion against God and ruin to himself.

Or suppose he had been tried by torments, whose extremity and continuance had vehemently oppressed his nature. This had only lessened the guilt, the action had still been voluntary; for no external force can compel the will to choose any thing but under the notion of comparative goodness. Now to choose sin rather than pain, and to prefer ease before obedience, is highly dishonourable to God, whose glory ought to be infinitely more valuable to us than life and all its endearments, Job xxxvi. 21. And though sharp pains, by discomposing the body, make the soul unfit for its highest and noblest operations, so that it cannot perform the acts of virtue with delight and freedom; yet then it may abstain from evil. But this was not Adam's case: the devil had no power over him (as over Job, who felt the extremity of his rage, and yet came off more than conqueror) to disturb his felicity; he prevailed by a simple suasion. Briefly, though Adam had strength sufficient to repel all the powers of darkness, yet he was vanquished by the assault of a single temptation. Now, that man, so richly furnished with all the perfections of the mind, and the excellent virtues of which original righteousness was composed; endued with knowledge to foresee the incomparable evils that would redound to himself and be universal to his posterity by his disobedience; so well tempered in his constitution, that all his appetites were subject to reason; notwithstanding these preservatives, should be deceived by the false persuasions of an erring mind and overcome by carnal concupiscence, these are the circumstances which derive a crimson guilt to his rebellious sin, and render it above measure sinful.

III. This will more fully appear in the dreadful effects that ensued. By his disobedience he lost original righteousness, and made a deadly forfeiture of felicity.

1. He lost the original righteousness; for that so depended on the human faculties, that the actual violation of the law was presently attended with the privation of it. Besides, the nature of his sin contained an entire forsaking of God as envious of his happiness, and a conversion to the creature as the supreme good. And whatever is desired as the last end perfective of man, virtually

includes all subordinate ends, and regulates all means for obtaining it. So that, when that was changed, a universal change of moral qualities in Adam necessarily followed. Instead of the rectitude and excellent holiness of the soul, succeeded a permanent viciousness and corruption.

Now holiness may be considered in the notion of purity and beauty, or of dominion and liberty, in opposition to which sin is represented in Scripture by foul deformity and servitude.

(1.) His soul degenerated from its purity; the faculties remained, but the moral perfections were lost, wherein the brightness of God's image was most conspicuous. The holy wisdom of his mind, the divine love that sanctified his will, the spiritual power to obey God, were totally quenched. How is man disfigured by his fall! How is he transformed, in an instant, from the image of God into the image of the devil! He is defiled with the filthiness of flesh and spirit; he is ashamed at the sight of his own nakedness that reproached him for his crime; but the most shameful was that of the soul: the one might be covered with leaves, the other nothing could conceal. To see a face of exquisite beauty devoured by a cancer, how doth it move compassion! But were the natural eye heightened, to such clearness and perspicacity, as to discover the deformity which sin hath brought upon the soul, how would it strike us with grief, horror, and aversion!

(2.) He was deprived of his dominion and liberty. The understanding was so wounded by the violence of the fall, that not only its light is much impaired, but its power is so weakened as to the lower faculties, that those which, according to the order of nature, should obey, have cast off its just authority and usurped the government. The will then lost its true freedom, whereby it was enlarged to the extent and amplitude of the divine will, in loving whatsoever was pleasing to God, and is contracted to mean and base objects. What a furious disorder is in the affections! The restraint of reason to check their violent course, provokes them to swell higher and to be more impetuous; and the more they are gratified, the more insolent and outrageous they grow. The senses, whose office is to be the intelligencers of the soul, to make discovery and to give a naked report without disturbing the higher faculties, sometimes mistake disguised enemies for friends; and sometimes by a false alarm move the lower appetites, and fill the soul with disorder and confusion, so that the voice of reason cannot be heard. By the irritation of grief, the insinuation of pleasure, or some other perturbation, the soul is captivated and wounded through the senses. In short, when man turned rebel to God, he became a slave to all the creatures. By their primitive institution they were appointed to be subservient to the glory of God and the use of man, to be motives of love and obedience to the Creator; but sin hath corrupted and changed them into so many instruments of vice; they are "made subject to vanity." And man is so far sunk into the dregs of servitude, that he is subject to them; for by forsaking God, the supreme object of love, with as much injustice as folly, and choosing the creature in his stead, he becomes a servant to the meanest thing upon which he places an inordinate affection. Briefly, man, who by his creation was the son of God, is made a slave to Satan that damned spirit and most cursed creature. Deplorable degradation, and worthy of the deepest shame and sorrow!

2. Man lost his felicity. Besides the trouble that sin hath in its own nature, which I have touched on before, there is a consequent guilt and torment attending it. Adam whilst obedient enjoyed peace with God, a sweet serenity of mind, a divine calm in the conscience, and full satisfaction in himself; but after his sin he trembled at God's voice, and was tormented at his presence. "I heard thy voice, and was afraid," saith guilty Adam. He looked on God as angry and armed against him, ready to execute the severest sentence. Conscience began an early hell within him: paradise with all its pleasures, could not secure him from that sting in his breast, and that sharpened by the hand of God. What confusion of thoughts, what a combat of passions was he in! When the temptation which deceived him, vanished,

and his spirit recovered out of the surprise, and took a clear view of his guilt in its true horror, what indignation did it kindle in his breast! How did shame, sorrow, revenge, despair, those secret executioners, torment his spirit! The intelligent nature, his peculiar excellency above the brutes, armed misery against him, and put a keener edge to it—by his reflecting upon the foolish exchange he made of God himself for the fruit of a tree; that so slender a temptation should cheat him of his blessedness. His present misery is aggravated by the sad comparison of it with his primitive felicity: nothing remains of his first innocence, but the vexatious regret of having lost it—by the foresight of the death he deserved: the conscience of his crimes racked his soul with the certain and fearful expectation of judgment.

Besides the inward torment of his mind, he was exposed to all miseries from without. Sin having made a breach into the world, the whole army of evils entered with it; the curse extends itself to the whole creation; for the world being made for man, the place of his residence, in his punishment it hath felt the effects of God's displeasure. The whole course of nature is set on fire. Whereas a general peace and amicable correspondence was established between heaven and earth, whilst all were united in subjection to the Creator; sin, that broke the first union between God and man, hath ruined the second. As in a state when one part of the subjects fall from their obedience, the rest which are constant in their duty, break with the rebels, and make war upon them till they return to their allegiance: so universal nature was armed against rebellious man, and had destroyed him without the merciful interposition of God.

The angels with flaming swords expelled him from paradise. The beasts, who were all innocent whilst man remained innocent, espouse God's interest, and are ready to revenge the quarrel of their Creator. The insensible creation, which at first was altogether beneficial to man, is become hurtful. The heavens sometimes are hardened as brass in a long and obstinate serenity, sometimes are dissolved in a deluge of rain: the earth is barren, and unfaithful to the sower, "it bringeth forth thorns and thistles" instead of bread. In short, man is an enemy to man. When there were but two brothers to divide the world, the one stained his hands in the blood of the other; and since the progeny of Adam is increased into vast societies, all the disasters of the world, as famine, pestilence, deluges, the fury of beasts, have not been so destructive of mankind, as the sole malignity of man against those that partake of the human nature.

To conclude; who can make a list of the evils to which the body is liable by the disagreeing elements that compose it? The fatal seeds of corruption are bred in itself. It is a prey to all diseases, from the torturing stone to the dying consumption. It feels the strokes of death a thousand times before it can die once. At last life is swallowed up of death. And if death were a deliverance from miseries, it would lessen its terror, but it is the consummation of all. The first death transmits to the second. As the body dies by the soul's forsaking it, so the soul, by separation from God, its true life, dies to its well-being and happiness for ever.

CHAPTER III.

THE CORRUPTION OF HUMAN NATURE.

1. THE rebellion of the first man against the great Creator was a sin of universal efficacy, that derives a guilt and stain to mankind in all ages of the world. The account the Scripture gives of it, is grounded on the relation which all men have to Adam, as their natural and moral principle.—Their natural. God created one man in the beginning from whom all others derive their being: and that the unity might be the more entire, he formed of him that aid which was necessary for the communicating kind to the world. "He made of one blood all nations of men, for to dwell on all the face of the earth." Acts xvii. 26. And as the whole race of mankind was virtually in Adam's loins, so it was presumed to give virtual consent

to what he did. When he broke, all suffered shipwreck, that were contained in him as their natural original. The angels were created immediately and distinctly, without dependence upon one another as to their original; therefore, when a great number revolted from God, the rest were not complicated in their sin and ruin. But when the universal progenitor of men sinned, there was a conspiracy of all the sons of Adam in that rebellion, and not one subject left in his obedience. He was the moral principle of mankind. In the first treaty between God and man, Adam was considered as a single person, but as "caput gentis," and he contracted for all his descendants by ordinary generation. His person was the fountain of theirs, and his will the representative of theirs. From hence his vast progeny became a party in the covenant, and had a title to the benefits contained in it upon his obedience, and was liable to the curse upon his violation of it. Upon this ground the apostle institutes a parallel between Adam and Christ, that "as by one man's disobedience, many were made sinners, so by the obedience of one, shall many be made righteous," Rom. v. 19. As Christ, in his death on the cross, did not suffer as a private person, but as a surety and sponsor representing the whole church, according to the testimony of Scripture, "if one died for all, then were all dead;" so the first Adam, who was "the figure of him that was to come," in his disobedience was esteemed a public person representing the whole race of mankind; and by a just law it was not restrained to himself, but is the sin of the common nature. Adam broke the first link in the chain whereby mankind was united to God, and all the other parts which depended upon it are necessarily separated from him. From hence the Scripture saith, that by nature we are "the children of wrath," Eph. ii. 3; that is, liable to punishment, and that hath relation to guilt.

And of this we have convincing experience in the common evils which afflict mankind before the commission of any actual sin. The cries of infants who are only eloquent to grief, but dumb to all things else, discover that miseries attend them. The tears which are born with their eyes, signify that they are come into a state of sorrow. How many troops of deadly diseases are ready to seize on them immediately after their entrance into the world, which are the apparent effects of God's displeasure, and therefore, argue man to be guilty of some great crime from his birth! The ignorance of this made the heathens accuse nature, and blaspheme God under that mask, as less kind and indulgent to man than to the creatures below him. They are not under so hard a law of coming into the world. They are presently instructed to swim, to fly, to run for their preservation. They are clothed by nature, and their habits grow in proportion with their bodies, some with feathers, some with wool, others with scales, which are both habit and armour: but man, who alone is sensible of shame, is born naked, and though of a more delicate temper, is more exposed to injuries by distempered seasons, and utterly unable to repel or avoid the evils that encompass him. Now the account the Scripture gives of original sin silences all these complaints. Man is a transgressor from the womb; and how can he expect a favourable reception into the empire of an offended God? Briefly; sometimes death enters into the retirements of nature, and changes the womb into a grave; which proves, that as soon as we partake of the human nature, we are guilty of the sin that is common to it; " for the wages of sin is death," Rom. vi. 23. Adam, in his innocent state had the privilege of immortality, but by him " sin entered into the world, and death by sin; and so death passed upon all men" as a just sentence upon the guilty, "for that all have sinned," v. 12.

An hereditary corruption is transmitted to all that naturally descend from him. If Adam had continued in his obedience, the spiritual as well as the natural life had been conveyed to his children; but for his rebellion he lost his primitive rectitude, and contracted a universal corruption; which he derives to all his posterity. And as in a disease there is a defect of health, and a distemper of the humours that affect the body; so in the depravation of nature, there is not the mere want of holiness, but a strong proclivity to sin. This privation of original righteousness, considered as a sin, is naturally from Adam, the principle of lapsed and corrupt nature: but, as a punishment, it is meritoriously from him, and falls under the ordination of divine justice. Man cast it away, and God righteously refuses to restore it.

It is a solicitous impertinency to inquire nicely about the manner of conveying this universal corruption; for the bare knowledge of it is ineffectual to the cure. And what greater folly than to make our own evils the object of simple speculation? I shall consider only that general account of it, which is set down in the Scripture.

It is the universal and unchangeable law of nature, that every thing should produce its like, not only in regard of the same nature that is propagated from one individual to another without a change of the species, but in respect of the qualities with which that nature is evidently affected. This is visible in the several kinds of creatures in the world; they all preserve the nature of the principle from whence they are derived, and retain the vein of their original, the quality of their extraction. Thus our Saviour tells us, Matt. vii. 18, that the fruit partakes of the rottenness of the tree; and whatever "is born of the flesh, is flesh," John iii. 6. The title of flesh doth not signify the material part of our humanity, but the corruption of sin with which the whole nature is infected. This is evident by the description the apostle gives of it, that the flesh " is not subject to the law of God;" and that which aggravates the evil is, that it cannot be, Rom. viii. 7. Sinful corruption is expressed by this title, partly in regard it is transmitted by the way of carnal propagation; " Behold, I was shapen in iniquity, and in sin did my mother conceive me," Psalm li. 5; and partly in regard it is exercised by the carnal members. This corruption is a poison so subtle, that it pierces into all the powers of the soul; so contagious, that it infects all the actions; so obstinate, that only omnipotent grace can heal it. More particularly;

1. It is an innate habit, not merely acquired by imita-

tion. The root of bitterness is planted in the human nature, and produces its fruits in the various seasons of life. No age is free from its working; every imagination of the thoughts of man's heart is only evil, and continually evil, Gen. vi. 5. We see this verified in children, when the most early acts of their reason and the first instances of their apprehension are in sin. If we ascend higher and consider man in his infant state, the vicious inclinations which appear in the cradle, the violent motions of anger which disturb sucklings, their endeavours to exercise a weak revenge on those that displease them, convince us that the corruption is natural, and proceeds from an infected original.

2. As it is natural, so universal. " Who can bring a clean thing out of an unclean?" Job xiv. 4; that is, how can a righteous person be born of a sinner? The answer is peremptory, " Not one." The fountain was poisoned in Adam, and all the streams partake of the infection. All that are derived from him in a natural way, and have a relation to him as their common father, are sharers in this depravation. What difference soever there is in their climates, colours, and external conditions of life, yet the blood from whence they spring, taints them all.

3. Corrupt nature is pregnant with the seeds of all sin, though they do not shoot forth together: and for this, several accounts may be given. Though all sins agree in their cause and end, yet some are contrary in their exercise. The human spirit is not capable of many passions in their height at the same time; and it is the art of our spiritual enemies to suit their temptations to the capacity of man. As the same produces different effects in different bodies, according to those various humours which are predominant in them; so the same corruption of nature works variously according to the different tempers of men. For though the conception of sin depends immediately upon the soul, yet to the bringing of it forth, the concurrence of the external faculties is requisite. Thus a voluptuary who is restrained from the gross acts of sensuality by a disease or age, may be as vicious in his desires, as another who follows

the pernicious swing of his appetite, having a vigorous constitution. Briefly; the variety of circumstances by which the inward corruption is excited and drawn forth, makes a great difference as to the open and visible acts of it. Thus an ambitious person who uses clemency to accomplish his design, would exercise cruelty if it were necessary to his end. It is true, some are really more temperate, and exempted from the tyranny of the flesh than others; Cicero was more virtuous than Catiline, and Socrates than Aristophanes: but these are privileged persons, in whom the efficacy of divine providence either by forming them in the womb, or in their education, or by conducting them in their maturer age, hath corrected the malignity of nature. All have sinned, and come short of the glory of God's image, Rom. iii. 23. And that sin breaks not forth so outrageously in some as in others, the restraint is from a higher principle than common and corrupt nature.

4. This corruption, though natural, is yet voluntary and culpable.

(1.) In some respects it is voluntary; in its principle and cause, the will of Adam that originally was ours. All habits receive their character from those acts by which they are produced; and as the disobedience of Adam was voluntary, so is the depravation that sprung from it. It is inherent in the will. If Adam had derived a leprosy to all men, it were an involuntary evil, because the diseases of the body are foreign to the soul; but when the corruption invades the internal faculties, it is denominated from the subject wherein it is seated. It is voluntary in its effects, the numberless actual sins proceeding from it: and if the acts that freely flow from this corruption are voluntary, the principle must be of the same nature.

(2.) It is culpable. The formality of sin consists in its opposition to the law, according to the definition of the apostle, "sin is a transgression of the law." Now the law requires an entire rectitude in all the faculties. It condemns corrupt inclinations, the originals as well as the acts of sin. Besides, concupiscence was not inherent in the human nature in its creation, but was contracted by the fall. The soul is stripped of its native righteousness and holiness, and invested with contrary qualities. There is as great a difference between the corruption of the soul in its degenerate state, and its primitive purity, as between the loathsomeness of a carcass, and the beauty of a living body. Sad change, and to be lamented with tears of confusion!

II. That the sin of Adam should be so fatal to all his posterity, is the most difficult part in the whole order of divine providence. Nothing more offends carnal reason, which forms many specious objections against it. I will briefly consider them.

1. " Since God saw that Adam would not resist the temptation, and that upon his fall the whole race of mankind which he supported as the foundation, would sink into ruin, why did he not confirm him against it? Was it not within his power, and more suitable to his wisdom, holiness, and goodness?" To this I answer;

(1.) The divine power could have preserved man in his integrity, either by laying a restraint on the apostate angels, that they should never have made an attempt upon him; or by keeping the understanding waking and vigilant to discover the danger of the temptation, and by fortifying the will, and rendering it impenetrable to the fiery darts of Satan, without any prejudice to its freedom; for that doth not consist in an absolute indifference, but in a judicious and deliberate choice; so that when the soul is not led by a blind instinct, nor forced by a foreign power, but embraces what it knows and approves, it then enjoys the most true liberty. Thus, in the glorified spirits above, by the full and constant light of the mind, the will is indeclinably fixed upon its supreme good, and this is its crown and perfection.

(2.) It was most suitable to the divine wisdom, to leave man to stand or fall by his own choice; to discover the necessary dependence of all second causes upon the first. No creature is absolutely impeccable, but the most perfect is liable to imperfection. He that is essentially, is only unchangeably good. Infinite goodness alone excludes all possibility of receiving corruption. The fall of angels and man convinces us, that there is one sole Being immutably pure and holy, on whom all depend, and without whose influence they cannot be, or must be eternally miserable. It was very fit that Adam should be first in a state of trial, before he was confirmed in his happiness. The reason of it is clear; he was left to his own judgment and election, that obedience might be his choice, and in the performance of it he might acquire a title to the reward. A determining virtue over him had crossed the end of his creation, which was to glorify God in such a free manner. Therefore, in paradise there were amiable objects to allure the lower faculties, before they were disordered by him. The forbidden fruit had beauty to invite the eye, and sweetness to delight the palate. And if upon the competition of the sensual with the intellectual good, he had rejected the one and chosen the other, he had been raised to an unchangeable state; his innocence had been crowned with perseverance; as the angels who continued in their duty when the rest revolted, are finally established in their integrity and felicity. And the apostle gives us an account of this order, when he tells us, that was first which was natural, then that which is spiritual and supernatural, 1 Cor. xv. 46. Man was created in a state of perfection, but it was natural, therefore, mutable; the confirming of him immediately had been grace, which belongs to a more excellent dispensation. Now to bring man from not being to a supernatural state, without trial of the middle state of nature, was not so congruous to the divine wisdom.

(3.) The permission of the fall doth not reflect on the divine purity; for man was made upright; he had no inward corruption to betray him; there was antidote enough in his nature to expel the strongest temptation. God was not bound to hinder the commission of sin. It is a true maxim, that "*in debitis causa deficiens efficit moraliter;*" but God is not only free from subjection to a law, as having no superior, but was under no voluntary obligation by promise to prevent the fall. Neither doth that first act of sin reflect on God's unspotted providence which suffered it, as if sin were in any degree allowed by him. The holy law which God gave to direct man, the terrible threatening annexed to warn him, declare his irreconcilable hatred against sin. He permits innumerable sins every day, yet he is as jealous of the honour of his holiness now, as in the beginning. It is the worst impiety for the sinner to think God like himself, Psalm l. 21; as if he took complacency in sin, because he is silent for a time, and suffers the commission of it. In the next state he will fully vindicate his glory, and convince the whole world of his eternal aversion to sin, by inflicting on sinners the most dreadful and durable torments.

(4.) The goodness of God is not disparaged by permitting the fall: this appears by considering that God bestowed on man an excellent being, and a happiness that might satisfy his nature, considered as human or holy. But he perverted the favours of God to his dishonour; and this doth not lessen the goodness that gave them. It is unreasonable to judge of the value of a benefit by the ungrateful abuse of the receiver, and not from its own nature. It is a chosen misery that is come upon man, and not to be imputed to any defect of the divine goodness. God is infinitely good, notwithstanding the entrance of sin and misery into the world. We must distinguish between natural and voluntary agents. Natural agents have no power to suspend their acts, but are entirely determined, and their operations are "*ad extremum virium,*" to the utmost of their efficacy. If there were infinite degrees of heat, there would be no cold, it being overcome by the force of its contrary. But God is a wise and free agent; and as he is infinite in goodness, so the exercise of it is voluntary, and only so far as he pleases. God is an omnipotent good, and it is his peculiar glory to bring good out of evil, that by the opposition and lustre of contraries, his goodness might be the more conspicuous. To speak strictly, sin is the only evil in the world; for all the rest which appear so to our fancies and appetites, are either absolutely good, or upon the supposal of sin, viz. either for the reformation of sinners, or for the ruin of the obstinate. Now the evil of sin God permitted as a fit occasion for the more glorious discovery of his attributes, in sending his Son into the world to repair his image which was defaced, and to raise man from an earthly to celestial happiness. I shall conclude with the excellent answer of St. Augustin to the adversary of the law and prophets: " *Quibus autem videtur sic hominem fieri debuisse ut peccare nollet, non eis displiceat sic esse factum, ut non peccare posset, si nollet. Nunquid enim si melior esset qui non posset peccare, ideo non benefactus est qui posset et non peccare? An vero usque adeo desipiendum est, ut homo videat melius aliquid fieri debuisse, et hoc Deum vidisse non putet? Aut putet vidisse et credat facere noluisse? Aut voluisse quidem et minime potuisse? Avertat hoc Deus a cordibus piorum.*" The substance of which is this, that it is an impious folly to imagine that God was either defective in wisdom, not to know what was the best state for man in his creation; or defective in goodness, that knowing it, he would not confer it upon him; or defective in power, that willing, he was unable to make him better.

2. There is another objection vehemently urged, that " the imputation of Adam's sin to all his posterity who were not existent at that time, and did not give their personal consent to the treaty between God and him, is inconsistent with justice." To this I answer;

(1.) The terms of the first covenant are such, that the common reason of mankind cannot justly refuse; for suppose all the progeny of Adam had appeared with him before their Creator, and this had been propounded, that God would make an agreement with their common father on their behalf, that if he continued in his obedience, they should enjoy a happy immortality; if he declined from it, they should be deprived of blessedness; what shadow of exception can be formed against this proposal? For God who is the master of his own favours, and gives them upon what terms he pleases, might, upon their refusal, have justly annihilated them. The command was equal, and his obedience for all was as easy, as that of every particular person for himself. Besides, Adam was as much concerned to observe the conditions of the covenant, for securing his own interest, as theirs; and after a short time of trial they should be confirmed in their blessedness. By all which it is apparent how reasonable the conditions of the original agreement between God and man are.

(2.) God hath a power over our wills superior to what we ourselves have. If God offers a covenant to the creature, the terms being equal, it becomes a law, and consent is due as an act of obedience. And if a community may appoint one of their number to be their representative, to transact affairs of the greatest moment, and according to his management, the benefit or damage shall accrue to them, because he is reckoned to perform the wills of them all; may not God, who hath a supreme dominion over us, constitute Adam the representative of mankind, and unite the consent of all in his general will, so that as he fulfilled or neglected his duty, they should be happy or miserable? This consideration alone, that the first covenant was ordered by God, may perfectly satisfy all inquiries; as Salvian having confessed his ignorance in the reasons of some dispositions of providence, silences all objections with this: "*Nihil in hac re opus est aliquid audire; satis sit pro universis rationibus, Auctor Deus.*" Neither is this a mere extrinsic argument, as authority usually is, because there is an intrinsic reason of this authority, the absolute rectitude and justice of God's nature, who is "righteous in all his ways, and holy in all his works," Psalm cxlv. 17.

CHAPTER IV.

THE MORAL IMPOTENCE OF MAN.

When Adam was expelled from paradise, the entrance was guarded by a flaming sword, to signify that all hopes of return by the way of nature are cut off for ever. He lost his right, and could not recover it by power. The chiefest ornaments of paradise are the image and favour of God, of which he is justly deprived, and there is no possibility for him to regain them. What can he expect from his own reason, that betrayed him to ruin? If it did not support him when he stood, how can it raise him when he is fallen? If there were a power in lapsed man to restore himself, it would exceed the original power he had to will and obey; it being infinitely more difficult for a dead man to rise, than for a living man to put forth vital actions.

For the clearer opening of this point concerning man's absolute disability to recover his primitive state, I will distinctly consider it with respect to the image and favour of God, upon which his blessedness depends.

I. He cannot recover his primitive holiness. This will appear by considering, that whatsoever is corrupted in its noble parts, can never restore itself; the power of an external agent is requisite for the recovering of its integrity. This is verified by innumerable instances in things artificial and natural. If a clock be disordered by a fall, the workman must mend it, before it can be useful. If wine that is rich and generous, decline by the loss of spirits, it can never be revived without a new supply. In the human body, where is a more noble form and more power to redress any evil that may happen to the parts, if a gangrene seize on any member, nothing can resist its course but the application of outward means; it cannot be cured by the internal principles of its constitutiou. And proportionably in moral agents, when the faculties which are the principles of action are corrupted, it is impossible, without the virtue of a divine cause, they should ever be restored to their original rectitude. As the image of God was at first imprinted on the human nature by creation, so the renewed image is wrought in him by the same creating power, Ephes. iv. 24. This will be more evident, by considering that inward and deep depravation of the understanding and will, the two superior faculties which command the rest.

1. The understanding hath lost the right apprehension of things. As sin began in the darkness of the mind, so one of its worst effects is the increasing of that darkness which can only be dispelled by a supernatural light. Now what the eye is to the body, that the mind is for directing the will, and conducting the life; and if the

light that is in us be darkness, how great is that darkness!" How irregular and dangerous must our motions be! Not only the lower part of the soul is under a dreadful disorder; but the "spirit of the mind," the divinest part, is depraved with ignorance and error. The light of reason is not pure; but as the sun, when with its beams it sends down pestilential influences, corrupts the air in the enlightening of it, so the carnal mind corrupts the whole man, by representing good as evil, and evil as good. The wisdom of the flesh is enmity against God; and the apostle describes the state of the Gentile world, that their understandings were darkened, " being alienated from the life of God, through the ignorance that is in them, because of the blindness of their heart," Ephes. iv. 18. The corruption of their manners proceeded from their minds: for all virtues are directed by reason in their exercise, so that if the understanding be darkened, all virtuous operations cease.

Besides, corrupt man being without light and life, can neither discern nor feel his misery. The carnal mind is insensible of its infirmity, ignorant of its ignorance, and suffers under the incurable extremes of being blind, and imagining that it is very clear-sighted. More particularly, the reasons why the carnal mind hath not a due sense of sinful corruption, are, because it is natural, and cleaves to the principles of our being from the birth and conception; and natural things do not affect us. It is confirmed by custom, which is a second nature, and hath a strange power to stupefy conscience, and render it insensible; as the historian observed concerning the Roman soldiers, that by constant use, their arms were no more a burthen to them than their natural members. In the transition from the infant state to the age of discerning, man is incapable of observing his native corruption; since at first he acts evilly, and is in constant conversation with sinners, who bring vice into his acquaintance; and, by making it familiar, lessen the horror and aversion to it. Besides, those corrupt and numerous examples wherewith he is encompassed, call forth his sinful inclinations, which, as they are heightened by repeated acts and become more strong and obstinate, so are less sensible to him.

And by this we may understand how irrecoverable man is by his own reason. The first step to our cure is begun in the knowledge of our disease, and this discovery is made by the understanding, when it is seeing and vigilant, not when it is blind. A disease in the body is perceived by the mind; but when the soul is the affected part, and the rectitude of reason is lost, there is no principle remaining to give notice of it. And as that disease is the most dangerous which strikes at the life, and is without pain, for pain is not the chief evil, but supposes it, it is the spur of nature urging us to seek for cure; so the corruption of the understanding is very fatal to man; for although he labours under many pernicious lusts, which in the issue will prove deadly, yet he is insensible of them, and from thence follows a carelessness and contempt of the means for his recovery.

2. The corruption of the will is more incurable than that of the mind; for it is full not only of impotence, but contrariety to what is spiritually good. There are some weak strictures of truth in lapsed man, but they die in the brain, and are powerless and ineffectual as the will, which rushes into the embraces of worldly objects. This the universal experience of mankind, since the fall, doth evidently prove, and the account of it is in the following considerations.

There is a strong inclination in man to happiness. This desire is born and brought up with him, and is common to all who partake of the reasonable nature. From the prince to the poorest wretch, from the most knowing to the meanest in understanding, every one desires to be happy; as the great flames and the little sparks of fire, all naturally ascend to their sphere.

The constituting of any thing to be our happiness, is the first and universal maxim, from whence all moral consequences are derived. It is the rule of our desires, and the end of our actions. As in natural things, the principles of their production operate according to their quality, so, in moral things, the end is as powerful to form the soul for its operations in order to it. Therefore, as all desire to be happy, so they apply themselves to those means which appear to be convenient for the obtaining of happiness.

Every one frames a happiness according to his temper. The apprehensions of it are answerable to the dispositions of the person; for felicity is the pleasure which arises from the harmonious agreement between the object and the appetite. Now man by his original and contracted corruption, is altogether carnal; he inherits the serpent's curse to creep on the earth; he cleaves to defiling and debasing objects, and is qualified only for sensual satisfactions. The soul is incarnated, and it shapes a happiness to itself, in the enjoyment of those things which are delicious to the senses. The shadow of felicity is pursued with equal ardour, as that which is real and substantial. The supreme part of man, the understanding, is employed to serve the lower faculties; reason is used to make him more ingenious and luxurious in sensuality: so much more brutish than the brutes is he become, when besides that part which is so by its natural condition, the most noble part is made so by unnatural choice and corruption. From hence the apostle gives a universal character of men in their corrupt state, that they are " foolish, disobedient, deceived, serving divers lusts and pleasures." Tit. iii. 3. This pursuit of sensual pleasure is the service of a slave, who hath no other law of his life but the will of his master. The servitude is diverse, but all are slaves; the chains are not the same, some are more glittering, but not less weighty; and every one is deprived of true liberty. But the bondage is so pleasing, that corrupted man prefers it before spiritual and real freedom. Sensual lusts blind the understanding, and bind the will so, that he is unable, because unwilling, to rescue himself. He is deluded with the false appearance of liberty, and imagines that to live according to rule is a slavish confinement; as if the horse were free, because his rider allows him a full career in a pleasant road, when the bridle is in his mouth, and he is under his imperious check at pleasure. or a galley-slave were free, because the vessel wherein he rows with so much toil, roams over the vast ocean. And whereas there are two considerations which are proper to convince man that the full and unconfined enjoyment of worldly things cannot make him happy, because they are wounding to the conscience and unsatisfying to the affections, yet these are ineffectual to take him off from an eager pursuit of them; I will particularly consider this, to show how unable man, in his lapsed condition, is to disentangle himself from miserable vanities, and consequently, to recover his lost holiness.

(1.) Sensual pleasures are wounding to the conscience. There is a secret acknowledgment in every man's breast of a superior power, to whom he must give an account; and though conscience be much impaired in its integrity, yet sometimes it recoils upon the sinner by the foulness of his actions, and its testimony brings such terror, as makes sin very unpleasant. The poet tells us, that of all the torments of hell, the most cruel, and that which exceeds the rest, is "*Nocte dieque suum gestare in pectore testem.*" And how can the sinner delight freely in that which vexes and frets the most vital and tender part? He cannot enjoy his charming lusts without guilt, nor embrace them without the reluctancy of a contradicting principle within him. As the fear of poison will embitter the sweetest cup, so the purest pleasures are alloyed with afflicting apprehensions of the future, and the presage of judgment to come.

Now man, in his sensual state, tries always to disarm conscience, that he may please the lower appetites without regret. I will instance in the principle. He uses many pleas and pretexts to justify or extenuate the evil, and, if possible, to justify carnality and conscience too. Self-love, which is the eloquent advocate of sense, puts a varnish upon sin, to take off from it its horrid appearance: and endeavours not only to colour the object, but to corrupt the eye by a disguising tincture, that the sight of things may not be according to truth, but the desire. Thus the heathens allowed intemperance, uncleanness, and other infamous vices, as innocent gratifications of nature. Now if the principles in man are poisoned, so that evil is esteemed good, he then lives in the quiet practice of sin, without reflection or remorse; there is no sting remaining to awaken him out of security. But if he cannot so far bribe conscience, as to make it silent, or favourable to that which delights the sense, if he cannot escape its internal condemnation, the next method is by a strong diversion to lessen the trouble. When the carnal mind sees nothing within but what torments, and finds an intolerable pain in conversing with itself, it runs abroad, and uses all the arts of oblivion to lose the remembrance of its true state; as Cain, to drown the voice of conscience, fell to building cities, and Saul to dispel his melancholy, called for music. The business and pleasures of this life are dangerous amusements to divert the soul, by the representation of what is profitable or pleasant, from considering the moral qualities of good and evil. Thus conscience, like an intermitting pulse, ceases for awhile. Miserable consolation, which doth not remove, but conceal the evil till it be past remedy! But if conscience, notwithstanding all these evasions, still pursues a sinner, and, at times, something disturbs his reason and his rest, yet he will not part with carnal pleasures; for being acquainted with those things only that affect the senses, and having no relish for that happiness which is sublime and supernatural, if he part with them, he is deprived of all delight, which is to him a state more intolerable than that wherein there is a mixture of delight and torment. From hence it appears that the interposition of conscience, though with a flaming sword, between man carnal, and his beloved objects, is not effectual to restrain him.

(2.) All worldly things are unsatisfying to the affections. There are three considerations which depreciate and lessen the value of any good—the shortness of its duration—if it brings only a slight pleasure—if that pleasure is attended with torments: all which are contrary to the essential properties of the supreme good, which is perpetual and sincere, without the least mixture of evil, and produces the highest delight to the soul. Now all these concur to vilify worldly things. They are short in their duration. Not only the voice of heaven, but of the earth declares this, that "all flesh is grass, and the glory of it as the flower of the grass," Isa. xl. 6, 7; 1 Pet. i. 24, 25. Life, the foundation of all temporal enjoyments, is but a span: the longest liver can measure in a thought the space of time between his infant state and the present hour; how long soever, it seems as short to him as the twinkling of an eye. And all the glory of the flesh, as titles, treasures, delights, are as the flower of the grass, which is the most tender amongst vegetables, and so weak a subsistence, that a little breath of wind, the hand of an infant, the teeth of a worm, can destroy it. The pleasures of sin, under which secular greatness and wealth are comprehended, are but "for a season," Heb. xi. 25. They are so short lived, that they expire in the birth, and die whilst they are tasted. Again; they bring only a slight pleasure, being disproportionable to the desires of the soul. They are confined to the senses, wherein the beasts are more accurate than man, but cannot reach to the upper and more comprehensive faculties, Nay, they cannot satisfy the greedy senses, much less quiet the spiritual and immortal appetite. What the poet speaks with astonishment of Alexander's insatiable ambition, "*Æstuat infelix angusto limite mundi,*" that the whole world seemed to him as a narrow prison, wherein he was miserable, and, as it were, suffocated, is true of every one. If the world was seated in the heart of man, it can no more satisfy it, than the picture of a feast can fill the stomach. Besides, vexation is added to the vanity of worldly things; and that either because the vehement delights of sense corrupt the temperament of the body, in which the vital complexion consists, and expose it to those sharp diseases, that it may be said without an hyperbole, that a thousand pleasures are not equal to one hour's pain that attends them; or, because of the inward torture of the mind, arising from the sense of guilt and folly, which is the anticipation of hell itself, the beginning of eternal sorrows.

Now these things are not obscure articles of faith, nor abstracted doctrines, to be considered only by refined reason, but are manifest and clear as the light, and verified by continual experience: it is, therefore, strange to amazement, that man should search after happiness in these things, where he knows it is not to be found, and court real infelicity under a deceitful appearance, when the fallacy is transparent. Who, from a principle of reason, would choose for his happiness a real good, which after a little time he should be deprived of for ever? or a slight good for ever, as the sight of a picture, or the hearing of music? Yet thus unreasonable is man in his corrupt state, whose soul is truly immortal and capable of infinite blessedness, yet he chooses those delights which are neither satisfying nor lasting.

And because the human understanding from time to time is convinced of the vanity of all sublunary things, therefore, to lessen the vexation which arises from disappointment, and that the appetite may not be taken off from them, corrupted man tries, by variety of objects, to preserve uniformity in delight. The most pleasing, if confined to them, grow nauseous and insipid; after the expiring of a few moments, there remains nothing but satiety and sickly resentments; and then changes are the remedies, to take off the weariness of one pleasure by another. The human soul is under a perpetual instability of restless desires; it despises what it enjoys, and values what is new, as if novelty and goodness were the same in all temporal things. And as the birds remain in the air by constant motion, without which they would quickly fall to the earth as other heavy bodies, there being nothing solid to support them; so the spirit of man, by many unquiet agitations and continual changes, subsists for a time, till at last it falls into discontent and despair, the centre of corrupt nature.

When present things are unsatisfactory, he entertains himself with hope; for that being terminated on a future object, which is of a doubtful nature, the mind attends to those arguments which produce a pleasant belief to find that, in several objects, which it cannot in any single one, and to make up in number, what is wanting in measure; whereas the present is manifest, and takes away all liberty of thinking. Upon this ground sensual pleasure is more expectation than fruition; for hope by a marvellous enchantment, not only makes that which is future present, but, representing in one view that which cannot be enjoyed but in the intervals of time, it unites all the successive parts in one point, so that what is divided and lessened in the fruition, which is always gradual, is offered at once and entire. Thus man carnal, deceived by the imperfect light of fancy and the false glass of hope, chooses a fictitious felicity. "Man walketh in a vain show," Psalm xxxix. 6. His original error hath produced this in its own image. And although the complacency he takes in sensual objects is like the joy of a distracted person, the issue of folly and illusion, and experience discovers the deceit that is in them, as smelling to an artificial rose undeceives the eye; yet he will embrace his error. Man is in a voluntary dream, which represents to him the world as his happiness, and when he is awakened, he dreams again, choosing to be deceived with delight, rather than to discover the truth without it. This is set forth by the prophet, "Thou art wearied in the greatness of thy way, yet saidst thou not, There is no hope," Isa. lvii. 10; that is, Thou art tired in the chase of satisfaction from one thing to another, yet thou wouldst not give over, but still pursuest those shadows which can never be brought nearer to thee. And the true reason of it is, that in the human nature, there is an intense and continual desire of pleasure, without which life itself hath no satisfaction; for life consisting in the operations of the soul, either the external of the senses or the internal of the mind, it is sweetened by those delights which are suitable to them; so that if all pleasant operations cease, without possibility of returning, death is more desirable than life. And in the corrupt state there is so strict an alliance between the flesh and spirit, that there is but one appetite between them, and that is of the flesh. All the designs and endeavours of the carnal man are by fit means to obtain satisfaction to his senses; as if the contentment of the flesh and the happiness of the soul were the same thing; or as if the soul were to die with the body, and with both, all hopes and fears, all joys and sorrows were at an end. The flesh is now grown absolute, and hath acquired a perfect empire, and taken a full possession of all the faculties. For this reason the apostle tells us, "They that are in the flesh, cannot please God;" and "The carnal mind is enmity against God, it is not subject, neither can it be," Rom. viii. 7, 8. It is ensnared in the cords of concupiscence, and cannot recover itself from its foolish bondage. But that does not lessen the guilt; which will appear by considering there is a twofold impotence.

There is a natural impotence, which protects from the severity of justice. No man is bound to stop the sun in its course, or to remove mountains; for the human nature was never endued with faculties to do those things. They are indubitably beyond our power. Now the law enjoins nothing but what man had in his creation an original power to perform.

There is a moral impotence, which arises from a perverse disposition of the will, and is joined with a delight in sin, and a strong aversion to the holy commands of God; and the more deep and inveterate this is, the more worthy it is of punishment. Aristotle asserts, that those who contract invincible habits by custom, are inexcusable, though they cannot abstain from evil; for since liberty consists in doing what one wills, this impossibility doth not destroy liberty; the depravation of the faculties does not hinder their voluntary operations. The understanding conceives, the will chooses, the appetite desires, freely. A distracted person that kills, is not guilty of murder, and therefore is secure from the sentence of the law; for his understanding being distempered by the disorder of the images in his fancy, it did not judge aright, so that the action is involuntary, and therefore not culpable. But there is a vast difference between the causes of distraction, and those which induce a carnal man to sin. The first are seated in the distemper of the brain, over which the will hath no power; whereas there should be a regular subjection of the lower appetite to the will, enlightened and directed by the mind. The will itself is corrupted and brought into captivity by things pleasing to the lower faculties: it cannot disentangle itself, but its impotence lies in its obstinacy. This is the meaning of St. Peter, speaking concerning unclean persons, that "their eyes are full of adultery, and they cannot cease from sin." It is from their fault alone that they are without power. Therefore the Scripture represents man to be ἀσθενὴς and ἀσεβής, weak, but wicked. His disability to supernatural good arises from an inordinate affection to that which is sensual, so that it is so far from excusing, that it renders inexcusable, being voluntary and vicious. And in this, the diseases of the body are different from those of the soul. In the first, the desire of healing is ineffectual, through want of knowledge or power to apply the sovereign remedies; whereas, in the second, the sincere desire of their cure is insufficient, for the diseases are corrupt desires.

The natural man is wholly led by sense, by fancy, and the passions, and he esteems it his infelicity to be otherwise; as the degenerate slave, who was displeased with a jubilee, and refused liberty. Servitude is his sensuality. He is not only in love with the unworthy object, but with the vicious affection, and abhors the cure of it. As one in the poet that was so delighted in his pleasant madness, that he was offended at his recovery;

"————Cui sic extorta voluptas
Et demptus per vim mentis gratissimus error."

This is acknowledged by St. Austin in his Confessions, where he describes the strife between conviction and corruption in his soul. He tells us in the conflict between reason and lust, that he had recourse to God, and his prayer was "*Da mihi continentiam, sed noli modò;*" he desired chastity, but not too soon. He was afraid that God should hear his petition, it being more bitter than death to change his custom. This is the general sense, though not the general discourse of men. As the sick person desired his physician to remove his fever, but not his thirst, which made his drink very pleasing to him; so man, in his sensual state, would fain be freed from the estuations of conscience, but he cherishes those carnal desires which gives a high taste to objects suitable to them.

From hence it appears, that though in the corrupt nature there is no liberty of indifference to good and evil, yet there is a liberty of delight in evil; and though the will in its natural capacity may choose good, yet it is morally determined by its love to evil. In short, there is so much power not to sin as is sufficient to sin ; that is, that the forbidden action be free, and so become a sin. Which strange combination of liberty and necessity is excellently expressed by St. Bernard ; " that the soul which fell by its own choice, cannot recover itself, is from the corruption of the will, which, overcome by the vicious love of the body, rejects the love of righteousness; so that, in a manner as strange as evil, the will being corrupted with sin, makes a necessity to itself, yet so, the necessity being voluntary, doth not excuse the will ; nor the will, being pleasantly and powerfully allured, exclude necessity." The law, therefore, remains in its full force, and God is righteous in commanding and condemning sinners.

From all that hath been discoursed, it is evident how impossible it is for corrupt man to recover his lost holiness; for there are only two motives to induce the reasonable creature to seek after it—its beauty and loveliness—and the reward that attends it. And both these arguments are ineffectual to work upon him.

The beauty of holiness, which excels all other created perfections, it being a conformity to the most glorious attribute of the Deity, doth not allure him : for " *Unusquisque ut affectus est, ita judicat ;*" man understands according to his affections. The renewed mind only can see the essential and innate beauty of holiness. Now in fallen man the clearness of the discerning power is lost. As the natural eye, till it is purged from vicious qualities, cannot look on things bright and sublime, and if it had been long in darkness, suffers by the most pleasing object, the light ; so the internal eye of the mind, that it may see the lively lustre of holiness, must be cleansed from the filthiness of carnal affections, and having been so long under darkness, it must be strengthened, before it can sustain the brightness of things spiritual. Till it be prepared, it can see nothing amiable and desirable in the image of God.

The reward of holiness hath no attractive power on the carnal will, because it is future and spiritual. It is future, and therefore the conceptions of it are very dark and imperfect. The soul is sunk down into the senses, and they are short-sighted and cannot look beyond what is present to the next life. And as the images of things are weakened and confused proportionably to their distance, and make a fainter impression upon the faculty; so the representation of heaven and blessedness as a happiness to come hereafter, and therefore remote, doth but coldly affect the will. A present vanity, in the judgment of the carnal soul, outweighs the most glorious futurity. Till there be taken from before its eyes, in Tertullian's language, " the thick curtain of the visible world," it cannot discern the difference between them, nor value the reward for its excellency and duration. It is spiritual, and there must be a divine disposition of the soul before it is capable of it. The pure in heart only can see the pure God, Matt. v. 8. The felicity above is that which " eye hath not seen, nor ear heard, neither hath it entered into the heart of man to conceive," 1 Cor. ii. 9. Now the carnal man is affected only with gross and corporeal things. The certainty, immensity, and immortality of the heavenly reward, do not prevail with him to seek after it. He hath no palate for spiritual pleasures; it is vitiated by luscious vanities, and cannot relish rational joys. Till the temper of the soul be altered, the bread of angels is distasteful to it; for the appetite is according to the disposition of the stomach, and when that is corrupted, it longs for things hurtful, and rejects wholesome food. If a carnal man were translated to heaven, where the love of God reigns, and where the brightest and sweetest discoveries of his glory appear, he would not find paradise in heaven itself; for delight arises not merely from the excellency of the object, but from the proportionableness of it to the faculty. Though God is an infinite good in himself, yet if he is not conceived as the supreme good to man, he cannot make him happy.

Suppose some slight convictions to be in the mind, that happiness consists in the enjoyment of God, yet this being offered upon the terms of quitting all sensual lusts, the carnal man esteems the condition impossible, and therefore is discouraged from using any endeavours to obtain it; for to excite hope, it is not sufficient to propose a reward that is real and excellent, but that is attainable; for although hope hath its tendency to a difficult good as its proper object, and the difficulty is so far from discouraging, that it quickens the soul and draws forth all the active powers, by rendering it greater in our esteem; yet when the difficulty is excessive, and confines upon impossibility, it dejects the soul and inclines it to despair. Thus when the condition of obtaining some good is necessary, but insufferable, it takes off from all endeavours in order to it.

To consider it in a temporal case, will make it more clear. As one that labours under a dropsy, and is vexed with an intolerable and insatiable thirst, if a physician should assure him of cure upon condition he would abstain from drinking, he could not conceive any real hope of being healed, judging it impossible to resist the importunity of his drought; he therefore neglects the means, he drinks and dies; thus the corrupt heart of man, that is under a perpetual thirst of carnal pleasure, and is more inflamed by the satisfaction it receives, judges it an insuperable condition to part with them for the acquiring of spiritual happiness: and this sensual and sottish despair causes a total neglect of the means. It is thus expressed by the Israelites; when God commanded them to return from the evil of their ways in order to their happiness, they said, "There is no hope, but we will walk after own devices, and we will every one do the imagination of his evil heart." Jer. xviii. 12. They were slaves to their domineering appetites, and resolved to make no trial about that they judged impossible. "*Abstinere nequeo,*" Grotius.

Briefly: in fallen man there is something predominant, which he values above the favour and fruition of God, and that is the world; as in the parable where happiness is set forth under the familiar representation of a feast, those who were invited to it, excuse themselves by such reasons as clearly discover that some amiable lust charmed them so strongly, that in the competition it was preferred before heaven. One saith, "I have bought a piece of ground, and I must needs go and see it;" and another, "I have bought five yoke of oxen, and I go to prove them;" and a third, "I have married a wife, and therefore I cannot come," Luke xiv. 18. The objects of their passions are different, but they all produce the same effect, the rejection of happiness.

The sum of all is this, that as man fell from obedience, and lost the image of God, by seeking perfection and satisfaction, that is, happiness, in the creature; so he can never return to his obedience, acknowledge God as his supreme Lord, till he chooses him for his happiness. And this he can never entirely do, till he is born again, and hath a new principle of life that may change the complexion of the soul, and qualify it for those delights which are sublime and spiritual.

II. Fallen man can never recover the favour of God; and this is evident upon a double account—he is not able to make satisfaction to God's justice for the dishonour brought to him—he is incapable of real repentance, which might qualify him for pardon.

1. He is unable to satisfy justice for his offence, either by exact obedience for the future, or by enduring the punishment that is due to sin.

(1.) Supposing that man could perform exact obedience after his fall, yet that could not be satisfaction. It is essential to satisfaction, that the action by which it is made be in the power of the person that satisfies. A servant, as a servant, cannot make satisfaction for an injury done to his lord, for whatsoever service he performs was due before the offence, and is not properly a restitution, because it is not of his own. Now the complete obedience of the creature is due to God. He is the Lord of all our actions, and whatever man doeth is but the payment of the original debt. The law requires a perpetual reverence of the Lawgiver, and express obedience to his will in all things: so that it is impossible that the highest respect to it afterwards, should compensate for the least violation of it.

Besides, to make satisfaction for a fault, it is necessary the offender do some voluntary act, that may be as honourable to the person, and as much above what he was before obliged to, as the contempt was dishonourable, and below that which was due. Unless God receive that which is as estimable in the nature of obedience, as the injury he received is in the nature of contempt, there can be no satisfaction. Now there is a greater dishonour brought to God by the commission of one sin, than there is honour by the perfect obedience of all the angels; for, in their obedience, God is preferred by the creature before things infinitely beneath him, which is but a small honour; but by one sin he is undervalued in the comparison, which is infinite contempt.

(2.) Man cannot make satisfaction by suffering; for the punishment must be equal to the offence, which derives its guilt from the dignity of the person offended, and the indignity of the offender. Now, God is the universal King; his justice is infinite, which man hath injured, and his glory, which man hath obscured; and man is finite. And what proportion is there between finite and infinite? How can a worthless rebel that is hateful to God, expiate the offence of so excellent a majesty? If he sacrifice himself, he can never appease the divine displeasure; for what doth he offer but a mass of rebellion and ingratitude? He can make no other satisfaction but that of the devils, which continues for ever, and is not completed.

2. Fallen man, considered only in his own corrupt and miserable state, is incapable of real repentance, which is a necessary condition to qualify him for pardon; for whereas repentance includes an ingenuous sorrow for sin past and a sincere forsaking of it, he is utterly indisposed for both.

(1.) He cannot be ingenuously sorrowful for his offence. It is true, when the circumstances are changed, that which was pleasing will cause trouble of spirit; as when a malefactor suffers for his crimes, he reflects upon his actions with sorrow: but this hath no moral worth in it; for it is a forced act, proceeding from a violent principle, and is consistent with as great a love to sin as he had before, and is entirely terminated on himself. But that grief which is divine, and is accompanied with a change in heart and life, respects the stain more than the punishment of sin; and arises from love to God, who is disobeyed and dishonoured by it. Now, it is not conceivable, that the guilty creature can love God, whilst he looks on him as an irreconcilable enemy. Distrust of the favour of a person, which is a degree of fear, is attended with coldness of affection; a strong fear, which still intimates an uncertainty in the event, inclines to hatred; but when fear is turned into despair, it causeth direct hatred. An instance of this we have in the devils, who curse the fountain of blessedness. If the evil is past remedy, the sense of it is attended with rage, and transports of blasphemy against God himself. A despairing sinner begins in this life the gnashing of teeth against his Judge, and kindles the fire that shall torment him forever. It is for this reason the Scripture propounds the goodness of God, as the most powerful persuasive to lead men to repentance, Rom. ii. 4. There can be no kindly relentings without filial affection, and that is always tempered with the expectation of favour. Without hope of pardon, all other motives are ineffectual to melt the heart.

Now the first covenant obliged man to obedience or punishment: it required innocence, and did not accept of repentance. The final voice of law is, "Do," or "Die." Guilty man cannot look on God with comfort under the notion of a holy Creator, that delights to view his own resemblance in the innocent creature, nor of a compassionate Father that spares an offending son; but apprehends him to be an inexorable judge, who hath right and power to avenge the disobedience. He can find no expedient for his deliverance, nor conceive how mercy can save him without the violation of justice, an attribute as essential to the divine nature, as mercy. And what can induce him to make an humble confession of his fault, when he expects nothing but an irrevocable doom? An instance of this we have in Adam, who being under the conviction of his sin, and an apprehension that God would be severe, did not solicit for mercy, but endeavoured to transfer the guilt on God himself. "The woman thou gavest me, she gave me of the tree, and I did eat," Gen. iii. 12; as if she had been designed for a snare, and not to be an aid in his innocent state.

(2.) A sincere resolution to forsake sin, is built on the hopes of mercy. Till the reasonable creature knows that heaven is open to repentance, to his second and better thoughts, he is irreclaimable. He that never hopes to receive any good, will continue in doing evil. Despair of mercy causeth a despising of the law. The apostate angels, who are without the reserves of pardon, are confirmed in their rebellion: their guilt is mixed with fury; they persist in their war against God, though they know the issue will be deadly to them. And had there not been an early revelation of mercy to Adam, he had been incorrigibly wicked as the devils; for despair would have inflamed his hatred against God, which is, of all the passions, the most incurable. Those vicious affections that depend on the humours of the body, which are mutable, alter with them; but hatred is seated in the superior part of the soul, which is of a spiritual nature, and diabolical in obstinacy.

In short; when the reasonable creature is guilty, and vicious, and knows that God is just and holy, and that he will be severe in revenging all disobedience, he hath no care nor desire to reform himself. He will not lay a restraint on his pleasing appetites, when he expects no recompense; he esteems it lost labour to abstain; and all his design is, to allay and sweeten the fear of future evils by present enjoyments. When he is scorched with the apprehensions of wrath to come, he plunges himself into sensual excesses for some relief. He resolves to make his best of sin for a time: according to the principle of the epicures, "Let us eat and drink while we may; to-morrow we shall die."

The sum of all is this, that an unrelenting and unreformed sinner is incapable of pardon; for unless God should renounce his own nature and deny his deity, he cannot receive him to favour. And it is inconceivable how the rational creature once lapsed, should ever be encouraged to repentance without the expectation of mercy: and there being an inseparable alliance between the integrity and felicity of man by the terms of the first covenant, the one failing, he could not entertain the least degree of hope concerning the other. By all which it appears he is under an invincible necessity of sinning and suffering for ever; his misery is complete and desperate.

CHAPTER V.

THE WISDOM OF GOD IN REDEMPTION.

God, by his infallible prescience, to which all things are eternally present, viewing the fall of Adam, and that all mankind lay bleeding in him, out of deep compassion to his creature, and that the devil might not be finally victorious over him, in his counsel decreed the recovery of man from his languishing and miserable state. The design and the means are most worthy of God, and in both his wisdom appears.

This will be made visible, by considering that all understanding agents first propound an end, and then choose the means for the obtaining of it. And the more perfect the understanding is, the more excellent is the end it designs, and the more fit and convenient are the means it makes use of for acquiring it. Now when God, whose understanding is infinite, and, in comparison of whom, the most prudent and advised are but as dark shadows, when he determines to work, especially in a most glorious manner, the end and the means are equally admirable.

I. The end is of the highest consequence. Were it some low, inconsiderable thing, it were unworthy of one thought of God for the effecting of it. To be curious in contriving how to accomplish that which is of no importance, exposes to a just imputation of folly; but when the most excellent good is the end, and the difficulties which hinder the obtaining of it are insuperable to a finite understanding, it then becomes the " only wise" God to discover the divinity of his wisdom, in making a way where he finds none. And such was the end of God in the work of our redemption. This was declared by the angels, who were sent ambassadors extraordinary to bring tidings of peace to the world; they praised

God, saying, "Glory to God in the highest, and on earth peace, good will towards men," Luke ii. 14.

The supreme end is his own glory; and, in order to it, the salvation of man hath the nature and respect of a medium; the subordinate is the recovery of the world from its lapsed and wretched state.

1. The supreme end is the glory of God. This signifies principally his internal and essential glory; and that consists in the perfections of his nature, which can never be fully conceived by the angels, but overwhelm, by their excellent greatness, all created understandings. But the glory that results from God's works is properly intended in the present argument, and implies,

(1.) The manifestation whereby he is pleased to represent himself in the exercise of his attributes. As the divine nature is the primary and complete object of his love, so he takes delight in those actions wherein the image and brightness of his own virtues appear. Now, in all the works of God there is an evidence of his excellencies; but as some stars shine with a different glory, so there are some noble effects, wherein the divine attributes are so conspicuous, that, in comparison with them, the rest of God's works are but obscure expressions of his greatness. The principal are creation and redemption. "The heavens declare the glory of God, and the firmament sheweth his handy-work," Psalm xix. 1. And when God surveyed the whole creation, and saw that all which he had made was good, he ordained a sabbath, to signify the content and satisfaction he had in the discovery of his eternal perfections therein. But his glory is most especially resplendent in the work of redemption, wherein more of the divine attributes are exercised than in the creation, and in a more glorious manner. It is here that wisdom, goodness, justice, holiness, and power, are united in their highest degree and exaltation. Upon this account the apostle useth that expression, 1 Tim. i. 11, "the glorious gospel of the blessed God;" it being the clearest revelation of his excellent attributes, the unspotted mirror wherein the great and wonderful effects of the Deity are set forth; τὰ μεγαλεῖα τυ Θευ, Acts ii. 11.

(2.) The praise and thanksgiving that arise from the discovery of his perfections by reasonable creatures, who consider and acknowledge them; when there is a solemn veneration of his excellencies, and the most ardent affections to him for the communication of his goodness. Thus in God's account, whoso offers praise, glorifies him, Psalm l. 23. An eminent example of this is set down in Job xxxviii. 7, when at the birth of the world, " the morning stars sang together, and all the sons of God shouted for joy." And at its new birth, they descend and make his praise glorious in a triumphant song, Psalm lxvi. 2. It will be the eternal exercise of the saints in heaven, where they more fully understand the mystery of our redemption, and consider every circumstance that may add a lustre to it, to ascribe " blessing, and honour, and glory, and power, to him that sitteth on the throne, and unto the Lamb, for ever and ever," Rev. v. 13.

2. The subordinate end is the restoring of man; and this is inviolably joined with the other. It is expressed by " peace on earth, and good will towards men." Sin hath broken that sacred alliance which was between God and man, and exposed him to his just displeasure; a misery inconceivable! And what is more becoming God, who is the Father of mercies, than to glorify his dear attribute, (" God is love,") and that which in a peculiar manner characterizes his nature, by the salvation of the miserable? What is more honourable to him, than by his almighty mercy to raise so many monuments from the dust, wherein his goodness may live and reign for ever?

Now, for the accomplishing of these excellent ends, the divine wisdom pitched upon those means which were most fit and congruous, which I shall distinctly consider.

The misery of fallen man consisted in the corruption of his nature by sin, and the punishment that ensues; and his happiness is in restoring of him to his primitive holiness, and in reconciliation to God, and the full fruition of him. The way to effect this was beyond the compass of any finite understanding.

That God, who is rich in goodness, should be favourable to the angels who serve him in perfect purity, we may easily conceive; for though they do not merit his favour, yet they never provoked his anger; and it is impossible but that he should love the image of his holiness wherever it shines. Or suppose an innocent creature in misery, the divine mercy would speedily excite his power to rescue it; for God is love to all his creatures, as such, till some extrinsical cause intervenes, which God hates more than he loves the creature, and that is sin; which alone stops the effusion of his goodness, and opens a wide passage for wrath to fall upon the guilty. But how to save the creature that is undone by its own choice, and is as sinful as miserable, will pose the wisdom of the world. Heaven itself seemed to be divided. Mercy inclined to save, but justice interposed for satisfaction. Mercy regarded man with respect to his misery, and the pleas of it are, Shall the Almighty build to ruin? Shall the most excellent creature in the lower world perish, the fault not being solely his? Shall the enemy triumph for ever, and raise his trophies from the works of the Most High? Shall the reasonable creature lose the fruition of God, and God the subjection and service of the creature, and all mankind be made in vain? Justice considered man as guilty of a transcendent crime, and it is its nature to render to every one what is due. Now, " the wages of sin is death;" and " shall not the Judge of all the world do right?" All the other attributes seemed to be attendants on justice. The wisdom of God enforced its plea, it being most indecent that sin which provokes the execution should procure the abrogation of the law; this would encourage the commission of sin without fear. The majesty of God was concerned; for it was not becoming his excellent greatness to treat with defiled dust, and to offer pardon to a presumptuous rebel immediately after his offence, and before he made supplication to his Judge. The holiness of God did quicken his justice to execute the threatening; for " he is of purer eyes than to behold iniquity." As goodness is the essential object of his will, which he loves unchangeably wherever it is, so is sin the eternal object of his hatred, and where it is found in the love of it, it renders the subject odious to him. "He will not take the wicked by the hand," Job viii. 20, marginal reading. The law of contrariety forbids purity and pollution to mix together. And the veracity of God required the inflicting of the punishment; for the law being a declaration of God's will, according to which he would dispense rewards and punishments, either it must be executed upon the offender, or if extraordinarily dispensed with, it must be upon such terms, as the honour of God's truth may be preserved. This seeming conflict was between the attributes.

The sublimest spirits in heaven were at a loss how to unravel the difficulty, and to find out the miraculous way to reconcile infinite mercy with inflexible justice; how to satisfy the demands of the one, and the requests of the other. God was to overcome himself before he restored man. In this exigence, his mercy excited his wisdom to interpose as an arbiter, which, in the treasure of its incomprehensible light, found out an admirable expedient to save man without prejudice to his other perfections; this was by constituting a Mediator, both able and willing, between the guilty creature and himself; that by transferring the punishment on the surety, he might punish sin and pardon the sinner.

And here the more severe and rigorous justice is, the more admirable is the mercy that saves. In the same stupendous sacrifice he declared his respect to justice and his delight in mercy. The two principal relations of our Redeemer are, the one of a gift from God to man, the other of an oblation for men to God. By the one, God satisfies his infinite love to man, and, by the other, satisfies his infinite justice for man. Neither is it unbecoming God to condescend in accepting the returning sinner, when a Mediator of infinite dignity intercedes for favour. The divine majesty is not lessened, when "God is in Christ reconciling the world unto himself," 2 Cor. v. 19. Neither is the sanctity of God disparaged by his clemency to sinners, for the Redeemer is the principle and pattern of holiness to all that are saved. The same grace that inclined God to send his Son to die for us, gives his

Spirit to live in us, that we may be revived and renewed according to his image, and by conformity to God be prepared for communion with him. Here is a sweet concurrence of all the attributes; " Mercy and truth are met together; righteousness and peace have kissed each other," Psalm lxxxv 10. Who can count up this heap of wonders? Who can unfold all the treasures of this mysterious love? The tongue of an angel cannot explicate it according to its dignity. It is the fairest copy of the divine wisdom, the consummation of all God's counsels, wherein all the attributes are displayed in their brightest lustre. It is here " the manifold wisdom of God appears," Ephes. iii. 10. The angels of light bend themselves with extraordinary application of mind and ardent affections, to study the rich and unsearchable variety that is in it, 1 Pet. i. 12; παρακυψαι—an allusion to the posture of the cherubim looking into the ark. Only the same understanding comprehends it, which contrived it. But as one views the ocean, though he cannot see its bounds or bottom, yet he sees so much as to know that that vast collection of waters is far greater than what is within the compass of his short sight; so though we cannot understand all the depths of that immense wisdom which ordered the way of our salvation, yet we may discover so much, as to know with the apostle, that it surpasses knowledge. May he that is the brightness of his Father's glory and the light of the world, so illuminate our dark understandings, that we may conceive aright of this great mystery.

1. The first thing that offers itself to consideration, is the compass of the divine wisdom, in taking occasion from the sin and fall of man to bring more glory to God, and to raise man to a more excellent state. Sin, in its own nature, hath no tendency to good; it is not an apt medium, it hath no proper efficacy to promote the glory of God: so far is it from a direct contributing to it, that, on the contrary, it is the most real dishonour to him. But as a black ground in a picture, which in itself only defiles, when placed by art, sets off the brighter colours and heightens their beauty; so the evil of sin, considered absolutely, obscures the glory of God, yet by the over-

ruling disposition of his providence serves to illustrate his name, and to make it more glorious in the esteem of reasonable creatures. Without the sin of man there had been no place for the most perfect exercise of his goodness. "*O fœlix culpa quæ tantum et talem meruit habere Redemptorem.*" Happy fault, not in itself, but by the wise and merciful counsel of God, to be repaired in a way so advantageous, that the salvation of the earth is the wonder of heaven. The redemption of man ravishes the angels.

The glory of God is more visible in the recovery of lapsed man, than if the law had been obeyed or executed. If Adam had persevered in his duty, the reward had been from grace, for owing himself to God, he could receive nothing but as a gift from his bounty; so that goodness only had then been exercised, and not in its highest and most obliging acts, which are to save the guilty and miserable; for innocence is incapable of mercy. If the sentence had been inflicted, justice had been honoured with a solemn sacrifice; but mercy, the sweet, tender, and indulgent attribute, had never appeared. But now the wisdom of God is eminent in the accord of both these attributes. God is equally glorious, as equally God, in preserving the authority of his law by an act of justice upon our Surety, as in the exercise of mercy by remitting the punishment to the offender.

And it is no less honourable to God's wisdom to restore man with infinite advantage. It is a mystery in nature, that the corruption of one thing helps the generation of another; it is more mysterious in grace, that the fall of man should occasion his more noble restitution. Innocence was not his last end; his supreme felicity transcends the first. The holiness of Adam was perfect, but mutable; but holiness in the redeemed, though in a less degree, shall be victorious over all temptations; for they are joined to the heavenly Adam in a strict and inviolable union. And those graces are acted by them, for the exercise of which there were no objects and occasions in innocence; as compassion to the miserable, forgiveness of injuries, fortitude and patience; all which, as they are a most lively resemblance of the divine perfections, so an excellent ornament to the soul, and infinitely endear it to God, 1 Pet. iv. 14. And the happiness of our renewed state exceeds our primitive felicity. Whether we consider the nature of it, it is wholly spiritual; or the place of it, heaven the sanctuary of life and immortality; or the constitution of the body, which shall be clothed with celestial qualities; but this will be particularly discussed in its proper place.

These are the effects of infinite wisdom, to the production of which sin affords no causality, but hath merely an accidental respect; as the apostle interprets the words of David, "Against thee only have I sinned," "that thou mightest be justified in thy sayings, and mightest overcome when thou art judged," Rom. iii. 4; Psalm li. 4; which doth not respect the intention of David, but the event only. The greater his injustice was in the commission, the more clear would God's justice be in the condemnation of his sin.

2. The wisdom of God appeared in ordaining such a Mediator who was qualified to reconcile God to man, and man to God. The first and most admirable article in the mystery of godliness, and the foundation of all the rest is, that "God was manifest in the flesh," 1 Tim. iii. 16. The middle must equally touch the extremes. A mediator must be capable of the sentiments and affections of both the parties he will reconcile. He must be a just esteemer of the rights and injuries of the one and the other, and have a common interest in both. The Son of God assuming the human nature, perfectly possesses these qualities; he hath zeal for God and compassion for man. He hath taken pledges of heaven and earth, the supreme nature in heaven and the most excellent on the earth, to make the hostility cease between them. He is Immanuel by nature and office. And if no less than an inspired wisdom could devise how to frame the earthly tabernacle, (Exod. xxxvi.) wherein God dwelt in a shadowy and typical manner, what wisdom was requisite to frame the human nature of Christ, wherein the Deity was really to dwell!

Now to discover more clearly the divine wisdom in uniting the two natures in Christ, to qualify him for his office, it is requisite to consider, that the office of Mediator hath three charges annexed to it; the priestly, which respects God, the prophetical and kingly, which regard men. These have a respect to the evils which oppress fallen man; and they are guilt, ignorance, sin, and death. Man was capitally guilty of the breach of God's law, and under the tyranny of his lusts, and in the issue liable to death. The Redeemer is made to him wisdom, righteousness, sanctification, and redemption. These benefits are dispensed by him in his threefold office. As a priest he expiates sin, as a prophet he instructs the church, as a king he regulates the lives of his subjects, delivers them from their enemies, and makes them happy. Now the divine and human nature are requisite for the performance of all these; for nothing is effectual to an end, but what is proportionable and commensurate thereunto; and to proportion, excesses, as well as defects, are opposite. This will appear by taking a distinct view of the several offices of our Mediator.

(1.) The priestly office hath two parts—to make expiation for sin—and intercession for sinners.

Now, for making expiation for sin, there was a necessary concurrence of the two natures in our Redeemer. He must be man; for the Deity was not capable of those submissions and sufferings which were requisite to expiate sin; and he must be man, that the sinning nature might suffer, and thereby acquire a title to the satisfaction that is made. The meritorious imputation of Christ's sufferings to man, is grounded on the union between them, which is as well natural in his partaking of flesh and blood, as moral in the consent of their wills. As the apostle observes, Heb. ii. 11, that " he that sanctifieth, and they who are sanctified, are all of one ;" so he that suffers, and they for whom he suffers, must have communion in the same nature. For this reason, God having resolved never to dispense mercy to the fallen angels, the Redeemer did not assume the angelical nature, but the seed of Abraham.

And as the human nature was necessary to qualify him for sufferings, and to make them suitable, so the divine was to make them sufficient. The lower nature, considered in itself, could make no satisfaction. The dignity of the divine person makes a temporal punishment to be of an infinite value in God's account. Besides, the human nature had sunk under the weight of wrath, if the Deity had not been personally present to support it. Briefly; to perform the first part of his office, he must suffer, yet be impassible; die, yet be immortal; and undergo the wrath of God, to deliver man from it.

To make intercession for us, it was requisite that he should partake of both natures, that he might have credit with God, and compassion to man. The Son hath a prevailing interest in the Father, as he testifies, "I know thou hearest me always," John xi. 42, a privilege which neither Abraham, Moses, nor any other who were the most favoured saints, enjoyed. And, as man, he was fit for passion and compassion. The human nature is the proper subject of feeling pity, especially when it hath felt misery. God is capable of love, not in strictness of compassion; for sympathy proceeds from an experimental sense of what one hath suffered; and the sight of the like affliction in others, revives the affections which were felt in that state, and inclines to pity. The apostle offers this to believers as the ground of comfort, that he who took our nature, and felt our griefs, intercedes for us; " For we have not an High-Priest which cannot be touched with the feeling of our infirmities, but was in all points tempted like as we are, yet without sin;" that with an humble confidence we may come to the " throne of grace," Heb. iv. 15. He hath drunk deepest of the cup of sorrows, that he may be an all-sufficient comforter to those that mourn. He hath such tender bowels, we may trust him to solicit our salvation. In short, it is the great support of our faith, that " we have access to the Father by the Son," and present all our requests by a Mediator so worthy and so dear to him; and by one who left the joys of heaven, that by enduring affliction on earth, his heart might be made tunable to the hearts of the afflicted.

(2.) For the discharge of the prophetical office, it was necessary the Mediator should be God and man.

He must be God, that he might deliver his counsels

with more authority and efficacy than any mere creature could. He must be a teacher sent from heaven, that reveals to us the will of God concerning the way thither, and the certainty and excellency of that state. Now, Christ is the original of all wisdom; it is not said, " The word of the Lord came to him," as to the prophets; he is the fountain of all sacred knowledge. The Son came from the " bosom of the Father," the seat of his counsels and compassions, to reveal those secrets which were concealed from the angels in that light which is inaccessible. And it is God alone who can teach the heart and convince the conscience, so as to produce a saving belief of the heavenly doctrine, and a delight in the discovery, and a resolution to follow it wherever it directs.

It was fit he should be man, that he might be familiarly conversant with us, and convey the counsels of God in such a way as man could receive. All saving truth comes from God, and it follows, by just consequence, that the nearer he is to us, the better we are likely to be instructed.

Now there are two things which render sinful man incapable of immediate converse with God—the infirmity of his nature, and the guilt that cleaves to him.—The infirmity of man's nature cannot endure the glory of God's appearance. When the law was delivered on Mount Sinai, the Israelites were under great terrors at the sights and prodigies which accompanied the divine presence, and they desired that God would speak to them no more in his majesty and greatness, lest they should die, Deut. v. 25. There is such a disproportion between our meanness and his excellencies, that Daniel, though a favourite with heaven, yet his comeliness was turned into corruption at the sight of a vision, Dan. x. 17. And the beloved disciple fell down as dead at the appearance of Christ in his glory, Rev. i. 17. When the eye gazes on the sun, it is more tormented with the brightness, than pleased with the beauty of it; but when the beams are transmitted through a coloured medium, they are more temperate and sweetened to the sight. The eternal Word shining in his full glory, the more bright, the less visible is he to mortal eyes; but the incarnate Word is eclipsed and allayed by a "veil of flesh," and so made accessible to us. God, out of a tender respect to our frailty and fears, promised to raise up a prophet clothed in our nature, that we might comfortably and quietly receive his instructions, Deut. xviii. 15. Guilt makes us fearful of his presence. The approach of God awakens the conscience, which is his spy in our bosoms, and causes a dreadful apparition of sin in its view. When one beam of Christ's divinity broke forth in the miraculous draught of fishes, Peter cries out, "Depart from me, for I am a sinful man, O Lord," Luke v. 8. Holiness, armed with terror, strikes a sinner into consternation. Now when the mind is shaken with a storm of fear, it cannot calmly attend to the counsels of wisdom. But the Son of God appearing in our nature to expiate sin and appease divine justice, we are encouraged to draw near to him, and sit at his feet, to hear the "words of eternal life." Thus God complied with our necessity, that with a freer dispensation we might receive the counsels of our Saviour.

(3.) He is qualified for the kingly office, by the union of the two natures in him. He must be God to conquer Satan, and convert the world. As eminent an act of power was necessary to redeem, as to create; for although the supreme Judge were to be satisfied by humble sufferings, yet Satan, who usurped the right of God (for man had no power to alienate himself) was to be subdued: having no just title, he was to be cast out by power. And no less than the divine power could accomplish our victorious rescue from him. In his love he pitied us, and "his holy arm got him the victory." He is the author of "eternal salvation," which no inferior agent could ever accomplish. It is God alone "can overcome death," and him that had "the power of death," and bring us safely to felicity.

Besides, our king must be man, that by the excellency of his example, he might lead us in the way of life. The most rational method to reform the world, is, not only to enact laws to be the rule of virtuous actions, but for lawgivers to make virtue honourable and imitable by their own practice. And to encourage us in the holy war against our enemies visible and invisible, it was congruous that the prince of our salvation should take the human nature, and submit to the inconveniences of our warfaring state; as kings, when they design a glorious conquest, go forth in person, and willingly endure the hardships of a military condition, to animate their armies The apostle tells us, Heb. ii. 10, that it "became him for whom are all things, and by whom are all things, in bringing many sons unto glory, to make the Captain of their salvation perfect through sufferings." God, the great designer of all things, foreseeing the sufferings to which the godly would be exposed in the world, ordained it as most convenient, that the author of their deliverance, should, by sufferings obtain the reward, that by his example, he might strengthen and deliver those that suffer to the end. Again; the Son of God entered into our family, and is not "ashamed to call us brethren," Heb. ii. 11. To make his sceptre amiable to us, he exerciseth his dominion with a natural and sensible touch of pity; he pardons our failings, and puts a value on our sincere though mean services, as an honour done to him. Briefly, in him there is a combination of power and love; the power of the Deity with the tenderness and clemency of the human nature.

He is the mighty God and Prince of Peace, Isa. ix. 6. He is a king just and powerful against our enemies, but mild and gentle to his people, Zech. ix. 9. He is willing to remove from us all the evils we cannot endure, our sins and sorrows; and able to convey to us all the blessings we are capable to enjoy. In all his glory, he remembers that he is our Saviour. At the day of judgment, when he shall come with a train of mighty angels, he will be as tender of man, as when he suffered on the cross.

And from hence we may discover the excellency of God's contrivance in uniting the divine and human nature in our Redeemer, that he might have ability and affection to qualify him for that great and blessed work.

3. The divine wisdom appears in the designation of the person; for God resolving to save man in a way that

is honourable to his justice, it was expedient a person in the blessed Trinity should be put into a state of subjection, to endure the punishment due to sin, but it was not convenient the Father should; for he must then have been sent into the world, which is incongruous to the relations that are between those glorious persons; for as they subsist in a certain order, so their operations are according to the manner of their subsistence. The Father is from himself, and the first motions in all things are ascribed to him; the Son is from the Father, and all his actions take their rise from him. "The Son can do nothing of himself, but what he seeth the Father do," John v. 19. The effecting of our redemption is referred to the Father's will as the supreme cause; our Saviour, upon his entrance into the world to undertake that work, declares, "I come to do thy will, O God," Heb. x. 7. Upon this account the apostle addresses his thanks to the Father as the first agent in our salvation, Col i. 12; which is not to lessen the glory of the Son and Spirit, but to signify, that in the accomplishment of it, their working follows their being. It was not fit that the Father should be incarnate; for he must then have sustained the part of a criminal, and appeared in that quality before the supreme Judge; but this was not consonant to the order among the persons; for although they are of equal majesty, being one God, yet the Father is the first person, and to him belongs most congruously to be the guardian of the laws and rights of heaven, to exact satisfaction for offences, and to receive intercessions for the pardon of the penitent.

Neither was it fit that the third person should undertake that work; for besides the sacrifice of propitiation, it was necessary the divine power should be exerted, to enlighten the minds and incline the wills of men to receive the Redeemer, that the benefits of his death might be applied to them. Now, the Redeemer is considered as the object, and the Holy Spirit as the disposer of the faculty to receive it; and in the natural order of things, the object must exist before the operation of the faculty upon it. There must be light before the eye can see. So in the disposition of the causes of our salvation, the

Redeemer must be ordained and salvation purchased before the divine power is put forth to enable the soul to receive it; and accordingly it is the office of the Spirit, who is the power of God, Luke i. 35, and by whom the Father and the Son execute all things, to render effectual the redemption procured by the Son.

Briefly, the mission of the persons is according to their principle. The Father sends the Son to acquire salvation for us, John iii. 17; the Son sends the Spirit to apply it, John xvi. 7. Thus there is no disturbing of their sacred order.

More particularly; in appointing the Son to assume the human nature, and to restore lapsed man, the wisdom of God is evident; for by that,

(1.) The properties of the sacred persons are preserved entire: the same title is appropriated to both natures in our Mediator. His state on earth corresponds with his state in heaven. He is the only Son from eternity, and the first born in time: and the honour due to the eternal and divine, and to the temporal but supernatural sonship, is attributed to him.

(2.) To unite the glorious titles of Creator and Redeemer in the same person. The Father made the world by the Son, Heb. i. 2. By this title he had an original propriety in man, which could not be extinguished. Though we had forfeited our right in him, he did not lose his right in us. Our contract with Satan could not nullify it. Now it was consonant that the Son should be employed to recover his own, that the Creator in the beginning should be the Redeemer in the fulness of time.

(3.) Who could more fitly restore us to favour and the right of children, than the only begotten and only beloved Son, who is the singular and everlasting object of his Father's delight? Our relation to God is an imitation and expression of Christ's. He is a son by nature, a servant by condescension; we are servants by nature, and sons by grace and favour. Our adoption into the line of heaven is by the purchase of his blood. The eternal Son "took flesh," and "was made under the law, that we might receive the adoption of sons," Gal. iv. 5;

Rom. viii. 29. Who was more fit to repair the image of God in man, and beautify his nature that was defiled with sin, than the Son who is "the express image" of his Father's person, and brightness and beauty itself? Who can better communicate the divine counsels to us, than the eternal Word?

4. The wisdom of God appears in making the remedy to have a proportion to the cause of our ruin; that as we fell in Adam, our representative, so we are raised by Christ, the head of our recovery, 1 Cor. xv. 22. The apostle makes the comparison between the first and second Adam; "Therefore as by the offence of one, judgment came upon all men to condemnation; even so by the righteousness of one, the free gift came upon all men unto justification of life. For as by one man's disobedience many were made sinners, so by the obedience of one shall many be made righteous," Rom. v. 18, 19. They are considered as causes of contrary effects. The effects are sin and righteousness, condemnation and justification. As the disobedience of the first Adam is meritoriously imputed to all his natural posterity, and brings death upon all; so the righteousness of the second is meritoriously imputed to all his spiritual progeny, to obtain life for them. The carnal Adam, having lost original righteousness, derives a corrupt nature to all that descend from him; and the spiritual, having by his obedience purchased divine grace for us, (that being the price without which so rich a treasure as holiness could not be obtained,) conveys a vital efficacy to renew his people. The same spirit of holiness which anointed our Redeemer, does quicken all his race, that as they have borne the image of the earthly, they may bear the image of the heavenly Adam, 1 Cor. xv. 49.

5. The divine wisdom is visible in the manner whereby our redemption is accomplished; that is, by the humiliation of the Son of God. By this he did counterwork the sin of angels and man. Pride is the poison of every sin, for in every one the creature prefers his pleasure, and sets up his will above God's; but it was the special sin of Adam. The devil would have leveled heaven by an unpardonable usurpation; he said, "I will be like the

Most High:" and man infected with his breath, " You shall be like God," became sick of the same disease. Now Christ, that by the quality of the remedy he might cure our disease in its source and cause, applied to our pride an unspeakable humility.

Man was guilty of the highest robbery in affecting to be equal with God; and the eternal Son, who was " in the form of God," and equal to him in majesty and authority without sacrilege or usurpation, emptied himself by assuming the human nature in its servile state, Phil. ii. 6. " The Word was made flesh;" the meanest part is specified, to signify the greatness of his abasement. There is such an infinite distance between God and flesh, that the condescension is as admirable as the contrivance. So great was the malignity of our pride, for the cure of which such a profound humility was requisite. By this he destroyed the first work of the devil, 1 John iii. 8.

6. The wisdom of God appears in ordaining such contemptible, and, in appearance, opposite means, to accomplish such glorious effects. The way is as wonderful as the work. That Christ by dying on the cross, a reputed malefactor, should be made our eternal righteousness; that descending to the grave, he should bring up the lost world to life and immortality, is so incredible to our narrow understandings, that he saves us and astonishes us at once. And in nothing is it more visible, that the thoughts of God are far above our thoughts, and his ways above our ways, as heaven is above the earth, Isa. lv. 8. It is a secret in physic to compound the most noble remedies of things destructive to nature, and thereby make one death victorious over another; but that eternal life should spring from death, glory from ignominy, blessedness from a curse, is so repugnant to human sense, that to render the belief of it easy, it was foretold by many prophecies, that when it came to pass, it might be looked on as the effect of God's eternal counsel. The apostle tells us, that Christ crucified was " to the Jews a stumbling-block, and to the Gentiles foolishness," 1 Cor. i. 23. The grand sophies of the world esteemed it absurd and unreasonable to believe, that he who was exposed to sufferings, could save others: but those who are

called, discover that the doctrine of salvation, by the cross of Christ, which the world counted folly, is the great " wisdom of God," and most convenient for his end.

A double reason is given of this method.

(1.) Because the heathen world did not find and own God in the way of nature. " For after that, in the wisdom of God, the world by wisdom knew not God, it pleased God, by the foolishness of preaching, to save them that believe," 1 Cor. i. 21. The frame of the world is called the wisdom of God; the name of the cause is given to the effect in regard the divine wisdom is so clearly discovered there, as if it had taken a visible form, and presented itself to the view of men. But those who professed themselves wise, did not acknowledge the Creator; for some conceited the world to be eternal, others that it was the product of chance, and became guilty of the most absolute contradiction to reason; for who can believe that one who is blind from his birth, and by consequence perfectly ignorant of all colours and of the art of painting, should take a bundle of pencils into his hand, and dipping them into colours mixed and corrupted, paint a great battle with that perfection in the design, propriety in the colours, distinction in the habits and countenances, as if it were not represented, but present to the spectators? Who ever saw a temple, or palace, or any regular building, spring from the stony bowels of a mountain? Yet some famous philosophers " became thus vain in their imaginations," fancying that the world proceeded from the casual concourse of atoms: and the rest of them neglected to know God so far as they might, and to honour him so far as they knew, Rom. i. 21. They debased the Deity by unworthy conceptions of his nature, and by performing such acts of worship, as were not fit for a rational spirit to offer, nor for the pure majesty of heaven to receive. Besides, they ascribed his name, attributes, and honour, to creatures. Not only the lights of heaven, and the secret powers which they supposed did govern them; not only kings, and great men who were, by their authority, raised above others, but the most despicable things in nature, beasts and birds, were the objects of their adoration. "They changed the glory of the incorruptible God, into an image made like to corruptible man, and to birds, and four-footed beasts, and creeping things;" a sin so foul, that it betrayed them to brutish blindness, and to the most infamous lusts natural and unnatural, Rom. i. 23. Now since the most clear and open discovery of God's wisdom was ineffectual to reclaim the world, he was pleased to change his method. They neglected him appearing in his majesty, and he now comes clothed with infirmities. And since by natural light they would not see God the Creator, he is imperceptible to the light of nature as Redeemer: the discovery of him depends on revelation. The wisdom of God in making the world is evident to every eye, but the gospel is "wisdom in a mystery," 1 Cor. ii. 7. The Deity was conspicuous in the creation, but concealed under a veil of flesh when he wrought our redemption. He was more easily discovered when invisible, than when visible. He created the world by power, but restored it by sufferings.

(2.) That the honour of all might solely redound to him. "God hath chosen the foolish things of the world to confound the wise; and the weak things of the world to confound the things which are mighty; and base things of the world, and things which are despised, hath God chosen; yea, and things which are not, to bring to nought things which are; that no flesh should glory in his presence," 1 Cor. i. 27—29. Thus Moses, the redeemer of Israel, was an infant exposed to the mercy of the waters, drawn forth from an ark of bulrushes, and not employed whilst he lived in the splendour of the court, but when banished as a criminal, and deprived of all power. And our Redeemer took not on him the nature of angels equal to Satan in power, but took part of flesh and blood, the more signally to triumph over that proud spirit in the human nature which was inferior to his, and had been vanquished by him in paradise: therefore he did not immediately exercise omnipotent power to destroy him, but managed our weakness and infirmity to foil the roaring lion. He did not enter into the combat in the glory of his Deity, but disguised under the human nature which was subject to mortality. And thus the devil is overcome in the same manner as he first got the victory; for as the whole race of man was captivated by him in Adam the representative, so believers are victorious over him as the tempter and tormentor, by the conquest that Christ their representative obtained in the wilderness and on the cross. And as our ruin was effected by the subtilty of Satan, so our recovery is wrought by the wisdom of God, who " taketh the wise in their own craftiness," 1 Cor. iii. 19. The devil excited Judas by avarice, the Jews by malice, and Pilate from reason of state to accomplish the death of Christ; and he then seemed to be victorious. Now what was more honourable to the Prince of our salvation, than the turning of the enemy's point upon his own breast, and by dying, to overcome him that had the power of death? Heb. ii. 14. This was signified in the first promise of the gospel, where the salvation of man is enclosed in the curse of the serpent, that is the devil clothed with that figure; " It shall bruise thy head, and thou shalt bruise his heel," Gen. iii. 15; that is, the Son of God should, by suffering in our flesh, overcome the enemy of mankind and rescue innumerable captives from his tyranny: here the events are most contrary to the probability of their cause. And what is more worthy of God, than to obtain his ends in such a manner, as the glory of all may be, *in solidum,* ascribed to him?

7. The divine wisdom appears in laying the design of the gospel in such a manner, as to provide for the comfort, and promote the holiness of man.

(1.) This is God's signature upon all heavenly doctrines, which distinguishes them from carnal inventions —they have a direct tendency to promote his glory and the real benefit of the rational creature. Thus the way of salvation by Jesus Christ, is most fit, as to reconcile God to man by securing his honour, so to reconcile man to God by encouraging his hope. Till this be effected, he can never be happy in communion with God; for that is nothing else but the reciprocal exercise of love between God and the soul. Now nothing can represent

God as amiable to a guilty creature, but his inclination to pardon. Whilst there are apprehensions of inexorable severity, there will be hard thoughts burning in the breast against God : till the soul is released from terrors, it can never truly love him. To extinguish our hatred, he must conquer our fears, and this he hath done by giving us the most undoubted and convincing evidence of his affections—by contracting the most intimate alliance with mankind. In this, God is not only lovely, but love, 1 John iv. 8, 9 ; and his love is not only visible to our understandings, but to our senses. The divine nature in Christ is joined to the human in a union that is not typical or temporary, but real and permanent. " The Word was made flesh," John i. 14, and " in him dwelleth all the fulness of the Godhead bodily," Col. ii. 9. Now, as love is an affection of union, so the strictest union is an evidence of the greatest love. The Son of God " took the seed of Abraham," the original element of our nature, that our interest in him might be more clear and certain, Heb. ii. 16. He stooped from the height of his glory to our low embraces, that we might with more confidence lay hold on his mercy.—By providing complete satisfaction to offended justice. The guilty convinced creature is restless and inquisitive after a way to escape " the wrath to come ;" for being under the apprehension that God is an incensed judge, it is very sensible of the greatness and nearness of the danger, there being nothing between it and eternal torments but a thin veil of flesh. Now an abundant satisfaction is made, that most effectually expiates and abolishes the guilt of sin. That is a temporary act, but of infinite evil, being committed against an infinite object ; the death of Christ was a temporary passion, but of infinite value, in respect of the subject : the honour of the law is fully repaired, so that God is justly merciful, and dispenses pardon to the glory of his righteousness. He hath set forth his Son " to be a propitiation through faith in his blood, to declare his righteousness, that he might be just, and the justifier of him which believeth in Jesus," Rom. iii. 25, 26. And what stronger security can be given, that God is ready to pardon man, upon his accepting the terms of the gospel, than the giving of his Son to be our atonement? If the stream swell so high as to overflow the banks, will it stop in a descending valley? Hath he, with so dear an expense, satisfied his justice, and will he deny his mercy to relenting and returning sinners? This argument is powerful enough to overcome the most obstinate infidelity.—By the unspeakable gift of his Son, he assures our hopes of heaven, which is a reward so great and glorious, that our guilty hearts are apt to suspect we shall never enjoy it. We are secure of his faithfulness, having his infallible promise; and of his goodness, having such a pledge in our hands; as the apostle argues, Rom. viii. 32; " He that spared not his own Son, but delivered him up for us all, how shall he not with him also freely give us all things?" Will he give us the tree of life, and not permit us to eat of its fruit? Is it conceivable, that, having laid the foundation of our happiness in the death of his Son, an act to which his tender affection seemed so repugnant, he will not perform the rest, which he can do by the mere signification of his will? It is an excellent encouragement St. Austin propounds from hence; *Securus esto acceptu-rum te vitam ipsius, qui pignus habes mortis ipsius,*" &c. "Be assured thou shalt partake of his life, who hast the pledge of it in his death." He hath performed more than he promised. It is more incredible that the Eternal should die, than that a mortal creature should live for ever.

In short; since no mortal eye can discover the heavenly glory to convince us of the reality of the invisible state, and to support our departing souls in their passage through the dark and terrible valley, our Saviour rose from the grave, ascended in our nature to heaven, and is the model of our happiness: he is at the right hand of God to dispense life and immortality to all that believe on him. And what can be more comfortable to us, than the assurance of that blessedness, which, as it eclipses all the glory of the world, so it makes death itself desirable in order to the enjoyment of it?

(2.) As the comfort, so the holiness of man is most promoted in this way of our redemption. Suppose we had been recovered upon easier terms, the evil of sin would have been lessened in our esteem, and the mercy that saves us, had not appeared so great. We are apt to judge of the danger of a disease from the difficulty of its cure; hunger is reputed a small trouble, (although, if it be not satisfied, it will prove deadly,) because a small price will procure what may remove it. He that falls into a pit, and is drawn forth by an easy pull of the hand, doth not think himself greatly obliged to the person that helped him, though if he had remained there, he must have perished. But when the Son of God had suffered for us more than ever one friend suffered for another, or a father for a son, or than the strength and patience of an angel could endure; who would not be struck with horror at the thought of that poison which required such a dreadful cure? And the benefit we receive in so costly a way, is justly magnified by us. Now, what is more apt to inflame our love to God, than the admirable expression of his love to us, in that with the most precious blood he ransomed us from hell? How did it endear obedience, that God had sacrificed his Son to keep us from acts of hostility! So that the grace of the gospel is so far from indulging sin, that it gives the most deadly wound to it: especially when the tenor of the new covenant is, that the condemned creature, in order to receive pardon and the benefits that are purchased, must receive the Benefactor, with the most entire consent, for his Prince and Saviour. The law of faith requires us to submit to his sceptre, as well as to depend upon his sacrifice. The gospel is a conditional act of oblivion, that none may venture to sin upon confidence of pardon.

And since the occasion of the fall was from a conceit, that man could better his estate by complying with the tempter, and obtain a more desirable happiness in the creature than in the favour of God; his recovery is by revealing to him wherein true blessedness consists, and giving him an assurance that he may obtain it; for man will never subject himself to God as his highest Lord, till he looks on him as his last end and sovereign good. Now the gospel offers to us the most effectual means to convince man of the folly of his choice in making the creature his happiness: for the Son of God, who was heir of all things, during his continuance in the world, was in the perpetual exercise of self-denial. He lived a despised life and died an ignominious death, to discover to us, that as the miseries of this life cannot make us truly miserable, so the prosperities of it cannot make us truly happy. Besides, how is it possible that the wretched enjoyment of this world should be the blessedness for which he spent his sweat, his tears, his blood? The rich price he laid down doth most powerfully convince us, that our felicity is infinitely more valuable than all earthly things, and can be no less than the fruition of God himself. Thus the divine wisdom hath so ordered the way of our salvation, that as mercy and justice in God, so holiness and comfort may be perfectly united in the reasonable creature.

CHAPTER VI.

PRACTICAL INFERENCES.

1. WHAT a superlative degree of praise and thankfulness is due to God, for revealing his eternal and compassionate counsel in order to our salvation!

The fall of man was so wounding and deadly, that only an infinite understanding could find out the means for his recovery. And if that mercy which moved the Lord to ordain the remedy, had not discovered it, a thick cloud of despair had covered mankind, being for ever unable to conceive the way of our redemption. It is a mystery which " eye hath not seen, nor ear heard, nor hath entered into the heart of man to conceive," 1 Cor. ii. 9. All human knowledge is acquired by two sorts of faculties; the external and internal. Of the first, sight and hearing are the most spiritual, and convey the knowledge of the most worthy objects; they are the senses of discipline; the other three are immersed in matter, and are incapable to make such clear discoveries.

Besides those impressions that are made upon the senses, we may form some ideas in the imagination; upon which the mind reflecting may argue and discourse: thus far only the light and vigour of the understanding can go; so that the apostle declares, that the whole plot of the gospel was without the compass of our most searching faculties.

This will be evident by considering,

1. There was no discovery of it in the creation. The voice of the heavens instructs us concerning the being of God, but not in the secrets of his will. The economy of man's redemption is the merciful design of God, which hath no connection with the existence of the creatures, but depends only upon his good pleasure. It is as impossible to read the divine decrees in the volume of the world, as for the eye to discover a sound, which hath neither figure, colour, nor visible motion. Besides the glorious nature of God in three persons, which is the foundation of this mysterious mercy, is not made known by the visible frame of the universe. It is true, in all external works the three persons are equally concerned: being of one essence, they are of one efficacy; and the essential perfections of the Deity, as they concur, so they are evident in the production of all things. The first motive is goodness; that which orders and directs, is wisdom; that which executes, is power, Rom. i. 20. And the several ranks of creatures, according to their state, reflect an honour on their Author. Things endued with life, declare him to be the fountain of life, and intellectual creatures represent him to be the Father of lights. But the personal being, as personal, operating nothing out of the divine nature, there is no resemblance in the world that expresses the distinction, propriety, and singularity of the persons, so as to discover them to the human understanding. Those deeper mysteries of the Deity, are made known only by the word of God.

2. It is above the strain and reach of natural reason to attain the knowledge of it. There are seminal sparks of the law in the heart of man, Rom. ii. 15; some common principles of piety, justice, and charity, without which the world would soon disband and fall into confu-

sion; but there is not the least presumption or conjecture of the contrivance of the gospel. Though misery sharpens the mind and makes it more ingenious to find out ways of deliverance, yet here reason was utterly at a loss. How could it ever enter into the thoughts of the Israelites, that by erecting a brazen serpent upon a pole and looking towards it, the wounds made by the fiery serpents should be healed? And how should guilty man find out a way to satisfy infinite justice by the sufferings of a Mediator, and to heal the wounded spirit by believing on him? The most inquiring reason could never have thought of the wonders of the incarnation, that a virgin should conceive, and a God be born; or of the death of the Prince of life, and the resurrection, and ascension of the Lord of glory.

We may see how impossible it is for the natural understanding to discover the mystery of redemption, when those that had the highest reputation for wisdom were ignorant of the creation. The philosophers were divided in nothing more, than in their account of the world's original. Some imagined it to proceed from water, others from fire; some from order, others from confusion; some to be from eternity, others in time. If the soul's eye be so weakened as not to see that eternal power which is so apparent in its effects, much less could it pierce into the will and free determinations of God, of which there is not the least intimation or shadow in the things that are made. This wisdom comes from above, and "was hidden from ages and generations," Col. i. 26. It is called the "mystery of Christ," Ephes. iii. 4; he is the object and revealer of it:—the "mystery of the faith," the discovery of which was by pure revelation, 1 Tim. iii. 9;—"the mystery of his will," an inviolable secret, till he was pleased to make it known, Ephes. i. 9. Were the human understanding as clear as it is corrupt, yet it cannot, by the strength of discourse, arrive at the knowledge of it. Supernatural revelation was necessary to discover it to the angels. The thoughts of men are a secret, into which the Creator alone had a right to enter, 2 Chron. vi. 30, it being his prerogative to search the heart. The angels conjecture only, from the dispositions of men, from outward circumstances, from the images in the fancy, and from material impressions on the blood and spirits, what are the thoughts of the heart: and much less can they discover the counsel of God himself. The apostle tells us, to principalities and powers in heavenly places, by the church, the manifold wisdom of God is made known, Ephes. iii. 10. By the first coming of Christ and the conversion of the world, the depths of the divine wisdom were opened, and there remains much undiscovered which his second coming shall gloriously make known. Before the first, they understood not the foundation; till the second, not the perfection of our recovery. Briefly: the Spirit that searches the mysterious counsel of God, is the alone intelligencer of heaven, that reveals them to the world, 1 Cor. ii. 10. And the more to incite us with sincere and humble thankfulness to acknowledge this invaluable mercy, it will be useful to reflect on the state of the heathen world, who are entirely ignorant of this mystery.

The apostle describes the case of the Gentiles in such terms as argue it to be extremely dangerous, if not desperate; their understanding was darkened, being alienated from the life of God, through the ignorance that is in them;" they were " without Christ, aliens from the commonwealth of Israel, strangers from the covenants of promise, without hope," Ephes. ii. 12; iv. 18. They had no sense of their misery, no expectation, nor desire of mercy. Not only the barbarous and savage, but the polished and civilized nations are called ἄθεοι, being without the knowledge of the true God and of a Saviour. Philosophy never made one believer. And as the want of a sovereign remedy exposes a man that hath a mortal disease to certain ruin, so the single ignorance of the gospel leaves men in a state of perdition. It is true, where the faculties are not capable, or the object is not revealed, God doth not impute the want of knowledge as a crime; but salvation is obtained only by the covenant of grace, which is founded in the satisfaction of the Redeemer; and it is by the knowledge of him that he justifies many, Isa. liii. 11. God would have all men saved by coming " to the knowledge of the truth;" that is, the doctrine of the gospel, so called in respect to its excellency, being the most profitable that ever was revealed, 1 Tim. ii. 4. The infants of believers are saved by special privilege, for the merits of Christ, without any apprehension of him; but others who are come to the use of reason, are made partakers of blessedness by the knowledge of God in Christ; "This is life eternal, that they might know thee, the only true God, and Jesus Christ whom thou hast sent," John xvii. 3. The sun quickens some creatures by its vital influences, which are buried in the caves of the earth and never see the light, but the Sun of righteousness illuminates all whom he saves. What degree of knowledge is necessary of the dignity of his person and the efficacy of his mediation, I cannot determine; but that the heathens who are absolutely strangers to the only means of our recovery, and do not believe on God reconciled in the Son of his love, should partake of saving mercy; I do not see any thing in the gospel, which is the revelation of God's will concerning our salvation, upon which to build a rational hope. Indeed if any heathen were seriously penitent, God is so merciful, that he would rather dispatch an angel from heaven, saying, "Deliver him from going down into the pit, I have found a ransom;" or by some extraordinary way instruct him in the necessary knowledge of our Saviour, than suffer him to perish. But repentance as well as forgiveness, is purchased and dispensed by our Saviour alone; and that any receive this benefit, who are entirely ignorant of the Benefactor, we cannot tell. Now this should raise our esteem of the discriminating favour of God to us.

What a flood of errors and miseries covered the earth, when "the grace of God that bringeth salvation" first appeared? The deluge was universal, and so was the destruction. Those that were most renowned for wisdom, the philosophers of Greece and the orators of Rome, were swallowed up, only the church of Christ is triumphant over the merciless waters. When Noah, from the top of the mountain, saw the sad remains of that dreadful inundation, what a lively sense of joy possessed his breast! As misery is heightened, so happiness is set off by comparison: not that there is any regular content to see the destruction of others, but the sense of our own preservation from a common ruin, raises our joy to its highest elevation. The first work of Noah, after his deliverance, was to build an altar, on which to offer the sacrifices of thanksgiving to his Preserver. We should imitate his example.

How many nations, unknown to our world, remain in the darkness and shadow of death, while "the day-spring from on high hath visited us!" This special favour calls for special thankfulness. Were there any qualities in us to incline God to prefer us before others, it would lessen our esteem of the benefit. But this distinguishing mercy is one of those free acts of God, for which there is no reason in the objects on which they are exercised. St. Austin calls it "*Profundum crucis.*" As the lowest part of the cross is under ground, unseen, but the upper part is exposed to sight; so the effects of the divine predestination, the fruits of the cross, are visible, but the reasons are not within our view. When "God divided the world," and chose Israel for his heritage to receive the promise of the Messiah, and left the rest in thick and disconsolate darkness, there was no apparent cause of this inequality; for they all sprang from the same corrupt root, and equally deserved a final rejection. There was no singular good in them, nor transcendent evil in others. The unaccountable pleasure of God was the sole motive of the different dispensation. Our Saviour breaks forth in an ecstasy of joy, "I thank thee, O Father, Lord of heaven and earth, that thou hast hid these things from the wise and prudent, and hast revealed them unto babes: even so, Father, for so it seemed good in thy sight," Luke x. 21. It is the prerogative of God to reveal the secrets of the kingdom to whom he pleases, Matt. xiii. 11. It is an act of pure grace, putting a difference between one nation and another, with the same liberty, as, in the creation, of the same indigested matter he formed the earth, the dregs of the universe, and the sun and stars, the ornaments of the heavens, and the glory of the visible world. How can we reflect on our spiritual obligations to divine grace without a rapture of soul? The corruption of nature was universal; our ignorance as perverse, and our manners as profane, as of other nations, and we had been condemned to an eternal night, if the light of life had not graciously shined upon us. This should warm our hearts in affectionate acknowledgments to God, who hath "made known to us the riches of the glory of this mystery, among the Gentiles," Col. i. 26, 27; and with that revelation the concomitant power of the Spirit, to translate us "from the kingdom of darkness into the kingdom of his dear Son." If the publication of the law by the ministry of angels to the Israelites were such a privilege, that it is reckoned their peculiar treasure; "he hath showed his statutes unto Israel; he hath not dealt so with any nation," Psalm cxlvii. 19, 20; what is the revelation of the gospel by the Son of God himself? For although the law is obscured and defaced since the fall, yet there are some ingrafted notions of it in the human nature; but there is not the least suspicion of the gospel. The law discovers our misery, but the gospel alone shows the way to be delivered from it. If an advantage so great and so precious doth not touch our hearts; and in possessing it with joy, if we are not sensible of the engagement the Father of mercies hath laid upon us, we shall be the ungratefulest wretches in the world.

II. This incomprehensible mystery is worthy of our most serious thoughts and study, that we may arrive to a fuller knowledge of it. And to incite us, it will be fit to consider those excellencies, which will render it most desirable.

Knowledge is a quality so eminent, that it truly ennobles one spirit above another. As reason is the singular ornament of the human nature, whereby it excels the brutes; so in proportion, knowledge, which is the perfection of the understanding, raises those who are possessors of it above others that want it. The testimony of Solomon confirms this, "Then I saw that wisdom excelleth folly, as far as light excelleth darkness," Eccles. ii. 13. And according to the nature and quality of knowledge, such is the advantage it brings to us. Now the doctrine of the gospel excels the most noble sciences, as well contemplative as practical.

It excels the contemplative in the sublimity of the object, and in the certainty of its principle.

(1.) In the sublimity and greatness of the object; and this is no less than the highest design of the eternal wisdom, the most glorious work of the great God. In the creation his footsteps appear, in our redemption his image; in the law his justice and holiness, but in the gospel all his perfections shine forth in their brightest lustre. The bare theory of this enriches the mind, and the contemplation of it affects the soul that is conversant about it, with the highest admiration, and most sincere and lasting delight.

It affects the soul with the highest admiration. The strongest spirits cannot comprehend its just greatness: the understanding sinks under the weight of glory. The apostle who had seen the light of heaven, and had such knowledge as never any man had before, yet, upon considering one part of the divine wisdom, breaks forth in astonishment, " O the depth of the riches both of the wisdom and knowledge of God! How unsearchable are his judgments, and his ways past finding out!" Rom. xi. 33. It is fit when we have spent the strength of our minds in the consideration of this excelling object, and are at the end of our subtilty, to supply the defects of our understandings with admiration; as the psalmist expresses himself, " Lord, how wonderful are thy thoughts to us-ward!" The angels adore this glorious mystery with an humble reverence, 1 Pet. i. 12. The admiration that is caused by it, is a principal delight of the mind. It is true, the wonder that proceedeth from ignorance, when the cause of some visible effect is not known, is the imperfection and torment of the spirit; but that which arises from the knowledge of those things which are most above our conception and our hope, is the highest advancement of our minds, and brings the greatest satisfaction to the soul. Now the contrivance of our redemption, was infinitely above the flight of reason and our expectation. When the Lord turned the captivity of Zion, they were as in a dream, Psalm cxxvi.

1. The way of accomplishing it was so incredible, that it seemed rather the picture of fancy, than a real deliverance. And there is far greater reason that the rescuing of us from the powers of hell, and the restoring of us to liberty and glory by Christ, should raise our wonder. The gospel is called a "marvelous light," upon the account of the objects it discovers, 1 Pet. ii. 9. But such a perverse judgment there is in men, that they neglect those things which deserve the highest admiration, and spend their wonder on meaner things. Art is more admired than nature; a counterfeit eye of crystal, which hath neither sight nor motion, than the living eye, the sun of the little world, that directs the whole man. And the effects of nature are more admired, than the sublime and supernatural works of grace; yet these infinitely exceed the other. The world is the work of God's hand, but the gospel is his plot, and the chiefest of all his ways. What a combination of wonders is there in the great mystery of godliness! That he who fills heaven and earth, should be confined to the virgin's womb; that life should die, and, being dead, revive! that mercy should triumph without any disparagement to justice! These are miracles that transcend all that is done in nature. And this appears by the judgment of God himself, who best knows the excellency of his own works; for whereas upon finishing the first creation, he ordained the seventh day, that reasonable creatures might more solemnly ascribe to him the glory of his attributes, which are visible in the things which are made; he hath upon the completing of our redemption by the raising of Christ from the dead, made the first day sacred for his service and praise, there being the clearest illustration of his perfections in that blessed work. God is more pleased in the contemplation of the new world, than of the old. The latter, by its extraordinary magnificence, hath lessened the dignity of the former, as the greater light obscures the less. Therefore the sabbath is changed into the Lord's day. And what a just reproach is it to man that he should be unobservant and unaffected with this glorious mercy, wherein he may always find new cause of admiration! "O Lord, how great are thy

works! and thy thoughts are very deep! A brutish man knoweth not, neither doth a fool understand this," Psalm xcii. 5, 6. The admiring of any other thing in comparison of this mystery, is the effect of inconsideration or infidelity.

It produces the most sincere and lasting pleasure. As the taste is to meat, to allure us to feed for the support of our bodies; that is delight to knowledge, to excite the mind to seek after it. But its vast capacity can never be satisfied with the knowledge of inferior things. The pleasure is more in the acquisition, than in the possession of it; for the mind is diverted in the search, but having attained to that knowledge which cannot fill the rational appetite, it is disgusted with the fruits of its travail, and seeks some other object to relieve its languor. From hence it is, that variety is the spring of delight, and pleasure is the product of novelty. We find that the pleasure of the first taste, in learning something new, is always most sensible. The most elegant compositions and excellent discourses, which ravished at the first reading, yet repeated often, are nauseous and irksome. The exercise of the mind on an object fully known, is unprofitable, and therefore tedious; whereas by turning the thoughts on something else, it may acquire new knowledge. But the apostle tells us that the mystery of our redemption contains all the "treasures of wisdom and knowledge," to signify their excellence and abundance: the "unsearchable riches" of grace are laid up in it. There is infinite variety, and perpetual matter for the inquiry of the most excellent understanding. No created reason is able to reach its height, or sound its depths. By the continual study, and increase in the knowledge of it, the mind enjoys a persevering pleasure, that far exceeds the short vehemence of sensual delights.

(2.) It excels other sciences in the certainty of its principle, which is divine revelation. Human sciences are built upon uncertain maxims, which being admitted with precipitation and not confirmed by sufficient experiments, the mind is satisfied with appearances, instead of real certainty. And from hence it is, that upon severe inquiry into matters of fact, those doctrines which were received in one age, are discovered to be false in another. Modern philosophy discards the ancient; but the doctrine of salvation is the "word of truth," that came from heaven, and bears the character and marks of its divine descent. It is confirmed by the "demonstration of the Spirit and of power." It is always the same, unchangeable as God the Author, and Christ the object of it, who is the same "yesterday, to-day, and for ever." And the knowledge which the sincere and enlightened mind hath of it, is not uncertain opinion, but a clear, solid, and firm apprehension. It is a contemplation of the glory of God with open face, 2 Cor. iii. 18. This appears by the effects it produces in those that have received the true tincture of it in their souls; they despise all things which carnal men admire, in comparison of this inestimable treasure.

2. The doctrine of the gospel exceeds all practical sciences in the excellency of its end, and the efficacy of the means to obtain it.

The end of it is the supreme happiness of man; the restoring of him to the innocence and excellency of his first state. And the means are appointed by infinite wisdom, so that the most insuperable obstacles are removed, and these are the justice of God that condemns the guilty, and that strong and obstinate aversion which is in corrupted man to true felicity. Here is a Mediator revealed, who is "able to save to the uttermost;" who hath quenched the wrath of God by the blood of his divine sacrifice; who hath expiated sin by the value of his death, and purifies the soul by the virtue of his life, that it may consent to its own salvation. No less than a divine power could perform this work. From hence the superlative excellency of evangelical knowledge doth arise; all other knowledge is unprofitable without it, and that alone can make us perfectly blessed; "This is life eternal, to know thee, and Jesus Christ, whom thou hast sent," John xvii. 3.

I will briefly consider how ineffectual all other knowledge is, whether natural, political, or moral, to recover us from our misery.

The most exact insight into natural things leaves the

mind blind and poor, ignorant of happiness and the way to it. Solomon, who had an extraordinary measure of natural knowledge and was able to set a just price upon it, tells us, that the increase of knowledge was attended with proportionable degrees of sorrow, Eccles. i. 18 ; for the more a man knows, the more he discerns the insufficiency of that knowledge to supply his defects and satisfy his desires : he was therefore weary of his wisdom, as well as of his folly. The devils know more than the profoundest philosophers ; yet their knowledge doth not alleviate their torments. It is not only insufficient to prevent misery, but will more expose to it by enlarging the faculties, and making them more capable of torment. It is the observation of St. Ambrose, that when God discovered the creation of the world to Moses, he did not inform him of the greatness of the heavens, the number of the stars, their aspects and influences ; whether they derive their light from the sun, or have it inherent in their own bodies ; from whence eclipses are caused ; how the rainbow is painted ; how the winds fly in the air ; or the causes of the ebbing and flowing of the sea : but so much as might be a foundation of faith and obedience, and left the rest, *quasi marcescentis sapientiæ vanitates,* as the vanities of perishing wisdom. The most knowing philosopher, though encompassed with these sparks, yet if ignorant of the Redeemer, shall lie down in sorrow forever.

And as natural, so political knowledge, in order to the governing of kingdoms and states, hath no power to confer happiness upon man. It concerns not his main interest ; it is terminated within the compass of this short life, and provides not for death and eternity. The wisdom of the world is folly in a disguise, a specious ignorance, which, although it may secure the temporal state, yet it leaves us naked and exposed to spiritual enemies " who war against the soul."

And all the moral knowledge which is treasured up in the books of the heathens, is insufficient to restore man to his original integrity and felicity. Reason sees that man is ignorant and guilty, mortal and miserable ; that he is transported with vain passions, and tormented with accusations of conscience; but it could not redress these evils. Corrupt nature is like an imperfect building that lies in rubbish, the imperfection is visible, but not the way how to finish it; for through the ignorance of the first design, every one follows his own fancy; whereas when the architect comes to finish his own project, it appears regular and beautiful. Thus the various directions of philosophers to recover fallen man out of his ruins, and to raise him to his first state, were vain. Some glimmerings they had, that the happiness of the reasonable nature consisted in its union with God; but in order to this, they propounded such means as were not only ineffectual, but opposite. Such is the pride and folly of carnal wisdom, that to bring God and man together, it advances man and depresses God. The Stoics ascribed to their wise man those prerogatives whereby he equalled their supreme god. They made him the architect of his virtue and felicity, and to vie with Jupiter himself, to be one of his peers. Others reduced the gods to live like men, and men like beasts, by placing happiness in sensual pleasures. Thus, instead of curing, they fomented the hereditary and principal diseases of mankind, pride and concupiscence, which at first caused the separation of man from God, and infinitely increase the distance between them; for what sins are more contrary to the majesty and purity of God than pride, which robs him of his honour; and carnal lust, which turns a man into a beast? Besides, all their inventions to expiate sin, to appease the Deity and make him favourable, to calm the conscience, were frivolous and unprofitable. And their most generous principles and accurate precepts were short of that purity and perfection wherewith moral duties are performed to God and men. Briefly, they wasted their candle in vain, in searching for the way to true happiness.

But God who created man for the enjoyment of himself, hath happily accomplished his eternal decree, by the work of our redemption, wherein his own glory is most visible. And the gospel which reveals this to us, humbles whom it justifies, and comforts those that were condemned; it abases more than the law, but without despair; and advances more than nature could, but without presumption. The Mediator takes away the guilt of our old sins, and our inclination to new sins. We are not only restored, but exalted, made "heirs of God, joint-heirs with Christ," Rom. viii. 17. For these reasons the apostle sets so high a value upon the heavenly doctrine, that reveals a Saviour to the undone world. He desires to "know nothing but Jesus Christ, and him crucified," 1 Cor. ii. 2. He despiseth all pharisaical and philosophical learning "in comparison of the excellency of the knowledge of Christ Jesus," Phil. iii. 8. Other knowledge swells the mind, and increases the esteem of ourselves; this gives us a sincere view of our state. It discovers our misery in its causes, and the almighty mercy that saves us. Other knowledge enlightens the understanding without changing the heart, but this inspires us with the love of God, with hatred of sin, and makes us truly better. In seeking after other knowledge, the mind is perplexed by endless inquiries; here it is at rest, as the wavering needle is fixed when turned to its beloved star. Ignorance of other things may be without any real damage to us, for we may be directed by the skilful how to preserve life and estate; but this knowledge is absolutely necessary to justify, sanctify, and save us. All other knowledge is useless at the hour of death; then the richest stock of learning is lost, the vessel being split wherein the treasure was laid; but this pearl of inestimable price is both the ornament of our prosperity, and the support of our adversity. A little ray of this is infinitely more desirable, than the light of all human science in their lustre and perfection.

And what an amazing folly is it, that men who are possessed with an earnest passion of knowing, should waste their time and strength in searching after things, the knowledge of which cannot remove the evils that oppress them, and be careless of the saving knowledge of the gospel! Were there no other reason to diminish the esteem of earthly knowledge, but the difficulty of its acquisition, that error often surprises those who are searching after truth, this might check our intemperate pursuit of it. Sin hath not only shortened our understandings, but our lives, so that we cannot arrive to the perfect discovery of inferior objects. But suppose that one, by his vast mind, should comprehend all created things, from the centre of the earth to the circumference of the heavens, and were not savingly enlightened in the mystery of our redemption, with all his knowledge he would be a prey to Satan, and increase the triumphs of hell. The historian Pliny upbraids the Roman luxury, that with so much cost and hazard they should send to foreign parts for trees that were beautiful but barren, and produced a shadow only without fruit. With greater reason we may wonder, that men should, with the expense of their precious hours, purchase barren curiosities, which are unprofitable to their last end. How can a condemned criminal, who is in suspense between life and death, attend to study the secrets of nature and art, when all his thoughts are taken up how to prevent the execution of the sentence? And it is no less than a prodigy of madness, that men who have but a short and uncertain space allowed them to escape the wrath to come, should rack their brains in studying things impertinent to salvation, and neglect the knowledge of a Redeemer. Especially when there is so clear a revelation of him: the righteousness of faith doth not command us to ascend to the heavens, or descend into the deep to make a discovery of it; but the word is nigh us, that discovers the certain way to a happy immortality, Rom. x. 6, 7. Seneca, a philosopher and a courtier, valued his being in the world only upon this account, that he might contemplate the starry heaven. He saw only the visible beauty of the firmament, but was ignorant of the glory within it, and of the way that leads to it; yet, to our shame, he speaks that the sight of it made him despise the earth, and without the contemplation of the celestial bodies, he esteemed his continuance in the world not the life of a man, but the toil of a beast. " *Quid erat cur in numero viventium me positum esse gauderem? an ut cibos et potum percolarem? ut hoc corpus casurum, ac fluidum, periturumque nisi subinde impleatur, farcirem? et viverem ægri minister? ut morti timerem cui omnes nascimur? Detrahe hoc inæstimabile bonum; non est vita tanti ut sudem, ut æstuem. O quam contempta res est homo nisi supra humana se erexerit!"* But what transports had he been in, if he had been acquainted with the contrivance of our redemption, the admirable order of its parts, and the beauty that results from the composition of the whole? But we that with open face may in the glass of the gospel behold the glory of the Lord, turn away our eyes from it to vanity. Here the complaint is more just, *"Ad sapientiam quis accedit? quis dignam judicat, nisi quam in transitu noverit?"* We content ourselves with slight and transient glances, but do not seriously and fixedly consider this blessed design of God, upon which the beginning of our happiness in this, and the perfection of it in the next life, is built. Let us provoke ourselves by the example of the angels who are not concerned in this redemption as man is; for they continued in their fidelity to their Creator, and were always happy in his favour, and where there is no alienation between parties, reconcilement is unnecessary; yet they are students with us in the same book, and unite all their powers in the contemplation of this mystery: they are represented stooping to pry into these secrets, to signify their delight in what they know, and their desire to advance in the knowledge of them, 1 Pet. i. 12. With what intentness then should we study the gospel, who are the subject and end of it!

CHAPTER VII.

THE CAUSES AND UNREASONABLENESS OF UNBELIEF.

THE simple speculation of this glorious mystery will be of no profit without a real belief of it, and a cordial acceptance of salvation upon the terms which the divine wisdom prescribes. The gospel requires the obedience of the understanding, and of the will; unless it obtains a full possession of the soul, there is no saving efficacy derived from it. And such is the sublimity and purity of the object, that till reason is sanctified and subdued, it cannot sincerely entertain it. I will, therefore, distinctly consider the opposition which carnal reason hath made against it; and show how just it is that the human understanding should, with reverence, yield up itself to the word of God, that reveals this great mystery to us.

1. The apostle tells us, that Jews and Gentiles conspired in the contempt of the gospel, 1 Cor. i. 22. Reason cannot hear without great astonishment, for the appearing contradiction between the terms, that God should be made man, and the Eternal die. The Jews esteemed it an intolerable blasphemy, and without any process of law were ready to stone the Lord Jesus, that, being a man, he should make himself equal with God, John x. 33. And they upbraided him in his sufferings, that he could not save himself; "If he be the king of Israel, let him now come down from the cross, and we will believe him," Matt. xxvii. 42. The Gentiles despised the gospel as an absurd, ill-contrived fable, 1 Cor. i. 23; for what in appearance is more unbecoming God and injurious to his perfections, than to take the frail garment of flesh, to be torn and trampled on? Their natural knowledge of the Deity inclined them to think the incarnation impossible. There is no resemblance of it in the whole compass of nature; for natural union supposes the parts incomplete, and capable of perfection by their joining together; but that a being infinitely perfect should assume by personal union a nature inferior to itself, the heathens looked on it as a fable, forged according to the model of the fictions concerning Danae and Antiope; Origen cont. Cels. And the doctrine of our Saviour's death on the cross they rejected, as an impiety contumelious to God; they judged it inconsistent with the majesty and happiness of the Deity, to ascribe to him that which is the punishment of the most guilty and miserable. In the account of carnal reason, they thought more worthily of God by denying that of him, which is due only to the worst of men. Celsus, who, with as much subtilty as malice, urges all that with any appearance could be objected against our Saviour, principally insists on his poverty and sufferings, the meanness and misery of his condition in the world. "It was fit," says

he, "that the Son of God should appear as the sun, which renders itself conspicuous by its own light; but the gospel having declared the Word to be the Son of God, relates, that he was a man of sorrows, one that had no power to defend himself, and was deserted by his Father and followers, scourged with rods, and shamefully executed." He could not reconcile so many things that seemed utterly incompatible, as sovereignty and servitude, innocence and punishment, the lowest of human miseries, death, with the highest of divine honours, adoration. Briefly; nothing was more contrary to flesh and blood, than to believe that person to be the Redeemer of the world, who did not rescue himself from his enemies; and to expect immortality from him that was overcome by death.

Now the causes of this infidelity are,

1. The darkness of the mind, which is so corrupted by original pravity, that it cannot behold heavenly mysteries in their proper light, so as to acquiesce in the truth of them. "The natural man receiveth not the things of the Spirit of God; for they are foolishness to him; neither can he know them, because they are spiritually discerned," 1 Cor. ii. 14. The apostle takes notice of the disaffection of the heart, and the incapacity of the mind, not prepared and illustrated by grace, to embrace and discern spiritual things in their verity and beauty. There is a great disproportion between the natural understanding, though elevated and enlarged by secular learning, and supernatural truth; for though the rational soul is a spirit, as it is distinguished from corporeal beings, yet till it is purged from error and vicious affections, it can never discover the divinity of things spiritual, so as to embrace them with certainty and delight. As there must be a spirit of revelation to unveil the object, so of wisdom to enlighten the eye, that it may be prepared for the reception of it. As heaven is seen only by its own light, so Christ is by his own Spirit. Divine objects, and faith that discerns them, are of the same original and of the same quality. The natural understanding, as the effects declare, is like the funeral lamps, which, by the ancients, were put into sepulchres to

guard the ashes of their dead friends, which shine so long as they are kept close, a thick moist vapour feeding them and repairing what was consumed: but, in opening the sepulchres and exposing them to the free air, they presently faint and expire. Thus natural reason, whilst conversant in things below and watching with the dead, that is, in the phrase of the ancients, studying the books of men who have left the world, discovers something, although it is rather twilight than clear; but when it is brought from the narrow sphere of things sensible, to contemplate the immensity of things spiritual and supernatural, its light declines and is turned into darkness.

2. The pride of the human understanding, which disdains to stoop to those great and heavenly mysteries. It is observable, that those who most excelled in natural wisdom, were the greatest despisers of evangelical truths. The proud wits of the world chose rather to be masters of their own, than scholars to another. They made reason their supreme rule, and philosophy their highest principle, and would not believe what they could not comprehend. They represented Christians under scornful titles, as captives of a blind belief, and derided their faith as the effect of folly; and rejected revelation, the only means to convey the knowledge of divine mysteries to them. They presumed by the light and strength of their own reason and virtue to acquire felicity, and slighted the doctrine that came from heaven to discover a clear way thither, and divine grace that was necessary to assist them. Therefore the apostle, by way of upbraiding, inquires, " Where is the wise ? Where is the scribe? Where is the disputer of this world ? Hath not God made foolish the wisdom of this world ?" As those who are really poor and would appear rich in the pomp of their habits and attendants, are made poor by that expense; so the philosophers who were destitute of true wisdom, and would appear wise in making reason the judge of divine revelation and the last resolution of all things, by that false affectation of wisdom, became more foolish: by all their disputes against the apparent

absurdities of the Christian religion, they were brough into a more learned darkness.

3. The prejudice which arose from sensual lusts hindered the belief of the gospel. As the carnal understanding rebels against the sublimity of its doctrine, so the carnal appetite against the purity of its precepts. And according to the dispositions of men from whence they act, such light they desire to direct them in acting. The gospel is a mystery of godliness, and those who are under the love of sin, cherish an affected ignorance, lest the light should inflame conscience by representing to them the deadly guilt that cleaves to sin, and thereby make it uneasy. This account our Saviour gives of the infidelity of the world, that "men love darkness rather than light, because their deeds are evil," John iii. 19. And that this was the real cause, whatever was pretended, is clear, in that the Gentiles who opposed Christ, adored those impure deities whose infamous lusts were acknowledged by them. And with what colour then could they reject our Redeemer because crucified? As if vice were not more incompatible with the Deity, than sufferings.

Now, though reason, enslaved by prejudice and corrupted by passion, despises the gospel, yet when it is enlightened by faith, it discovers such a wise economy in it, that, were it not true, it would transcend the most noble created mind to invent it. It is so much above our most excellent thoughts, that no human understanding would ever attempt to feign it, with confidence of persuading the world into a belief of it. How is it possible that it should be contrived by natural reason, since no man can believe it sincerely when it is revealed without a supernatural faith?

II. To confirm our belief of these great and saving mysteries, I will show how just it is that the understanding should resign itself to divine revelation which hath made them known.

In order to this, we must consider,

First, There are some doctrines in the gospel, which the understanding could not discover; but when they are revealed, it hath a clear apprehension of them upon a rational account, and sees the characters of truth visibly stamped on their forehead; as the doctrine of satisfaction to divine justice, that pardon might be dispensed to repenting sinners; for our natural conception of God includes his infinite purity and justice; and when the design of the gospel is made known, whereby he hath provided abundantly for the honour of those attributes, so that he doth the greatest good without encouraging the least evil, reason acquiesces and acknowledges, 'This I sought, but could not find.' Now, although the primary obligation to believe such doctrines ariseth from revelation, yet being ratified by reason, they are embraced with more clearness by the mind.

Secondly, There are some doctrines which, as reason by its light could not discover, so when they are made known, it cannot comprehend; but they are by a clear necessary connection joined with the other that reason approves; as the mystery of the Trinity and the incarnation of the Son of God, which are the foundations of the whole work of our redemption. The nature of God is repugnant to plurality; there can be but one essence; and the nature of satisfaction requires a distinction of persons; for he that suffers as guilty, must be distinguished from the person of the judge that exacts satisfaction, and no mere creature is able, by his obedient sufferings, to repair the honour of God; so that a divine person assuming the nature of man, was alone capable to make that satisfaction which the gospel propounds, and reason consents to. Now, according to the distinction of capacities in the Trinity, the Father required an honourable reparation for the breach of the divine law, and the Son bore the punishment in the sufferings of the human nature, that is peculiarly his own. Besides, it is clear that the doctrine of the Trinity, that is, of three glorious relations in the godhead, and of the incarnation, are most firmly connected with all the parts of the Christian religion, left in the writings of the apostles, which, as they were confirmed by miracles, the divine signatures of their certainty, so they contain such authentic marks of their divinity, that right reason cannot reject them.

Thirdly, Whereas there are three principles by which

we apprehend things, sense, reason, and faith, these lights have their different objects that must not be confounded. Sense is confined to things material; reason considers things abstracted from matter; faith regards the mysteries revealed from heaven: and these must not transgress their order. Sense is an incompetent judge of things about which reason only is conversant; it can only make a report of those objects, which, by their natural characters, are exposed to it. And reason can discourse only of things within its sphere; supernatural things, which derive from revelation, and are purely the objects of faith, are not within its territories and jurisdiction. Those superlative mysteries exceed all our intellectual abilities.

It is true, the understanding is a rational faculty, and every act of it is really, or in appearance, grounded on reason; but there is a wide difference between proving a doctrine by reason, and giving a reason why we believe the truth of it. For instance; we cannot prove the Trinity by natural reason, and the subtilty of the schoolmen who affect to give some reason of all things, is here more prejudicial than advantageous to the truth: for he that pretends to maintain a point by reason and is unsuccessful, doth weaken the credit which the authority of revelation gives: and it is considerable, that the scripture in delivering supernatural truths, produces God's authority as their only proof, without using any other way of arguing. But although we cannot demonstrate these mysteries by reason, yet we may give a rational account why we believe them. Is it not the highest reason to believe the discovery that God hath made of himself and his decrees? For he perfectly knows his own nature and will; and it is impossible he should deceive us. This natural principle is the foundation of faith. When God speaks, it becomes man to hear with silence and submission. His naked word is as certain as a demonstration.

And is it not most reasonable to believe, that the Deity cannot be fully understood by us? The sun may more easily be included in a spark of fire, than the infinite perfections of God be comprehended by a finite mind. The angels who dwell so near the fountain of light, cover their faces in a holy confusion, not being able to comprehend him; how much less can man in this earthly state, distant from God, and oppressed with a burden of flesh?

Now from hence it follows,

1. That ignorance of the manner how divine mysteries exist is no sufficient plea for infidelity, when the scripture reveals that they are; for reason that is limited and restrained, cannot frame a conception that is commensurate to the essence and power of God.

This will appear more clearly by considering the mysterious excellencies of the divine nature, the certainty of which we believe, but the manner we cannot understand; as, that his essence and attributes are the same, without the least shadow of composition; yet his wisdom and power are, to our apprehensions, distinct, and his mercy and justice in some manner opposite;—that his essence is entire in all places, yet not terminated in any;—that he is above the heavens and beneath the earth, yet hath no relation of high or low, distant or near;—that he penetrates all substances, but is mixed with none;—that he understands, yet receives no ideas within himself;—that he wills, yet hath no motion that carries him out of himself; that in him time hath no succession, that which is past is not gone, and that which is future is not to come;—that he loves without passion, is angry without disturbance, repents without change. These perfections are above the capacity of reason fully to understand, yet essential to the Deity. Here we must exalt faith, and abase reason. Thus in the mystery of the incarnation, that two such distant natures should compose one person, without the confusion of properties, reason cannot reach unto, but it is clearly revealed in the word: here therefore we must obey, not inquire.

The obedience of faith is, to embrace an obscure truth with a firm assent, upon the account of divine testimony. If reason will not assent to revelation till it understands the manner how divine things are, it doth not obey it at all. The understanding then sincerely submits, when it is inclined by those motives which demonstrate that such a belief is due to the authority of the revealer, and to the quality of the object. To believe only in proportion to our narrow conceptions, is to disparage the divine truth and debase the divine power. We cannot know what God can do; he is omnipotent, though we are not omniscient; it is just we should humble our ignorance to his wisdom, and that every lofty imagination and "high thing that exalteth itself against the knowledge of God, should be cast down," and every thought captivated to the obedience of Christ. 2 Cor. x. 5. It is our wisdom to receive the great mysteries of the gospel in their simplicity; for in attempting to give an exact and curious explication of them, the understanding, as in a hedge of thorns, the more it strives, the more it is wounded and entangled. God's ways are far above ours, and his thoughts above ours, as heaven is above the earth. To reject what we cannot comprehend, is not only to sin against faith, but against reason, which acknowledges itself finite, and unable to "find out the Almighty to perfection," Job xi. 7.

2. We are obliged to believe those mysteries that are plainly delivered in scripture, notwithstanding those seeming contradictions wherewith they may be charged. In the objects of sense, the contrariety of appearances doth not lessen the certainty of things. The stars to our sight, seem but glittering sparks, yet they are immense bodies. And it is one thing to be assured of a truth, another to answer all the difficulties that encounter it; a mean understanding is capable of the first; the second is so difficult, that in clear things the profoundest philosophers may not be able to untie all the intricate and knotty objections which may be urged against them. It is sufficient the belief of supernatural mysteries is built on the veracity and power of God; this makes them prudently credible; this resolves all doubts, and produces such a stability of spirit as nothing can shake. A sincere believer is assured that all opposition against revealed truths is fallacious, though he cannot discover the fallacy.

Now the transcendent mysteries of the Christian religion, the Trinity of persons in the divine nature, the incarnation of the Son of God, are clearly set down in the scripture. And although subtile and obstinate opponents have used many guilty arts to dispirit and enervate those texts by an inferior sense, and have racked them with violence to make them speak according to their prejudices, yet all is vain, the evidence of truth is victorious. A heathen who considers not the gospel as a divine revelation but merely as a doctrine delivered in writing, and judges of its sense by natural light, will acknowledge, that those things are delivered in it. And notwithstanding those who usurp a sovereign authority to themselves to judge of divine mysteries according to their own apprehensions, deny them as mere contradictions, yet they can never conclude them impossible; for no certain argument can be alleged against the being of a thing, without a clear knowledge of its nature: now although we may understand the nature of man, we do not the nature of God, the economy of the persons, and his power to unite himself to a nature below him.

It is true, no article of faith is really repugnant to reason; for God is the author of natural as well as of supernatural light, and he cannot contradict himself: they are emanations from him, and though different, yet not destructive of each other. But we must distinguish between those things that are above reason and incomprehensible, and things that are against reason and utterly inconceivable. Some things are above reason, in regard of their transcendent excellency or distance from us. The divine essence, the eternal decrees, the hypostatical union, are such high and glorious objects, that it is an impossible enterprise to comprehend them: the intellectual eye is dazzled with their overpowering light: we can have but an imperfect knowledge of them. And there is no just cause of wonder that supernatural revelation should speak incomprehensible things of God; for he is a singular and admirable Being, infinitely above the ordinary course of nature. The maxims of philosophy are not to be extended to him. We must adore what we cannot fully understand. But those things are against reason and utterly inconceivable, that involve a contradiction, and have a natural repugnancy to our understandings, which cannot conceive any thing that is formally impossible: and there is no such doctrine in the Christian religion.

We must distinguish between reason corrupted, and right reason. Since the fall, the clearness of the human understanding is lost, and the light that remains is eclipsed by the interposition of sensual lusts. The carnal mind cannot out of ignorance, and will not from pride and other malignant habits, receive things spiritual. And from hence arise many suspicions and doubts concerning supernatural verities, the shadows of darkened reason and of dying faith. If any divine mystery seems incredible, it is from the corruption of our reason not from reason itself; from its darkness, not its light. And as reason is obliged to correct the errors of sense, when it is deceived either by some vicious quality in the organ, or by the distance of the object, or by the falseness of the medium that corrupts the image in conveying it; so it is the office of faith to reform the judgment of reason, when, either from its own weakness, or the height of things spiritual, it is mistaken about them. For this end supernatural revelation was given, not to extinguish reason, but to redress it, and enrich it with the discovery of heavenly things.

Faith is called wisdom and knowledge: it doth not quench the vigour of the faculty wherein it is seated, but elevates it, and gives it a spiritual perception of those things that are most distant from its commerce. It doth not lead us through a mist to the inheritance of the saints in light. Faith is a rational light; for—it arises from the consideration of those arguments which convince the mind, that the scripture is a divine revelation. "I know," saith the apostle, "whom I have believed," 2 Tim. i. 12; and we are commanded always to be ready to give an account of the hope that is in us, 1 Peter iii. 15. Those that owe their Christianity merely to the felicity of their birth, without a sight of that transcendent excellency in our religion which evidences that it came from heaven, are not true believers. He that absolves an innocent person for favour, without considering sufficient proofs offered, though his sentence is just is an unjust judge; and the eye that is clouded with a suffusion, so that all things appear yellow to it, when it judges things to be yellow that are so, yet is erroneous, because its judgment proceeds not from the quality of the object, but from the jaundice that discolours the organs: so those who believe the doctrine of the gospel upon the account of its civil establishment in their country, are not right believers, because they assent to the word of truth upon a false principle. It is not judgment, but chance, that inclines them to embrace it. The Turks are zealous votaries of Mahomet, upon the same reason as they are disciples of Christ.—Faith makes use of reason to consider what doctrines are revealed in the scripture, and to deduce those consequences which have a clear connection with supernatural principles. Thus reason is an excellent instrument to distinguish those things which are of a divine original, from what is spurious and counterfeit; for sometimes that is pretended to be a mystery of religion, which is only the fruit of fancy; and that is defended by the sacred respect of faith that reason ought not to violate, which is but a groundless imagination; so that we remain in an error, by the sole apprehension of falling into one, as those that die for fear of death. The Bereans are commended for their searching the scriptures, whether the doctrines they heard were consentaneous to them, Acts xvii. 11. But it is a necessary duty, that reason, how stiff soever, should fully comply with God, where it appears reasonable that He hath spoken.

Briefly; the richest ornament of the creature is humility, and the most excellent effect of it is the sense of the weakness of our understanding. This is the temper of soul that prepares it for faith—partly as it puts us on a serious consideration of those things which are revealed to us in the word: infidelity proceeds from the want of consideration, and nothing hinders that so much as pride:—partly as it stops all curious inquiries into those things which are unsearchable:—and, principally, as it entitles to the promise, God will instruct and give grace to the humble, 1 Pet. v. 5. The knowledge of heaven, as well as the kingdom of heaven, is the inheritance of the poor in spirit. A greater progress is made in the knowledge and belief of these mysteries by humble prayer, than by the most anxious study; as at court, an hour of favour is worth a year's attendance. Man cannot acquire so much as God can give.

And as humility, so holiness prepares the soul for the receiving of supernatural truths. The understanding is clarified by the purification of the heart. It is not the difficulty and obscurity of things revealed, that is the real cause of infidelity, since men believe other things upon far less evidence; but it is the prejudice of the lower faculties that hinders them. When all affections to sin are mortified, the soul is in the best disposition to receive divine revelation. He that doth the will of God, shall know whether the doctrine of the gospel came from heaven, John vii. 17.

The Spirit of God is the alone instructer of the spirit of man in these mysteries, so as to produce a saving belief of them. That knowledge is more clear and satisfying, that we have by his teaching, than by our own learning. The rational mind may discern the literal sense of the propositions in the gospel, and may yield a naked assent to the truth of them; but without supernatural irradiation by the Spirit of life, there can be no transforming and saving knowledge and belief of them. And as the vast expansion of air that is about us, doth not preserve life, but that part which we breathe in; so it is not the compass of our knowledge and belief, though it were equal to the whole revealed will of God, that is vital to the soul, but that which is practised by us. The apostle saith, though he had the understanding of all mysteries, and all knowledge, and all faith; yet if it were not joined with love, the principle of obedience, it were unprofitable, 1 Cor. xiii. 2. There is the same difference between the speculative knowledge of these mysteries, and that which is affectionate and operative, as between the wearing of pearls for ornament, and the taking of them as a cordial to revive the fainting spirits. In short; such a belief is required, as prevails upon the will, and draws the affections, and renders the whole man obsequious to the gospel; for such a faith alone is answerable to the quality of the revelation. The gospel is not a mere narrative, but a promise. Christ is not represented only as an innocent person dying, but as the Son of God dying to deliver men from sin and the effects of it. The fallen angels may understand and believe it without any affections, being unconcerned in it; to them it is a naked history; but to men it is a promise, and cannot be rightly conceived without the most ardent affections. " This is a faithful saying, and worthy of all acceptation, that Christ Jesus came into the world to save sinners," 1 Tim. i. 15.

It is, essentially, as good as true; its sweetness and profit are equal to its certainty: so that it commends itself to all our faculties. There are severe and sad truths which are attended with fearful expectation, and the mind is averse from receiving them; as the law, which, like lightning, terrifies the soul with its amazing brightness: and there are pleasant illusions which have no solid foundation: and as truth doth not delight the mind unless united to goodness, such as is suitable to its palate, so goodness doth not affect the will, unless it be real. Now the doctrine of the gospel is as certain as the law, and infinitely more comfortable than all the inventions of men. It is in the knowledge of it alone, that the sensible and considering soul enjoys perfect satisfaction and the most composed rest. It is evident, that the understanding doth not behold these truths in their proper light, when the will doth not embrace them; for the rational appetite follows the last judgment of the mind. When the apostle had a powerful conviction of "the excellency of the knowledge of Christ," this made him so earnest to gain an interest in him, Phil. iii. 8. For this reason, those who are only Christians in title, " having a form of godliness, and denying the power of it," are, in scripture language, styled infidels; it being impossible that those who truly and heartily believe this great mystery of godliness, should remain ungodly. It is a strong and effectual assent that descends from the brain to the heart and life, that denominates us true believers; so that when the death of Christ is propounded as the cause of our reconciliation with God, the wonder of the mystery doth not make it incredible, when as the reason of the mortification of our lusts, the pleasures of sin do not disguise its horror. When salvation is offered upon our accepting of Christ for our Prince and Saviour, the soul is ravished with its beauty, and chooses it for an everlasting portion.

To conclude; the doctrine of the gospel clearly discovers its divine original. It is so reasonable in itself, and profitable to us, so sublime and elevated above man, yet hath such an admirable agreement with natural truths; it is so perfectly corresponding in all its parts, that without affected obstinacy, no man can reject it. And if, after the open revelation of it, we are so stupid and wicked as not to see its superlative excellency, and not to receive it with the faith, love, and obedience which are due to it, what contempt is this of that infinite wisdom which contrived the astonishing way of our salvation! what a reproach to the divine understanding, as if it had been employed from eternity about a matter of no moment, and that deserves not our serious consideration and acceptance! The neglect of it will justly bring a more severe punishment than the hell of the uninstructed heathens, who are strangers to supernatural mysteries.

CHAPTER VIII.

THE FREENESS OF THE DIVINE MERCY IN REDEMPTION.

Though all the divine attributes are equal as they are in God, (for one infinite cannot exceed another,) yet in their exercise and effects, they shine with a different glory. And mercy is represented in scripture with peculiar advantages above the rest. It is God's natural offspring; he is styled "the Father of mercies," 2 Cor. i. 3. It is his dear attribute, that which he places next to himself; he is proclaimed, "The Lord God merciful and gracious," Exod. xxxiv. 6. It is his delight, mercy pleases him, Mic. vii. 18. It is his treasure, "he is rich in mercy," Ephes. ii. 4. It is his triumphant attribute, and the special matter of his glory ; mercy rejoices over judgment, Jam. ii. 13. Now, in the performance of our redemption, mercy is the predominant attribute, that sets all the rest a working. The acts of his wisdom, justice, and power, were in order to the illustration of his mercy. And if we duly consider that glorious work, we shall find in it all the ingredients of the most sovereign mercy. In discoursing of it, I shall principally consider two things, wherein this attribute is eminently glorified, the freeness and the greatness of it.

The freeness of this mercy will appear by considering the original and object of it.

1. The original is God: and the notion of a Deity includes infinite perfections, so that it necessarily follows that he hath no need of the creature's service to preserve or heighten his felicity. "If thou be righteous, what givest thou him ? or what receiveth he of thine hand ?" Job xxxv. 7. From eternity he was without external honour, yet in that infinite duration he was perfectly joyful and happy. He is the fountain of his own blessedness, the theatre of his own glory, the glass of his own beauty. One drop increases the ocean, but to God a million of worlds can add nothing. Every thing hath so much of goodness as it derives from him. As there was no gain to him by the creation, so there can be no loss by the annihilation of all things. The world proceeded from his wisdom as the idea and exemplar, and from his power as the efficient cause ; and it so proceeds from him, as to remain more perfectly in him. And as the possession of all things, and the obedience of angels and men, is of no advantage to God, so the opposition of impenitent rebels cannot lessen his blessedness. "If thou sinnest, what doest thou against him ? or, if thy transgressions be multiplied, what doest thou unto him ?" Job xxxv. 6. The sun suffers no loss of his light by the darkness of the night or an eclipse, but the world loses its day : if intelligent beings do not esteem God for his greatness, and love him for his goodness, it is no injury to him, but their own infelicity. Were it for his interest, he could by one act of power conquer the obstinacy of his fiercest enemies. If he require subjection from his

creatures, it is not that he may be happy, but liberal, that his goodness may take its rise to reward them. Now this is the special commendation of divine love, it doth not arise out of indigency as created love, but out of fulness and redundancy. Our Saviour tells us, there is " none good but God ;" not only in respect of the perfection of that attribute, as it is in God in a transcendent manner; but as to the effects of his goodness, which are merely for the benefit of the receiver. He only is rich in mercy, to whom nothing is wanting or profitable. The most liberal monarch doth not always give, for he stands in need of his subjects. And where there is an expectation of service for the support of the giver, it is traffic, and no gift. Human affection is begotten, and nourished by something without; but the love of God is from within : the misery of the creature is the occasion, but the cause of it is from himself. And how free was that love, that caused the infinitely blessed God to do so much for our recovery, as if his felicity were imperfect without ours!

It doth not prejudice the freeness of redeeming mercy, that Christ's personal glory was the reward of his sufferings. It is true, that our Redeemer for " the joy that was set before him, endured the cross, despising the shame, and is set down at the right hand of the throne of God," Heb. xii. 2 ; but he was not first drawn to the undertaking of that hard service by the interest of the reward : for if we consider him in his divine nature, he was the second person in the Trinity, equal to the first; he possessed all the supreme excellencies of the Deity : and by assuming our nature, the only gain he purchased to himself was to be capable of loss for the acomplishing of our salvation. Such was " the grace of our Lord Jesus Christ, that though he was rich, yet for our sakes he became poor, that we through his poverty might be rich," 2 Cor. viii. 9. And although his human soul was encouraged by the glorious recompence the Father promised, to make him King and Judge of the world, yet his love to man was not kindled from that consideration, neither is it lessened by his obtaining of it; for immediately upon the union of the human nature to the Eternal Son, the highest honour was due to him. When the first-begotten was brought into the world, it was said, " Let all the angels of God worship him," Heb. i. 6. The sovereign power in heaven and earth was his inheritance, annexed to the dignity of his primogeniture. " The name above every name " was a preferment due to his person. He voluntarily renounced his right for a time, and appeared in the " form of a servant " upon our account, that by humbling himself he might accomplish our salvation. He entered into glory after a course of sufferings, because the economy of our redemption so required; but his original title to it was by the personal union. To illustrate this by a lower instance: the mother of Moses was called to be his nurse by Pharaoh's daughter, with the promise of a reward, as if she had no relation to him. Now the pure love of a mother, not the gain of a nurse, was the motive that inclined her to nourish him with her milk. Thus the love of Christ was the primary active cause that made him liberal to us of his blood; neither did the just expectation of the reward take off from it.

The sum is this—the essence of love consists in desiring the good of another without respect to ourselves; and love is so much the more free, as the benefit we give to another is less profitable or more damageable to us. Now among men it is impossible that to a virtuous benefactor there should not redound a double benefit, from the eternal reward which God hath promised, and from the internal beauty of an honest action, which, the philosopher affirms, doth exceed any loss that can befal us; for if one dies for his friend, yet he loves himself most, for he would not choose to be less virtuous than his friend, and by dying for him he excels him in virtue, which is more valuable than life itself. But to the Son of God no such advantage could accrue; for being infinitely holy and happy in his essence, there can be no addition to his felicity or virtues by any external emanation from him. His love was for our profit, not his own.

The freeness of God's mercy is evident by considering there was no tie upon him to dispense it. Grace, strictly taken, differs from love; for love may be a debt, and without injustice not denied. There are inviolable obligations on children to love their parents: and duty lessens desert; the performance of it doth not so much deserve praise, as the neglect merits censure and reproof. But the love of God to man is a pure, free, and liberal affection, no way due. "The grace of God, and the gift by grace, hath abounded unto many," Rom. v. 15. The creation was an effusion of goodness, much more redemption. "Thou art worthy, O Lord, to receive glory and honour, and power; for thou hast created all things, and for thy pleasure they are, and were created," Rev. iv. 11. It is grace that gave being to the angels, with all the prerogatives that adorn their natures. It is grace that confirmed them in their original integrity, for God owes them nothing and they are nothing to him. It was grace that placed Adam in paradise, and made him as a visible god in the lower world. And if grace alone dispensed benefits to innocent creatures, much more to those who are obnoxious to justice: the first was free, but this is merciful. And this leads to the second consideration, which exalts redeeming love.

II. The object of it is man in his lapsed state. In this respect it excels the goodness that created him at the beginning. In the creation as there was no object to invite, so nothing repugnant to man's being and happiness. The dust of the earth did not merit such an excellent condition as it received from the pure bounty of God, but there was no moral unworthiness. But the grace of the gospel hath a different object, the wretched and unworthy; and it produces different operations, it is healing and medicinal, ransoming and delivering, and hath a peculiar character among the divine attributes. It is goodness that crowns the angels, but it is mercy, the sanctuary of the guilty and refuge of the miserable, that saves man. The scripture hath consecrated the name of grace in a special manner, to signify the most excellent and admirable favour of God in recovering us from our justly deserved misery. We are "justified freely by his grace," Rom. iii. 24;—"By grace we are saved," Eph. ii. 5;—"Grace and truth came by Jesus Christ,"

John i. 17;—it is "the grace of God that bringeth salvation," Tit. ii. 11.

And this is gloriously manifested towards man in that, 1, considered in himself, he is altogether unworthy of it; 2, as compared with the fallen angels who are left under perfect, irremediable misery.

1. Man, considered in himself, is unworthy of the favour of God.

The usual motives of love are—the goodness of things or persons. This is the proper allective of the rational appetite: there is such a ravishing beauty in it, that it powerfully calls forth affection. When there is a union of amiable qualities in a person, every one finds an attractive. A conformity in disposition hath a mighty force to beget love. Resemblance is the common principle of union in nature: social plants thrive best when near together: sensitive creatures associate with those of their kind. And love, which is an affectionate union and voluntary band, proceeds from a similitude of wills and inclinations. The harmony of tempers is the strongest and sweetest tie of friendship.—Love is an innocent and powerful charm to produce love: it is of universal virtue, and known by all the world. None are of such an unnatural hardness, but they are softened and receive impression from it. Now there are none of these inducements to incline God to love man.

(1.) He was utterly destitute of moral goodness. As the exact temperament of the body, so the order and beauty of the soul, was spoiled by sin. Nothing remained but deformity and defilements. The love of God makes us amiable, but did not find us so. Redemption is a free favour, not excited by the worth of him that receives it, but the grace of him that dispenses it; "God commendeth his love toward us, that while we were yet sinners, Christ died for us," Rom. v. 8. Our goodness was not the motive of his love, but his love the original of our goodness.

(2.) There is a fixed contrariety in the corrupted nature of man to the holy nature and will of God, for which he is not only unworthy of his love, but worthy of his wrath. We are opposite to him in our minds, affections, and actions: a strong antipathy is seated in all our faculties. How unqualified were we for his love! There is infinite holiness in him, whereby he is eternally opposite to all sin, yet he expressed infinite love to sinners in saving them from misery.

(3.) There was not the least spark of love in man to God. Notwithstanding his infinite beauty and bounty to us, yet we renewed acts of hostility against him every day, Rom. v. 10. And it was the worst kind of hostility, arising from the hatred of God, Rom. i. 30; and that for his holiness, his most amiable perfection. Yet then in his love, he pitied us. The same favour bestowed on an enemy, is morally more valuable than given to a friend; for it is love that puts a price on benefits: and the more undeserved they are, the more they are endeared by the affection that gives them. "Herein is love, not that we loved God, but that he loved us, and sent his Son to be the propitiation for our sins," 1 John iv. 10. We were rebels against God and at enmity with the Prince of life, yet then he gave himself for us.

(4.) It will further appear that our salvation comes from pure favour, if we consider man not only as a rebellious enemy to God, but impotent and obstinate, without power to resist justice and without affection to desire mercy. Sometimes the interest of a prince may induce him to spare the guilty; he may be compelled to pardon, whom he cannot punish. The multitude is the greatest potentate. The sons of Zeruiah were too strong for David; and then it is not pity, but policy to suspend the judgment, 2 Sam. iii. 39. But our condition is described by the apostle, that when we were sinners and "without strength," then Christ died for us, Rom. v. 6. Man is a despicable creature, so weak that he trembles at the appearance of a worm, and yet so wicked that he lifts up his head against heaven. How unable is he to encounter with offended omnipotence! How easily can God destroy him, when by his sole word he made him! If he unclasps his hand that supports all things, they will presently relapse into their first confusion. The whole world of sinners was shut up, utterly unable to repel or avoid his displeasure; and what amazing love

THE DIVINE ATTRIBUTES.

is it to spare rebels that were under his feet! "If a man find his enemy, will he let him go well away?" 1 Sam. xxiv. 19: But God, when we were all at his mercy, spared and saved us.

Besides, rebels sometimes solicit the favour of their prince by their acknowledgments, their tears and supplications, the testimonies of their repentance; but man persisted in his fierce enmity, and had the weapons of defiance in his hands against his Creator; he trampled on his laws, and despised his Deity; yet then the Lord of hosts became the God of peace.

In short; there was nothing to call forth the divine compassion but our misery: the breach began on man's part, but reconciliation on God's. Mercy opened his melting eye, and prevented not only our desert, but our expectation and desires. The design was laid from eternity. God foresaw our sin and our misery, and appointed a Saviour "before the foundation of the world," 1 Pet. i. 20. It was the most early and pure love to provide a ransom for us before we had a being; therefore we could not be deserving, nor desirous of it; and after we were made, we deserved nothing but damnation.

2. The grace of God eminently appears in man's recovery, by comparing his state with that of the fallen angels who are left under misery. This is a special circumstance that magnifies the favour; and to make it more sensible to us, it will be convenient briefly to consider the first state of the angels, their fall, and their punishment.

God, in creating the world, formed two natures capable of his image and favour, to glorify and enjoy him, angels and men; and placed them in the principal parts of the universe, heaven and earth. The angels were the eldest offspring of his love, the purest productions of that supreme light: man in his best state was inferior to them, Psalm viii. 5. A great number of them kept not their first state of integrity and felicity. Their sin is intimated in scripture; "Not a novice, lest being lifted up with pride, he fall into the condemnation of the devil," 1 Tim. iii. 6; that is, lest he become guilty of that sin which brought a severe sentence on the devil. The prince of darkness was blinded with the lustre of his own excellencies, and attempted upon the regalia of heaven, affecting an independent state. He disavowed his Benefactor, enriched with his benefits: and, in the same moment, he, with his companions in rebellion, was banished from heaven. "God spared not the angels that sinned, but cast them down to hell, and delivered them into chains of darkness to be reserved unto judgment," 2 Pet. ii. 4. Mercy did not interpose to avert or suspend their judgment, but immediately they were expelled from the divine presence. A solemn triumph in heaven followed: "A voice came out of the throne, saying, Praise our God, all ye his servants. And I heard as it were the voice of mighty thunderings, saying, Hallelujah, for the Lord God omnipotent reigneth." They are now the most eminent examples of revenging wrath. Their present misery is inuspportable, and they expect worse. When our Saviour cast some of them out of the possessed persons, they cried out, "Art thou come to torment us before the time?" "*Miserrimum est timere cum speres nihil;*" it is the height of misery to have nothing to hope, and something to fear. Their guilt is attended with despair. They are in "everlasting chains;" he that "carries the keys of hell and death" will never open their prison. If the sentence did admit a revocation after a million of years, their torment would be nothing in comparison of what it is; for the longest measure of time bears no proportion to eternity, and hope would allay the sense of the present sufferings with the prospect of future ease: but their judgment is irreversible; they are under the "blackness of darkness for ever." There is not the least glimpse of hope to allay their sorrows, no starlight to sweeten the horrors of their eternal night. They are "*servi pœnæ,*" that can never be redeemed. It were a kind of pardon to them to be capable of death; but God will never be so far reconciled, as to annihilate them. His anger shall be accomplished, and his fury rest upon them, Ezek. iii. 5. Immortality, the privilege of their nature, infinitely increases their torment; for when the understanding, by a strong and active apprehension, hath a terrible and unbounded prospect of the continuance of their sufferings, that what is intolerable must be eternal, this inexpressibly exasperates their misery: there wants a word beyond death to set it forth.

This is the condition of the sinning angels, and God might have dealt in as strict justice with rebellious man. It is true, there are many reasons may be assigned, why the wisdom of God made no provision for their recovery.

(1.) It was most decent that the first breach of the divine law should be punished, to secure obedience for the future. Prudent lawgivers are severe against the first transgressors, the leaders in disobedience. He that first presumed to break the sabbath, was by God's command put to death; and Solomon, the king of peace, punished the first attempt upon his royalty with death, though in the person of his brother.

(2.) The malignity of their sin was in the highest degree; for such was the clearness of the angelical understanding, that there was nothing of ignorance and deceit to lessen the voluntariness of their sin. It was no mistake, but malice. They fell in the light of heaven, and rendered themselves incapable of mercy: as under the law, those who sinned "with a high hand," that is, not out of ignorance or imbecility, to please their passions, but knowingly and proudly despised the command, their presumption was inexpiable; no sacrifice was appointed for it. And the gospel, though the declaration of mercy, yet excepts those who sin the great transgression against the Holy Ghost. Now of such a nature was the sin of the rebellious angels, it being a contemptuous violation of God's majesty, and therefore unpardonable. Besides, they are wholly spiritual beings, without any allay of flesh, and so fell to the utmost in evil, there being nothing to suspend the entireness of their will; whereas the human spirit is more slow by its union with the body. And that which extremely aggravates their sin is, that it was committed in the state of perfect happiness; they despised the full fruition of God. It was, therefore, congruous to the divine wisdom, that their final sentence should depend upon their first election: whereas man's rebellion, though inconceivably great, was against a lower light and less grace dispensed to him.

(3.) They sinned without a tempter, and were not in the same capacity with man to be restored by a Saviour. The devil is an original proprietor in sin, it is of his own, John viii. 44. Man was beguiled by the serpent's subtilty. As he fell by another's malice, so he is recovered by another's merit.

(4.) The angelical nature was not entirely lost. Myriads of blessed spirits still continue in the place of their innocency and glory, and for ever ascribe to the great Creator that incommunicable honour which is due to him, and perfectly do his commandments. But all mankind was lost in Adam, and no religion was left in the lower world.

Now, although in these and other respects it was most consistent with the wisdom and justice of God, to conclude them under an irrevocable doom, yet the principal cause that inclined him to save man, was mere and perfect grace. The law made no distinction, but awarded the same punishment: mercy alone made the difference; and the reason of that is in himself. Millions of them fell sacrifices to justice, and guilty man was spared. It is not for the excellency of our nature, for man in his creation was lower than the angels; nor upon the account of service, for they, having more eminent endowments of wisdom and power, might have brought greater honour to God; nor for our innocence, for though not equally, yet we had highly offended him; but it must be resolved "into that love which passeth knowledge." It was the unaccountable pleasure of God that preferred babes before the wise and prudent, and herein grace is most glorious. He in no wise took the nature of angels, though immortal spirits; he did not put forth his hand to help them, and break the force of their fall; he did nothing for their relief, they are under unallayed wrath: but he took " the seed of Abraham," and plants a new colony of those who sprung from the earth, in the heavenly country, to fill up the vacant places of those apostate spirits. This is just matter of our highest admiration, why the milder attribute is exercised towards man, and the severer on them! Why the vessels of clay are chosen, and the vessels of gold neglected! How can we reflect upon it without the warmest affections to our Redeemer? We shall never fully understand the riches of distinguishing grace, till our Saviour shall be the Judge, and receive us into the kingdom of joy and glory, and condemn them to an eternal separation from his presence.

CHAPTER IX.

THE GREATNESS OF THE DIVINE MERCY IN REDEMPTION.

THE next circumstance to be considered in the divine mercy is the degree of it; and this is described by the apostle in all the dimensions which can signify its greatness. He prays for the Ephesians, that they "may be able to comprehend with all saints, what is the breadth, and length, and depth, and height of the love of Christ which passeth knowledge," Ephes. iii. 18. No language is sufficient to express it: if our hearts were as large as the sand on the sea shore, yet they were too strait to comprehend it. But although we cannot arrive at the perfect knowledge of this excellent love, yet it is our duty to study it with the greatest application of mind; for our happiness depends upon it; and so far we may understand it, as to inflame our hearts with a superlative affection to God. And the full discovery, which here we desire and search after, in the future state shall be obtained by the presence and light of our Redeemer.

Now the greatness of the divine love in our redemption appears by reflecting on,

I. The mighty evils from which we are freed.

II. The means by which our redemption is accomplished.

III. The excellent state to which we are advanced by our Redeemer.

I. If we reflect upon the horror of our natural state, it will exceedingly heighten the mercy that delivered us. This I have in part opened before, therefore I will be the shorter in describing it. Man by his rebellion had forfeited God's favour, and the honour and happiness he enjoyed in paradise. And as there is no middle state between sovereignty and misery, he that falls from the throne stops not till he comes to the bottom; so when man fell from God and the dignity of his innocent state, he became extremely miserable. He is under the servitude of sin, the tyranny of Satan, the bondage of the law, and the empire of death.

1. Man is a captive to sin. He is fallen from the hand of his counsel, under the power of his passions. Love, hatred, ambition, envy, fear, sorrow, and all the other stinging affections (of which is true what Solinus speaks of the several kinds of serpents in Africa, " *Quantus nominum, tantus mortium numerus* ") exercise a tyranny over him. And if " no man can serve two masters," as our Saviour tells us, how wretched is the slavery of man, whose passions are so opposite, that in obeying one, he cannot escape the lash of many imperious masters! He is possessed with a legion of impure lusts. And as the demoniac in the gospel was sometimes cast into the fire and sometimes into the water; so he is hurried by the fury of contrary passions.

This servitude to sin is in all respects complete; for those who serve, are either born servants, or bought with a price, or made captives by force; and sin hath all these kinds of title to man.

He is conceived and born in sin, Psalm li. 5;—he is " sold under sin," Rom. vii. 14.—and sells himself to do evil, Isa. xxviii. 15. As that which is sold passeth into the possession of the buyer, so the sinner exchanging himself for the pleasure of sin, is under its power. Original sin took possession of our nature, and actual sin of our lives. He is the servant of corruption by yielding to it: " for of whom a man is overcome, of the same is he brought in bondage," 2 Pet. ii. 19.

The condition of the most wretched bondslave is more sweet and less servile than that of a sinner; for the severest tyranny is exercised only upon the body, the soul remains free in the midst of chains: slaves are called σώματα, bodies, Rev. xviii. 13: but the power of sin oppresses the soul, the most noble part, and defaces the bright character of the Deity that was stamped upon its visage. The worst slavery is terminated with this present life. In the grave "the prisoners rest together; they hear not the voice of the oppressor. The small and the great are there; and the servant is free from his master," Job iii. 18, 19. But there is no exemption from this servitude by death, it extends itself to eternity.

2. Man since his fall is under the tyranny of Satan, who is called "the god of this world," and is more absolute than all temporal princes, his dominion being over the will. He overcame man in paradise, and by the right of war rules over him. The soul is kept in his bondage by the subtile chains, of which the spiritual nature is capable. The understanding is captivated by ignorance and errors; the will, by inordinate and dangerous lusts; the memory, by the images of sinful pleasures, those mortal visions which enchant the soul and make it not desirous of liberty. Never did cruel pirate so incompassionately urge his slaves to ply their oars in charging or flying from an enemy, as Satan incites those who are his captives to do his will, 2 Tim. ii. 26. And can there be a more afflicting calamity, than to be a slave of one's enemy, especially if base and cruel? This is the condition of man; he is a captive to the devil, who was a liar and a murderer from the beginning. He is under the rage of that bloody tyrant, whose ambition was to render man as miserable as himself; who in triumph upbraids him for his folly, and adds derision to his cruelty.

3. Fallen man is under the curse and terror of the law; for being guilty, he is justly exposed to the punishment threatened against transgressors, without the allowance of repentance to obtain pardon. And conscience, which is the echo of the law in his bosom, repeats the dreadful sentence. This is an accuser which none can silence, a judge that none can decline: and from hence it is that men all their life are "subject to bondage,"

being obnoxious to the wrath of God, which the awakened conscience fearfully sets before them.

This complicated servitude of a sinner the scripture represents under a great variety of similitudes, that the defects of one may be supplied by another. Every sinner is a servant, John viii. 34. Now a servant by flight may recover his liberty; but the sinner is a captive in chains, 2 Tim. ii. 26. A captive may be freed by laying down a ransom; but the sinner is deeply in debt. Every debtor is not miserable by his own fault; it may be his infelicity, not his crime, that he is poor; but the sinner is guilty of the highest offences. A guilty person may enjoy his health; but the sinner is sick of a deadly disease, an incurable wound, Isa. i. 6. He that is sick and wounded may send for the physician in order to his recovery; but the sinner is in a deep sleep, 2 Tim. ii. 26. The apostle sets forth the conversion of a sinner by the word ἀνανήφειν, which signifies an awaking out of sleep, caused by the fumes of wine or strong liquor; which is an excellent resemblance of the sinner's state, wherein the spiritual senses are bound up, and the passions, as thick and malignant vapours, cloud the mind, that it cannot reflect upon his miseries. He that is asleep may awake; but the sinner is in a state of death, which implies, not only a cessation from all vital actions, but an absolute disability to perform them. The understanding is disabled for any spiritual perception, the will for any holy inclinations, the whole man is disabled for the sense of his wretched state. This is the spiritual death which justly exposes the sinner to death temporal and eternal.

4. Every man as descending from Adam, is born a sacrifice to death. His condition in this world is so wretched and unworthy the original excellency of his nature, that it deserves not the name of life. It is a continual exercise of sinful actions dishonourable to God and damning to himself; and after the succession of a few years in the defilements of sin and the accidents of this frail state, in doing and suffering evil, man comes to his fatal period, and falls into the bottomless pit, the place of pollutions and horrors, of sin and torments. It is there that the wrath of God abides on him; and "who knoweth

the power of his wrath? According to his fear, so is his wrath," Psalm xc. 12. Fear is an unbounded passion, and can extend itself to the apprehension of such torments, as no finite power can inflict: but the wrath of God exceeds the most jealous fears of the guilty conscience. It proceeds from infinite justice, and is executed by almighty power, and contains eminently all kinds of evils. A lake of burning brimstone, and whatever is most dreadful to sense, is but an imperfect allusion to represent it.

And how great is that love which pitied and rescued us from sin and hell! This saving mercy is set out for its tenderness and vehemence by the commotion of the bowels, at the sight of one in misery, Luke i. 78, especially the working of the mother, when any evil befalls her children: such an inward deep resentment of our distress was in the Father of mercies. When we were in our blood, he said unto us, Live, Ezek. xvi. 6.

And that which farther discovers the eminent degree of his love is this—he might have been unconcerned with our distress, and left us under despair of deliverance. There is a compassion which arises from self-love, when the sight of another's misery surprises us, and affects us in such a manner as to disturb our repose and embitter our joy, by considering our liableness to the same troubles; and from hence we are inclined to help them. And there is a compassion that proceeds from pure love to the miserable, when the person that expresses it, is above all the assaults of evil, and incapable of all affections that might lessen his felicity, and yet applies himself to relieve the afflicted; and such was God's towards man.

If it had been a tolerable evil under which we were fallen, the mercy that recovered us, had been less; for benefits are valued by the necessity of the receiver. But man was disinherited of paradise, an heir of hell, his misery was inconceivably great. Now the measure of God's love is proportionable to the misery from whence we are redeemed. If there had been any possible remedy for us in nature, our engagements had not been so great: but only he that created us by his power, could restore us by his love.

Briefly; it magnifies the divine compassion, that our deliverance is full and entire. It had been admirable favour to have mitigated our misery, but we have a perfect redemption, sweetened by the remembrance of those dreadful evils that oppressed us. As the three Hebrew martyrs came unhurt out of the fiery furnace; the hair of their heads was not singed, nor their coats ·changed, nor the smell of the fire passed on them, Dan. iii. 27; so the saints above have no marks of sin or misery remaining upon them, not the " least spot or wrinkle " to blast their beauty, nor the least trouble to diminish their blessedness; but forever possess the fulness of joy and glory, a pure and triumphant felicity.

II. The greatness of the divine love towards fallen man appears in the means by which our redemption is accomplished; and those are the incarnation and sufferings of the Son of God.

1. The incarnation manifests his love upon a double account—in regard of the essential condition of the nature he assumed—its servile state and meanness.

(1.) The essential condition of the human nature assumed by our Redeemer, discovers his transcendent love to us; for what proportion is there between God and man? Infinite and finite are not terms that admit comparison, as greater and less; but are distant, as all and nothing. The whole world before him is but " the drop of a bucket," that hath scarce weight to fall; and " the small dust of the balance," that is not of such moment as to turn the scales; it is " as nothing," and " counted less than nothing, and vanity," Isa. xl. 15, 17. The Deity in its own nature includes independence and sovereignty. To be a creature implies dependence and subjection. The angelical nature is infinitely inferior to the divine, and man is lower than the angels; yet " the Word was made flesh."

Add to this, he was not made as Adam in the perfection of his nature, and beginning the first step of his life in the full exercise of reason and dominion over the creatures, but he came into the world by the way of a natural birth and dependence upon a mortal creature. The eternal wisdom of the Father stooped to a state of infancy, which is most distant from that of wisdom, wherein though the life, yet the light of the reasonable soul is not visible; and the mighty God, to a condition of indigence and infirmity. The Lord of nature submitted to the laws of it. Admirable love, wherein God seemed to forget his own greatness and the meanness of the creature! This is more endeared to us by considering,

(2.) The servile state of the nature he assumed. An account of this we have in the words of the apostle, Phil. ii. 5—8; "Let this mind be in you which was also in Christ Jesus: who being in the form of God;" that is, enjoying the divine nature with all its glory, eternally and invariably; as to be in the form of a king, signifies not only to be a king, but to have all the conspicuous marks of royalty, the crown, sceptre, throne, the guards and state of a king. Thus our Saviour possessed that glory that is truly divine, before he took our nature, John xvii. 5. The angels adored him in heaven, and by him princes reigned on the earth. It is added, "he thought it not robbery to be equal with God," that is, being the essential image of the Father, he had a rightful possession of all his perfections; yet " he made himself of no reputation, and took upon him the form of a servant, and was made in the likeness of men:" this is a lower degree of condescension, than assuming the naked human nature. A servant is not simply a man, there being many men of higher quality, but a man in a low state. Now he that was in the form of God, lessened himself into the form of a servant; that is, he took the human nature without honour, attended with its infirmities; so that by the visible condition of his life, he was judged to be an ordinary person, and not that under that meanness the Lord of angels had been concealed.

This will more distinctly be understood, if we consider the lowness of his extraction, the poverty of his birth, and the tenor of his life whilst he conversed with men. What nation was more despicable in the esteem of the world than the Jews? They are called by Tacitus, '*Vilissima pars servientum.*' Yet of their stock Christ disdained not to descend. And among the Jews, none were more vilified than the Galileans; and in Galilee, Nazareth was a contemptible village; and in Nazareth, the family of Joseph was very obscure, and to him our Saviour was nearly allied. His reputed father was a carpenter, and his mother a poor virgin, that offered two pigeons for her purification. He first breathed in a stable, and was covered with poor swaddling clothes, who was Master of heaven and earth, and adorns all creatures with their glory. But love made him, who is heir of all things, renounce the privilege of his supernatural Sonship. Inconceivable condescension! Therefore an angel was despatched from heaven, who appeared with a surprising miraculous light, the visible character of his dignity, to prevent the scandal which might arise from the meanness of his condition, and to assure the shepherds that the babe which lay in the manger, was the Redeemer of the world. The course of his life was a preface and preparative for the death of the cross. He had a just right to all that glory, which a created nature personally united to the Deity could receive. An eminent instance of it there was in his transfiguration, when glory descended from heaven to encompass him. That which was so short should have been continual, but he presently returned to the lowness of his former condition. "The fulness of the Godhead dwelt in him bodily," yet in his humble state he was voluntarily deprived of those admirable effects which should proceed from that union. Strange separation between the Deity and the glory that results from it! God is light, and the Son is "the brightness of his Father's glory," yet in his pilgrimage upon the earth he was always under a cloud." Astonishing miracle, transcending all those in the compass of nature! yet the power of love effected it. He was made not only "lower than the angels," but less than all men, joining (O amazing abasement!) the majesty of God, with the meanness of a worm, Heb. ii. Psalm xxii. The "high and lofty One," whom the prophet saw "exalted on a high throne," and all the powers of heaven in a posture of reverence about him, "was despised and rejected of men;" they turned their eyes from him, not for the lustre of his countenance, but for shame, Isa. vi. liii.

If the Lord had assumed our nature in its most honourable condition, and appeared in its beauty, the condescension were infinite; for although men are distinguished among themselves by titles of honour, yet as two glow-worms that shine with an unequal brightness in the night, are equally obscured by the light of the sun; so all men, those that are advanced to the most eminent degree, as well as the most abject and wretched, are in the same distance from God: but he emptied himself of all his glory. "He grew up as a tender plant, and as a root out of a dry ground; there was no form or comeliness in him," Isa. liii. 2. From his birth to the the time of his preaching, he lived so privately, as to be known only under the quality of the carpenter's son. There was a continual repression of that inconceivable glory that was due to him the first moment of his appearing among men. In short, his despised condition was an abasement not only of his divinity, but his humanity. And how conspicuous was his love in this darkening condescension! "Ye know the grace of our Lord Jesus Christ, that though he was rich, yet for your sakes he became poor," 2 Cor. viii. 9. He did not assume that which was due to the excellency of his nature, but what was convenient for our redemption, which was to be accomplished by sufferings.

Where can be found an example of such love? Some have favourable inclinations to help the distressed, and will express so much compassion as is consistent with their state and quality; but if, in order to the relieving of the miserable, one must submit to what is shameful, who hath an affection so strong and vehement, as to purchase his brother's redemption at the loss of his own honour? Yet the Son of God descended from his throne, and put on our vile mortality; he parted with his glory, that he might be qualified to part with his life for our salvation. How doth this exalt his compassion to us!

(3.) Add further, he took our nature after it had lost its primitive innocency. The natural distance between God and the creature is infinite; the moral between God and the sinful creature, if possible, is more than infinite;

yet the mercy of our Redeemer overcame this distance. What an ecstasy of love transported the Son of God so far as to espouse our nature after it was depraved and dishonoured with sin? He was essential innocence and purity, yet he came " in the likeness of sinful flesh," which to outward view was not different from what was really sinful. He was the holy Lawgiver, yet he submitted to that law which made him appear under the character and disreputation of a sinner. He paid the bloody tribute of the children of wrath, being circumcised as guilty of Adam's sin; and he was baptized as guilty of his own.

2. The most evident and sensible proof of the greatness of God's love to mankind, is in the sufferings of our Redeemer to obtain our pardon. He is called in scripture, " a man of sorrows :" the title signifies their number and quality. His whole life was a continual passion. He suffered the contradiction of sinners, who by their malicious calumnies obscured the lustre of his miracles and most innocent actions; he endured the temptations of Satan in the desert; he was often in danger of his life. But all these were nothing in comparison of his last sufferings. It is therefore said, that at the bare apprehension of them, he " began to be sorrowful," as if he had never felt any grief till then. His former afflictions were like scattered drops of rain: but as in the deluge, all the fountains beneath, and all the windows of heaven above were opened; so in our Saviour's last sufferings, the anger of God, the cruelty of men, the fury of devils, broke out together against him. And that the degrees of his love may be measured by those of his sufferings, it will be fit to consider them with respect of his soul and his body. The gospel delivers to us the relation of both.

Upon his entrance into the garden, he complains, " My soul is exceeding sorrowful, even unto death." There were present only Peter, James, and John, his happy favourites, who assured him of their fidelity: there was no visible enemy to afflict him; yet his soul was environed with sorrows. It is easy to conceive the injuries he suffered from the rage of men, for they were terminated upon his body; but how to understand his inward sufferings, the wounds of his spirit, the cross to which his soul was nailed, is very difficult: yet these were inexpressibly greater, as the visible effects declare. The anguish of his soul so affected his body, that his "sweat was, as it were, great drops of blood," the miraculous evidence of his agony. The terror was so dreadful, that the assistance of an angel could not calm it. And if we consider the causes of his grief, the dispositions of Christ, and the design of God in afflicting him, it will further appear that no sorrow was ever like his. The causes were,

(1.) The evil of sin, which inconceivably exceeds all other; for the just measure of an evil is taken from the good to which it is opposite, and of which it deprives us. Now sin is formally opposite to the holy nature and will of God, and meritoriously deprives us of his blessed presence for ever. Therefore God being the supreme good, sin is the supreme evil. And grief being the resentment of an evil, that which is proportioned to the evil of sin must be infinite. Now, the Lord Christ alone had perfect light to discover sin in its true horror, and perfect zeal to hate it according to its nature: for who can understand the excellency of good and the malignity of evil, but the author of the one and the judge of the other? Who can fully conceive the guilt of rebellion against God, but the Son of God, who alone is able to comprehend his own majesty? On this account the grief of our Redeemer exceeded all the sorrows of repenting sinners from the beginning of the world; for our knowledge is so imperfect and our zeal so remiss, that our grief for sin is much beneath what it is worthy of; but sin was as hateful to Christ as it is in itself, and his sorrow was equal to its evil.

(2.) The death he was to suffer, attended with all the curses of the law, and the terrible marks of God's indignation. From hence it is said, "he began to be sore amazed, and to be very heavy." It is wonderful that the Son of God, who had perfect patience, and the strength of the Deity to support him, who knew that his passion would soon pass away, and that the issue would be his own glorious resurrection and the recovery of lapsed man, that he should be shaken with fear and oppressed with sorrow at the first approaches of it. How many of the martyrs have, with an undisturbed courage, embraced a more cruel death! But to them it was disarmed; whereas our Saviour encountered it with all its formidable pomp, with its darts and poison.

(3.) The wrath of God was inflamed against him; for although he was perfectly innocent, and more distant from sin than heaven is from the earth, yet by the ordination of God, and his own consent, being made our sponsor, the iniquity of us all was laid upon him. —He suffered as deeply as if he had been guilty. Vindictive justice was inexorable to his prayers and tears. Although he renewed his request with the greatest ardency; as it is said by the evangelist, that "being in an agony, he prayed more earnestly," yet God would not spare him. The Father of mercies saw his Son humbled in his presence, prostrate on the earth, yet deals with him in extreme severity. He was "stricken, smitten of God, and afflicted." And who is able to conceive the weight of God's hand, when he punishes sin according to its desert? Who can understand the degrees of those sufferings, when God exacts satisfaction from one that was obliged and able to make it? How piercing were those sorrows whereby divine justice, infinitely incensed, was to be appeased! Who knows the consequence of those words, "My God, my God, why hast thou forsaken me?" It is impossible to comprehend or represent that great and terrible mystery. But thus much we may understand, that holiness and glory being essential to the Deity, they are communicated to the reasonable nature when united to it; but with this difference, that holiness necessarily results from union with God, for sin being infinitely repugnant to his nature, makes a separation between him and the creature; but glory and joy are dispensed in a free and arbitrary manner. This dereliction of our Saviour must be understood with respect to the second, not the first communication. In the extremity of his torments, all his affections were innocent and regular, being raised to that degree only, which the vehemency of the object required.

He expressed no murmur against God, nor anger against his enemies. His faith, love, humility, and patience, were then in their exaltation. But that glorious and unspeakable joy, which in the course of his life, the Deity conveyed to him, was then withdrawn. An impetuous torrent of pure, unmixed sorrows broke into his holy soul; he felt no refreshing emanations; so that having lost the sense of present joy, there remained in his soul only the hope of future joy. And in that sad moment his mind was so intent upon his sufferings, that he seems to have been diverted from the actual consideration of the glory that attended the issue of them.

Briefly; all comforting influences were suspended, but without prejudice to the personal union, or the perfection of his grace, or the love of his Father toward him. His soul was liable to sorrows, as his body to death; for the Deity is the principle of life as well as of joy, and as the body of Christ was three days in the state of death, and the hypostatical union remained entire; so his soul was left for a time under the fearful impressions of wrath, yet was not separated from the Godhead. And although he endured whatever was necessary for the expiation of sin, yet all vicious evils, as blasphemy, hatred of God, and any other which are not inflicted by the Judge, but in strictness are accidental to the punishment, and proceed from the weakness or wickedness of the patient, he was not in the least guilty of. Besides, when his Father appeared an enemy against him, at that time he was infinitely pleased in his obedience. But with these exceptions, our blessed Lord suffered whatever was due to us.

The sorrows of his forsaken state were inexpressibly great; for according to the degree and sense we have of happiness, such in proportion is our grief for the loss of it. Now Christ had the fullest enjoyment and the highest valuation of God's favour. His enjoyment was raised above what the most glorious spirits are capable of: all his faculties were pure and vigorous, never blunted with sin, and intimately united to the Deity. How cutting then was it to his soul, to be suspended from the perfect vision of God! To be divorced, as it were, from himself, and to lose that paradise he always had within him! If all the angels of light were at once deprived of their glory, the loss were not equal to this dreadful eclipse of the Sun of Righteousness; as if all the stars were extinguished, the darkness would not be so terrible, as if the sun, the fountain of light, were put out. Whatever his sufferings were in kind, yet in degree they were answerable to the full and just desert of sin, and surpassed the power of the human or angelical nature to endure. In short, his sorrows were equalled only by that love which procured them.

And as the sufferings inflicted by the hand of God, so the evils he endured from men, declare the infiniteness of our Redeemer's love to us. For the farther discovery of it, it is necessary to reflect upon his death, which is set down by the apostle as the lowest degree of his humiliation, in which the succession of all his bodily sufferings is included, it being the complement of all. And if we consider the quality of it, the goodness of our Redeemer will be more visible in his voluntary submission to it. Two circumstances make the kind of death which is to be suffered, very terrible to us, ignominy and torment; and they eminently concur in the death of the cross.

The greatest ignominy attended it, and that in the account of God and men. As honour is "*in honorante,*" and depends upon the esteem of others, so infamy consists in the judgment of others. Now in the account of the world, every death inflicted for a crime is attended with disgrace; but that receives its degrees from the manner of it. To be executed privately is a favour, but to be made a spectacle to the multitude increases the dishonour of one that suffers. When death is speedily inflicted, the sense of shame is presently past; but to be exposed to public view for many hours, as a malefactor, whilst the beholders detest the crime and abhor the punishment, is a heavy aggravation of it. Beheading, which is suddenly despatched by a sword or military instrument, and therefore more honourable, was a privilege; but to hang on the cross was the most conspicuous mark of the public justice and displeasure; a special infamy was concomitant with it. Among the Jews, hanging on a tree was branded with the curse; therefore God commanded that the bodies of those who were hanged on a tree should be taken down in the evening, that the land might not be defiled with a curse, Deut. xxi. 23. And the judgment of other nations was answerable; for it was inflicted only on the most infamous offenders, as fugitives, slaves, thieves, and traitors; such whom the lowness of their quality or the height of their crimes rendered unworthy of any respect. Hence it is that Cicero, to aggravate the cruelty of Verres in crucifying a Roman citizen calls it " a nameless wickedness:" no eloquence could express the indignity. *" Facinus est vincire Romanum civem; scelus est verberare; prope parricidium necare, quid dicam in crucem tollere? Verbo quidem satis digno tam nefaria res appellari nullo modo potest."*

The pain of that death was extreme. The hands and feet, those parts wherein the complexion of the nerves meet and are of an exquisite sense, were nailed. Crucified persons suffered a slow death; but quick torments; they felt themselves die; therefore in pity the soldiers broke their legs to put a period to their misery. And to complete their punishment, they were judged unworthy to enjoy the privilege of the grave, to repose in the bosom of the earth our common mother, the last consolation of the dead, but were exposed as a prey to birds and beasts.

Now the Son of God endured no gentler nor nobler death than that of the cross. His pure and gracious hands, which were never stretched out but to do good, were pierced; and those feet which bore the Redeemer of the world, and for which the waters had a reverence, were nailed. His body, the precious workmanship of the Holy Ghost, the temple of the Deity, was destroyed. He that is the glory of heaven, was made the scorn of the earth: the King of kings was crucified between two thieves in Jerusalem, at their sacred feasts, in the face of the world. His naked body was exposed on the cross for three hours, covered only with a veil of darkness. This was such a stupendous submission of the Son of God, that his death astonished the universe in another manner than his birth and life, his resurrection and ascension. Universal nature relented at his last sufferings. The sun was struck with horror, and withdrew its light; it did not appear crowned with beams, when the Creator was with thorns. The earth trembled, the rocks rent; the most insensible creatures sympathized with him: and it is in this we have the most visible instance of divine love to us.

The scriptures distinctly represent the love of God in giving his Son, and the love of Christ in giving himself to die for man, and both require our deepest consideration.

The Father expressed such an excess of love, that our Saviour himself speaks of it with admiration: " God so loved the world, that he gave his only begotten Son, that whosoever believeth in him should not perish, but have everlasting life," John iii. 16. If Abraham's resolution to offer his son, was in the judgment of God a convincing evidence of his affection, Gen. xxii. 12, how much more is the actual sacrificing of Christ the strongest proof of God's love to us? for God had a higher title to Isaac than Abraham had: the Father of spirits hath a nearer claim, than the fathers of the flesh. Abraham's readiness to offer up his son was obedience to a command, not his own choice; it was rather an act of justice than love, by which he rendered to God what was his own; but God " spared not his own Son " in whom he had an eternal right; and he was not only free from obligation, but not sued to for our salvation in that wonderful way. For what human or angelical understanding could have conceived such a thought, that the Son of God should die for our redemption? The most charitable spirits in heaven had not a glimmering inclination towards this admirable way of saving us: it had been an impious blasphemy to have desired it; so that Christ is the most absolute gift of God to us. Besides, the love of Abraham is to be measured by the reasons that might excite it; for according to the amiableness of the object, so much greater is the love that gives it. Many endearing circumstances made Isaac the joy of his father: he was an only son, miraculously obtained, after many prayers and long expectation of his parents, when natural vigour was spent, and all hopes dead of having a surviving heir; he was in the spring of his youth, and the root of all the promises, that in him a progeny as numerous as the stars, and that the Messiah infinitely more worthy than all the rest, should come; yet at the best he was an imperfect, mortal creature, so that but a moderate affection was regularly due to him. Whereas our Redeemer was not a mere man or an angel, but God's only begotten Son, which title signifies his unity with him in his state and perfections; and according to the excellency of his nature, such is his Father's love to him. John represents to us that "God is love;" not charitable and loving, that is too weak an expression, but love itself. The divine nature is infinite essential love, in which other perfections are included. And he produces the strongest and most convincing testimony of it, "In this was manifested the love of God toward us, because that God sent his only begotten Son into the world, that we might live through him," 1 John iv. 9. The love of God in all temporal blessings, is but faint in comparison with the love that is expressed in our Redeemer. As much as the Creator exceeds the creature, the gift of Christ is above the gift of the whole world. "Herein is love," saith the apostle, that is, the clearest and the highest expression of it that can be, "God sent his Son to be a propitiation for our sins." The wisdom and power of God did not act to the utmost of their efficacy in the creation; he could frame a more glorious world; but the love of God in our strange salvation by Christ, cannot in a higher degree be expressed. As the apostle, to set forth how sacred and inviolable God's promise is, saith that "because he could swear by no greater, he sware by himself;" so when he would give the most excellent testimony of his favour to mankind, he gave his eternal Son, the heir of his love and blessedness. The giving of heaven itself, with all its joys and glory, is not so perfect and full a demonstration of the love of God, as the giving of his Son to die for us.

It is an endearing circumstance of this love, that it warmed the heart of God from eternity, and was never interrupted in that vast duration. Great benefits that come from a sudden flush of affection, are not so highly estimable, as when dispensed with judgment and counsel; because they do not argue in the giver such a true valuation and fixed love of the person that receives them. The spring-tide may be followed by as low an ebb; the benefactor may repent of his labours as spent in vain; but our salvation by Christ is the product of God's eternal thoughts, the fruit of love that ever remains. He was delivered " by the determinate counsel and foreknowledge of God," to suffer for us, Acts ii. 23. Before the world began, we were before the eyes, nay, in the heart of God.

And yet the continuance of this love through infinite ages past, is less than the degree of it. According to the rule of common esteem, a greater love was expressed to wretched man, than to Christ himself; for we expend things less valuable for those that are more precious; so that God in giving him to die for us, declared that our salvation was more dear to him than the life of his only Son. When no meaner ransom than the blood royal of heaven could purchase our redemption, God delighted in the expense of that sacred treasure for us; " It pleased the Lord to bruise him." Though the death of Christ absolutely considered was the highest provocation of God's displeasure and brought the greatest guilt upon the Jews, for which " wrath came upon them to the uttermost," yet in respect of the end, namely, the salvation of men, it was the most grateful offering to him, " a sacrifice of a sweet smelling savour." God repented that he made man, but never that he redeemed him.

And as the love of the Father, so the love of Christ appears in a superlative manner in dying for us. " Greater love hath no man than this, that a man lay down his life for his friends," John xv. 13. There is no kind of love that exceeds the affection which is expressed in dying for another; but there are divers degrees of it, and the highest is to die for our enemies. The apostle saith, Rom. v. 7, " Peradventure for a good man some would even dare to die:" it is possible, gratitude may prevail upon one who is under strong obligations, to die for his benefactor: or some may, from a generous principle, be willing with the loss of their lives to preserve one who is a general and public good. But this is a rare and almost incredible thing. It is recorded as a miraculous instance of the power of love, that the two Sicilian philosophers, Damon and Pythias, each had courage to die for his friend; for one of them being condemned to die by the tyrant, and desiring to give the last farewell to his family, his friend entered into prison as his surety to die for him, if he did not return at the appointed time; and he came, to the amazement of all, that expected the issue of such a hazardous caution. Yet in this example there seems to be in the second, such a confidence of the fidelity of the first, that he was assured he should not die in being a pledge for him; and in the first it was not mere friendship or sense of the obligation, but the regard of his own honour that made him rescue his friend from death. And if love were the sole motive, yet the highest expression of it was to part with a short life, which in a little time must have been resigned by the order of nature. But the love of our Saviour was so pure and great, there can be no resemblance, much less any parallel of it; for he was perfectly holy, and so the privilege of immortality was due to him; and his life was infinitely more precious than the lives of angels and men; yet he laid it down, and submitted to a cursed death, and to that which was infinitely more bitter, the wrath of God: and all this for sinful men, who were under the just and heavy displeasure of the Almighty. He loved us, and gave himself for us, Gal. ii. 20. If he had only interposed as an advocate to speak for us, or only had acted for our recovery, his love had been admirable; but he suffered for us. He is not only our Mediator, but Redeemer; not only Redeemer, but Ransom.

It was excellent goodness in David, when he saw the destruction of his people, to offer himself and family as a sacrifice to avert the wrath of God from them; but his pride was the cause of the judgment, whereas our Redeemer was perfectly innocent, 2 Sam. xxiv. 17. David interceded for his subjects, Christ for his enemies.

He received the arrows of the Almighty into his breast to shelter us. "He hath borne our griefs and carried our sorrows; he was wounded for our transgressions, he was bruised for our iniquities; the chastisement of our peace was upon him, and with his stripes we are healed," Isa. liii. 4, 5. Among the Romans the despotic power was so terrible, that if a slave had attempted upon the life of his master, all the rest had been crucified with the guilty person; but our precious master died for his slaves who had conspired against him. He shed his blood for those who spilt his.

And the readiness of our Lord to save us, though by the sharpest sufferings, magnifies his love. When the richest sacrifices under the law were insufficient to take away sin, and no lower price than the blood of God could obtain our pardon, upon his entering into the world to execute that wonderful commission which cost him his life, with what ardour of affection did he undertake it! "Lo, I come to do thy will, O God." Heb. x. 5—7. When Peter, from carnal affection, looking with a more tender eye on his master's life than our redemption, deprecated his sufferings, "Master, spare thyself;" he who was incarnate goodness, and never quenched the smoking flax, expresses the same indignation against him, "Get thee behind me, Satan," as he did formerly against the devil tempting him to worship him, Matt. xvi. 23. He esteemed him the worst adversary that would divert him from his sufferings: he longed for the baptism of his blood. And when death was in his view, with all the circumstances of terror, and the supreme Judge stood before him, ready to inflict the just punishment of sin; though the apprehension of it was so dreadful that he could scarcely live under it, yet he resolved to accomplish his work. Our salvation was amiable to him in his agony. This is specially observed by the evangelist, that Jesus having loved his own, he loved them unto the end, John xiii. 1. When the soldiers came to seize upon him, though by one word he could have commanded legions of angels for his rescue, yet he yielded up himself to their cruelty. It was not any defect of power, but the strength of his love that made him to suffer. He was willing to be crucified, that we might be glorified; our redemption was sweeter to him than death was bitter, by which it was to be obtained. It was excellently said by Pherecides, that God transformed himself into love when he made the world: but with greater reason it is said by the apostle, " God is love," when he redeemed it. It was love that by a miraculous condescension took our nature, accomplishing the desire of the mystical spouse, " Let him kiss me with the kisses of his mouth." It was love, that stooped to the form of a servant, and led a poor despised life here below. It was love that endured a death, neither easy nor honourable, but most unworthy of the glory of the divine and the innocency of the human nature. Love chose to die on the cross, that we might live in heaven, rather than to enjoy that blessedness and leave mankind in misery.

CHAPTER X.

THE GREATNESS OF THE DIVINE MERCY IN REDEMPTION.

III. The third consideration which makes the love of God so admirable to lapsed man, is, the excellency of that state to which he is advanced by the Redeemer. To be only exempted from death is a great favour. The grace of a prince is eminent in releasing a condemned person from the punishment of the law: this is sufficient for the mercy of man, but not for the love of God. He pardons and prefers the guilty: he rescues us from hell, and raises us to glory; he bestows eternity upon those who were unworthy of life.

The excellency of our condition under the gospel will be set off by comparing it with that of innocent man in paradise. It is true, he was then in a state of holiness and honour, and in perfect possession of that blessedness which was suitable to his nature; yet in many respects our last state transcends our first, and redeeming love exceeds creating.

If man had been only restored to his forfeited rights, to the enjoyment of the same happiness which was lost, his first state were most desirable; and it had been greater goodness to have preserved him innocent, than to recover him from ruin: as he that preserves his friend from falling into the hands of the enemy, by interposing between him and danger in the midst of the combat, delivers him in a more noble manner, than by paying a ransom for him after many days spent in woful captivity: and that physician is more excellent in his art, who prevents diseases, and keeps the body in health and vigour, than another that expels them by sharp remedies. But the grace of the gospel hath so much mended our condition, that if it were offered to our choice, to enjoy either the innocent state of Adam or the renewed by Christ, it were folly like that of our first parents, to prefer the former before the latter. The jubilee of the law restored to the same inheritance, but the jubilee of the gospel gives us the investiture of that which is transcendently better than what we at first possessed. Since " the day-sping from on high hath visited us " in tender mercy, we are enriched with higher prerogatives, and are under a better covenant, and entitled to a more glorious reward, than was due to man by the law of his creation.

1. The human nature is raised to a higher degree of honour, than if man had continued in his innocent state;

(1.) By its intimate union with the Son of God. He assumed it as the fit instrument of our redemption, and preferred it before the angelical, which surpassed man's in his primitive state. The fullness of the Godhead dwells in our Redeemer bodily, Col. ii. 9. From hence it is, that the angels descended to pay him homage at his birth, and attended his majesty in his disguise. The Son of man hath those titles which are above the dignity of any mere creature; he is King of the church, and Judge of the world; he exercises divine power, and receives divine praise. Briefly; the human nature in our Redeemer is an associate with the divine; and being made a little lower than the angels for a time, is now "advanced far above all principality and power," Eph. i. 21.

(2.) In all those who are partakers of grace and glory by the Lord Jesus. Adam was the Son of God by creation, but to be joined to Christ as our head by a union so intimate, that he lives in us and counts himself incomplete without us, and by that union to be adopted into the line of heaven, and thereby to have an interest in the "exceeding great and precious promises" of the gospel; to be "constituted heirs of God, and co-heirs with Christ," are such discoveries of the dignity of our supernatural state, that the lowest believer is advanced above Adam in all his honour. Nay, the angels, though superior to man in the excellency of their nature, yet are accidentally lower by the honour of our alliance: their King is our brother. And this relative dignity, which seems to eclipse their glory, might excite their envy; but such an ingenuous goodness dwells in those pure and blessed spirits, that they rejoice in our restoration and advancement.

To this I shall add, that as the Son of God hath a special relation to man, so the most tender affections for him. To illustrate this by a sensible instance: angels and men are as two different nations in language and customs, but under the same empire; and if a prince that commands two nations should employ one for the safety and prosperity of the other, it were an argument of special favour. Now the angels are "sent forth to minister for them who shall be heirs of salvation," Heb. i. 14. Besides, in two other things the peculiar affection of the prince would be most evident to that nation—if he put on their habit, and attire himself according to their fashion—if he fixed his residence among them. Now, the Son of God was clothed with our flesh, and "found in fashion as a man," and for ever appears in it in heaven; and will at the last day invest our bodies with glory like to his own. He now dwells in us by his Spirit, and when our warfare is accomplished, he shall in a special manner be present with us in the eternal mansions. As God incarnate, he conversed with men on earth, and as such he will converse with them in heaven. There he reigns as the first-born in the midst of many brethren.

Now all these prerogatives are the fruits of our redemption. And how great is that mercy which hath raised mankind more glorious out of its ruins! The apostle breaks out with a heavenly astonishment, "Behold, what manner of love the Father hath bestowed upon us, that we should be called the sons of God!" that we who are strangers and enemies, children of wrath by nature, should be dignified with the honourable and amiable title of his sons! 1 John iii. 1. It was a rare and most merciful condescension in Pharaoh's daughter, to rescue an innocent and forsaken infant from perishing by the waters, and adopt him to be her son; but how much greater kindness was it for God to save guilty and wretched man from eternal flames, and to take him into his family! The ambition of the prodigal rose no higher than to be a servant; what an inestimable favour is it to make us children! When God would express the most dear and peculiar affection to Solomon, he saith, "I will be his Father, and he shall be my son," 2 Sam. vii. 14; this was the highest honour he could promise; and all believers are dignified with it. It is the same relation that Christ hath. When he was going to heaven, he comforted his disciples with these words, "I ascend to my Father and your Father, to my God and your God." There is indeed a diversity in the foundation of it. Christ is a Son by nature, we are by mere favour; he is by generation, we are by adoption. Briefly; Jesus Christ hath made us "kings and priests unto God and his Father:" these are the highest offices upon earth, and were attended with the most conspicuous honour; and the Holy Spirit chose those bright images, to convey a clearer notice of the glory to which our Redeemer hath raised us. Not only all the crowns and sceptres in the perishing world are infinitely beneath this dignity, but the honour of our innocent state was not equal to it.

2. The gospel is a better covenant than that which was established with man in his creation; and the excellency of it will appear, by considering,

(1.) It is more beneficial, in that it admits repentance and reconciliation after sin, and accepts of sincerity instead of perfection. The apostle magnifies the office of Christ; " By how much he is the Mediator of a better covenant, which was established upon better promises," Heb. viii. 6. The comparison here is between the ministry of the gospel, and the Mosaical economy ; and the excellency of the gospel is specified, in respect of those infinitely better promises that are in it. The ceremonial law appointed sacrifices for sins of ignorance and error, and to obtain only legal impunity ; but the gospel upon the account of Christ's all-sufficient sacrifice, offers full pardon for all sins that are repented of and forsaken. Now with greater reason the covenant of grace is to be preferred before the covenant of works ; for the law considered man as holy, and endued with perfection of grace equal to whatsoever was commanded; it was the measure of his ability as well as duty, and required exact obedience, or threatened extreme misery. The least breach of it is fatal : a single offence as certainly exposes to the curse, as if the whole were violated : and in our lapsed state we are utterly disabled to comply with its purity and perfection. But the gospel contains the promises of mercy, and is in the " hands of a Mediator." The tenor of it is, that repentance and remission of sins be preached in the name of Christ, Acts ii. 38. And " if we would judge ourselves, we should not be judged," 1 Cor. xi. 31. It is not, if we are innocent, for then none could be exempt from condemnation ; but if the convinced sinner erect a tribunal in conscience, and strip sin of its disguise, to view its native deformity ; if he pronounce the sentence of the law against himself, and glorify the justice of God which he cannot satisfy, and forsake the sins which are the causes of his sorrow, he is qualified for pardoning mercy.

Besides, the gospel doth not only apply pardon to us for all forsaken sins, but provides a remedy for those infirmities to which the best are incident. Whilst we are in this mortal state, we are exposed to temptations from without, and have corruptions within that often betray us : now to support our drooping spirits, our Redeemer sits in heaven to plead for us, and perpetually renews the pardon that was once purchased, to every contrite spirit, for those unavoidable frailties which cleave to us here. The promise of grace is not made void by the sudden surprises of passions. "If any man sin, we have an advocate with the Father, Jesus Christ the righteous," 1 John ii. 1. The rigour of the law is mollified by his mediation with "the Father"—a title of love and tenderness. God deals not with the severity of a judge, but he spareth us "as a man spareth his own son that serveth him," Mal. iii. 17.

And as he pardons us upon our repentance, so he accepts our hearty, though mean services. Now the legal, that is, unsinning and complete obedience cannot be performed; the evangelical, that is, the sincere, though imperfect, is graciously received. God doth not require the duties of a man by the measures of an angel. Unfeigned endeavours to please him, unreserved respect to all his commands, single and holy aims at his glory, are rewarded. Briefly, although the law is continued as a rule of living, yet not as the covenant of life. And what an admirable exaltation of mercy is there in this new treaty of God with sinners! It is true, the first covenant was "holy, just, and good," but it made no abatements of favour, and it is now "weak through the flesh;" that is, the carnal corrupt nature is so strong and impetuous, that the restraints of the law are ineffectual to stop its desires, and therefore cannot bring man to that life that is promised, by the performance of the condition required. But the gospel provides an indulgence for relenting and returning sinners. This is the language of God in that covenant, "I will be merciful to their unrighteousness, and their sins and their iniquities will I remember no more," Heb. viii. 12.

(2.) The excellency of the evangelical covenant above the legal, is, in that supernatural assistance which is conveyed by it to believers, whereby they shall certainly be victorious over all opposition in their way to heaven. It is true Adam was endued with perfect holiness and freedom, but he might entagle himself in the snares of sin and death. The grace of the Creator given to him was always present, but it depended on the natural use of his faculties, without the interposing of any extraordinary operation of God's Spirit. The principle of holiness was in himself, and it was subjected to his will: he had a power to obey if he would, but not a power that actually determined his will, for then he had persevered. But the grace of the Redeemer that flows from Christ as our quickening head, and is conveyed to all his members, inclines the will so powerfully that it is made subject to it. "God worketh in you both to will and to do of his good pleasure," Phil. ii. 13. The use of our faculties and the exercise of grace depend on the good pleasure of God who is unchangeable, and the operations of the Spirit, which are prevailing and effectual. And upon these two, the stability of the new covenant is founded.

First, It is founded on the love of God, who is as unchangeable in his will, as in his nature. This love is the cause of election, from whence there can be no separation. This gives Christ to believers, and believers to him. "Thine they were," saith our Saviour, "and thou gavest them me," John xvii. 6; which words signify, not the common title God hath to all by creation, for men thus universally considered compose the world, and our Saviour distinguishes those that are given him from the world, John xvii. 9; but that special right God hath in them by election. And all these are given by the Father to Christ in their effectual calling, which is expressed by his drawing them to the Son, and are committed to his care, to lead them through a course of obedience to glory. For them Christ prays absolutely as Mediator, "Father, I will that those also whom thou hast given me, be with me where I am, that they may behold my glory," John xvii. 24. And he is always heard in his requests.

It is from hence that the apostle challenges all creatures in heaven and earth, with that full and strong persuasion, that nothing could separate between believers and their happiness; "For I am persuaded, that neither death nor life, nor angels, nor principalities, nor powers, nor things present, nor things to come, nor height, nor depth, nor any other creature shall be able to separate us from the love of God which is in Christ Jesus our Lord,"

Rom. viii. 38. His assurance is not built on the special prerogatives he had as an apostle, not on his rapture to paradise, nor revelations, nor the apparition of angels, for of these he makes no mention; but on that which is common to all believers, the love of God declared in the word, and " shed abroad in their hearts." And it is observable that the apostle having spoken in his own person, changes the number, " I am persuaded that nothing shall separate us," to associate with himself in the partaking of that blessed privilege, all true believers who have an interest in the same love of God, the same promises of salvation, and had felt the sanctifying work of the Spirit, the certain proof of their election. For how is it possible that God should retract his merciful purpose to save his people ? He that chose them from eternity before they could know him, and from pure love (there being nothing in the creature to induce him) gave his Son to suffer death for them, will he stop there, without bestowing that grace which may render it effectual? What can change his affection ? He that prevented them in his mercy, when they were in their pollutions, will he leave them after his image is engraven upon them ? He that loved them so as to unite them to Christ when they were strangers, will he hate them when they are his members ? No; his loving-kindness is everlasting, and the covenant that is built on it, is more firm than the pillars of heaven and the foundations of the earth. This supported David in his dying hours, that " God had made with him an everlasting covenant, ordered in all things, and sure, for that was all his salvation," 2 Sam. xxiii. 5.

Secondly, The new covenant is secured by the efficacy of divine and supernatural grace. " This is the covenant that I will make with the house of Israel, saith the Lord ; I will put my laws into their minds, and write them in their hearts, and I will be to them a God, and they shall be to me a people," Heb. viii. 10. The elect are enabled to perform the conditions of the gospel, to which eternal life is promised. Our Redeemer blesses us in turning us from our iniquities, Acts iii. 26. And although the instability of the human spirit, by reason of remaining corruptions and those various temptations to which we are liable, may excite our fear lest we should fall short of the high prize of our calling, yet the grace of the gospel secures true believers against both.

Whilst we are in the present state, our corruptions are not perfectly healed, but there are some remains, which, like a gangrene, threaten to seize on the vital parts, wherein the spiritual life is seated. But the divine nature which is conveyed to all that are spiritually descended from Christ, is active and powerful to resist all carnal desires, and will prevail in the end; for if sin in its full vigour could not control the efficacy of converting grace, how can the relics of it, after grace hath taken possession, be strong enough to spoil it of its conquest? There is a greater distance from death to life, than from life to action. That omnipotent grace that visited us in the grave and restored life to the dead, can much more perpetuate it in the living. That which was so powerful as to pluck the heart of stone out of the breast, can preserve the heart of flesh. It is true, the grace that is given to believers, in its own nature is a perishing quality, as that which was bestowed on Adam. Not only the slight superficial tincture in hypocrites will wear off, but that deep impression of sanctifying grace in true believers, if it be not renewed, would soon be defaced. But God hath promised to put his Spirit into their hearts, and to cause them to walk in his statutes, and they shall keep his commandments, Ezek. xxxvi. 27. He is a living, reigning principle in them, to which all their faculties are subordinate. The Spirit infused grace at first, and enlivens it daily: he confirms their faith, inflames their love, encourages their obedience, and refreshes in their minds the ideas of that glory which is invisible and future. In short his influence cherishes the blessed beginnings of the spiritual life; so that sincere grace, though weak in its degree, yet is in a state of progress till it come to perfection. The waters of the Spirit have a cleansing virtue upon believers, till every spot be taken away, and their purified souls ascend to heaven.

The grace of the Spirit shall make true Christians finally victorious over temptations to which they may be exposed. And these are various. Some are pleasant and insinuating, others are sharp and furious, and are managed by the devil, our subtle and industrious enemy, to undermine, or by open battery, to overthrow us. And how difficult is it for the soul, whilst united to flesh, to resist the charms of what is amiable, or to endure the assaults of what is terrible to sense! But the renewed Christian hath no reason to be affrighted with disquieting fears that any sinful temptation may come, which, notwithstanding his watchfulness, may overcome him irrecoverably; for—temptations are external, and have no power over our spirits but what we give them. A voluntary resistance secures the victory to us. And the apostle tells us, " greater is he that is " in believers, "than he that is in the world," 1 John iv. 4. God is stronger, not only in himself, but as working in us, by the vigorous assistance of his grace to confirm us, than the devil, assisted with all the delights and terrors of the world, and taking advantage of that remaining concupiscence which if not entirely extinguished, is to corrupt and destroy us. All temptations, in their degrees and continuance, are ordered by God's providence. He is the president of the combat: none enter into the lists but by his call. In all ages the promise shall be verified, " God will not suffer " his people " to be tempted above that they are able," 1 Cor. x. 13. They shall come off " more than conquerors," through Christ that loved them, Rom. viii. 37. And as St. Austin observes, " More powerful grace is necessary to fortify Christians in the midst of all opposition, than Adam at first received." This is visible in the glorious issue of the marytrs, " who loved not their lives unto the death;" for Adam, when no person threatened him, nay, against the prohibition of God, abusing his liberty, did not abide in his happiness, when it was most easy for him to avoid sin; but the martyrs remained firm in the faith, not only under terrors, but torments. And which is more admirable, in that Adam saw the happiness present, which he should forfeit by his disobedience, and the martyrs believed only the future glory they were to receive. This proceeded only from God who was so merciful, as to make them faithful. Briefly, unless there is a power above the divine, the elect are secured from final apostasy. Our Saviour tells us, that his Father " is greater than all, and none is able to pluck them out of his hand." His invariable will and almighty power prevent their perishing. Indeed, if it were only by the strength of natural reason or courage, that we are to overcome temptations, some might be so violent as to make the strongest to faint and fall away: but if the divine power be the principle that supports us, it will make the weakest victorious; for the grace of God makes us strong, and is not made weak by us.

From hence we may fully discover the advantage we have by the gospel, above the terms of the natural covenant. Restoring mercy hath bettered our condition: we have lost the integrity of the first, and got the perfection of the second Adam: our salvation is put into a stronger and safer hand. "I give," saith our Redeemer, " unto my sheep eternal life, and they shall never perish, neither shall any pluck them out of my hand." John x. 28. That is an inviolable sanctuary, from whence no believer can be taken. Christ is our friend, not only to the altar, but now in the throne. Our reconciliation is ascribed to his death; our conservation to his life, Rom. v. 10. He that was created in a state of nature could sin and die; but he that is born of God cannot sin unto death, 1 John iii. 9. The new birth is unto eternal life. In short; as the mercy of God is glorified in the whole work of our salvation, so especially in the first and last grace it confers upon us, in vocation that prevents us, and perseverance that crowns us; according to the double change made in our state, translating us from darkness to light, and from the imperfect light of grace, to the full light of glory.

I have more particularly discoursed of this advantage by the new covenant, in regard that the glory of God and the comfort of true Christians are so much concerned in it; for if grace and free will are put in joint commission, so that the efficacy of it depends on the mutability of the will, which may receive or reject it, the consequence is visible, that (which is impious to suppose) the Son of God might have died in vain; for that which is not effectual without a contingent condition, must needs be as uncertain as the condition on which it depends; so that although the wisdom of God so admirably formed the design of our salvation, and there is such a connection in his counsels, yet all may be defeated by the mutability of man's desires. And the most sincere Christians would be always terrified with perplexing jealousies, that notwithstanding their most serious resolutions to continue in their duty, yet one day they may perish by their apostasy. But the gospel assures us, that God will not reverse his own eternal decrees; and that the Redeemer "shall see of the travail of his soul, and be satisfied;" and that believers are "kept by the power of God through faith unto salvation."

3. There is an excellent manifestation of divine love in the glorious reward that is promised to believers, which far exceeds the primitive felicity of man.

Adam was under the covenant of nature, that promised a reward suitable to his obedience and state. The manner of declaring that covenant was natural—external, by the discovery of God's attributes in his works, from which it was easy for man to collect his duty and his reward—internal, by his natural faculties. By the light of reason he understood that so long as he continued in his original innocence, the Creator, who from pure goodness gave him his being and all the happiness which was concomitant with it, would certainly preserve him in the perpetual enjoyment of it. But there was no promise of heaven annexed to that covenant, without which Adam could attain no knowledge, nor conceive any hopes of it. If there had been a necessary connection between his perfect obedience and the life of glory, it would have been revealed to him, to allure his will; for there can be no desire of an unknown good. And whereas, in the covenant, God principally and primarily regards the promise, and but secondarily the threatening, (the exercise of goodness being more pleasing to him than of avenging justice) it is said, that God expressly threatened death, but he made no promise of heaven: by which it is evident it did not belong to that covenant: for it was easier for man to understand the quality of the punishment that attended sin, than to conceive of celestial happiness of which he was incapable in his animal state. It is true, God might have bestowed heaven as an absolute gift upon man, after a course of obedience; but it was not due by the condition of the first covenant. A natural work can give no title to a supernatural reward. Man's perseverance in his duty, according to the original treaty, had been attended with immortal happiness upon the earth; but the "blessed hope," is promised in the gospel only, and unspeakably transcends the felicity of nature in its consummate state.

This reward is answerable to the invaluable treasure which was laid down for it. The blood of the Son of God, as it is a ransom to redeem us from misery, so it is a price to purchase glory for believers. It is called the "blood of the new testament," Matt. xxvi. 28, because it conveys a title to the heavenly inheritance. Our impunity is the effect of his satisfaction; our positive happiness, of his redundant merit. God was so well pleased with his perfect obedience, which infinitely surpasses that of any mere creature, that he promised to confer upon those who believe in him, all the glorious qualities becoming the sons of God, and to make them associates with him in his eternal kingdom. The complete happiness of the redeemed is the Redeemer's recompense, in which he is fully satisfied for all his sufferings.

Now the transcendent excellency of this above the first state of man, will more distinctly appear by considering,

(1.) The place where it is enjoyed; and that is the heaven of heavens. Adam was put into the terrestrial paradise, a place suitable to his natural being, and abounding with all pleasing objects; but they were such as creatures of a lower kind enjoyed with him. But heaven is the element of angels, their native seat, who are the most noble part of the creation. It is the true palace of God, entirely separated from the impurities and imperfections, the alterations and changes, of the lower world; where he reigns in eternal peace. It is the temple of the divine majesty, where his excellent glory is revealed in the most conspicuous manner. It is "the habitation of his holiness, the place where his honour dwelleth." It is the sacred mansion of light, and joy, and glory. Paradise with all its pleasures was but a shadow of it.

(2.) The life of Adam was attended with innocent infirmities; for the body being composed of the same principles, with other sensitive creatures, was in a perpetual flux, and liable to hunger, and thirst, and weariness, and was to be repaired by food and sleep. Adam was made a "living soul;" therefore subject to those inclinations and necessities which are purely animal. And though, whilst innocent, no disease could seize on him, yet he was capable of hurtful impressions. Immortality was not the essential property of man as compounded of soul and body, but conditional upon his obedience, and consequent to his eating the fruit of the tree of life, Gen. iii. 22; therefore man, after his sin, was expelled from paradise, that he might not eat of it and live for ever. By which it appears that eternal life in that happy state was not from the temperament of the body, but to be preserved by the divine power in the use of means. From hence it follows that Adam in his natural state was not capable of the vision of God. Heaven is too pure an air for him to have lived in. The glory of it is inconsistent with such a tempered body: "Flesh and blood cannot inherit the kingdom of God," 1 Cor. xv. 50; the faculties would be confounded with its overcoming brightness. Till the sensitive powers are refined and exalted to that degree that they become spiritual, they cannot converse with glorified objects. Now the bodies of the saints shall be invested with celestial qualities. The natural shall be changed into a spiritual body, and be preserved, as the angels, by the sole virtue of the quickening Spirit. The life above shall flourish in its full vigour, without any other support than the divine power that first created it. As the body shall be spiritual, so truly immortal, and free from all corruptive change; as the sun, which for so many ages hath shined with an equal brightness to the world, and hath a durable fullness of light in it. In this respect, the "children of the resurrection, are equal to the angels," who being pure spirits, do not marry to perpetuate their kind, for they never die, Luke xx. 36. And the glorified body shall be clothed with a more divine beauty in the resurrection, than Adam had in the creation. The glory of the second temple shall excel that of the first. In short; the first "man was of the earth, earthy," and could derive but an earthly condition to his descendants; but the Lord Christ is from heaven, and is the principle of a heavenly and glorious life to all that are united to him.

(3.) The felicity of heaven exceeds the first, in the manner and degrees of the fruition, and the continuance of it.

The vision of God in heaven is immediate. Adam was a spectator of God's works, and his understanding being full of light, he clearly discovered the divine attributes in their effects. The strokes of the Creator's hand are engraven in all the parts of the universe. The heavens and earth, and all things in them, are evident testimonies of the excellency of their Author. The "invisible things of God, from the creation of the world, are clearly seen," Rom. i. 20. And the knowledge that shined in his soul, produced a transcendent esteem of the Deity, in whom wisdom and power are united in their supreme degree, and a superlative love and delight in him for his goodness. Yet his sight of God was but "through a glass," an eclipsing medium; for inferior beings are so imperfect, that they can give but a weak resemblance of his infinite perfections. But the sight of God in heaven, is called the " seeing of him as he is," and signifies the most clear and complete knowledge which the rational soul, when purified and raised to its most perfect state, can receive, and outshines all the discoveries of God in the lower world. Adam had a visible copy of his invisible beauty, but the saints in heaven see the glorious original. He saw God in the reflection of the creature, but the saints are under the direct beams of glory, and " see him face to face." All the attributes appear in their full and brightest lustre to them: wisdom, love, holiness, power, are manifested in their exaltation. And the glorified soul, to qualify it for converse with God in this intimate manner, hath a more excellent constitution than was given to it in the creation. A new edge is put upon the faculties, whereby they are fitted for those objects which are peculiar to heaven. The intellectual eye is fortified for the immediate intuition of God. Adam in paradise was absent from the Lord, in comparison of the saints who encompass his throne, and are in the presence of his glory.

Besides, it is the peculiar excellency of the heavenly life, that the saints every moment enjoy it without any allay, in the highest degree of its perfection. The life of Adam was always in a circle of low and mean functions of the animal nature, which being common to him and beasts, the acts of it are not strictly human: but the spiritual life in heaven is entirely freed from those servile necessities, and is spent in the eternal performance of the most noble actions of which the intelligent nature is capable. The saints do always contemplate, admire, love, enjoy, and praise their everlasting Benefactor. God is to them "all in all."

In short; that which prefers the glory of heaven infinitely before the first state of man, is the continuance of it for ever; it is an unwithering and never-fading glory. Adam was liable to temptations and capable of change; he fell in the garden of Eden, and was sentenced to die.

But heaven is the sanctuary of life and immortality; it is inaccessible to any evil. The serpent that corrupted paradise with its poison, cannot enter there. As there is no seed of corruption within, so no cause of it without. Our Redeemer offered himself by the eternal Spirit, and purchased an eternal inheritance for his people. Their felicity is full and perpetual, without increase, for in the first moment it is perfect, and shall continue without declination. The day of judgment is called the "last day;" for days, and weeks, and months, and years, the revolutions which now measure time, shall then be swallowed up in an unchangeable eternity. The saints shall be for ever with the Lord, 1 Thess. iv. 17. And in all these respects, the glory of the redeemed as far exceeds the felicity of man in the creation, as heaven, the bright seat of it, is above the fading beauty of the terrestrial paradise.

CHAPTER XI.

PRACTICAL INFERENCES.

1. This redeeming love deserves our highest admiration and most humble acknowledgments.

If we consider God aright, it may raise our wonder, that he is pleased to bestow kindness upon any created being; for in him is all that is excellent and amiable; and it is essential to the Deity to have perfect knowledge of himself, and perfect love to himself. His love being proportioned to his excellencies, the act is infinite, as the object: and the perfections of the divine nature being equal to his love, it is a just cause of admiration that it is not confined to himself, but is transient, and goes forth to the creature. When David looked up to the heavens, and saw the majesty of God written in characters of light, he admires that love which first "made man a little lower than the angels, and crowned him with glory and honour," and that providential care which is mindful of him, and visits him every moment, Psalm viii. Such an inconceivable distance there is between God and man, that it is wonderful God will spend a thought upon us. "Lord, what is man, that thou takest knowledge of him? or the son of man, that thou makest account of him? Man is like to vanity; his days are as a shadow that passeth away," Psalm cxliv. 3, 4. His being in this world hath nothing firm or solid; it is like a shadow that depends upon a cause that is in perpetual motion, the light of the sun, and is always changing, till it vanishes in the darkness of the night. But if we consider man in the quality of a sinner, and what God hath wrought for his recovery, we are overcome with amazement. All temporal favours are but foils to this miraculous mercy, and unspeakably below the least instance of it. Without it, all the privileges we enjoy above inferior creatures in this life, will prove aggravations of our future misery. God saw us in our degenerate state, destroyed by ourselves; and yet (O goodness truly divine!) he loved us so far, as to make the way for our recovery. High mountains were to be leveled, and great depths to be filled up, before we could arrive at blessedness: all this hath been done by mighty love. God laid the curse of the guilty upon the innocent, and exposed his beloved Son to the sword of his justice, to turn the blow from us. What astonishing goodness is it, that God, who is the author and end of all things, should become the means of our salvation, and by the lowest abasement? What is so worthy of admiration, as that the Eternal should become mortal? that being in the form of God, he should take on him the form of a servant? that the Judge of the world should be condemned by the guilty? that he should leave his throne in heaven, to be nailed to the cross? that the Prince of life should taste of death? These are the great wonders which the Lord of love hath performed, and all for sinful, miserable, and unworthy man, who deserved not the least drop of that sweat and blood he spent for him; and without any advantage to himself, for what content can be added to his felicity by a cursed creature? Infinite love, that is as admirable as saving! "Love that passeth knowledge," and is as much above our comprehension as desert! In natural things, admiration is the effect of ignorance, but here it is increased by knowledge: for the more we understand the excellent greatness of God, and the vileness of man, the more we shall be instructed to admire the glorious wonder of saving mercy. A deliberate admiration springing from our most deep thoughts, is part of the tribute and adoration we owe to God, who so strangely saved us "from the wrath to come."

And the most humble acknowledgments are due for it. When David told Mephibosheth, that he should "eat bread with him at his table continually;" he bowed himself, and said, "What is thy servant, that thou shouldst look upon such a dead dog as I am?" 2 Sam. ix. 8; a speech full of gratitude and humility; yet he was of a royal extraction, though at that time in a low condition. With a far greater sense of our unworthiness, we should reflect upon that condescending love that provides the "bread of God" for the food of our souls, without which we had perished for want. David in that divine thanksgiving recorded in the scripture, reflects upon his own meanness, and from that magnifies the favour of God towards him. "Who am I, O Lord God? and what is my house, that thou hast brought me hitherto? And this was yet a small thing in thy sight, O Lord God, but thou hast spoken also of thy servant's house for a great while to come: and is this the manner of man, O Lord God?" 2 Sam. vii. 18. If such humble and thankful acknowledgments were due for the sceptre of Israel, what is for the crown of heaven; and that procured for us by the sufferings of the Son of God? Briefly; goodness is the foundation of glory, therefore the most solemn and affectionate praise is to be rendered for transcendent goodness. The consent of heaven and earth, is, in ascribing "blessing, and honour, and glory, and power, unto him that sitteth on the throne, and to the Lamb for ever." Rev. v. 13.

II. The love of God discovered in our redemption is the most powerful persuasive to repentance.

For the discovery of this we must consider, that real repentance is the consequent of faith, and always in proportion to it; therefore the law, which represents to us the divine purity and justice without any allay of mercy, can never work true repentance in a sinner. When conscience is under the strong conviction of guilt and of God's justice as implacable, it causes a dreadful flight from him, and a wretched neglect of means. Despair hardens. The brightest discoveries of God in nature are not warm enough to melt the frozen heart into the current of repentance. It is true, the visible frame of the world, and the continual benefits of providence, instruct men in those prime truths, the being and bounty of God to those that serve him; and invite them to their duty. "God never left himself without a witness" in any age: his goodness is designed "to lead men to repentance." And the apostle aggravates the obstinacy

of men, that rendered that method entirely fruitless
But the declaration of God's goodness in the gospel is
infinitely more clear and powerful, than the silent revelation by the works of creation and providence; for
although the patience and general goodness of God
offered some intimations that he is placable, yet not a
sufficient support for a guilty and jealous creature to rely
on. The natural notion of God's justice is so deeply
rooted in the human soul, that till he is pleased to proclaim an act of grace and pardon, on the conditions of
faith and repentance, it is hardly possible that convinced
sinners should apprehend him otherwise than an enemy;
and that all the common benefits they enjoy, are but
provisions allowed in the interval between the sentence
pronounced by the law, and the execution of it at death.
Therefore, God, to overcome our fears and to melt us
into a compliance, hath given in the scripture the highest
assurance of his willingness to receive all relenting and
returning sinners. He interposes the most solemn oath
to remove our suspicions. "As I live, saith the Lord
God, I have no pleasure in the death of the wicked, but
that the wicked turn from his way and live," Ezek.
xxxiii. 11. And, "Have I any pleasure at all that the
wicked should die? saith the Lord God: and not that
he should return from his ways, and live," Ezek. xviii.
23. The majesty and ardency of the expressions testify
the truth and vehemency of his desire, so far as the excellency of his nature is capable, to move our affections.
And the reason of it is clear; for the conversion of a
sinner implies a thorough change in the will and affections from sin to grace, and that is infinitely pleasing to
God's holiness; and the giving of life to the converted
is most suitable to his mercy. The angels, who are infinitely inferior to him in goodness, rejoice in the repentance and salvation of men: much more doth God.
There is an eminent difference between his inclinations to
exercise mercy and justice. He uses expressions of
regret when he is constrained to punish, "O that my
people had hearkened unto me, and Israel had walked
in my ways!" Psalm lxxxi. 13. And "How shall I
give thee up, Ephraim? How shall I deliver thee,

Israel? Mine heart is turned within me," Hos. xi. 8; as a merciful judge, that pities the man, when he condemns the malefactor. But he dispenses acts of grace with pleasure. He pardons iniquity and passes by transgressions, " because he delighteth in mercy," Mic. vii. 18. It is true, when sinners are finally obdurate, God is pleased in their ruin, for the honour of his justice, yet it is not in such manner as in their conversion and life; he doth not invite sinners to transgress, that he may condemn them; he is not pleased when they give occasion for the exercise of his anger. And, above all, we have the clearest and surest discovery of pardoning mercy in the death of Christ; for what stronger evidence can there be of God's readiness to pardon, than sending his Son into the world to be a sacrifice for sin, that mercy, without prejudice to his other perfections, might, upon our repentance, forgive us? And what more rational argument is there, and more congruous to the breast of a man, to work in him a serious grief and hearty detestation of sin, not only as a cursed thing, but as it is contrary to the divine will, than the belief that God, in whose power alone it is to pardon sinners, is most desirous to pardon them, if they will return to obedience? The prodigal, in his extreme distress, resolved to go to his father with penitential acknowledgments and submission: and, to use the words of a devout writer, his guilty conscience as desperate, asked him, " *Qua spe!*" " With what hope?" He replied to himself, " *Illa qua pater est. Ego perdidi quod erat filii; ille quod patris est non amisit.*" " Though I have neglected the duty and lost the confidence of a Son, he hath not lost the compassion of a Father." That parable represents man in his degenerate, forlorn state, and that the divine goodness is the motive that prevails upon him to return to his duty.

III. The transcendent love that God hath expressed in our redemption by Christ, should kindle in us a reciprocal affection to him; for what is more natural than that one flame should produce another? " We love him, because he first loved us," 1 John iv. 19. The original of our love to God is from the evidence of his to us; this alone can strongly and sweetly draw the heart to him. It is true, the divine excellencies, as they deserve a superlative esteem, so the highest affection; but the bare contemplation of them is ineffectual to fire the heart with a zealous love to God; for man hath a diabolical seed in his corrupt nature; he is inclined not only to sensuality, which is an implicit hatred of God, (for an eager appetite to those things which God forbids, and a fixed aversion to what he commands, are the natural effects of hatred;) but to malignity and direct hatred against God. He is an enemy in his mind through wicked works, Col. i. 21; and this enmity ariseth from the consideration of God's justice and the effects of it. Man cannot sin and be happy; therefore he wishes there were no God to whom he must be accountable. He is no more wrought on by the divine perfections and beauties to love the Deity, than a guilty person who resolvedly goes on to break the laws, can be persuaded to love the judge, for his excellent knowledge and his inflexible integrity, who will certainly condemn him.

Besides, the great and abundant blessings, which God as Creator and Preserver, bestows upon all, cannot prevail upon guilty creatures to love him. Indeed the goodness that raised us from a state of nothing, is unspeakably great, and lays an eternal obligation upon us. The whole stock of our affections is due to him for conferring upon us the human nature, that is common to kings and the meanest beggar. All the riches and dignity of the greatest prince, whereby he exceeds the poorest wretch, compared to this benefit which they both share in, have no more proportion than a farthing to an immense treasure. The innumerable expressions of God's love to us every day should infinitely endear him to us; for who is so inhuman as not to love his parents, or his friend who defended him from his deadly enemies, or relieved him in his poverty, especially if the vein of his bounty is not dried up, but always diffuses itself in new favours? If we love the memory of that emperor, who, reflecting upon one day that passed without his bestowing some benefit, with grief said, "*Diem perdidi*," "I have lost a day;" how much more should we love God, who every moment bestows innumerable blessings upon his creatures! But sinful man hath contracted such an unnatural hardness, that he receives no impressions from the renewed mercies of God. He violates the principles of nature, and reason; for how unnatural is it not to love our benefactor, when the dull ox and the stupid ass serve those that feed them! and how unreasonable when the publicans return love for love!

Now there is nothing that can perfectly overcome our hatred, but the consideration of that love which hath freed us from eternal misery; for the guilty creature will be always suspicious, that notwithstanding the ordinary benefits of providence, God is an enemy to it; and till man is convinced, that in loving God, he most truly loves himself, he will never sincerely affect him. This was one great design of God in the way, as well as in the work of our redemption, to gain our hearts entirely to himself. He saves us in the most endearing and obliging manner. As David's affection declared itself, " I will not serve the Lord with that which doth cost me nothing;" so God would not save man with that which cost him nothing; but with the dearest price he hath purchased a title to our love. " God was in Christ reconciling the world unto himself," as well as through Christ reconciling himself to the world. He hath propounded such arguments for our love, so powerful and sublime, that Adam in innocence was unacquainted with. He sent down his own bowels to testify his affection to us. And that should be the greatest endearment of our love, which was the greatest evidence of his.

And if we consider the person of our Redeemer, what more worthy object of our affection than Christ? and Christ enduring the most terrible things, and at last dying with all the circumstances of dishonour and pain, for love to man? If he had no attractive excellencies, yet his cruel sufferings for us should make him infinitely precious and dear to our souls. If by solemn regards we contemplate him in the garden, amazed at the first approaches of that cup mixed with all the ingredients of divine displeasure, sweating like drops of blood under a weight of unspeakable sorrow, and without the least relief of man whose sins he then bore; what kind of marble are our hearts, if they do not tenderly relent at this doleful spectacle? Can we stand by him prostrate on the earth, and " offering up prayers and supplications with strong cryings and tears," (the effects of the travail of his soul,) without the most passionate sensibility? Can we see him contemned by impure worms, abused in his sacred offices, spitefully represented as a mock king, buffeted and flouted as a mock prophet, his sacred face defiled with loathsome spittle, his back torn with sharp scourges; and all endured with a victorious patience; can we behold this with an unconcerned eye? without the mournings of holy love? Can we accompany him in the dolorous way, and see him fainting and sinking under his heavy cross, and not feel his sufferings? Can we ascend to mount Calvary, and look on him hanging on the infamous tree in the midst of thieves, suffering the utmost fury of malicious enemies, and not be crucified with him? Can we hear the astonishing complaint of his deserted soul to the Judge of all the world doing extreme right on him as our Surety, and not be overcome with grief and love? Shall not the warm streams sadly running from his wounded head, and hands, and feet, melt our congealed affections? His pierced side discovers his heart, the vital fountain opened to wash away our guilt, and shall our hearts be untouched? His bloody, undeserved death, the precious ransom of our souls, makes him our life, and shall it not render him full of loveliness to our inflamed thoughts? He is more amiable on the cross than in the throne; for there we see the clearest testimony and the most glorious triumph of his love. There he endured the anger of heaven, and the scorn of the earth. There we might see joy saddened, faith fearing, salvation suffering, and life dying. Blessed Redeemer, what couldst thou have done or suffered more, to quicken our dead powers and inflame our cold hearts toward thee? How can we remember thy bleeding dying love without an ecstasy of affection? If we are not more insensible than the rocks, it is impossible but we must be touched and softened by it.

Suppose an angel by special delegation had been enabled to tread Satan under our feet, our obligations to him had been inexpressible, and our love might have been intercepted from ascending to our Creator; for salvation is a greater benefit, than mere giving to us our natural being; as the privation of felicity with the actual misery that is joined with it, is infinitely worse than the negation of being. Our Lord pronounced concerning Judas, "It had been good for that man if he had not been born." Redeeming goodness exceeds creating. Now the Son of God, to procure our highest love, alone wrought salvation for us.

And what admirable goodness is it, that puts a value upon our affection, and accepts such a small return! Our most intent and ardent love bears no more proportion to his, than a spark to the element of fire. Besides, his love to us was pure, and without any benefit to himself; but ours to him is profitable to our souls, for their eternal advantage. Yet with this he is fully satisfied; when we love him in the quality of a Saviour, we give him the glory of that he designs most to be glorified in, that is, of his mercy to the miserable. For this reason he instituted the sacrament of the supper, the contrivance of his love, to refresh the memory of his death, and quicken our fainting love to him.

Now the love that our Saviour requires must be,

1. Sincere and unfeigned. This declares itself by a care to please him in all things. "If a man love me," saith our Saviour, "he will keep my commandments." Obedience is the most natural and necessary product of love; for love is the spring of action, and employs all the faculties in the service of the person loved. The apostle expresses the force of it by an emphatical word, συνεχει, 2 Cor. v. 16; "The love of Christ constraineth us;" it signifies to have one bound and so much under power, that he cannot move without leave; as the inspired prophets were carried by the Spirit, and acted entirely by his motions. Such an absolute empire had the love of Christ over him, ruling all the inclinations of his heart and actions of his life, Acts xviii. 5. It is this alone that makes obedience cheerful, and constant; for love is seated in the will, and the obedience that proceeds from it, is

out of choice and purely voluntary. No commandment is grievous that is performed from love, 1 John v. 3. And it makes obedience constant. That which is forced from the impression of fear, is unsteadfast; but what is mixed with delight, is lasting.

2. Our love to Christ must be supreme, exceeding that which is given to all inferior objects. The most elevated and entire affection is due to him who saves us from torments that are extreme and eternal, and bestows upon us an inheritance immortal and undefiled. By the offering of himself to divine justice he has obliged us to present our bodies a living sacrifice to God, which is our reasonable service; life itself and all the endearments of it, relations, estates are to be disvalued when set in comparison with him. Nay if, by an impossible supposition, they could be separated, our Saviour should be more dear to us than salvation; for he declared greater love in giving himself for our ransom, than in giving heaven to be our reward. When we love him in the highest degree we are capable of, we have reason to mourn for the imperfection of it. In short; a superlative love, as it is due to our Redeemer, so it only is accepted by him. He that loveth father or mother, son or daughter, more than him, is not worthy of him. And he tells us in other places that we must hate them, to show that our love to him should so far exceed the affection that is due to those relations, that on all occasions where they divide from Christ, we should demean ourselves as if we had for them only an indifference, and even an aversion. Indeed, the preferring of any thing before him who is altogether desirable in himself and infinitely deserves our love, is brutishly to undervalue him, and in effect not to love him; for in a temptation, where Christ and the beloved object are set in competition, as a greater weight turns the scales, so the stronger affection will cause a person to renounce Christ for the possession of what he loves better. It is the love of Christ reigning in the heart that is the only principle of perseverance.

IV. What a high provocation is it to despise redeeming mercy, and to defeat that infinite goodness which hath been at such expense for our recovery!

The Son of God hath emptied all the treasures of his love, to purchase deliverance for guilty and wretched captives; he hath passed through so many pains and thorns to come and offer it to them; he solicits them to receive pardon and liberty, upon the conditions of acceptance and amendment, which are absolutely necessary to qualify them for felicity: now if they slight the benefit and renounce their redemption, if they sell themselves again under the servitude of sin and gratify the devil with a new conquest over them, what a bloody cruelty is this to their own souls, and a vile indignity to the Lord of glory! And are there any servile spirits so charmed with their misery, and so in love with their chains, who will stoop under their cruel captivity, to be reserved for eternal punishment! Who can believe it? But, alas, examples are numerous and ordinary. The most, by a folly as prodigious as their ingratitude, prefer their sins before their Saviour, and love that which is the only just object of hatred, and hate him who is the most worthy object of love. It is a most astonishing consideration, that love should persuade Christ to die for men, and that they should trample upon his blood, and choose rather to die by themselves, than to live by him! that God should be so easy to forgive, and man so hard to be forgiven! This is a sin of that transcendent height, that all the abominations of Sodom and Gomorrah are not equal to it. This exasperates mercy, that dear and tender attribute, the only advocate in God's bosom for us. This makes the judge irreconcilable. The rejecting of life upon the gracious terms of the gospel, makes the condemnation of men most just, certain, and heavy.

1. Most just: for when Christ hath performed what was necessary for the expiation of sin, and hath opened the throne of grace, which was before shut against us, and by this God hath declared how willing he is to save sinners; if they are wilful to be damned, and frustrate the blessed methods of grace, it is most equal they should inherit their own choice: "they judge themselves unworthy of eternal life." Conscience will justify the severest doom against them.

2. It makes their condemnation certain and final. The sentence of the law is reversible by an appeal to a higher court; but that of the gospel against the refusers of mercy will remain in its full force forever. " He that believeth not, is condemned already," John iii. 18. It is some consolation to a malefactor, that the sentence is not pronounced against him; but an unbeliever hath no respite. The gospel assures the sincere believer, that " he shall not enter into condemnation," to prevent his fears of an after sentence; but it denounces a present doom against those who reject it. " The wrath of God abideth on them." Obstinate infidelity sets beyond all possibility of pardon; there is no sacrifice for that sin. Salvation itself cannot save the impenitent infidel; for he excludes the only means whereby mercy is conveyed. How desperate then is the case of such a sinner. To what sanctuary will he fly ? All the other attributes condemn him; holiness excites justice, and justice awakens power for his destruction; and if mercy interpose not between him and ruin, he must perish irrecoverably. Whoever loveth not the Lord Christ, is " *anathema maranatha;*" he is under an irrevocable curse, which the Redeemer will confirm at his coming.

3. Wilful neglect of redeeming mercy aggravates the sentence, and brings an extraordinary damnation upon sinners. Besides the doom of the law which continues in its vigour against transgressors, the gospel adds a more heavy one against the impenitent, " because he believeth not in the name of the only begotten Son of God," John iii. 18. Infidelity is an outrage, not to a man or an angel, but to the eternal Son; for the redemption of souls is reckoned as a part of his reward; " He shall see of the travail of his soul and be satisfied," Isa. liii. 11. Those therefore who spurn at salvation, deny him the honour of his sufferings; and are guilty of the defiance of his love, of the contempt of his clemency, of the provocation of the most sensible and severe attribute when it is incensed. This is to strike him at the heart, and to kick against his bowels. This increases the anguish of his sufferings, and imbitters the cup of his passion. This renews his sorrows, and makes his wounds bleed

afresh. Dreadful impiety, that exceeds the guilt of the Jews. They once killed him, being in his humble, inglorious state, but this is a daily crucifying him now glorified. Ungrateful wretches, that refuse to bring glory to their Redeemer, and blessedness to themselves; that choose rather that the accuser should triumph in their misery, than their Saviour rejoice in their felicity! This is the great condemnation, that Christ came into the world to save men from death, and they refuse the pardon, John iii. 19. It is an aggravation of sin above what the devils are capable of, for pardon was never offered to those rebellious spirits. In short; so deadly a malignity there is in it, that it poisons the gospel itself, and turns the sweetest mercy into the sorest judgment. The Sun of righteousnes, who is a reviving life to the penitent believer, is "a consuming fire" to the obdurate. How much more tolerable had been the condition of such sinners, if saving grace had never appeared unto men, or they had never heard of it! for the degrees of wrath shall be in proportion to the riches of neglected goodness. The refusing of life from Christ, makes us guilty of his death. And when he shall come in his glory and be visible to all that pierced him, what vengeance will be the portion of those who despised the majesty of his person, the mystery of his compassions and sufferings! Those that lived and died in the darkness of heathenism, shall have a cooler climate in hell than those who neglect the great salvation.

CHAPTER XII.

THE JUSTICE OF GOD IN REDEMPTION

The Deity in itself is simple and pure, without mixtuie or variety: the scripture ascribes attributes to God for our clearer understanding. And those as essential in him are simply one: they are distinguished only with respect to the divers objects on which they are terminated, and the different effects that proceed from them.

The two great attributes which are exercised towards reasonable creatures in their lapsed state, are mercy and justice. These admirably concur in the work of our redemption. Although God spared guilty man for the honour of his mercy, yet he "spared not his own Son," who became a surety for the offender, but delivered him up to a cruel death for the glory of his justice.

For the clearer understanding of this, three things are to be considered:

I. The reasons why we are redeeemed by the satisfaction of justice;

II. The reality of the satisfaction made by our Redeemer;

III. The completeness and perfection of it.

1. Concerning the first, there are three different opinions among those who acknowledge the reality of satisfaction.

The first opinion is that it is not possible that sin should be pardoned without satisfaction; for justice being a natural and necessary excellency in God, hath an unchangeable respect to the qualities which are in the creatures; that as the divine goodness is necessarily exercised towards a creature perfectly holy, so justice is in punishing the guilty, unless a satisfaction intervene. And if it be not possible, considering the perfection of the Deity, that holiness should be unrewarded, far less can it be, that sin should be unpunished; since the exercise of justice, upon which punishment depends, is more necessary than that of goodness, which is the cause of remuneration; for the rewards which bounty dispenses, are pure favour, whereas the punishments which justice inflicts, are due. In short; since justice is a perfection, it is in God in a supreme degree, and being infinite, it is inflexible. This opinion is asserted by several divines of eminent learning.

The second opinion is, that God, by his absolute dominion and prerogative, might have released the sinner from punishment without any satisfaction: for, as by his sovereignty he transferred the punishment from the guilty to the innocent, so he might have forgiven sin, if no Redeemer had interposed. From hence it follows, that the death of Christ for the expiation of sin, was necessary only with respect to the divine decree.

The third opinion is, that considering God in this transaction, as qualified with the office of supreme Judge and Governor of the world, who hath given just laws to direct his creatures in their obedience, and to be the rule of his proceedings with them as to rewards and punishments, he hath so far restrained the exercise of his power, that upon the breach of the law, either it must be executed upon the sinner, or if extraordinarily dispensed with, it must be upon such terms as may secure the ends of government; and those are his own honour, and public order, and the benefit of those that are governed. And upon these accounts it was requisite, supposing the merciful design of God to pardon sin, that his righteousness should be declared in the sufferings of Christ. I will distinctly open this.

In the law, the sovereignty and holiness of God eminently appear: and there are two things in all sins which expose the offender justly to punishment;—a contempt of God's sovereignty, and in that respect there is a kind of equality between them. He that offends in one point, is guilty of all, they being ratified by the same authority, Jam. ii. 10. And from hence it is, that guilt is the natural passion of sin, that always adheres to it; for as God has a judicial power to inflict punishment upon the disobedient by virtue of his sovereignty, so the desert of punishment arises from the despising of it in the violation of his commands. In every sin there is a contrariety to God's holiness. And in this the natural turpitude of sin consists, which is receptive of degrees. From hence arises God's hatred of sin, which is as essential as his love to himself: the infinite purity and rectitude of his nature, infers the most perfect abhorrence of whatever is opposite to it. "The righteous Lord loveth righteousness, but the wicked his soul hateth," Psalm xi. 5, 7.

Now the justice of God is founded in his sovereignty and in his holiness; and the reason why it is exercised against sin, is not an arbitrary constitution, but his holy nature, to which sin is repugnant.

These things being premised, it follows, that God, in the relation of a governor, is protector of those sacred laws which are to direct the reasonable creature. And, as it was most reasonable, that in the first giving of the law, he should lay the strongest restraint upon man for preventing sin by the threatening of death, the greatest evil in itself, and in the estimation of mankind, so it is most congruous to reason, when the command was broken by man's rebellion, that either the penalty should be inflicted on his person, according to the immediate intent of the law, or satisfaction equivalent to the offence should be made; that the majesty and purity of God might appear in his justice, and there might be a visible discovery of the value he puts on obedience.

The life of the law depends upon the execution of it; for impunity occasions a contempt of justice, and by extenuating sin in the account of men, encourages to the free commission of it. If pardon be easily obtained, sin will be easily committed. Crimes unpunished seem authorised. The first temptation was prevalent by this persuasion, that no punishment would follow. Besides, if upon the bold violation of the law, no punishment were inflicted, not only the glory of God's holiness would be obscured, as if he did not love righteousness and hate sin, but suffered the contempt of the one and the commission of the other, without control; but it would reflect either upon his wisdom, as if he had not upon just reason established an alliance between the offence and the penalty, or upon his power, as if he were not able to vindicate the rights of heaven. And after his giving a law, and declaring that, according to the tenor of it, he would dispense rewards and punishments, if sin were unrevenged, it would lessen the sacredness of his truth in the esteem of men; so that the law and Lawgiver would be exposed to contempt. By all which it appears, that the honour of God was infinitely concerned in his requiring satisfaction for the breach of his laws.

Temporal magistrates are bound to execute wise and equal laws, for the preservation of public order and civil societies. It is true, there are some cases wherein the lawgiver may be forced to dispense with the law, as when the sparing of an offender is more advantage to the state than his punishment: besides, there is a superior tribunal to which great offenders are obnoxious, and good magistrates, when through weakness they are fain to spare the guilty, refer them to God's judgment. But it is otherwise in the divine government; for God is infinitely free from any necessity of compliance. There is no exigency of government that requires that any offenders should escape his severity. Neither is there any justice above his, which might exact satisfaction of them. Besides, the majesty of his laws is more sacred than of those which preserve earthly states, and ought to be more inviolable.

The sum is this—to declare God's hatred of sin, which is essential to his nature; to preserve the honour of the law, which otherwise would be securely despised, and lose its effect; to prevent sin, by keeping up in men a holy fear to offend God, an eternal respect in the rational creature to him; it was most fit that the presumptuous breach of God's command should not be unpunished. Now when the Son of God was made a sacrifice for sin, and by a bloody death made expiation of it, the world is convinced how infinitely hateful sin is to him, the dignity of the law is maintained, and sin is most effectually discouraged. There is the same terror, though not the same rigour, as if all mankind had been finally condemned. Thus it appears, how becoming God it was, to accomplish our salvation in such a manner, that justice and mercy are revealed in their most noble and eminent effects and operations.

II. The reality of the satisfaction made to divine justice is next to be proved. This is the centre and heart of the Christian religion, from whence all vital and comforting influences are derived: and for the opening of it, I will first consider the requisites in order to it: which are,

1. The appointment of God, whose power and will are to be considered in this transaction.

(1.) His power; for it is an act of supremacy to admit, that the sufferings of another should be effectual to redeem the offender. God doth not in this affair sustain the person of a judge, who is the minister of the law, and cannot free the guilty by transferring the punishment on another; but is to be considered as governor, who may by pure jurisdiction dispense with the execution of the law, upon those considerations which fully answer the ends of government.

The law is not executed according to the letter of it, for then no sinner can be saved; but repenting believers are free from condemnation. Nor is it abrogated, for then no obligation remains as to the duty or penalty of it; but men are still bound to obey it, and impenitent infidels are still under the curse: " the wrath of God abideth on them." But it is relaxed as to the punishment, by the merciful condescension of the Lawgiver.

Some laws are not, in their own nature, capable of relaxation, because there is included moral iniquity in the relaxation; as the commands to love God and obey conscience, can never lose their binding force. It is a universal rule that suffers no exception, " God cannot deny himself;" therefore he can never allow sin, that directly opposes the perfections of his nature. Besides, some laws cannot be relaxed, *ex hypothesi*, upon the account of the divine decree which makes them irrevocable; as that all who die in their impenitence, shall be damned. Now there was no express sign annexed to the sanction of the original law, to intimate, that it should be unalterable as to the letter of it. The threatening declared the desert of sin in the offender, and the right of punishing in the superior; but it is so to be understood, as not to frustrate the power of the Lawgiver to relax the punishment upon wise and just reasons.

The law did neither propound nor exclude this expedient: for judging without passion against the sinner, it is satisfied with the punishment of the crime; for it is not the evil of the offender that is primarily designed by the law, but the preservation of public order, for the honour of the Lawgiver, and the benefit of those that are subjects: so that the relaxing of the punishment, as to the person of the sinner, by compensation, fully answers the intent of the law.

(2.) As by the right of jurisdiction God might relax

the law, and appoint a Mediator to interpose by way of ransom, so he hath declared his will to accept of him. The law in strictness obliged the sinning person to suffer, so that he might have refused any other satisfaction; therefore the whole work of our redemption is referred to his will as the primary cause. Our Saviour was sent into the world by the order of God, John iii. 17. He was sealed, that is, authorized for that great work by commission from him, John vi. 27. He was called to his office, by the voice of his Father from heaven, "this is my beloved Son, in whom I am well pleased," Matt. iii. 17. "God anointed him with the Holy Ghost and with power," Acts x. 38; which signifies, as the enduing of him with the graces of the Spirit, so the investing of him in the dignity of Mediator, as kings, priests, and prophets were: and both were necessary; for his graces without his office are unprofitable to us, and his office without his capacity, of no advantage. In short: the apostle observes this as the peculiar excellency of the new covenant and the foundation of our hopes, that the Mediator was constituted by a solemn oath: "The Lord sware, and will not repent, Thou art a priest for ever after the order of Melchisedec," Heb. vii. 21.

2. The consent of our Redeemer was necessary, that he might by sufferings satisfy for us; for being the "Lord from heaven," there was no superior authority to command, or power to compel him. It is true, having become our Surety, it was necessary he should be accountable to the law; but the first undertaking was most free. When one hath entered into bonds to pay the debt of an insolvent person, he must give satisfaction; but it is an act of liberty and choice to make himself liable. Our Saviour tells us, "It behoved Christ to suffer;" he doth not say that the Son of God should suffer, but Christ. This title signifies the same person in substance, but not in the same respect and consideration. Christ is the second person clothed with our nature. There was no necessity that obliged God to appoint his Son, or the Son to accept the office of Mediator; but when the eternal Son had undertaken that charge, and was made Christ, that is, assumed our

nature, in order to redeem us, it was necessary that he should suffer.

Besides, his consent was necessary upon another account; for the satisfaction doth not arise merely from the dignity of his person, but from the law of substitution, whereby he put himself in our stead, and voluntarily obliged himself to suffer the punishment due to us. The efficacy of his death is by virtue of the contract between the Father and him, of which there could be no cause but pure mercy, and his voluntary condescension.

Now the scripture declares the willingness of Christ, particularly at his entrance into the world and at his death. Upon his coming into the world, he begins his life by the internal oblation of himself to his Father, Heb. x. 6, 7. " Sacrifice and offering thou didst not desire; mine ears hast thou opened;" that is, he entirely resigned himself to be God's servant; " burnt-offering and sin-offering hast thou not required. Then said I, Lo, I come: in the volume of the book it is written of me: I delight to do thy will, O my God ; yea, thy law is within my heart," Psalm xl. 6—8. He saw the divine decree, and embraced it; the law was in his heart, and fully possessed all his thoughts and affections, and had a commanding influence upon his life.—and his willingness was fully expressed by him, when he approached his last sufferings; for although he declined death as man, having natural and innocent desires of self-preservation, yet as Mediator he readily submitted to it; " Not my will, but thine be done," was his voice in the garden. And this argued the completeness and fixedness of his will, that notwithstanding his aversion to death absolutely considered, yet with an unabated election he still chose it as the means of our salvation. No involuntary constraint did force him to that submission : but the sole causes of it were his free compliance with his Father's will, and his tender compassion towards men. He saith, " I have power to lay down my life, and I have power to take it again: this commandment have I received of my Father," John x. 18. In his death, obedience and sacrifice were united. The typical sacrifices were led to the altar, but the Lamb of God presented himself: it is said, "he gave himself for us," Gal. i. 4; to signify his willingness in dying, Tit. ii. 14. Now the freeness of our Redeemer in dying for us qualified his sufferings to be meritorious. The apostle tells us, Rom. v. 19, that "by the obedience of one many are made righteous;" that is, by his voluntary sufferings we are justified; for without his consent his death could not have the respect of a punishment for our sins. No man can be compelled to pay another's debt, unless he make himself surety for it.

Briefly : the appointment of God and the undertaking of Christ, to redeem us from the curse of the law by his suffering it, are the foundation of the new testament.

3. He that interposed as Mediator, must be perfectly holy ; otherwise he had been liable to justice for his own sin; and guilty blood is impure and corrupt, apter to stain by its effusion and sprinkling, than to purge away sin. The apostle joins these two as inseparable ; "He was manifested to take away our sin, and in him is no sin," 1 John iii. 5. The priesthood under the law was imperfect, as for other reasons, so for the sins of the priests; Aaron, the first and chief of the Levitical order, was guilty of gross idolatry, so that reconciliation could not be obtained by their ministry; for how can one captive ransom another, or sin expiate sin? But our Mediator was absolutely innocent, without the least tincture of sin original or actual. He was conceived in a miraculous manner, infinitely distant from all the impurities of the earth. That which is produced in an ordinary way, receives its propriety from second causes, and contracts the defilement that cleaves to the whole species. Whatever is born "of blood" and "of the will of the flesh," that is formed of the substance of the flesh and by the sensual appetite, is defiled : but though he was formed of the substance of the virgin, yet it was by virtue of a heavenly principle according to the words of the angel to her. "The Holy Ghost shall come upon thee, and the power of the highest shall overshadow thee ; therefore also that holy thing which shall be born of thee, shall be called the Son of God," Luke i. 35. He came in the appearance only "of sinful flesh;" as the brazen serpent had the figure, and not

the poison, of the fiery serpent. He was without actual sin. He foiled the tempter in all his arts and methods wherewith he tried him. He resisted the lust of the flesh, by refusing to make the stones bread to assuage his hunger; and the lust of the eyes in despising the kingdoms of the world with all their treasures; and the pride of life, when he would not throw himself down, that by the interposing of angels for his rescue, there might be a visible proof that he was the Son of God. The accuser himself confessed him to be the "Holy One of God;" he found no corruption within him, and could draw nothing out of him. Judas that betrayed him, and Pilate that condemned him, acknowledged his innocence. He perfectly fulfilled the law, and did always what pleased his Father. In the midst of his sufferings, no irregular motion disturbed his soul, but he always expressed the highest reverence to God and unspeakable charity to men. He was compared, for his passion and his patience, to a lamb, that quietly dies at the foot of the altar.

Besides, we may consider in our Mediator not only a perfect freedom from sin, but an impossibility that he should be touched by it. The angelical nature was liable to folly; but the human nature, by its intimate and unchangeable union with the divine, is established above all possibility of falling. The Deity is holiness itself and, by its personal presence, is a greater preservative from sin, than either the vision of God in heaven, or the most permanent habit of grace. Our Saviour tells us, "the Son can do nothing of himself," but according to the pattern the Father sets him, John v. 19.

Now the perfect holiness of our Redeemer hath a special efficacy in making his death to be the expiation of sin, as the scripture frequently declares; "For such an High Priest became us, who is holy, harmless, undefiled, separate from sinners," Heb. vii. 26. And he that knew no sin, was made sin for us, "that we might be made the righteousness of God in him," 2 Cor. v. 21. "We are redeemed not with corruptible things, as silver and gold, but with the precious blood of Christ, as of a lamb without blemish, and without spot," 1 Pet. i. 18. And, "By his knowledge shall my righteous servant justify many," Isa. liii. 11.

4. It was requisite the Mediator should be God and man.

He must assume the nature of man, that he might be put in his stead in order to make satisfaction for him. He was to be our representative, therefore such a conjunction between us must be, that God might esteem all his people to suffer in him. By the law of Israel the right of redemption belonged to him that was next in blood. Now Christ took the seed of Abraham, the original element of our nature, that having a right of propriety in us as God, he might have a right of propinquity as man. He was allied to all men, as men, that his sufferings might be universally beneficial.

And he must be God. It is not his innocency only or deputation, but the dignity of his person that qualifies him to be an all-sufficient sacrifice for sin, so that God may dispense pardon in a way that is honourable to justice; for justice requires a proportion between the punishment and the crime; and that receives its quality from the dignity of the person offended. Now since the majesty of God is infinite against whom sin is committed, the guilt of it can never be expiated but by an infinite satisfaction. There is no name under heaven nor in heaven, that could save us, but the Son of God, who, being equal to him in greatness, became man.

If there had been such compassion in the angels as to have inclined them to interpose between justice and us, they had not been qualified for that work; not only upon the account of their different nature, so that by substitution they could not satisfy for us; nor that being immaterial substances, they are exempted from the dominion of death, which was the punishment denounced against the sinner, and to which his surety must be subjected; but principally that being finite creatures, they are incapable to atone an incensed God. Who among all their glorious orders durst appear before so consuming a fire? Who could have been an altar whereon to sanctify a sacrifice to divine justice? No mere creature how worthy soever could propitiate the supreme majesty when justly provoked. Our Redeemer was to be the Lord of angels. The apostle tells us, that it "pleased the Father that in him should all fulness dwell :" this respects not his original nature, but his office ; and the reason of it is, to reconcile by the blood of the cross, things in heaven and in the earth, Col. i. 19. From the greatness of the work we may infer the quality of the means, and from the quality of the means, the nature of the person that is to perform it. Peace with God, who was provoked by our rebellion, could only be made by an infinite sacrifice. Now in Christ the Deity itself, not its influences, and the fulness of it, not any particular perfection only, dwelt really and substantially. God was present in the ark in a shadow, and representation; he is present in nature by his sustaining power, and in his saints by special favour, and the eminent effects, the graces and comforts, that proceed from it; but he is present in Christ in a singular and transcendent manner. The humanity is related to the Word, not only as a creature to the author of its being, for in this regard it hath an equal respect to all the persons, but by a peculiar conjunction ; for it is actuated by the same subsistence, as the divine essence is in the Son, but with this difference, the one is voluntary, the other necessary ; the one is espoused by love, the other received by nature.

Now from this intimate union, there is a communication of the special qualities of both natures to the person of Christ: man is exalted to be the Son of God, and the Word abased to be the Son of man ; as by reason of the vital union between the soul and body, the essential parts of man, it is truly said that he is rational in respect of his soul, and mortal in respect of his body.

This union derives an infinite merit to the obedience of Christ; for the human nature having its complement from the divine person, it is not the nature simply considered, but the person, that is the fountain of actions. To illustrate this by an instance : the civil law determines that a tree transplanted from one soil to another, and taking root there, belongs to the owner of that ground, in regard that receiving nourishment from a new earth, it becomes as it were another tree, though there be the same individual root, the same body and the same soul of vegetation as before. Thus the human nature taken from the common mass of mankind, and transplanted by personal union into the divine, is to be reckoned as entirely belonging to the divine, and the actions proceeding from it are not merely human, but are raised above their natural worth, and become meritorious. One hour of Christ's life glorified God more than an everlasting duration spent by angels and men in the praises of him; for the most perfect creatures are limited and finite, and their services cannot fully correspond with the majesty of God; but when the Word was made flesh, and entered into a new state of subjection, he glorified God in a divine manner and most worthy of him. " He that cometh from above, is above all," John iii. 31. The all-sufficiency of his satisfaction arises from hence—he that " was in the form of God, and thought it not robbery to be equal with God ;" that is, in the truth of the divine nature was equal with the Father, and without sacrilege or usurpation possessed divine honour; he became obedient to the death of the cross. The Lord of glory was crucified. We are purchased by the blood of God, Acts xx. 28. " The blood of Jesus Christ his Son cleanseth us from all sin," 1 John i. 7. The divine nature gives it an infinite and everlasting efficacy.

And it is observable, that the Socinians, the declared enemies of his eternity, consentaneously to their first impious error, deny his satisfaction; for if Jesus Christ were but a titular God, his sufferings, how deep soever, had been insufficient to expiate our offence; in his death he had been only a martyr, not a mediator; for no satisfaction can be made to divine justice, but by suffering that which is equivalent to the guilt of sin, which as it is inconceivably great, such must the satisfaction be

CHAPTER XIII.

THE JUSTICE OF GOD IN REDEMPTION.

HAVING premised these things, I shall now prove that the divine justice is really declared and glorified in the obedient sufferings of Christ.

For the opening of this point, it is necessary to consider the account the scripture gives of his death; which is threefold—it is represented under the relation of a punishment inflicted on him for sin, and the effect of it is satisfaction to the law—as a price to redeem us from hell—under the notion of a sacrifice to reconcile God to sinners.

1. As a punishment inflicted on him for sin. This will appear by considering that man by his rebellion against God was capitally guilty: he stood sentenced by the law to death. Christ, with the allowance of the supreme Judge, interposed as our Surety, and in that relation was made liable to punishment. Sins are by resemblance called debts. As a debt obliges the debtor to payment, so sin doth the sinner to punishment. And as the creditor hath a right to exact the payment from the debtor, so God hath a right to inflict punishment on the guilty; but with this difference—the creditor by the mere signification of his will may discharge the debtor, for he hath an absolute power over his estate; whereas public justice is concerned in the punishment of the guilty. This is evident by many instances; for it is not sufficient that a criminal satisfy his adversary, unless the prince, who is the guardian of the laws, give him pardon.—The interest of a private person who hath received an injury, is so distinct from that of the state, that sometimes the injured party solicits the pardon of the offender without success: which shows, that it is not principally to satisfy the particular person, that the crime is punished, but to satisfy the law, and prevent future disorders.

Now our debt was not pecuniary, but penal: and as in civil cases, where one becomes surety for another, he is obliged to pay the debt, for in the estimate of the law they are but one person; so the Lord Jesus Christ entering into this relation, he sustained the persons of sinners, and became judicially one with them, and according to the order of justice, was liable to their punishment. The displeasure of God was primarily and directly against the sinner, but the effects of it fell upon Christ, who undertook for him. The apostle tells us, that "when the fulness of time was come, God sent forth his Son, made under the law, to redeem them that were under the law," Gal.

iv. 4, 5. He took our nature and condition: he was made under the law moral and ceremonial. The directive part of the moral law he fulfilled by the innocency of his life; the penalty he satisfied as our Surety, being under an obligation to save us. And he appeared as a sinner in his subjection to the law of Moses.—That "hand-writing was against us;" he therefore entered into the bond that we had forfeited. In his circumcision he signed it with those drops of blood, which were an earnest of his shedding the rest on the cross; for whosoever was circumcised, became a debtor to the whole law, Gal. v. 3. And we may observe, it is said, that as Moses lifted up the brazen serpent, so the law, of which Moses was a type and minister, lifted up the Messiah on the cross.

The scripture is very clear and express in setting down the part that God had in the sufferings of Christ as supreme Judge, the impulsive cause that moved him, their proportion to the punishment of the law, and the effect of them for our deliverance. He was "delivered by the determinate counsel and foreknowledge of God," Acts ii. 23. All the various and vicious actions of men were overruled by his providence; the falseness of Judas, the fearfulness of Pilate, and the malice of the Jews were subservient to God's eternal design. And as he wills not the death of a sinner, much less of his Son, but for the most weighty reasons, these are declared by the prophet; "All we like sheep, have gone astray; we have turned every one to his own way;" our errors were different, but the issue was the same, that is, eternal death: "and the Lord hath laid on him the iniquity of us all;" that is, the punishment of our iniquities, Isa. liii. 6. His sufferings had such a respect to sin, as included the imputation of it. It was an act of sovereignty in God to appoint Christ as man to be our Surety, but an act of justice to inflict the punishment, when Christ had undertaken for us. It is said, "he hath borne our griefs, and carried our sorrows." The expressions are comprehensive of all the miseries of his life, especially his last sufferings. The Hebrew words signify such a taking away, as is by laying upon one who bears it from us. And thus it is interpreted by Peter; "Who his own self bare our sins in his own body on the tree," 1 Pet. iii. 24. This necessarily implies the derivation of our guilt to him, and the consequent of it, the transferring of our punishment. Those words are full and pregnant to the same purpose; " He was wounded for our transgressions, he was bruised for our iniquities, the chastisement of our peace was upon him, and with his stripes we are healed," Isa. liii. 5 ; where the meritorious cause of his sufferings is set down, as appears by the connection of the words with the former. The Jews thought " him stricken, smitten of God, and afflicted ;" that is, justly punished for blasphemy and usurping divine honour. In opposition to this conceit, it is added, " but he was wounded for our transgressions." This the apostle expressly tells us, when he declares that " Christ died for our sins."

This will appear more fully, by considering what the desert of sin is. By our rebellion we made the forfeiture of soul and body to divine justice : death, both the first and the second, was the sentence of the law. Now the sufferings of Christ were answerable to his punishment. The death which the law threatened for sin, was to be accompanied with dishonour and pain. And he suffered the death of the cross, in which the equal extremities of ignominy and torment were joined. A special curse was annexed to it, not only in respect of the judgment of men, before whom a crucified person was made a spectacle of public vengeance for his crimes, but in respect of God's declaration concerning it. The Jews were commanded, that none should hang on a tree longer than the evening, lest the holy land should be profaned by that which was an express mark of God's curse. Now the legal curse was a typical signification of the real, that should be suffered by our Redeemer. Besides, his death was attended with exquisite pains : he suffered variety of torments by the scourges, the thorns, the nails that pierced his hands and feet, the least vital, but most sensible parts. He refused the wine mixed with myrrh, that was given to stupefy the senses ; for the design of his passion required, that he should have the quickest sense of his sufferings, which were the punishment of sin. And his inward sorrows were equivalent to the pains of loss and sense that are due to sinners. It is true, there are circumstances in the sufferings of the damned, as blasphemy, rage, impotent fierceness of mind, which are not appointed by the law, but are accidental, arising from the perverseness of their spirits; for the punishment of the law is a physical evil, but these are moral; and that punishment is inflicted by the Judge, but these are only from the guilty sufferers: now to these he was not possibly liable. Besides, the death that the sinner ought to suffer is eternal, attended with despair and intolerable anguish of conscience. Now our Redeemer having no real guilt, was not liable to the worm of conscience, and his temporary sufferings were equivalent to the eternal upon the account of his divine person; so that he was not capable of despair. But he endured the unknown terrors of the second death, so far as was consistent with the perfection of his nature. The anguish of his soul was not merely from sympathy with his body, but immediately from divine displeasure. "It pleased the Lord to bruise him;" this principally respects the impressions of wrath made upon his inward man. Had the cup he feared been only death, with the bitter ingredients of dishonour and pain, many have drunk it with more apparent resolution. The martyrs have endured more cruel torments without complaint; nay, in their sharpest conflicts have expressed a triumphant joy. Whereas our Redeemer was under all the innocent degrees of fear and sorrow at the approach of his sufferings. From whence was the difference? Had Christ less courage? He was the fountain of their fortitude. The difference was not in the dispositions of the patients, but in the nature of the suffering. He endured that which is infinitely more terrible than all outward torments. The light of joy that always shined in his soul, a sweet image of heaven, was then totally eclipsed. God, the fountain of compassion, restrained himself; his Father appeared a severe, inexorable Judge, and dealt with him not as his Son, but our Surety. Under all the cruelties exercised by men, the Lamb of God opened not his mouth; but when the "Father of mercies, and the God of all consolation" forsook him, then he broke forth into a mournful complaint.

Now by this account of Christ's sufferings from scripture, it is evident, they were truly penal; for they were inflicted for sin by the supreme Judge, and were equivalent to the sentence of the law. And the benefit we receive upon their account, proves that they are a satisfaction to divine justice, for we are exempted from punishment by his submission to it. He freed us "from the curse of the law, being made a curse for us," Gal. iii. 13. "The chastisement of our peace was upon him," by whose "stripes we are healed," Isa. liii. 5. So that his death being the meritorious cause of freeing the guilty, is properly satisfaction.

Before I proceed to the second consideration of Christ's death, I will briefly answer the objection of the Socinians, viz., that it is a violation of justice to transfer the punishment from one to another; so that the righteous God could not punish his innocent Son for our sins.

Now to show the invalidity of this pretence, we must consider,—that justice is not an irregular appetite for vengeance, arising from hatred that cannot be satisfied but with the destruction of the guilty. It preserves right with pure affections, and is content when the injury is repaired, from whomsoever satisfaction comes.—Though an innocent person cannot suffer as innocent without injustice, yet he may voluntarily contract an obligation, which will expose him to deserved sufferings. The wisdom and justice of all nations agree in punishing one for another's fault, where consent is preceding, as in the case of hostages. And although it is essential to the nature of punishment to be inflicted for sin, yet not on the person of the sinner; for *in conspectu fori*, the sinner and surety are one.—That exchange is not allowed in criminal causes, where the guilty ought to suffer in person, is not from any injustice in the nature of the thing, for then it would not be allowed in civil; but there are special reasons why an innocent person is not ordinarily admitted to suffer for an offender. No man hath absolute power over his own life. It is a *depositum* consigned to him for a time, and must be preserved till God, or the public good, calls for it. The public, too, would suffer prejudice by the loss of a good subject.

Therefore the rule of the law is just, *Non auditur perire volens.* The desire of one that devotes himself to ruin, is not to be heard. And the guilty person who is spared, might grow worse by impunity, and cause great disorders by his evil example. But these considerations are of no force in the case of our Saviour; for he had full power to dispose of his life; "I have power to lay it down, and I have power to take it again: this commandment have I received of my Father," John x. 18. He declares his power as God, that his life entirely depended on his will, to preserve it, or part with it; and his subjection as Mediator to the order of his Father.

Our Saviour, too, could not finally perish. It was not possible he should be held under the power of death, Acts ii. 24. Otherwise it had been against the laws of reason, that the precious should for ever suffer for the vile. Better ten thousand worlds had been lost, than that the Holy One of God should perish. He saved us through his sufferings, though as by fire; and had a glorious reward in the issue. There is also an infinite good redounds from his suffering: for sinners are exempted from death, and the preservation of the guilty is for the glory of God's government; for those who are redeemed by his death, are renewed by his Spirit. He covers their sins, that he may cure them. He is made righteousness and sanctification to his people, 1 Cor. i. 30. The serious belief that Christ, by dying, hath rescued us from hell, produces a superlative love to him; an ingenuous and grateful fear lest we should offend him; an ambition to please him in all things; briefly, universal obedience to his will, as its most natural and necessary effect. So that in laying the punishment on Christ, under which mankind must have sunk for ever, there is nothing against justice.

2. The death of Christ is the price which redeems us from our woful captivity. Mankind was fallen under the dominion of Satan and death, and could not obtain freedom by escape, or mere power; for by the order of divine justice, we were detained prisoners: so that till God, the supreme Judge, is satisfied, there can be no discharge. Now the Lord Christ hath procured our de-

liverance by his death, according to the testimony of the apostle; " We have redemption through his blood, even the forgiveness of sins, Col. i. 14. His blood is congruously called a " price," because in consideration of it, our freedom is purchased. He is our Redeemer by ransom; " he gave himself a ransom for all;" and that signifies the price paid for the freeing of a captive, 1 Tim. ii. 6. The word used by the apostle, ἀντίλυτρον, hath a special emphasis; it signifies an exchange of conditions with us, the redeeming of us from death by dying for us; as the ἀντίψυχοι, who devoted themselves to death, for the rescuing of others. Our Saviour told his disciples, that the Son of man came " to give his life a ransom for many;" λύτρον ἀντὶ πολλῶν, Matt. xx. 28. 'Ἀντὶ signifies a commutation or exchange, with respect of things or persons. Thus we are commanded to render to none " evil for evil:" and, " if a son ask of his father a fish, will he *for* a fish give him a serpent ?" ἀντὶ ἰχθύος ὄφιν, Luke xi. 11. When it is used in respect of persons, it imputes a substitution in another's place. Archelaus reigned " in the room of his father Herod;" ἀντὶ Ἡρώδου, Matt. ii. 22. Peter paid tribute " for Christ," that is, representing him. The effect, therefore, of our Saviour's words, that " he gave his life a ransom for many," is evidently this, that he died in their stead, and his life as a price intervened to obtain their redemption. It is for this reason the glorified saints sung a hymn of praise to the divine Lamb, saying, " Thou art worthy, for thou wast slain, and hast redeemed us to God by thy blood." Rev. v. 9.

The singular and blessed effect of Christ's death, distinguishes it from the death of the most excellent martyrs. If he had died only for the confirmation of the gospel, or to exhibit to us a pattern of suffering graces, what were there peculiar and extraordinary in his death? How can it be said that he alone was crucified for us? For the martyrs sealed the truth with their blood, and left admirable examples of love to God, of zeal for his glory, of patience under torments, and of compassion to their persecutors: yet it were intolerable blasphemy to say that they redeemed us by their death. And it is observable, when the death of Christ is propounded in scripture as a pattern of patience, it is with a special circumstance that distinguishes it from all others. " Christ suffered for us, leaving us an example that we should follow his steps: who his own self bare our sins in his own body on the tree; by whose stripes ye were healed." 1 Pet. ii. 21, 24. The truth is, if the sole end of Christ's death were to induce men to believe his promises and to imitate his graces, there had been no such necessity of it; for the miracles he did, had been sufficient to confirm the gospel, yet remission of sins is never attributed to them; and the miseries he suffered during the course of his life, had been sufficient to instruct us how to behave ourselves under indignities and persecutions: and at the last he might have given as full a testimony to the truth of his doctrine by his descent from the cross, as by dying for us. But no lower price than his blood could make compensation to the law, and satisfaction to God; and to deny this, is to rob him of the glory of his death, and to destroy all our comfort.

It is objected by those who nullify the mystery of the cross of the Lord Jesus; how could God receive this price, since he gave up his Son to that death which redeems us? And how can our Redeemer, supposing him God, make satisfaction to himself? To this I answer,

(1.) The infinite goodness of God in giving our Redeemer, doth not divest him of the office of supreme Judge, nor prejudice his examining of the cause according to his sovereign jurisdiction, and his receiving a ransom to preserve the rights of justice inviolable. There is an eminent instance of this in Zaleucus, the prince of the Locrians, who passed a law that adulterers should lose both their eyes; and when his son was convicted of that crime, the people who respected him for his excellent virtues, out of pity to him, interceded for the offender. Zaleucus, (vid. Ælian, Var. Histor. 1. 13. c. 24.) in a conflict between zeal for justice and affection to his son, took but one eye from him, and parted with one of his own to satisfy the law: and thus he paid and received the punishment; he paid it as a father, and received it as the conservator of public justice. Thus when guilty mankind in its poverty could not pay the forfeiture to the law, God, the Father of mercies, was pleased to give it from the treasures of his love; that is, the blood of his Son for our ransom. And this he receives from the hand of Christ offered upon the cross, as the supreme Judge, and declares it fully valuable, and the rights of justice to be truly performed.

(2.) It is not inconsistent with reason, that the Son of God, clothed with our nature, should by his death make satisfaction to the Deity, and therefore to himself. In the according of two parties, a person that belongs to one of them, may interpose for reconciliation, provided that he divests his own interest, and leaves it with the party from whom he comes. Thus when the senate of Rome and the people were in dissension, one of the senators, Menenius Agrippa, trusted his own concernment with the council of which he was a member, and mediated between the parties to reconcile them, Liv. lib. 2. Thus when the Father and the Son, both possessed of the imperial power, have been offended by rebellious subjects, it is not inconvenient that the Son interpose as a Mediator, to restore them to the favour of the Prince. And by this he reconciles them to himself, and procures them pardon of an offence by which his own majesty was violated. This he doth as Mediator, not as a party concerned. Now this is a fit illustration of the great work of our redemption, so far as human things can represent divine; for all the persons of the glorious Trinity were equally provoked by our sin; and to obtain our pardon, the Son with the consent of the Father deposits his interest into his hands, and as a Mediator intervenes between us and him, who in this transaction is the depositary of the rights of heaven; and having performed what justice required, he reconciled the world to God, that is, to the Father, himself, and the eternal Spirit. In this cause his person is the same, but his quality is different: he made satisfaction as mediator, and received it as God. It is in this sense that the apostle saith, 1 John ii. 2. "We have an Advocate with the Father, Jesus Christ the righteous;" not to exclude the other persons, but in regard the Father as the first person is the protector of justice, our Mediator in appeasing him appeases the other also.

3. The death of Christ is represented under the notion of a sacrifice offered up to God.

For the more full understanding of this, we must consider that sacrifices were of two kinds.

Some were eucharistical; they are called peace-offerings, by which the sacrificer acknowledged the bounty of God and his own unworthiness, and rendered praise for a favour received, and desired the divine blessing.

Others were expiatory; the sin offerings for the averting of God's wrath. The institution of these was upon a double reason—that man is a sinner, and therefore obnoxious to the just indignation and extreme displeasure of the holy and righteous God—that God was to be propitiated, that he might pardon them. These truths are engraven in the natural consciences of men, as appears by the pretended expiations of sin among the heathens; but are more clearly revealed in the scripture. Under the law, without the " shedding of blood, there was no remission;" to signify, that God would not forgive sin without the atonement of justice, which required the death of the offender, but it being tempered with mercy, accepted a sacrifice in his stead. And that there was a substitution of the beast in the place of the guilty offender, appears by the law concerning sacrifices. None were instituted for capital offences, as murder, idolatry, adultery, because the sinner himself was to be cut off; but for other sins, which although in strictness they deserved death, yet God, who was the King of Israel, was pleased to remit the forfeiture, and to accept the life of the sacrifice for the life of the sinner. The guilty person was to offer a clean beast of his own; to signify the surrogation of it in his stead, for in the relation of a possessor he had a dominion over it, to apply it to that use. The priest, or the person that offered was to lay his hands on the head of the sacrifice, thereby consecrating it to God, and devoting it in his stead to bear the punishment. For this reason it was called a sin, and a curse. The confession of sin by the people or the priest, as in the day of atonement, signified that the guilt of all met on the sacrifice for expiation. The blood was to be shed, wherein the vital spirits are, an express representation of what the sinner deserved, and that it was accepted for his life. Lastly; the deprecating of God's anger was joined with the sacrifice; as when a man was slain and the murderer was not found, the elders of the city next to the dead body, were to kill an heifer in a valley, and pray that innocent blood might not be laid to their charge; otherwise the land could not be cleansed from the guilt of blood, but by the blood of the murderer.

The effects of these sacrifices declare their nature; and they are answerable to their threefold respect, to God, to sin, to man—to God, that his anger might be appeased; to sin, that the fault might be expiated; to man, that the guilty person might obtain pardon, and freedom from punishment. Thus when a sacrifice was duly offered, it is said to be " of a sweet savour unto the Lord," and to atone him, Lev. i. 17; and the remission of sins, with the release of the sinner, followed. " The priest shall expiate it," that is, declaratively, " and it shall be forgiven him."

Now there was a double guilt contracted by those that were under the Mosaical dispensation.

(1.) Typical, from the breach of a ceremonial constitution, which had no relation to morality. Such were natural pollutions, accidental diseases, the touching of a dead body, which were esteemed vicious according to the law, and the defiled were excluded from sacred and civil society. Now these impurities, considered in themselves, deserved no punishment; for involuntary and inevitable infirmities, and corporeal things which do not infect the inward man, are the marks of our abject and weak state, but are not themselves sinful. Therefore ceremonial guilt was expiated by a ceremonial offering; for it is according to the nature of things, that obligations should be dissolved by the same means by which they are contracted. As therefore those pollutions were penal merely by the positive will of God, so (the exercise of his supreme right being tempered with wisdom and equity) he ordained that the guilt should be abolished by a sacrifice, and that they should be fully restored to their former privileges. Thus the apostle tells us, that the blood of those sacrifices " sanctifieth to the purifying of the flesh;"

that is, it communicated a legal purity to the offerers, and consequently a right to approach the holy place. Now the reason of these institutions was that the legal impurity might represent the true defilements of sin, and the expiatory sacrifices prefigure that great and admirable oblation which should purge away all sin.

(2.) A real guilt, which respects the conscience, and was contracted from the breach of the moral law, and subjected the offender to death temporal and eternal. This could not be purged away by those sacrifices; for how is it possible the blood of a beast should cleanse the soul of a man, or content the justice of an offended God? Nay, on the contrary, they revived the guilt of sin, and reinforced the rigour of the law, and were a public profession of the misery of men: for this reason the law is called "the ministry of death." As the moral contained a declaration of our guilt, and God's right to punish, so all the parts of the ceremonial were either arguments and convictions of sin, or images of the punishment due for them. But as they had a relation to Christ who was their complement, so they signified the expiation of moral guilt by his sacrifice, and freed the sinner from that temporal death to which he was liable; as the representative of our freedom from eternal death by the blood of the cross.

This will appear more clearly by considering—that all kinds of placatory sacrifices are referred to Christ in the new testament.—that all their effects are attributed to him in a sublimer and most perfect manner. He is called a Lamb in the notion of a sacrifice; "The Lamb slain from the foundation of the world," Rev. xiii. 8. A lamb was used in the expiation of moral and legal impurities, Lev. v. 6; xiv. 12. He is called " our passover that was sacrificed for us," 1 Cor. v. 7. The paschal lamb in its first institution had an expiatory efficacy; for God, by looking on that blood, averted the destruction from the Israelites, which seized on the Egyptians, Exod. xii. 13. This was the reason of the prohibition, that none should go out of the house till the morning, lest they should be struck by the destroying angel. Not but that the angel could distinguish the

Israelites from the Egyptians abroad, but it was typical, to show their security was in being under the guard of the lamb's blood, which was shed to spare theirs. Thus the apostle Peter tells us, that we are redeemed by the blood of the pure and perfect Lamb, 1 Pet. i. 19. And he was represented by the red heifer, whose ashes were the chief ingredient in the water of purification; " For if the blood of bulls and of goats, and the ashes of an heifer sprinkling the unclean, sanctifieth to the purifying of the flesh, how much more shall the blood of Christ purge your conscience?" Heb. ix. 13, 14. Especially the anniversary sacrifice, which was the abridgment and recapitulation of all the rest, had an eminent respect to Christ. The whole epistle to the Hebrews is tinctured with this divine doctrine.

The effects of Christ's death are infinitely more excellent than those that proceeded from the Levitical sacrifices. The law had " a shadow of good things to come," Heb. x. 1; but the real virtue and efficacy is found only in Christ.

The averting of God's wrath is ascribed to his death; according to the words of the apostle, " Whom God has set forth to be a propitiation through faith in his blood, to declare his righteousness for the remission of sins that are past, through the forbearance of God; to declare, I say, at this time his righteousness; that he might be just, and the justifier of him which believeth in Jesus," Rom. iii. 25, 26; " a propitiation," $ἱλαστήριον$, the title of the mercy-seat, partly in regard it covered the tables of the law which were broken by us, to signify that by him pardon is procured for us; and principally because God was rendered propitious by the sprinkling of the blood of the sacrifice on it, and exhibited himself there, as on a throne of grace favourable to his people. For this reason he gives the name of the figure to Christ; for he alone answers the charge of the law, and interposes between justice and our guilt, and by his own blood hath reconciled God to us. Now the design of God in this appointment was to " declare his righteousness;" that is, that glorious attribute that inclines him to punish sinners; for in the legal propitiations, although the guilt of men was publicly declared in the death of the sacrifices, yet the justice of God did not fully appear, since he accepted the life of a beast in compensation for the life of a man; but in the death of Christ he hath given the most clear demonstration of his justice, a sufficient example of his hatred to sin, condemning and punishing it in the person of his beloved Son; that the whole world may acknowledge it was not from any inadvertency but merely by the dispensation of his wisdom and goodness that he forbore so long. And by the death of Christ he hath declared that glorious mystery which no created understanding could ever have conceived, that he is inflexibly just, and will not suffer sin to pass unpunished, and that he justifies those who are guilty in themselves, if by a purifying faith they receive Christ for pardon. The same apostle tells us, that Christ "hath given himself for us an offering and a sacrifice to God for a sweet smelling savour;" Προσφοράν καὶ θυσίαν, an allusion to the peace-offering and sin-offering; for the truth of both is in the death of Christ, which appeases God, and obtains the blessings that depend on his favour; Eph. v. 2. He is qualified as a priest, whose office it was to present to God an offering for appeasing his anger; he gave himself; the oblation that is added to his death, gives the complete formality of a sacrifice to it; for it is the priest who gives being to the sacrifice: and the effect of it is, to be a sweet smelling savour to God, that is to conciliate his favour to us. The same phrase is applied to the sin offering under the law. We may observe that upon this account, our reconciliation to God is attributed to the death of Christ in distinction from his glorified life; "For if, when we were enemies, we were reconciled to God by the death of his Son, much more being reconciled, we shall be saved by his life," Rom. v. 10. And the same apostle tells us, that "God was in Christ reconciling the world unto himself, not imputing their trespasses unto them; we pray you in Christ's stead, be ye reconciled to God," 1 Cor. v. 19, 20. A double reconciliation is mentioned, that of God to men, and of men to God; the first is the ground of the apostle's exhortation, the latter the effect of it. The first was obtained by the death of Christ, who by imputation had our guilt transferred upon him, and consequently our punishment ; and in consideration of it, God who is just and holy, is willing to pardon penitent believers ; the latter is by the powerful working of the Spirit, who assures men that are guilty and therefore suspicious and fearful of God's anger, that he is most willing to pardon them upon their repentance, since he hath in such an admirable manner found out the means to satisfy his justice.

The true expiation of sin is the effect of Christ's death. He is called "the Lamb of God which taketh away the sin of the world," John i. 29. Now sin may be taken away in two manners ;—by removing its guilt, and exempting the person that committed it from death ; and when this is effected by enduring the punishment that was due to sin, it is properly expiation ;—by healing the corrupt inclinations of the heart, from whence actual sins proceed. It is true, our Redeemer takes away sin in both these respects ; he delivers from the damnation and dominion of it ; for he is made of God our righteousness and sanctification. But the first sense only is convenient here ; for it is evident that the Lamb took away sin, that is, the guilt of it, by dying instead of the sinner, and had no effect for the destroying of the malignant habits of sin in the person who offered it. And it is more apparent, that this divine Lamb hath taken away the guilt of our sins, in that "he bare them in his own body on the tree ;" for the native force of the word $\alpha\iota\rho\epsilon\iota\nu$ signifies, not only to take away, but to carry and bear, which, applied to sin, is nothing else but to suffer the penalty of it. And it is to be observed, when cleansing, purifying, and washing are attributed to the blood of Christ, they have an immediate respect to the guilt of sin, and declare its efficacy to take off the obligation to punishment. Thus it is said, that his "blood cleanseth from all sin," 1 John i. 7; and that it "purgeth the conscience from dead works," Heb. ix. 14 ; and that we are washed from our sins in his blood, Rev. i. 5. The frequent sprinklings and purifications with water under the law, prefigured our cleansing from the defilements of sin by the grace of the Spirit; but the shedding of the blood of sacrifices was to purge away sins so far as they were made liable to a curse.

Our exemption from punishment, and our restoration to communion with God in grace and glory, are the fruits of his expiating sin. For this reason the blood of the Mediator " speaketh better things than that of Abel;" for that cried for revenge against the murderer, but his procures remission to believers. And as the just desert of sin is separation from the presence of God, who is the fountain of felicity, so when the guilt is taken away, the person is received into God's favour and fellowship. A representation of this is set down in the 24th of Exodus, where we have described the manner of dedicating the covenant between God and Israel by bloody sacrifices. After Moses had finished the offering, and sprinkled the blood on the altar and the people, the elders of Israel, who were forbid to approach near to the Lord, were then invited to come into his presence, and in token of reconciliation, feasted before him. Thus the eternal covenant is established by the blood of the Mediator, and all the benefits it contains, as remission of sins, freedom to draw near to the throne of grace, and the enjoyment of God in glory, are the fruits of his reconciling sacrifice.

The sum of all is this, that, as under the law, God was not appeased without shedding of blood, nor sin expiated without suffering the punishment, nor the sinner pardoned without the substitution of a sacrifice; so all these are eminently accomplished in the death of Christ. He reconciled God to us by his most precious blood, and expiated sin by enduring the curse, and hath procured our pardon by being " made sin for us." So that it is most evident, that the proper and direct end of the death of Christ was, that God might exercise his mercy to the guilty sinner in a way that is honourable to his justice.

It is objected, that if God from infinite mercy gave his Son to us, then antecedently to the coming of Christ, he had the highest love for mankind, and consequently there was no need that Christ by his death should satisfy justice, to reconcile him to us. But a clear answer may be given to this by considering—that anger and love are consistent at the same time, and may in several respects be terminated on the same subject. A father feels a double affection towards a rebellious son ; he loves him as his son, is angry with him as disobedient. Thus in our lapsed state, God had compassion on us as his creatures, and was angry with us as sinners. As the injured party he laid aside his anger, but as the preserver of justice, he required satisfaction.—We must distinguish between a love of good will and compassion, and a love of complacency. The first is that which moved God to ordain the means, that without prejudice to his other perfections, he might confer pardon and all spiritual benefits upon us; the other is that whereby he delights in us, being reconciled to him, and renewed according to his image. The first supposes him placable ; the latter, that he is appeased. There is a visible instance of this in the case of Job's friends. The Lord said to Eliphaz the Temanite, " My anger is kindled against thee and against thy two friends; for ye have not spoken of me the thing that is right, as my servant Job hath :" here is a declaration of God's anger, yet with the mixture of love ; for it follows, " therefore take unto you now seven bullocks and seven rams, and go to my servant Job, and offer up for yourselves a burnt-offering ; and my servant Job shall pray for you, for him will I accept," Job xlii. 7, 8. He loved them when he directed the way that they might be restored to his favour ; yet he was not reconciled, for then there had been no need of sacrifices to atone his anger.

It is further objected, that supposing the satisfaction of Christ to justice, both the freeness and greatness of God's love in pardoning sinners, will be much lessened. But it will appear that the divine mercy is not prejudiced in either of those respects.

The freeness of God's love is not diminished ; for that is the original mover in our salvation, and hath no cause above it to excite or draw it forth, but arises merely from his own will. This love is so absolute, that it hath no respect to the sufferings of Christ as Mediator ; for "God so loved the world, that he gave his Son" to die for us: and that which is the effect and testimony of his love, cannot be the impulsive cause of it. This first love of God to man is commended to us in Christ, who is the medium to bring it honourably about. Grace, in scripture, is never opposed to Christ's merits, but to ours. If we had made satisfaction, justice itself had absolved us; for the law having two parts, the command of our duty, which consists in a moral good, and the sanction of the punishment that is a physical evil, to do or to suffer is necessary, not both: or if we had provided a surety, such as the judge could not reject, we had been infinitely obliged to him, but not to the favour of the Judge. But it is otherwise here. God sent the Reconciler when we were enemies, and the pardon that is dispensed to us upon the account of his sufferings, is the effect of mere mercy.—We are "justified freely by his grace, through the redemption that is in Jesus Christ," Rom. iii. 24. It is pure love that appointed and accepted, that imputes and applies, his righteousness to us.

And as the freeness, so the riches of his mercy, is not lessened by the satisfaction Christ made for us. It is true, we have a pattern of God's justice, never to be parallelled, in the death of Christ: but to the severity of justice towards his only beloved Son, his clemency towards us guilty rebels is fully commensurate; for he pardons us without the expense of one drop of our blood, though the soul of Christ was poured forth as an offering for sin. Nay, hereby the divine clemency is more commended, than by an absolute forgiveness of sin without respect to satisfaction; for the honour of God being concerned in the punishment of sin, that man might not continue under a sad obligation to it, he was pleased, by the astonishing wonder of his Son's death, to vindicate his glory, that repenting believers may be justified before him. Thus in an admirable manner he satisfies justice and exalts mercy; and this could have been no other way effected; for if he had by mere sovereignty dissolved our guilt, and by his Spirit renewed his image in us, his love had eminently appeared, but his justice had not been glorified. But in our redemption they are both infinitely magnified: his love could give no more than the life of his Son, and justice required no less; for death being the "wages of sin," there could be no satisfaction without the death of our Redeemer.

CHAPTER XIV.

THE JUSTICE OF GOD IN REDEMPTION.

THE third thing to be considered, is the completeness of the satisfaction that Christ hath made, by which it will appear that God's justice as well as mercy is fully glorified in his sufferings. For the proof of this, I will consider the causes from whence the completeness of his satisfaction arises, and the effects that proceed from it, which are convincing evidences that God is fully appeased.

1. The causes of his complete satisfaction are two.

(1.) The quality of his person derives an infinite value to his obedient sufferings. Our Surety was equally God, and as truly infinite in his perfections, as the Father who was provoked by our sins; therefore he was able to make satisfaction for them. He is the Son of God, not merely in virtue of his office, or the special favour of God, for on such accounts that title is communicated to others; but his only Son by nature. The sole preeminence in gifts and dignity would give him the title of "the first-born," but not deprive them of the quality of brethren.

Now the wisdom and justice of all nations agree, that punishments receive their estimate from the quality of the persons that suffer. The poet observes, "*Pluris enim Decii, quam qui servantur ab illis,*" Juvenal; that the death of a virtuous person is more precious than of legions. Of what inestimable value then is the death of Christ, and how worthy a ransom for lost mankind! For although the Deity is impassible, yet he that was a divine person suffered. A king suffers more than a private person, although the strokes directly inflicted on his body, cannot immediately reach his honour. And it is specially to be observed, that the efficacy of Christ's blood is ascribed to his divine nature: this the apostle declares; "In whom we have redemption through his blood, even the forgiveness of sins, who is the image of the invisible God;" not an artificial image which imperfectly represents the original, as a picture that sets forth the colour and figure of a man, but not his life and nature; but the essential and exact image of his Father, that expresses all his glorious perfections in their immensity and eternity, Col. i. 14. This is testified expressly in Heb. i. 3; the Son of God, "the brightness of his glory, and the express image of his person, when he had by himself purged our sins, sat down on the right hand of the majesty on high." From hence arises the infinite difference between the sacrifices of the law, and Christ's, in their value and virtue. This with admirable emphasis is set down in Heb. ix. 13, 14; "For if the blood of bulls and of goats, and the ashes of an heifer sprinkling the unclean, sanctifieth to the purifying of the flesh; how much more shall the blood of Christ, who through the eternal Spirit, offered himself without spot to God, purge your consciences from dead works to serve the living God?" Wherein the apostle makes a double hypothesis,—that the legal sacrifices were ineffectual to purify from real guilt—that by their typical cleansing, they signified the washing away of moral guilt by the blood of Christ.

Their insufficiency to expiate sin, appears, if we consider the subject. Sin is to be expiated in the same nature wherein it was committed. Now the beasts are of an inferior rank, and have no communion with man in his nature. Or if we consider the object, God was provoked by sin, and he is a spirit, and not to be appeased by gross material things. His wisdom requires that a rational sacrifice should expiate the guilt of a rational creature: and justice is not satisfied without a proportion between the guilt and the punishment. This weakness and insufficiency of the legal sacrifices to expiate sin, is evident from their variety and repetition:

for if full remission had been obtained, " the worshippers once purged, should have had no more conscience of sin," Heb. x. 2. It was the sense of guilt, and the fear of condemnation, that required the renewing of the sacrifice. Now under the law, the ministry of the priests never came to a period or perfection. The millions of sacrifices in all ages, from the erecting of the tabernacle, to the coming of Christ, had not virtue to expiate one sin. They were only shadows which could give no refreshment to the inflamed conscience, but as they depended on Christ, the body and substance of them. But the Son of God, who " offered himself up by the eternal Spirit to the Father," is a sacrifice not only intelligent and reasonable, but incomparably more precious than the most noble creatures in earth or in heaven itself. He was priest and sacrifice in respect of both his natures; his entire person was the offerer and offering: therefore, the apostle from the excellency of his sacrifice, infers the unity of its oblation, and from thence concludes its efficacy. Christ, not " by the blood of bulls and goats, but by his own blood, entered in once into the holy place, having obtained eternal redemption for us," Heb. ix. 12; and, " by one offering he hath perfected for ever them that are sanctified," Heb. x. 14. Upon this account, God promised in the new covenant, that " their sins and iniquities" he would " remember no more," having received complete satisfaction by the sufferings of his Son. It is now said, that " once in the end of the world hath he appeared, to put away sin by the sacrifice of himself. And as it is appointed unto men once to die, but after this the judgment; so Christ was once offered to bear the sins of many, and unto them that look for him, shall he appear the second time without sin," Heb. ix. 26—28. As there is no other natural death to suffer between death and judgment, so there is no other propitiatory sacrifice between his all-sufficient death on the cross, and the last coming of our Redeemer.

There is one consideration I shall add, to show the great difference between legal sacrifices and the death of Christ, as to its saving virtue. The law absolutely forbids the eating of blood, and the people's tasting of the sin-offerings, to signify the imperfection of those sacrifices: for since they were consumed in their consecration to God's justice, and nothing was left for the nourishment of the offerers, it was a sign they could not appease God. The offerers had communion with them when they brought them to the altar, and in a manner derived their guilt to them, but they had no virtue by them in coming from it. The sinner conveyed death to the sacrifice, but did not receive life from it. But Christ, the Lamb of God, was not swallowed up in his offering to divine justice. It is his peculiar glory that he hath completely made satisfaction. We may feed upon the flesh of this precious victim, and drink his blood. As he entered into communion of death with us, so we are partakers of life by him.

(2.) The completeness of his satisfaction is grounded on the degrees of his sufferings. There was no defect in the payment he made. We owed a debt of blood to the law, and his life was offered up as a sacrifice; otherwise the law had remained in its full vigour, and justice had been unsatisfied. That a divine person hath suffered our punishment, is properly the reason of our redemption; as it is not the quality of the surety that releases the debtor from prison, but the payment which he makes in his name. The blood of Christ shed, poured forth from his veins, and offered up to God, in that precise consideration, ratifies the new testament, Matt. xxvi. 28.

The sum is—our Saviour by his death, suffered the malediction of the law, and his divine nature gave a full value to his sufferings, so that the satisfaction proceeding from them was not merely *ex pacto*, as brass money is current by composition, but *ex merito*, as pure gold hath an intrinsic worth; and God who was infinitely provoked, is infinitely pleased.

2. The effects and evidences of his complete satisfaction are,

(1.) His resurrection from the grave; for if we consider the Lord Christ in the quality of our Surety, he satisfied the law in his death; and having made complete payment of our debt, he received acquittance in his resurrection. His death appeased God, his resurrection assures men. As he rose himself, so in one concurrent action God is said to raise him, Rom. vi. 4. He was released from the grave, as from prison, by public sentence; which is an indubitable argument of the validity and acceptance of the payment made by him in our name: for being under such bonds as the justice and power of God, he could never have loosed the pains of death, if his sufferings had not been fully satisfactory, and received by him for our discharge. And it is observable, that the raising of Christ is ascribed to God as reconciled; "Now the God of peace, that brought again from the dead the great Shepherd of the sheep, through the blood of the everlasting covenant," Heb. xiii. 20. The divine power was not put forth till God was pacified. Justice incensed exposed him to death; and justice appeased freed him from the dead. And his resurrection is attributed to his blood, that being the full price of his and our liberty. In short; when inflexible justice ceases to punish, there is the strongest proof it is satisfied.

(2.) His ascent into heaven, and intercession for us, prove the completeness and all-sufficiency of his sacrifice. If he had been excluded from the divine presence, there had been just cause to suspect that anger had been still remaining in God's breast; but his admission into heaven is an infallible testimony that God is reconciled. This our Saviour produces as the argument by which the Holy Ghost will overcome the guilty fears of men, "He shall convince the world of righteousness, because I go to my Father," John xvi. 10. Christ in his suffering was numbered among transgressors; he died as a guilty person, not only in respect of the calumnies of men, but the curse of the law, and the wrath of God, which then appeared inexorable against sin; but having overcome death, and broken through the weight of the law, and retired to his Father, he made apparent the innocency of his righteous person, and that a complete righteousness is acquired by his sufferings sufficient to justify all that shall truly accept of it.

This will be more evident, by considering his entry into heaven as the true High-Priest, who carried the blood of the new covenant into the celestial sanctuary.

For opening this, we are to consider there are two parts of the priestly office—to offer sacrifice—to make intercession for the people by virtue of the sacrifice. This was performed by the high-priest in the feast of atonement, which was celebrated in the month Tisri, Lev. xvi. 14, 15. The oblation of the sacrifices was without, at the altar: the intercession was made in the holy of holies, into which none might enter but the high-priest once a year. And first he must expiate his own sins and the sins of the people by sacrifices, before he could remove the veil, and enter into that sacred and venerable place, where no sinner had right to appear. Then he was to present the precious incense, and the blood of the sacrifices, to render God favourable to them. Now these were shadows of what Christ was to perform. The holy of holies was the type of the third heaven, in its situation, quality and furniture. It was the most secret part of the tabernacle, separated by a double veil, by that which was between it and the first sanctuary, and by another that distinguished the first from the outward court. Thus the heaven of heavens is the most distant part of the universe, and separated from the lower world, by the starry heaven, and by the airy region which reaches down to the earth. Besides, the most holy part of the tabernacle was inaccessible to sinners; as heaven is styled by the apostle the place of inaccessible light. And it was the throne of God where he reigned; according to the language of the Psalmist, he dwelt "between the cherubims," Psalm lxxx. 1. The figures of the cherubim represented the myriads of holy angels that adore the incomprehensible Deity, and are always ready to execute his commands. The tables of the law were a symbol of that infinite wisdom and holiness which ordained them: and the high-priest's entering with the blood of the sacrifice, and carrying with him all the "tribes of Israel" upon his breast, signified that Jesus Christ, the true High-Priest, after he had really expiated sin by his divine sacrifice in the lower world, should enter into the eternal sanctuary with his own blood, and introduce, with him, all his people. Of this there was a marvellous sign given; for in the same moment that Christ expired, the veil of the temple that separated the oracle from the first part, was rent from the top to the bottom, to signify that the true High-Priest had authority and right to enter into heaven itself. And the special end of his ascending is expressed by the apostle, "For Christ is not entered into the holy places made with hands, which are the figures of the true; but into heaven itself, now to appear in the presence of God for us," Heb. ix. 24. As the high-priest might not enter into that sacred and terrible place, nor could propitiate God without sprinkling the blood of the slain sacrifice; so our Redeemer first perfomed what was necessary for the expiation of sin, and then passed through the visible heavens, and ascended before the throne of God to appear as our Advocate. He made an oblation of himself on the earth before he could make intercession for us in heaven, which is the consummation of his priestly office. The first was a proper sacrifice, the second is a commemoration of it; therefore he is said to appear before his Father by sacrifice, Heb. ix. 23—26.

Besides what hath been discoursed of the order and dependence of these parts of his priestly office, which proves that he had accomplished the expiation of sin before he was admitted into heaven to intercede for us, there are two other considerations which manifest the completeness of his satisfaction. The manner of it: he doth not appear in the form of a suppliant upon his knees before the throne, offering up tears and strong cries as in the days of his flesh, but he sits at God's right hand making intercession for us. He solicits our salvation, not as a pure favour to him, but as the price of his sufferings, and as due to his infinite merit. His blood in the same manner pleads for our pardon, as the blood of righteous Abel called for vengeance against the murderer; not by an articulate voice, but by suing to justice for a full recompense of it. In short; his intercession is the continual representation of his most worthy passion. The omnipotent efficacy of his intercession proves that God is fully satisfied. He frees us from the greatest evils, and obtains for us the greatest good, in quality of Mediator. "If any man sin, we have an Advocate with the Father, Jesus Christ the righteous; and he is the propitiation for our sins, and not for ours only, but also for the sins of the whole world," 1 John ii. 1, 2. He disarms the anger of God, and hinders the effects of his indignation against repenting sinners. Now the prevalence of his mediation is grounded on the perfection of his sacrifice. The blessedness of heaven is conferred on believers according to his will; "Father, I will that those also, whom thou hast given me, be with me where I am, that they may behold my glory," John xvii. 24. His request is effectual, not only because he is God's Son and in highest favour with him, but for his meritorious sufferings.

It is for this reason that the office of Mediator is incommunicable to any creature. "There is one God, and one Mediator between God and men, the man Christ Jesus, who gave himself a ransom for all," 1 Tim. ii. 5. The apostle makes a parallel between the unity of the Mediator and of the Deity, which is most sacred and inviolable. For the right of intercession, as it is an authoritative act, is founded in redemption; they cannot be divided. And we may observe, by the way, how the popish doctrine that erects as many advocates, as angels, or saints, or whoever are canonized, is guilty of impiety and folly:—of impiety, in taking the sovereign crown from the head of Christ to adorn others with it, as if they had more credit with God or compassion for men; and of folly, in expecting benefits by their intercession, who have no satisfactory merit to purchase them. The numerous advocates that are conceived by superstitious persons in their fancies, are like the counterfeit suns, that are drawn in the clouds by reflection as in a glass, which although they shine with a considerable brightness, yet they are suns in appearance only, and derive no quickening influences to the earth. The blessed spirits above, do enjoy a dependent light from the Sun of righteousness, yet convey no benefits to men by meritorious interceding for them. We obtain grace and glory only upon the requests of our Redeemer. Briefly, the acts of his priesthood respect the attributes, which in a special manner are to be glorified in our salvation. By his death he made satisfaction to justice, by his intercession he solicits mercy for us; and they both join together with the same readiness and warmth to dispense the benefits which he purchased for his people.

(3.) The completeness of his satisfaction is fully proved by the glorious issue of his sufferings. This will be most evident by considering the connexion and dependence which his glory hath upon his humiliation; and that is twofold. 1. A dependence of order. His abasement and sufferings were to precede his majesty and power; as in nature things pass from a lower state to perfection. This order was necessary: for being originally " in the form of God," it was impossible he should be advanced, if he did not voluntarily descend from his glory, that so he might be capable of exaltation. He was first made " a little lower than the angels," and afterwards raised above them. 2. A dependence of efficacy. Glory is the reward of his suffering. This is expressly declared by the apostle; Christ "humbled himself, and became obedient unto death, even the death of the cross, wherefore God also hath highly exalted him, and given him a name which is above every name, that at the name of Jesus every knee should bow;" the mark of that homage that all creatures pay to him, Phil. ii. 8. 9. This exaltation is correspondent to the degrees of his abasement. His body was restored to life and immortality, and ascended on a bright cloud. God's chariot being attended with angels, and the everlasting gates opened to receive the king of glory, he is set down " on the right hand of the throne of the Majesty in the heavens;" Heb. viii. 1; this signifies that divine dignity to which he is advanced, next to his Father; for God being an infinite spirit, hath neither right nor left hand in strict sense. Our Redeemer's honour is the same, and his empire of the same extent with his Father's. Thus the apostle interprets the words of the Psalmist, Psalm cx. 1; that the Messiah should sit at the right hand of God, till he made his enemies his footstool, by reigning; " for he must reign till he hath put all his enemies under his feet," 1 Cor. xv. 25. And Peter tells us, " that the Father hath made him Lord and Christ:" that is, by a sovereign trust hath committed to him the government of the church and the world; not divesting himself of his essential dominion, but exercising it by

Christ. The height of this dignity is emphatically set forth by the apostle, Eph. i. 21; the Father hath seated him "at his own right hand in the heavenly places, far above all principality, and power, and might, and dominion," (which titles signify the several degrees of glory among the angels,) "and every name that is named not only in this world, but also, in that which is to come:" that is, hath given him a transcendent and incommunicable glory, the use of names being to signify the quality of persons. In short; he is made the head of the church and judge of the world: angels and men shall stand before the tribunal, and receive their eternal decision from him.

Now in the economy of our Mediator, his humiliation was the cause of his exaltation upon a double account; 1. as the death of Christ was an expression of such humility, such admirable obedience to God, such divine love to men, that it was perfectly pleasing to his Father, and his power being equal to his love, he infinitely rewarded it; 2. the death of Christ was for satisfaction to justice, and when he had done that work, he was to enter into rest. It behoved Christ to suffer, and "to enter into his glory," Luke xxiv. 26. It is true, divine honour was due to him upon another title, as the Son of God; but the receiving of it was deferred by dispensation for a time. First, he must redeem us, and then reign. The scripture is very clear in referring his actual possession of glory, as a just consequent to his complete expiation of sin; "When he had by himself purged our sins, he sat down on the right hand of the Majesty on high," Heb. i. 3. "After he had offered one sacrifice for sins, for ever sat down on the right hand of God," Heb. x. 12.

And not only the will of the Father, but the nature of the thing itself required this way of proceeding: for Jesus Christ by voluntary susception, undertaking to satisfy the law for us, as he was obliged to suffer what was necessary, in order to our redemption, so it was reasonable, after justice was satisfied, that the human nature should be freed from its infirmities, and the glory of his divine be so conspicuous, that every tongue should confess that Jesus, who was despised on earth, is supreme Lord.

The apostle sums up all together, in that triumphant challenge, Rom. viii. 33, 34; "Who shall lay any thing to the charge of God's elect? It is God that justifieth: who is he that condemneth? It is Christ that died, yea, rather, that is risen again; who is even at the right hand of God, who also maketh intercession for us."

(4.) The excellent benefits which God reconciled, bestows upon us, are the effects and evidences of the completeness of Christ's satisfaction; and these are pardon of sin, grace, and glory. The apostle tells us, that "the law made nothing perfect:" all its sacrifices and ceremonies could not expiate the guilt, nor cleanse the stain of sin, nor open heaven for us; which three are requisite to our perfection.—But "Christ, by one offering, hath perfected forever, them that are sanctified," Heb. x. 14. By him we obtain full justification, renovation and communion with God: therefore, his sacrifice, the meritorious cause of procuring them, must be perfect.

First; our justification is the effect of his death, for the obligation of the law is made void by it. God forgives our trespasses, "blotting out the handwriting of ordinances that was against us; and took it out of the way, nailing it to his cross," Col. ii. 14. The terms are used, that are proper to the cancelling of a civil bond. The killing letter of the law is abolished by the blood of the cross; the nails and the spear have rent it in pieces, to signify that its condemning power is taken away.

Now the infinite virtue of his death in taking away the guilt of sin will more fully appear, if we consider, that it hath procured pardon for sins committed in all ages of world. Without the intervention of a sacrifice, God would not pardon, and the most costly that were offered up by sinners, were of no value to make compensation to justice; but the blood of Christ was the only propitiation for sins committed before his coming. The apostle tells us, he was not obliged to "offer himself often, as the high-priest entered into the holy place every year with the blood of others, but now once in the end of the world hath he appeared to put away sin by the sacrifice of himself," Heb. ix. 25, 26. The direct sense of the words is, that the virtue of his sacrifice extended itself to all times; for otherwise in regard men have always needed propitiation, he must have suffered often since the creation of the world. And if it be asked, how his death had a saving influence before he actually suffered, the answer is clear—we must consider the death of Christ, not as a natural, but moral cause; it is not as a medicine that heals, but as a ransom that frees a captive. Natural causes operate nothing before their real existence; but it is not necessary that moral causes should have an actual being; it is sufficient that they shall be, and that the person with whom they are effectual, accept the promise; as a captive is released upon assurance given that he will send his ransom, though it is not actually deposited. Thus the death of Christ was available to purchase pardon for believers before his coming; for he interposed as their Surety, and God, to whom all things are present, knew the accomplishment of it in the appointed time. He is therefore called the "Lamb slain from the foundation of the world," not only in respect of God's decree, but his efficacy. The salvation we derive from him, was ever in him. He appeared under the empire of Augustus, and died under Tiberius, but he was a Redeemer in all ages, otherwise the comparison were not just, that as by Adam all die, so by Christ all are made alive. 1 Cor. xv. 12.

It is true, under the Old Testament they had not a clear knowledge of him, yet they enjoyed the benefit of his unvalued sufferings; for the medium by which the benefits our Redeemer purchased are conveyed to men, is not the exact knowledge of what he did and suffered, but sincere faith in the promise of God. Now the divine revelation being the rule and measure of our faith, such a degree was sufficient to salvation, as answered the general discovery of grace. Believers depended upon God's goodness to pardon them in such a way as was honourable to his justice. They had some general knowledge that the Messiah should come, and bring salvation. Abraham rejoiced to see the day of Christ; Moses valued the afflictions of Christ, more than the treasures of Egypt; and believers in general are described to be "waiters for the consolation of Israel." In short, the Jewish and Christian church are essentially one; they differ no more than the morning and evening star, which is the same, but is diversely called from its appearance before the sun-rising or after its setting: so our faith respects a Saviour that is past, theirs respected him as to come.

Besides, the saving virtue of his death as it reaches to all former, so to all succeeding ages. "He is the same, yesterday, to-day, and for ever," not only in respect of his person, but his office. The virtue of the legal sacrifices expired with the offering; upon a new sin they were repeated. Their imperfection is argued from their repetition. But the precious oblation of Christ hath an everlasting efficacy to obtain full pardon for believers. His blood is as powerful to propitiate God, as if it were this day shed upon the cross. He is able to save to perpetuity all that shall address to God by him; since he ever lives to make intercession. The pardon that he once purchased, shall ever be applied to contrite believers. The covenant that was sealed with his blood is eternal, and the mercies contained in it.

The perfection of his sacrifice is evident by its expiating universally the guilt of all transgressions. It is true, sins in their own nature are different; some have a crimson guilt attending them, and accordingly conscience should be affected; but the grace of the gospel makes no difference. The apostle tells us, that "the blood of Christ cleanseth from all sin;" whatever the kinds, degrees, and circumstances are. As the deluge overflowed the highest mountains, as well as the least hills, so pardoning mercy covers sins of the first magnitude, as well as the smallest. Under the law, one sacrifice could expiate but one offence, though but against a carnal commandment; but this one washes away the guilt of all sins against the moral law. And in that dispensation no sacrifices were instituted for idolatry, adultery, murder, and other crimes, which were certainly punished with death; but under the gospel, sins, of what quality soever, if repented of, are pardoned. The apostle having reckoned up idolaters, adulterers, and many other notorious sinners that shall not inherit the kingdom of heaven, tells the Corinthians, that such were some of them; but they were sanctified, and justified in the name of the Lord Jesus Christ, 1 Cor. vi. 11. It is true, those who sin against the Holy Ghost, are excepted from pardon; but the reason is, because the death of Christ was not appointed for the expiation of it; and there being no sacrifice, there is no satisfaction, and consequently no pardon, Heb. x. 26. The wisdom and justice of God requires this severity against them; for if "he that despised Moses' law died without mercy, of how much sorer punishment shall he be thought worthy, who hath trodden under foot the Son of God, and hath counted the blood of the covenant wherewith he was sanctified an unholy thing, and hath done despite to the Spirit of grace?" Heb. x. 28, 29; that is, they renounce their Redeemer, as if he were not the Son of God, and virtually consent to the cruel sentence passed against him, as if he had blasphemed when he declared himself to be so; and thereby out-sin his sufferings. How reasonable is it they should be for ever deprived of the benefits, who obstinately reject the means that purchased them!

Secondly; the death of Christ hath procured grace for men. We made a forfeiture of our original holiness, and were righteously deprived of it: and till divine justice was appeased, all influences of grace were suspended. Now the death of Christ opened heaven, and brought down the Spirit, who is the principle of renovation in us. The world lay in wickedness, as a carcass in the grave, insensible of its horror and corruption, 1 John v. 19. The holy Spirit hath inspired it with a new life, and by a marvellous change hath caused purity to succeed pollution.

Thirdly; the receiving of believers into heaven is a convincing proof of the all-sufficiency of his sacrifice; for justice will not permit that glory and immortality, which are the privileges of the righteous, should be given to guilty and defiled creatures. Therefore our Saviour's first and greatest work was to remove the bar that excluded us from the place of felicity. It is more difficult to justify a sinner, than to glorify a saint. The goodness of God inclines him to bestow happiness on those who are not obnoxious to the law; but his justice was to be atoned by sufferings. Now what stronger argument can there be, that God is infinitely pleased with what his Son hath done and suffered for his people, than the taking of them into his presence to see his glory? The apostle sets down this order in the work of our redemption, that Christ " being made perfect" by sufferings; that is, having consummated that part of his office which respected the expiation of sin; " he became the author of eternal salvation unto all them that obey him," Heb. v. 9.

To sum up all, it is observable, that the scripture attributes to the death of Christ, not only satisfaction, whereby we are redeemed from punishment; but such a redundant merit, as purchases for us adoption, and all the glorious prerogatives of the children of God. Upon these accounts his blood hath a double efficacy; as the blood of the covenant, it procured our peace, Heb. xiii. 20; as the blood of the testament, Luke xxii. 20, it conveys to us a title to heaven itself; according to that of Paul, " We have boldness to enter into the holiest by his blood," Heb. x. 19.

I will remove two slender prejudices against this doctrine.

1. That repentance and faith are required in order to the partaking of the precious benefits which Christ hath purchased, doth not lessen the merit of his death, and the completeness of the satisfaction made to God by it. For we must consider, there is a great difference between the payment of that which the law requires by the debtor, and the payment of that which was not in the original obligation by another in his stead. Upon the payment of the first, actual freedom immediately follows. If a debtor pays the sum he owes, or a criminal endures the punishment of the law, they are actually discharged, and never liable to be sued or suffer again; but when the sum that the law requires is not paid, but something else, by another, the release of the guilty is suspended upon those conditions, which he that freely makes satis-

faction, and the governor who by favour accepts it, are pleased to appoint. Now it is thus in the transaction of our redemption. Christ laid down his life for us, and this was not the very thing in strict sense that the law required; for, according to the threatening, the soul that sins shall die; the delinquent, in his own person, was to suffer the penalty; and there was no necessity, natural or moral, that obliged God to admit of his satisfaction for our discharge, but in rigour of justice he might refuse it. If the law had expressed that the sinner or his surety should suffer, there had been no need of a "better covenant." But in this the grace of God so illustriously appears, that by his appointment the punishment of the guilty was transferred to the innocent, who voluntarily undertook for them. In this respect God truly pardons sin, though he received entire satisfaction, for he might in right have refused it.

Now these things being supposed, although the blood of Christ was a price so precious that it can be valued by God only that received it, and might worthily have redeemed a thousand worlds, yet the effects of it are to be dispensed according to the eternal covenant between the Father and the Son; and the tenor of it is revealed in the gospel, viz., that repentance and faith are the conditions, upon which the obtaining of pardon of sin, and all the blessings which are the consequence of it, depends; thus Christ, who makes satisfaction, and God, that accepts it, declare. The commission of the apostles from his own mouth, was, to preach "repentance and remission of sins in his name to all nations," Luke xxiv. 47; and he was exalted by God "to be a Prince and Saviour, for to give repentance to Israel, and forgiveness of sins," Acts v. 31.

The establishing of this order is not a mere positive command, wherein the will of the Lawgiver is the sole ground of our duty; but there is a special congruity and reason in the nature of the thing itself; for Christ hath satisfied justice, that God may exercise pardoning mercy in such a manner as is suitable to his other perfections. Now it is contrary to his wisdom to dispense the precious benefits of his Son's blood to impenitent unbelievers; to give such rich pearls, and so dearly bought, to swine that will trample them under their feet; to bestow salvation on those who despise the Saviour. It is contrary to his holiness to forgive those who will securely abuse his favour, as if his pardon were a privilege and license to sin against him. Nay, final impenitency is unpardonable to mercy itself; for the objects of justice and mercy cannot be the same. Now an impenitent sinner is necessarily under the avenging justice of God. It is no disparagement to his omnipotency that he cannot save such; for although God can do whatsoever he will, yet he can will nothing but what is agreeable to his nature. Not that there is any law above God that obliges him to act, but he is a law to himself. And the more excellent his perfections are, the less he can contradict them. As it is no reflection upon his power that he cannot die, neither is it that he can do nothing unbecoming his perfections. On the contrary, it implies weakness to be liable to any such act. Thus supposing the creature holy, it is impossible but he should love it; not that he owes any thing to the creature, but in regard he is infinitely good: and if impenitent and obstinate in sin, he cannot but hate and punish it; not that he is accountable for his actions, but because he is infinitely just. And from hence it appears, that the requiring of repentance and faith in order to the actual partaking of the blessings our Redeemer purchased, doth not diminish the value of his satisfaction, they being not the causes of pardon, but necessary qualifications in the subject that receives it.

2. It doth not lessen the completeness of his satisfaction, that believers are liable to afflictions and death; for these are continued, according to the agreement between God and our Redeemer, for other ends than satisfaction to justice, which was fully accomplished by him. This will appear by several considerations.—Some afflictions have not the nature of a punishment, but are intended only for the exercise of their graces; "that the trial of their faith, patience, and hope, being much more precious than of gold that perisheth, though it be tried with fire, might be found unto praise," 1 Peter i. 7.

Now these afflictions are the occasion of their joy, and in order to their glory. Of this kind are all the sufferings that Christians endure for the promotion of the gospel. Thus the apostles esteemed themselves dignified in suffering what was contumelious and reproachful for the name of Christ, Acts v. 41. And Paul interprets it as a special favour, that God called forth the Philippians to the combat: "To you it is given in the behalf of Christ to suffer," Phil. i. 29: not only the graces of faith and fortitude, but the affliction was given. So believers are declared happy, when they are "partakers of Christ's sufferings: for the spirit of glory resteth on them," 1 Peter iv. 14. Now it is evident that afflictions of this nature are no punishments; for since it is essential to punishment to be inflicted for a fault, and every fault hath a turpitude in it, it necessarily follows, that punishment, which is the brand of a crime, must be always attended with infamy, and the sufferer under shame. But Christians are honourable by their sufferings for God, as they conform them to the "image of his Son," who was consecrated by sufferings. Afflictions are sent sometimes not with respect to a sin committed, but to prevent the commission of it: and this distinguishes them from punishments; for the law deters from evil, not by inflicting, but threatening the penalty. But in the divine discipline there is another reason; God afflicts to restrain from sin: as Paul had "a thorn in the flesh" to prevent pride, 2 Cor. xii. 7. Those evils that are inflicted on believers for sin, do not diminish the power and value of Christ's passion; for we must distinguish between punishments which are merely castigatory for the good of the offender, and those which are purely vindictive for the just satisfaction of the law. Now believers are liable to the first, but are freed from the other; for "Christ hath redeemed them from the curse of the law, being made a curse for them."

The Popish doctrine of satisfaction to offended justice by our suffering temporal evils, is attended with many pernicious consequences.—It robs the cross of Christ of one part of its glory; as if something were left us to make up in the degrees and virtue of his sufferings. —It reflects on God's justice, as if he exacted two different satisfactions for sin; the one from Christ, our Surety, the other from the sinner.—It disparages his mercy, in making him to punish whom he pardons, and to inflict a penalty after the sin is remitted.—It is dangerous to man, by feeding a false presumption in him; as if by the merit of his sufferings, he could expiate sin, and obtain part of that salvation which we entirely owe to the death of our Redeemer.

The difference between chastisements, and purely vindictive punishments, appears in three things:

1. In the causes from whence they proceed. The severest sufferings of the godly are not the effects of the divine vengeance. It is true, they are evidences of God's displeasure against them for sin, but not of hatred; for being reconciled to them in Christ, he bears an unchangeable affection to them, and love cannot hate, though it may be angry. The motive that excites God to correct them, is love: according to that testimony of the apostle, "Whom the Lord loveth he chasteneth," Heb. xii. 6. As sometimes out of his severest displeasure he forbears to strike, and condemns obstinate sinners to prosperity here, so from the tenderest mercy he afflicts his own. But purely vindictive judgments proceed from mere wrath.

2. They differ in their measures. The evils that believers suffer are always proportioned to their strength. They are not the sudden eruptions of anger, but deliberate dispensations. David deprecates God's judgment as it is opposed to favour: "Enter not into judgment with thy servant, O Lord," Psalm cxliii. 2; and Jeremiah desires God's judgment, as it is opposed to fury: "O Lord, correct me, but with thy judgment, not in thine anger," Jer. x. 24. It is the gracious promise of God to David, 2 Sam. vii. 14, with respect to Solomon: "If he commit iniquity, I will chasten him with the rod of men, and with the stripes of the children of men;" that is, chastise him moderately; for in the style of the scripture, as things are magnified by the epithet "divine" or "of God," as "the cedars of God," that is, very tall; and Nineveh is called the city of God, that is, very great: so, to signify things that are in a mediocrity, the

scripture uses the epithet "human" or "of men." And according to the rule of opposition, the rod of God is an extraordinary affliction which destroys the sinner; it is such a punishment as a man can neither inflict nor endure: but the rod of men is a moderate correction, that doth not exceed the strength of the patient. But every purely vindictive punishment which the law pronounces, is in proportion to the nature of the crime, not the strength of the criminal.

3. They are distinguished by the intention and end of God in inflicting them.—In chastisements God primarily designs the profit of his people, that they may be "partakers of his holiness," Heb. xii. 10. When they are secure and carnal, he awakens conscience by the sharp voice of the rod, to reflect upon sin, to make them observant for the future, to render their affections more indifferent to the world, and stronger towards heaven. The apostle expresses the nature of chastisements, " When we are judged, we are chastened" or instructed " by the Lord," 1 Cor. xi. 32: they are more lively lessons than those which are by the word alone, and make a deeper impression upon the heart. David acknowledges, " Before I was afflicted, I went astray; but now I have kept thy word," Psalm cxix. 67. Corrupt nature makes God's favours pernicious, but his grace makes our punishments profitable. Briefly, they are not satisfactions for what is passed, but admonitions for the time to come. But purely vindictive judgments are not inflicted for the reformation of an offender, but to preserve the honour of the sovereign, and public order, and to make compensation for the breach of the law. If any advantage accrue to the offender, it is accidental, and beside the intention of the judge. The end of chastisements upon believers is to prevent their final destruction: " When we are judged, we are chastened of the Lord, that we may not be condemned with the world," 1 Cor. xi. 32. And this sweetens and allays all their sufferings; as the Psalmist declares, " Let the righteous smite me; it shall be a kindness: and let him reprove me; it shall be an excellent oil, which shall not break my head," Psalm cxli. 5. But the vindictive punish-

ment of a malefactor is not to prevent his condemnation; for death is sometimes the sentence. In this respect the temporal evils that befall the wicked and the godly, though materially the same, yet legally differ; for to the wicked they are so many earnests of the complete payment they shall make to justice in another world, the beginning of eternal sorrows; but to the godly they are in order to their salvation. They are as the Red Sea, through which the Israelites passed to the land of promise, but the Egyptians were drowned in it. Briefly, their sufferings differ as much in their issue, as the kingdoms of heaven and hell.

That death remains to believers, doth not lessen the perfection of Christ's satisfaction. It is true, considered absolutely, it is the revenge of the law for sin, and the greatest temporal evil; so that it may seem strange, that those who are redeemed by an all-sufficient ransom, should pay this tribute to the king of terrors: but the nature of it is changed. It is a curse to the wicked inflicted for satisfaction to justice, but a privilege to believers: as God appointing the rainbow to be the sign of his covenant, that he would drown the world no more, ordained the same waters to be the token of his mercy, which were the instrument of his justice. "Blessed are the dead that die in the Lord," Rev. xiv. 13. And the Psalmist tells us, that "precious in the sight of the Lord is the death of his saints," Psalm xvi. 15. Christ hath taken away what is truly destructive in it. It is continued for their advantage. Corruption hath so depraved the sensitive appetite, that during our natural state we are not entirely freed from it: but death, that destroys the natural frame of the body, puts an end to sin. And in this respect there is a great difference between the death of Christ and of believers; the end of his was to remove the guilt of sin, of theirs to extinguish the relics of it. It is a delivery from temporal evils, and an entrance into glory. Death and despair seize on the wicked at once, "but the righteous hath hope in his death." The grave shall give up his spoils at the last. It retains the body for a time, not to destroy, but purify it. Our Saviour tells us, that "whosoever believeth on him shall

not see death for he will raise him up at the last day."
He that dies a man, shall revive an angel, clothed with
light and immortality.

I will conclude this argument with the words of St.
Austin, Lib. 13. de Civ. Dei, c. 4; *" Ablato criminis
nexu, relicta est mors. Nunc vero majore et mirabiliore gratia Salvatoris in usum justitiæ peccati
pœna est conversa; tum enim dictum est homini;
' Morieris si peccaveris ;' nunc dictum est martyri ;
' Morere ne pecces.' Et sic per ineffabilem Dei misericordiam et ipsa pœna vitiorum transit in arma
virtutis, et fit justi meritum etiam supplicium peccatoris.*" Although the guilt of sin is removed, yet death
remains; but by the admirable grace of the Redeemer,
the punishment of sin is made an advantage to holiness.
The law threatened man with death if he sinned; the
gospel commands a martyr to die that he may not sin.
And thus by the unspeakable mercy of God, the punishment of vice becomes the security of virtue; and that
which was revenge upon the sinner, gives to the righteous a title to a glorious reward.

CHAPTER XV.

PRACTICAL INFERENCES.

I. FROM hence we may discover more clearly the evil of
sin, which no sacrifice could expiate but the blood of the
Son of God. It is true, the internal malignity of sin, abstracted from its dreadful effects, is most worthy of our
hatred; for it is in its own nature direct enmity against
God, and obscures the glory of all his attributes. It is
the violation of his majesty, who is the universal Sovereign of heaven and earth; a contrariety to his holiness,
which shines forth in his law; a despising of his goodness, the attractive to obedience; the contempt of his
omniscience, which sees every sin when it is committed;
the slighting of his terrible justice and power, as if the
sinner could secure himself from his indignation; a

denial of his truth, as if the threatening were a vain terror to scare men from sin. And all this done voluntarily, to please an irregular, corrupt appetite, by a despicable creature, who absolutely depends upon God for his being and happiness.

These considerations seriously pondered, are most proper to discover the extremity of its evil; but sensible demonstrations are most powerful to convince and affect us: and those are taken from the fearful punishments that are inflicted for sin. Now the torments of hell, which are the just and full recompense of sin, are not sensible till they are inevitable; and temporal judgments cannot fully declare the infinite displeasure of God against the wilful contempt of his authority. But in the sufferings of Christ it is expressed to the utmost. If justice itself had rent the heavens, and come down in the most visible terror to revenge the rebellions of men, it could never have made stronger impressions upon us than the death of Christ duly considered. The destruction of the world by water, the miraculous burning of Sodom and Gomorrah by showers of fire, and all the other most terrible judgments, do not afford such a sensible instruction of the evil of sin. If we regard the dignity of his person and the depth of his sufferings, he is an unparalleled example of God's indignation for the breach of his holy law: for he that was the Son of God and the Lord of Glory, was made a man of sorrows. He endured derision, scourgings, stripes, and at last a cruel and cursed death. The Holy of Holies was crucified between two thieves. By how much the life of Christ was more precious than the lives of all men, so much in his death doth the wrath of God appear more fully against sin, than it would in the destruction of the whole world of sinners. And his spiritual sufferings infinitely exceeded all his corporeal. The impressions of wrath that were inflicted by God's immediate hand upon his soul, forced from him those strong cries, that moved all the powers of heaven and earth with compassion. If the curtain were drawn aside, and we could look into the chambers of death, where sinners lie down in sorrow for ever, and hear the woful expressions and deep complaints of the damned, with what horror and distraction they speak of their torments, we could not have a fuller testimony of God's infinite displeasure against sin, than in the anguish and agonies of our Redeemer; for whatever his sufferings were in kind, yet in their degree and measure they were equally terrible with those that condemned sinners endure. Now, how is it possible that rational agents should freely, in the open light, for perishing vanities, dare to commit sin? Can they avoid or endure the wrath of an incensed God? If God spared not his Son when he came in the similitude of sinful flesh, how shall sinners who are deeply and universally defiled escape? Can they fortify themselves against the supreme Judge? Can they encounter with the fury of the Almighty, the apprehensions of which made the soul of Christ heavy unto death? Have they patience to bear that for ever, which was to Christ, who had the strength of the Deity to support him, intolerable for a few hours? If it were so with the green tree, what will become of the dry when exposed to the fiery trial? If he that was holy and innocent suffered so dreadfully, what must they expect, who add impenitency to their guilt, and live in the bold commission of sin, without reflection and remorse? What prodigious madness is it to drink iniquity like water, as a harmless thing, when it is a poison so deadly that the least drop of it brings certain ruin? What desperate folly, to have slight apprehensions of that which is attended with the first and second death? Nothing but unreasonable infidelity and inconsideration can make men venturous to provoke the "living God," who is infinitely sensible of their sins, and who both can and will most terribly punish them for ever.

II. The strictness of divine justice appears, that required satisfaction equivalent to the desert of sin.

The natural notion of the Deity, as the governor of the world, instructed the heathens, that the transgression of his laws was worthy of death, Rom. i. 32. This proves that the obligation to punishment doth not arise from the mere will of God, which is only discovered by revelation; but is founded in the nature of things, and by its own light is manifested to reasonable creatures. From hence they inferred, that it was not becoming the divine nature, as qualified with the relation of supreme Ruler, to pardon sin without satisfaction. This appears by the sacrifices and ceremonies, the religions and expiations which were performed by the most ignorant nations. And although they infinitely abused themselves in the conceit they had of their pretended efficacy and virtue, yet the universal consent of mankind in the belief that satisfaction was necessary, declares it to be true. This, as other natural doctrines, is more fully revealed by scripture. Under the law, " without shedding of blood there was no remission :" not that common blood could make satisfaction for sin, but God commanded there should be a visible mark of its necessity in the worship offered to him, and a prefiguration that it should be accomplished by a sacrifice eternally efficacious.

And the economy of our salvation clearly proves, that to preserve the honour of God's government, it was most fit sin should be punished, that sinners might be pardoned; for nothing was more repugnant to the will of God absolutely considered, than the death of his beloved Son; and the natural will of Christ was averse from it. What then moved that infinite wisdom, which wills nothing but what is perfectly reasonable, to ordain that event? Why should it take so great a circuit, if the way was so short, that by pure favour, without satisfaction, sin might have been pardoned? Our Saviour declares the necessity of his suffering death, supposing the merciful will of his Father to save us, when he saith, that " as Moses lifted up the serpent in the wilderness, even so must the Son of man be lifted up, that whosoever believeth in him should not perish." It is true, since God had foretold and prefigured his death by the oracles and actions under the law, it necessarily came to pass; but to consider things exactly, the unchangeable truth of types and prophecies is not the primitive and main reason of the necessity of things, but only a sign of the certainty of the event. In strictness, things do not arrive because of their prediction, but are foretold because they shall arrive. It is apparent there was a divine decree before the prophecies; and that in the light of God's infinite knowledge things are, before they were foretold. So it is not said, a man must be of a ruddy complexion, because his picture is so; but on the contrary because he is ruddy, his picture must be so. That Christ by dying on the cross should redeem man, was the reason that the serpent of brass was erected on a pole to heal the Israelites, and not on the contrary. Briefly, the apostle supposes this necessity of satisfaction is an evident principle, when he proves wilful apostates to be incapable of salvation, " because there remaineth no more sacrifice for sin ;" for the consequence were of no force, if sin might be pardoned without sacrifice, that is, without satisfaction.

III. This account of Christ's death takes off the scandal of the cross, and changes the offence into admiration.

It was foretold of Christ, " that he should be a stone of stumbling, and a rock of offence ;" not a just cause, but an occasion of offence to the corrupt hearts of men; and principally for his sufferings. The Jews were pleased with the titles of honour given to the Messiah, that he should be a king powerful and glorious; but that poverty, disgrace, and the suffering of death should be his character, they could not endure: therefore they endeavoured to pervert the sense of the prophets. His disciples who attended him in his mean state, expected those sad appearances would terminate in visible glory and greatness; but when they saw him arrested by his enemies, condemned and crucified, this was so opposite to their expectation, that they fainted under the disappointment; and when Christ was preached to the Gentile world, they rejected him with scorn. His death seemed so contrary to the dignity of his person and design of his office, that they could not relish the doctrine of the gospel. They judged it absurd to expect life from one that was subjected to death, and blessedness from him that was made a curse. To those who look upon the death of Christ with the eyes of carnal wisdom and according to the laws of corrupt reason, it appears folly and weakness, and most unworthy of God; but if we consider it in its principles and ends, all these prejudices vanish, and we clearly discover it to be the most noble and eminent effect of the wisdom, power, goodness, and justice of God. Accordingly the apostle tells the Jews, "Him being delivered by the determinate counsel and foreknowledge of God, ye have taken, and by wicked hands have crucified and slain," Acts ii. 23. The instruments were deeply guilty in shedding that immaculate blood, yet we must not terminate our thoughts on them, but ascend to the supreme Disposer, by whose wise and holy decree that event came to pass. To the eye of sense it was a spectacle of horror, that a perfect innocent should be cruelly tormented; but to the eye of faith, under that sad and ignominious appearance, there was a divine mystery, able to raise our wonder and ravish our affections; for he that was nailed to the cross, was really the Son of God and the Saviour of men; his death with all the penal circumstances of dishonour and pain, is the only expiation of sin, and satisfaction to justice. He, by offering up his blood, appeased the wrath of God, quenched the flaming sword that made paradise inaccessible to us; he took away sin, the true dishonour of our natures, and purchased for us the graces of the Spirit; the richest ornaments of the reasonable creature. The doctrine of the cross is the only foundation of the gospel, that unites all its parts and supports the whole building. It is the cause of our righteousness and peace, of our redemption and reconciliation. How blessed an exchange have the merits of his sufferings made with those of our sins! Life instead of death, glory for shame, and happiness for misery. For this reason the apostle with vehemence declares that to be the sole ground of his boasting and triumph, which others esteemed a cause of blushing; "God forbid that I should glory, save in the cross of Jesus Christ," Gal. vi. 14. He rejects with extreme detestation the mention of any other thing, as the cause of his happiness and matter of his glory. The cross was a tree of death to Christ, and of life to us. The supreme wisdom is justified of its children.

IV. The satisfaction of divine justice by the sufferings of Christ, affords the strongest assurance to man, who is a guilty and suspicious creature, that God is most ready to pardon sin.

There is in the natural conscience, when opened by a piercing conviction of sin, such a quick sense of guilt and God's justice, that it can never have an entire confidence in his mercy till justice be atoned. From hence the convinced sinner is restlessly inquisitive how to find out the way of reconciliation with a righteous God. Thus he is represented inquiring by the prophet, " Wherewith shall I come before the Lord, and bow myself before the high God? Shall I come before him with burnt-offerings, with calves of a year old? Will the Lord be pleased with thousands of rams, or with ten thousands of rivers of oil? Shall I give my first born for my transgression, the fruit of my body for the sin of my soul?" Mic. vi. 6, 7. The scripture tells us, that some consumed their children to render their idols favourable to them. But all these means were ineffectual; their most costly sacrifices were only food for the fire. Nay, instead of expiating their old, they committed new sins; and were so far from appeasing, that they inflamed the wrath of God by their cruel oblations. But in the gospel there is the most rational and easy way propounded for the satisfaction of God and the justification of man. "The righteousness of faith speaketh on this wise, Say not in thine heart, Who shall ascend into heaven? (that is, to bring Christ down from above:) or who shall descend into the deep? (that is, to bring up Christ again from the dead:) but if thou shalt confess with thy mouth the Lord Jesus, and shalt believe in thine heart that God hath raised him from the dead, thou shalt be saved," Rom. x. 6, 7, 9. The apostle sets forth the anxiety of an awakened sinner; he is at a loss to find out a way to escape judgment; for things that are on the surface of the earth, or floating on the waters, are within our view, and may be obtained; but those which are above our understanding to discover, or power to obtain, are proverbially said to be in the heavens above, or in the deeps. And it is applied here to the different ways of justification, by the law and by the gospel. The law propounds life upon an impossible condition, but the gospel clearly reveals to us,

that Christ hath performed what is necessary for our
justification, and that by a lively and practical faith we
shall have an interest in it. The Lord Jesus being
ascended, hath given us a convincing proof that the propitiation for our sins is perfect; for otherwise he had not
been received into God's sanctuary. Therefore to be
under perplexities how we may be justified, is to deny
the value of his righteousness and the truth of his ascension. And "say not, "Who shall descend into the
deep," to bear the torments of hell and expiate sin?
This is to deny the virtue of his death, whereby he appeased God, and redeemed us from the wrath to come.
In the law, the condemning righteousness of God is made
visible; in the gospel, his justifying righteousness is revealed, "from faith to faith." And this is an infallible
proof of its divine descent; for whereas all other religions either stupefy conscience and harden it in carnal
security, or terrify it by continual alarms of vengeance,
the gospel alone hath discovered how God may show
mercy to repenting sinners without injury to his justice.
The heathens robbed one attribute to enrich another.
Either they conceived God to be indulgent to their sins
and easy to pardon, to the prejudice of his justice; or
cruel and revengeful to the dishonour of his goodness:
but Christians are instructed how these are wonderfully
reconciled and magnified in our redemption. From
hence there is a divine calm in the conscience, and that
"peace which passeth understanding." The soul is not
only freed from the fear of God's anger, but hath a lively
hope of his favour and love. This is expressed by the
apostle, when he reckons among the privileges of believers, that they "are come to God, the Judge of all,
and to Jesus the Mediator of the new covenant, and to
the blood of sprinkling that speaketh better things than
that of Abel," Heb. xii. 23, 24. The apprehension
of God as the Judge of the world, strikes the guilty with
fear and terror; but as he is sweetened by the Mediator,
we may approach to him with confidence; for what sins
are there which so entire a satisfaction doth not expiate?
What torments can they deserve, which his wounds and
stripes have not removed? God is just, as well as mer-

ciful, in justifying those who believe in Jesus. It is not the quality of sins, but of sinners, that excepts them from pardon. Christ is the "golden altar in heaven" for penitent believers to fly to, from whence God will never pluck any one to destroy him.

V. From hence we may learn how absolute a necessity there is for our coming to Christ for justification.

There are but two ways of appearing before the righteous and supreme Judge,—in innocence and sinless obedience, or by the righteousness of Christ. The one is by the law, the other by grace. And these two can never be compounded; for he that pleads innocence, in that disclaims favour; and he that sues for favour, acknowledges guilt.

1. Now the first cannot be performed by us; for entire obedience to the law supposes the integrity of our natures, there being a moral impossibility that the faculties once corrupted should act regularly; but man is stained with original sin from his conception. And the form of the law runs universally; "Cursed is every one that continueth not in all things which are written in the book of the law to do them," Gal. iii. 10. In these scales, one evil work preponderates a thousand good. If a man were guilty but of one single error, his entire obedience afterwards could not save him; for that being always due to the law, the payment of it cannot discount for the former debt. So that we cannot in any degree be justified by the law; for there is no middle between transgressing and not transgressing it. He that breaks one article in a covenant, cuts off his claim to any benefit by it.

Briefly, the law justifies only the perfect, and condemns without distinction all that are guilty; so that to pretend justification by the works of it, is as unreasonable, as for a man to produce in court the bond which obliges him to his creditor, in testimony that he owes him nothing. Whoever presumes to appear before God's judgment-seat in his own righteousness shall be covered with confusion.

2. By the righteousness of Christ. This alone absolves from the guilt of sin, saves from hell, and can endure

the trial of God's tribunal. This the apostle prized as his invaluable treasure, in comparison of which all other things are but dross and dung; "That I may win Christ and be found in him, not having mine own righteousness, which is of the law, but that which is through the faith of Christ, the righteousness which is of God by faith," Phil. iii. 9. That which he ordained and rewarded in the person of our Redeemer, he cannot but accept. Now this righteousness is meritoriously imputed only to believers; for depending solely upon the will of God as to its being and effects, it cannot possibly be reckoned to any for their benefit and advantage, but in that way which he hath appointed. The Lord Christ, who made satisfaction, tells us, that the benefit of it is communicated only through our believing; "God so loved the world, that he gave his only begotten Son, that whosoever believeth on him, should not perish," John iii. 16. As all sins are mortal in respect of their guilt, but death is not actually inflicted for them upon account of the grace of the new covenant; so all sins are venial in respect of the satisfaction made by Christ, but they are not actually pardoned, till the performing of the condition to which pardon is annexed. Faith transfers the guilt from the sinner to the sacrifice. And this is not an act restrained to the understanding, but principally respects the will, by which we accept or refuse salvation. The nature of it is best expressed by the scripture phrase, "the receiving of Christ," which respects the terms upon which God offers him in the gospel, to be our Prince and Saviour. The state of favour begins upon our consent to the new covenant. And how reasonable is the condition it requires! How impossible is it to be otherwise! God is reconcilable by the death of Christ, so that he may exercise mercy without injury to his justice and holiness: he is willing and desirous to be upon terms of amity with men, but cannot be actually reconciled till they accept of them; for reconcilement is between two. Though God upon the account of Christ is made placable to the human nature, which he is not to the angelical in its lapsed state, and hath condescended so far as to offer conditions of peace to men, yet they are not reconciled at once. That Christ may become an effectual Mediator, there must be the consent of both parties. As God hath declared his by laying the punishment of our sins on Christ, so man gives his, by submitting to the law of faith. And the great end of preaching the gospel is, to overcome the obstinacy of men, and reconcile them to God and their happiness: "We are ambassadors for Christ; we pray you in Christ's stead, be ye reconciled to God;" with this difference—Christ furnished the means, they only bring the message of reconciliation, 2 Cor. v. 20.

Now men are with difficulty wrought on to comply with the conditions of pardon by Christ.

(1.) Upon the account of a legal temper that universally inclines them to seek for justification by their own works. This is most suitable to the law and light of nature; for the tenor of the first covenant was, Do and live. So that the way of gospel justification, as it is supernatural in its discovery, so in its contrariety to man's principles. Besides, as pride at first aspired to make man as God, so it tempts him to usurp the honour of Christ, to be his own Saviour. He is unwilling to stoop, that he may drink of the waters of life. Till the heart by the weight of its guilt is broken in pieces, and loses its former fashion and figure, it will not humbly comply with the offer of salvation for the merits of another. And it is very remarkable, that upon the first opening of the gospel, no evangelical doctrine was more disrelished by the Jews, than justification by imputed righteousness. The apostle gives this account of their opposition, that "being ignorant of God's righteousness, and going about to establish their own righteousness, they submitted not themselves to the righteousness of God," Rom. x. 3. They were prepossessed with this principle, that life was to be obtained by their works, because the express condition of the law was so; and mistaking the end of its institution by Moses, they set the law against the promises; for since the fall, the law was given, not absolutely to be a covenant of life, but with a design to prepare men for the gospel, that upon the sight of their guilt and the curse, they might have recourse to the Redeemer, and by faith embrace that satisfaction he hath made for them. " Christ is the end of the law for righteousness to every one that believeth," Rom. x. 4. From the example of the Jews we may see how men are naturally affected. And it is worthy of observation, that the reformation of religion took its rise by the same controversy with the papists, by which the gospel was first introduced into the world; for, besides innumerable abuses crept into the church, the people were persuaded, that by purchasing indulgences they should be saved from the wrath of God. And when this darkness covered the face of the earth, the zeal of the first reformers broke forth; who, to undeceive the world, clearly demonstrated from the scriptures, that justification is obtained alone by a lively and purifying faith in the blood of Christ—a strong proof that the same gospel which was first revealed by the apostles, was revived by those excellent men; and the same church which was first built by the apostles, was raised out of its ruins by them.

Now the gospel, to eradicate this disposition, which is so natural and strong in fallen man, is in nothing more clear and express, than in declaring, that " by the deeds of the law there shall no flesh be justified in God's sight." The apostle asserts without distinction, that by the works of the law justification cannot be obtained, whether they proceed from the power of nature, or the grace of the Spirit; for he argues against the merit of works to justification, not against the principle from whence they proceed, Rom. iii.—And where he most affectionately declares his esteem of Christ and his righteousness, as the sole meritorious cause of his justification, he expressly rejects " his own righteousness which is of the law," Phil. iii. 9. By his own righteousness he comprehends all the works of the renewed, as well as the natural state; for they are performed by man, and are acts of obedience to the law, which commands perfect love to God. These are slight, withering leaves, that cannot hide our nakedness, and conceal our shame, when we appear before God in judgment. Not but that good works are most pleasing to him, but not for this end, to expiate sin. We must distinguish between their substance, and the quality that error giveth them. The opinion of merit changes their nature, and turns gold into dross. And if our real righteousness, how exact soever, cannot absolve us from the least guilt, much less can the performance of some external actions, though specious in appearance, yet not commanded by God, and that have no moral value. All the disciplines and severities whereby men think to make satisfaction to the law, are like a crown of straw, that dishonours the head instead of adorning it. But that righteousness which was acquired by the obedience and meritorious sufferings of Christ, and is embraced by faith, is all-sufficient for our justification. This is as pure as innocence, to all the effects of pardon and reconciliation; this alone secures us from the charge of the law and the challenge of justice. Being clothed with this, we may enter into heaven, and converse with the pure society of angels, without blushing. The saints who now reign in glory, were not men who lived in the perfection of holiness here below; but repenting, believing sinners, who are washed white in the blood of the Lamb.

(2.) The most universal hinderance of men's complying with the conditions of pardon by Christ, is, the predominant love of some lust. Although men would entertain him as a Saviour to redeem them from hell, yet they reject him as their Lord. Those in the parable, who said, "We will not have this man to reign over us," expressed the inward sense and silent thoughts of all carnal men. Many would depend on his sacrifice, yet will not submit to his sceptre; they would have Christ to pacify their consciences, and the world to please their affections. Thus they divide between the offices of Christ, his priestly, and his regal.—They would have Christ to die for them, but not to live in them. They divide the acts of the same office; they lean on his cross to support them from falling into hell, but crucify not one lust on it. They are desirous he should reconcile them to God by his sacrifice, but not to bless them, in turning them away from their iniquities, Acts iii. 26. And thus in effect they absolutely refuse him, and render his death unavailable; for the receiving of Christ as

Mediator in all his offices, is the condition indispensably requisite to partake of the benefits of his sufferings. The resigning up of ourselves to him as our Prince, is as necessary an act of justifying faith, as the apprehending of the crucified Saviour. So that in every real Christian, faith is the principle of obedience and peace, and is as inseparable from holiness, as from salvation.

To conclude this argument: from hence we may see, how desperate the state is of impenitent unbelievers. They are cut off from any claim to the benefits of Christ's death.—The law of faith, like that of the Medes and Persians, is unalterable; "He that believeth not the Son, shall not see life." Christ died not to expiate final infidelity. This is the mortal sin, that actually damns. It charges all their guilt upon sinners; it renders the sufferings of Christ fruitless and ineffectual to them; for it is not the preparation of a sovereign remedy that cures the disease, but the applying of it. As our sins were imputed to him, upon the account of his union with us in nature and his consent to be our Surety; so his righteousness is meritoriously imputed to us, upon our union with him by a lively faith. The man that looked on the rainbow, when he was ready to be drowned, what relief was it to him, that God had promised not to drown the world, when he must perish in the waters? So though Christ hath purchased pardon for repenting believers, and a rainbow encompasses the throne of God, the sign of reconciliation, what advantage is this to the unbeliever, who dies in his sins and drops into the lake of fire? It is not from any defect of mercy in God, or righteousness in Christ, but for the obstinate refusal of it, that men certainly perish.—This enhances their guilt and misery. All the rich expense of grace for their redemption shall be charged upon them. The blood of Christ shall not be imputed for their ransom, but for their deeper damnation: and instead of speaking better things than the blood of Abel, shall call louder for vengeance against them, than that innocent blood which reached heaven with its voice against the murderer. Briefly, whom so precious a sacrifice doth not redeem, they are reserved entire victims, whole burnt-offerings to divine justice.

Every impenitent unbeliever shall be "salted with fire," Mark ix. 49.

CHAPTER XVI.

THE HOLINESS OF GOD IN REDEMPTION.

OF all the perfections of the Deity, none is more worthy of his nature, and so peculiarly admirable, as his infinite purity. It is the most shining attribute that derives a lustre to all the rest; he is "glorious in holiness," Exod. xv. 11. Wisdom degenerates into craft, power into tyranny, mercy loses its nature, without holiness. He swears by it as his supreme excellency: "Once have I sworn by my holiness, that I will not lie unto David," Psalm lxxxix. 35. It is the most venerable attribute, in the praise whereof the harmony of heaven agrees. The angels and saints above are represented, expressing their ecstacy and ravishment at the beauty of holiness; "Holy, holy, holy is the Lord of hosts; the whole earth is full of his glory," Isa. vi. 3. This only he loves and values in the creature, being the impression of his most divine and amiable perfection. Inferior creatures have a resemblance of other divine attributes: the winds and thunder set forth God's power, the firmness of the rocks and the incorruptibility of the heavens are an obscure representation of his unchangeableness; but holiness, that is the most orient pearl in the crown of heaven, shines only in the reasonable creature. Upon this account man only is said to be formed after his image. And in men there are some appearances of the Deity, that do not entitle to his special love. In princes there is a shadow of his sovereignty, yet they may be the objects of his displeasure; but a likeness to God in holiness attracts his eye and heart, and infinitely endears the creature to him.

Now this attribute is in a special manner provoked by man's sin, and we are restored to the favour and friendship of God, in such a manner as may preserve the honour of it entire and inviolable.

This will fully appear, by considering what our Redeemer suffered for the purchasing of our pardon; and the terms upon which the precious benefits of his death are conveyed to us: and what he hath done to restore our lost holiness, that we may be qualified for the enjoyment of God.

I. God's infinite purity is declared in his justice, in that he would not pardon sin, but upon such terms as might fully demonstrate how odious it was to him. What inflamed the wrath of God against his beloved Son, whom, by a voice from heaven, he declared to be the object of his delight? What made him inexorable to his prayers and tears, when he solicited the divine power and love, the attributes that relieve the miserable, crying, "Abba, Father, all things are possible to thee; let this cup pass from me?" What made him suspend all comforting influences, and, by a dreadful desertion, afflict him when he was environed with sorrows? It is sin only that caused this fierce displeasure, not inherent, (for the Messiah " was cut off, but not for himself,") but imputed by his voluntary undertaking for us. "God so loved the world," and so hated sin, that he gave his Son to purchase our pardon by sufferings. When his compassions to man were at the highest, yet then his antipathy against sin was so strong, that no less a sacrifice could reconcile him to us. Thus God declared himself to be unappeasable to sin, though not to sinners.

II. The privileges that are purchased by our Redeemer's sufferings, are dispensed upon those terms which are honourable to God's holiness. I will instance in the three great benefits of the evangelical covenant—the pardon of sin, adoption into God's family, and the inheritance of glory; all which are conditional, and annexed to special qualifications in the persons who have a title to them.

1. The death of Christ is beneficial to pardon and life, to those only who repent and believe. The holy God will by no means spare the guilty, that is, declare the guilty innocent, or forgive an incapable subject. All the promises of grace and mercy are with respect to repentance from dead works, and to a lively faith. The Son

of God is made a Prince and a Saviour, "to give repentance and remission of sins." And the apostle tells us, that "being justified by faith, we have peace with God, through our Lord Jesus Christ." The first includes a cordial grief for sins passed, and sincere effectual resolution to forsake them; and hath a necessary conjunction with pardon, as by virtue of the divine command, so from a condecency and fitness with respect to God, the giver of pardon, and to the quality of the blessing itself. The other qualification is faith, to which justification is in a special manner attributed; not in respect of efficiency or merit, for the mercy of God upon the account of Christ's satisfaction is the sole cause of our pardon; but as a moral instrument, that is the condition upon which God absolves man from his guilt. And this grace of faith, as it respects entire Christ in all his offices, so it contains the seed and first life of evangelical obedience. It crucifies our lusts, overcomes the world, works by love, as well as justifies the person by relying on the merits of Christ for salvation.

2. Adoption into God's family, the purchase of Christ's meritorious sufferings, who redeemed us from the servitude of sin and death, is conferred upon us in regeneration; for this prerogative consists not merely in an extrinsic relation to God and a title to the eternal inheritance, but in our participation of the divine nature, whereby we are the living images of God's holiness. Civil adoption gives the title, but not the reality of a son; but the divine is efficacious, and changes us into the real likeness of our heavenly Father. We cannot enter into this state of favour, but upon our cleansing from all impurity; "Be ye separate" from the pollutions of the profane world, " and I will receive you, and will be a father unto you, and ye shall be my sons and daughters, saith the Lord Almighty," 2 Cor. vi. 17. These are the indispensable terms upon which we are received into that honourable alliance. None can enjoy the privilege, but those that yield the obedience of children.

3. Holiness is the condition on which our future blessedness depends. Electing mercy doth not produce

our glorification immediately, but begins in our vocation and justification, which are the intermediate links in the chain of salvation; as natural causes work on a distant object, by passing through the medium. God first gives grace, then glory. The everlasting covenant that is sealed by the blood of Christ, establishes the connexion between them; " Blessed are the pure in heart, for they shall see God," Matt. v. 8. The exclusion of all others is peremptory and universal; "Without holiness no man shall see the Lord," Heb. xii. 14. The righteousness of the kingdom is the only way of entering into it. A few good actions scattered in our lives are not available, but a course of obedience brings to happiness. Those "who by patient continuance in well-doing, seek for glory, and honour, and immortality," shall inherit " eternal life," Rom. ii. 7. This is not a mere positive appointment, but grounded on the unchangeable respect of things. There is a rational convenience between holiness and happiness, according to the wisdom and goodness of God; and it is expressed in scripture by the natural relation of the seed to the harvest, both as to the quality and measure; " Whatsoever a man soweth, that shall he also reap," Gal. vi. 7. We must be like God in purity, before we can be in felicity. Indeed, it would be a disparagement to God's holiness, and pollute heaven itself, to receive unsanctified persons, as impure as those in hell. It is equally impossible for the creature to be happy without the favour of the holy God, and for God to communicate his favour to the sinful creature. Briefly, according to the law of faith, no wicked person hath any right to the satisfaction Christ made, nor to the inheritance he purchased for believers.

III. Man in his corrupt state is deprived of spiritual life, so that till revived by special grace, he can neither obey nor enjoy God. Now the Redeemer is made a quickening principle to inspire us with new life.

In order to our sanctification he hath done four things —he hath given us the most perfect laws as the rule of holiness—he exhibited the most complete pattern of holiness in his life upon the earth—he purchased and conveys the Spirit of holiness, to renew, and to enable us for the performance of our duties—he hath presented the strongest inducements and motives to persuade us to be holy.

1. He hath given to men the most perfect laws as the rule of holiness. The principal parts of the holy life, are, ceasing from evil and doing well, Isa. i. 16, 17. Now the commands of Christ refer to the purifying of us from sin, and the adorning of us with all the graces for the discharge of our universal duty.

They enjoin a real and absolute separation " from all filthiness of the flesh and spirit," 2 Cor. vii. 1. The outward and inward man must be cleansed, not only from pollutions of a deeper dye, but from all carnality and hypocrisy. " The grace of God that bringeth salvation hath appeared to all men, teaching us to deny ungodliness, and worldly lusts," all those irregular and impetuous desires which are raised by worldly objects, honours, riches, and pleasures, and reign in worldly men; pride, covetousness, and voluptuousness, Tit. ii. 11, 12. The gospel is most clear, full, and vehement, for the true and inward mortification of the whole body of corruption, of every particular darling sin. It commands us to pluck out the right eye, and to cut off the right hand, that is, to part with every grateful and gainful lust. It obliges us to " crucify the flesh, with the affections and lusts," Gal. v. 24. The laws of men regard external actions as prejudicial to societies; but of thoughts and resolutions that break not forth into act, there can be no human accusation and judgment; they are exempted from the jurisdiction of the magistrate. But the law of Christ reforms the powers of the soul, and all the most secret and inward motions that depend upon them. It forbids the first irregular impressions of the carnal appetite. We must hate sin in all its degrees, strangle it in the birth, destroy it in the conception. We are enjoined to fly the appearances and accesses of evil: whatever is of a suspicious nature and not fully consistent with the purity of the gospel, and whatever invites to sin and exposes us to the power of it, becomes vicious, and must be avoided. That glorious purity, that shall adorn the church when our Redeemer presents it " without spot or wrinkle, or any such thing," every Christian must aspire to in this life. In short, the gospel commands us " to be holy as God is holy," who is infinitely distant from the least conceivable pollution, 1 Pet. i. 15.

The precepts of Christ contain all solid, substantial goodness, that is essentially necessary in order to our supreme happiness, and prepares us for the life of heaven. In his sermon on the mount, he commends to us humility, meekness, and mercy, peaceableness and patience, and doing good for evil; which are so many beams of God's image, the reflections of his goodness upon intelligent creatures. And that comprehensive precept of the apostle describes the duties of all Christians: " Whatsoever things are true," Phil. iv. 8; truth is the principal character of our profession, and is to be expressed in our words and actions: " whatsoever things are honest " or venerable; that is, answer the dignity of our high calling, and agree with the gravity and comeliness of the Christian profession: " whatsoever things are just," according to divine and human laws: " whatsoever things are pure;" we must preserve the heart, the hand, the tongue, the eye, from impurity; " whatsoever things are lovely and of good report;" some graces are amiable and attractive in the view of men, as easiness to pardon, a readiness to oblige, compassion to the afflicted, liberality to the necessitous, sweetness of conversation without gall and bitterness; these are of universal esteem with mankind, and soften the most savage tempers: " if there be any virtue, and if there be any praise, think on these things." And Peter excites believers to join to their faith by which the gospel of Christ is embraced, intellectual and moral virtues, without which it is but a vain picture of Christianity: " Add to your faith, virtue; and to virtue, knowledge; and to knowledge, temperance; and to temperance, patience; and to patience, godliness; and to godliness, brotherly-kindness; and to brotherly-kindness, charity," 2 Pet. i. 5. He enforces the command; Give all diligence that these things abound in you, and " ye shall neither be barren nor unfruitful in the knowledge of Christ." Now these graces purify and perfect, refine and raise the human nature, and without a command their goodness is a strong obligation.

I will take a more distinct view of the precepts of Christ as they are set down in that excellent abridgment of them by the apostle: "The grace of God that bringeth salvation hath appeared to all men, teaching us, that denying ungodliness and worldly lusts, we should live soberly, righteously, and godly, in this present world," Tit. ii. 11. 12.

Here is a distribution of our duties with respect to their several objects, ourselves, others, and God. The first are regulated by temperance, the second by justice, the third by godliness. And from the accomplishment of these is formed that holiness without which no man shall see God.

In respect to ourselves, we must live soberly. Temperance governs the sensual appetites and affections by sanctified reason. The gospel allows the sober and chaste use of pleasures, but absolutely and severely forbids all excess in those that are lawful, and commands abstinence from all that are unlawful, that stain and vilify the soul, and alienate it from converse with God, and mortify its taste to spiritual delights. By sensual complacency man first lost his innocence and happiness, and till the flesh is subdued to the spirit, he can never recover them. "The carnal mind is enmity against God," Rom. viii. 7. "Fleshly lusts war against the soul," 1 Peter ii. 11; therefore we are urged with the most affectionate earnestness, to abstain from them, by withdrawing their incentives, and crucifying our corrupt inclinations. In short, the law of Christ obliges us to deal with the body, as an enemy that is disposed to revolt against the spirit, by watching over all our senses, lest they should betray us to temptations; so to preserve it, as a thing consecrated to God, from all impurity that will render it unworthy the honour of being the temple of the Holy Ghost.

We are commanded to live righteously, in our relation to others. Justice is the supreme virtue of human life that renders to every one what is due. The gospel gives rules for men in every state and place, to do what reason requires. As no condition is excluded from its blessedness, so every one is obliged by its precepts. Subjects are commanded to obey all the lawful commands of authority, and not to resist, and that upon the strongest motives, " not only for wrath, but also for conscience sake," Rom. xiii. 5. They must obey man for God's sake but never disobey God for man's sake. And princes are obliged to be an encouragement to good works, and " a terror to the evil," Rom. xiii. 3; that those who are under them " may lead a quiet and peaceable life, in all godliness and honesty," 1 Tim. ii. 2. It enjoins all the respective duties of husbands and wives, parents and children, masters and servants; and that in all contracts and commerce none " defraud his brother:" accordingly, in the esteem of Christians, he is more religious who is more righteous than others. Briefly, Christian righteousness is not to be measured by the rigour of the laws, but by that rule of universal equity delivered by our Saviour; " Whatsoever ye would that men should do to you, do ye even so to them," Matt. vii. 12.

We are instructed by the law of Christ to live godly. This part of our duty respects our apprehensions, affections, and demeanour to God, which must be suitable to his glorious perfections. The gospel hath revealed them clearly to us, viz., the unity, simplicity, eternity, and purity of the divine nature, that it subsists in three persons, the Father, Son, and Spirit; and his wisdom, power, and goodness, in the work of our redemption. It requires that we pay the special honour that is due to God, in the esteem and veneration of our minds, in the subjection of our wills, in the assent of our affections to him as their proper object; that we have an entire faith in his word, a firm hope in his promises, a holy jealousy for his honour, a religious care in his service; and that we express our reverence, love, and dependence on him in our prayers and praises; that our worship of him be in such a manner as becomes God who receives it, and man that presents it. God is a pure spirit, and man is a reasonable creature; therefore he " must worship him in spirit and truth." And since man in his fallen state cannot approach the holy and just God without a Mediator, he is directed by the gospel to address himself to the throne of grace, in the name of the Lord Jesus Christ, who alone can reconcile our persons, and render our services acceptable with his Father.

Besides the immediate service of the Deity, godliness includes the propension and tendency of the soul to him in the whole conversation; and it contains three things; 1. that our obedience proceeds from love to God as its vital principle. This must warm and animate the external action. This alone makes obedience both delightful to us and pleasing to God. He shows mercy to those who love him and keep his commandments, Exod. xx. 6. "Faith worketh by love," and inclines the soul to obey with the same affection that God enjoins the precept. 2. That all our conversation be regulated by his will as the rule. He is our Father and Sovereign, and the respect to his law gives to every action the formality of obedience. We must choose our duty, because he commands it. "Whatsoever ye do in word or deed, do all in the name of the Lord Jesus;" that is, for his command and by his assistance, Col. iii. 17. 3. That the glory of God be the supreme end of all our actions. This qualification must adhere, not only to necessary duties, but to our natural and civil actions. Our light must so "shine before men, that they may see our good works, and glorify our Father which is in heaven," Matt. v. 16. "Whether we eat or drink, or whatsoever we do," all must be done in a regular and due proportion, "to the glory of God," 1 Cor. x. 31. A general designation of this is absolutely requisite, 1 Peter iv. 11; and the renewing of our intentions actually in matters of moment; for he being the sole author of our lives and happiness, we cannot, without extreme ingratitude and disobedience, neglect to "glorify him in our bodies and spirits which are his." This religious tendency of the soul to God, as the supreme Lord and our utmost end, sanctifies our actions, and gives an excellency to them above what is inherent in their own nature. Thus moral duties towards men, when they are directed to God, become divine, Heb. xiii. 16. Acts of charity are so many sacred oblations to the Deity. Men are but the altars upon which we lay our presents: God receives them, as if immediately offered to his majesty, and consumed to his honour. Such was the charity of the Philippians towards the relief of the apostle, which he calls "an odour of a sweet smell, a sacrifice acceptable, well-pleasing to God," Phil. iv 18. The same bounty was an act of compassion to man, and devotion to God. This changes the nature of the meanest and most troublesome things. What was more vile and harsh than the employment of a slave? Yet a respect to God makes it a religious service, that is, the most noble and voluntary of all human actions; for the believer addressing his service to Christ, and the infidel only to his master, he doth cheerfully what the other doth by constraint, and " adorns the gospel of God our Saviour," as truly as if he were in a higher condition, Ephes. vi. 5. Tit. ii. 10.

All virtues are of the same descent and family, though in respect of the matter about which they are conversant and their exercise, they are different. Some are heroical, some are humble; and the lowest being conducted by love to God in the meanest offices, shall have an eternal reward. In short, piety is the principle and chief ingredient of righteousness and charity to men; for since God is the author of our common nature and the relations whereby we are united one to another, it is necessary that a regard to him should be the first, and have an influence upon all other duties.

I shall farther consider some particular precepts, which the gospel doth especially enforce upon us, and the reasons of them.

(1.) That concerning humility, the peculiar grace of Christians, so becoming our state as creatures and sinners; the parent and nurse of other graces; that preserves in us the light of faith and the heat of love; that procures modesty in prosperity and patience in adversity, that is the root of gratitude and obedience, and is so lovely in God's eyes, that he giveth grace to the humble. This our Saviour makes a necessary qualification in all those who shall enter into his kingdom : " Except ye be converted and become as little children, ye shall not enter into the kingdom of heaven," Matt. xviii. 3. As by humility he purchased our salvation, so by that grace we possess it. And since pride arises out of ignorance, the gospel, to cause in us a just and lowly sense of our unworthiness, discovers the nakedness and misery of the human nature, divested of its primitive righteousness. It reveals the transmission of original sin, from the first man to all his posterity, wherewith they are infected and debased; a mystery so far from our knowledge, that the participation of it seems impossible, and unjust to carnal reason. We are " dead in sins and trespasses," without any spiritual strength to perform our duty. The gospel ascribes all that is good in man to the free and powerful grace of God : he " worketh in us to will and to do of his good pleasure," Phil. ii. 13. He gives grace to some, because he is good; denies it to others, because he is just; but doth injury to none, because all being guilty, he owes it to none. Grace, in its being and activity, entirely depends upon him. As the drowsy sap is drawn forth into flourishing and fruitfulness by the approaches of the sun ; so habitual grace is drawn forth into act by the presence and influences of the Sun of righteousness. " Without me," our Saviour tells his disciples, " ye can do nothing," John xv. 5. " I have laboured more abundantly than they all," saith the apostle, " yet not I, but the grace of God with me," 1 Cor. xv. 10. The operations of grace are ours, but the power that enables us is from God. Our preservation from evil, and perseverance in good, is a most free, unmerited favour, the effect of his renewed grace in the course of our lives. Without his special assistance, we should every hour forsake him, and provoke him to forsake us. As the iron cannot ascend or hang in the air longer than the virtue of the loadstone draws it, so our affections cannot ascend to those glorious things that are above, without the continually attracting power of grace. It is by humble prayer, wherein we acknowledge our wants and unworthiness, and declare our dependence upon the divine mercy and power, that we obtain grace.

Now from these reasons the gospel commands humility in our demeanour towards God and men. And if we seriously consider them, how can any crevice be opened in the heart for the least breath of pride to enter ? How can a poor diseased wretch, that neither hath money, nor can by any industry procure nourishment or physic for his deadly diseases, and receives from a merciful person not only food, but sovereign medicines brought from another world (for such is the divine grace sent to us from heaven) without his desert or possibility of retribution, be proud towards his benefactor? How can he that lives only upon alms, boast that he is rich? How can a creature be proud of the gifts of God, which it cannot possess without humility, and without acknowledging that they are derived from mercy? If we had continued in our integrity, the praise of all had been entirely due to God; for our faculties and the excellent dispositions that fitted them for action, were bestowed upon us freely by him, and depended upon his grace in their exercise. But there is now greater reason to attribute the glory of all our goodness solely to him; for he revives our dead souls by the power of the Spirit, of the sanctifying Spirit, without which we are "to every good work reprobate." Since all our spiritual abilities are graces, the more we have received, the more we are obliged; and therefore should be more humble and thankful to the Author of them. And in comparing ourselves with others, the gospel forbids all proud reflections that we are dignified above them; "For, who maketh thee to differ from another? And what hast thou that thou didst not receive? Now if thou didst receive it, why dost thou glory, as if thou hadst not received it?" 1 Cor. iv. 7. If God discern one from another by special gifts, the man hath nothing of his own that makes him excellent. Although inherent graces command a respect from others to the person in whom they shine, yet he that possesses them, ought rather to consider himself in those qualities that are natural, and make him like the worst, than in those that are divine, proceeding from the sole favour of God, and that exalt him above them.

Add further, that God hath ordained in the gospel repentance and faith, which are humbling graces, to be the conditions of our obtaining pardon. By repentance we acknowledge that if we are condemned, it is just severity; and if we are saved, it is rich mercy. And faith absolutely excludes boasting; for it supposes the creature guilty, and receives pardon from the sovereign grace of God upon the account of our crucified Redeemer. The benefit, and the manner of our receiving it, was typified in the miraculous cure of the Israelites by looking up to the brazen serpent: for the act of seeing is performed by receiving the images derived from objects; it is rather a passion than an action; that it might appear that the healing virtue was merely from the power of God, and the honour of it entirely his. In short, God had respect to the lowliness of this grace, in appointing it to be the qualification of a justified person; for the most firm reliance on God's mercy, is always joined with the strongest renouncing of our own merits. Briefly, to excite humility in us, the gospel tells us, that the glorious reward is from rich bounty and liberality. "The gift of God is eternal life through Jesus Christ our Lord," Rom. vi. 23. As the election of us to glory, so the actual possession of it proceeds from pure favour. There is no more proportion between all our services, and that high and eternal felicity, than between running a few steps, and obtaining an imperial crown. Indeed not only heaven, but all the graces that are necessary to purify and prepare us for it, we receive from undeserved mercy; so that God crowns in us not our proper works, but his own proper gifts.

(2.) The gospel strictly commands self-denial, when the honour of God and religion is concerned. Jesus tells his disciples, "If any man will come after me, let him deny himself, and take up his cross, and follow me." Matt. xvi. 24. Life, and all the comforts of it, estates, honours, relations, pleasures, must be put under our feet, to take the first step with our Redeemer. This is absolutely necessary to the being of a Christian. In the preparation of his mind and the resolution of his will, he must live a martyr; and whensoever his duty requires, he must break all the *retinacula vitæ*, the voluntary bands that fasten us to the world, and die a martyr, rather than suffer a divorce to be made between his heart and Christ. Whatsoever is most esteemed and loved in the world, must be parted with as a snare, if it tempts us from obedience; or offered up as a sacrifice, when the glory of God calls for it. And this command that appears so hard to sense, is most just and reasonable; for God hath by so many titles a right to us, that we ought to make an entire dedication of ourselves and our most valuable interests to him. Our Redeemer infinitely denied himself to save us, and it is most just we should in gratitude deny ourselves to serve him. Besides, an infinite advantage redounds to us; for our Saviour assures us, that "whosoever will save his life," when it is inconsistent with the performance of his duty, "shall lose it; and whosoever will lose his life for his sake, shall find it," Matt. xvi. 25. Now what is more prudent, than of two evils that are propounded, to choose the least; that is, temporal death, rather than eternal? and of two goods that are offered to our choice, to prefer the greater, a life in heaven, before that on the earth? especially if we consider, that we must shortly yield the present life to the infirmities of nature; and it is the richest traffic to exchange that which is frail and mortal, for that which remains in its perfection for ever.

(3). The gospel enjoins universal love among men. This is "that fire which Christ came to kindle upon the earth." It is the abridgment of all Christian perfection, the fulfilling of the divine law; for all the particular precepts are in substance, love, Rom. xiii. 8, 9. He that loves his neighbour, will have a tender regard to his life, honour, and estate, which is the sum of the second table. The extent of our love must be to all that partake of the same common nature. The universal consanguinity between men, should make us regard them as our allies. Every man that wants our help, is our neighbour. "Do good unto all men," is the command of the apostle, Gal. vi. 10. For the quality of our love, it must be unfeigned, without dissimulation, 1 Pet. i. 22. The image of it in words, without real effects, provokes the divine displeasure; for as all falsehood is odious to the God of truth, so especially the counterfeiting of charity, that is, the impression of his Spirit and the seal of his kingdom. A sincere pure affection that rejoices at the good and resents the evils of others as our own, and expresses itself in all real offices, not for our private respects, but their benefit, is required of us. And as to the degree of our love, we are commanded "above all things to have fervent charity among yourselves," 1 Pet. iv. 8.

This principally respects Christians, who are united by so many sacred and amiable bands, as being formed of the same eternal seed, children of the same heavenly Father, and joint-heirs of the same glorious inheritance. Christian charity hath a more noble principle than the affections of nature, for it proceeds from the love of God shed abroad in believers, to make them of one heart and one soul: and a more divine pattern, the example of Christ, who hath by his sufferings restored us to the favour of God, that we should love one another, as he hath loved us. This duty is most strictly enjoined, for without love angelical eloquence is but an empty noise, and all other virtues have but a false lustre; prophecy, faith, knowledge, miracles, the highest outward acts of charity or self-denial, the giving of our estates to the poor, or bodies to martyrdom, are neither pleasing to God, nor profitable to him that does them, 1 Cor. xiii.

Besides, that special branch of love, the forgiving of injuries, is the peculiar law of our Saviour; for the whole world consents to the returning of evil for evil. The vicious love of ourselves makes us very sensible; and according to our perverse judgments, to revenge an injury seems as just as to requite a benefit. From hence revenge is the most rebellious and obstinate passion. An offence remains as a thorn in the mind, that inflames and torments it, till it is appeased by a vindication. It is more difficult to overcome the spirit, than to gain a battle. We are apt to revolve in our thoughts injuries that have been done to us, and after a long distance of time the memory represents them as fresh as at the first. Now the gospel commands a hearty and entire forgiveness of injuries, though repeated never so often, to "seventy times seven;" and allows not the least liberty of private revenges. We must not only quench the fire of anger, but kindle the fire of love towards our greatest enemies. "I say unto you, love your enemies, bless them that curse you, do good to them that hate you, and pray for them which despitefully use you and persecute you," Matt. v. 44. This is urged from the consideration of God's forgiving us, who being infinitely provoked, yet pardons innumerable faults to us, moved only by his mercy,

Col. iii. 13. And how reasonable is it that we should at his command, remit a few faults to our brethren! To extinguish the strong inclination that is in corrupt nature to revenge, our Saviour hath suspended the promise of pardon to us, upon our pardoning others; "For if ye forgive men their trespasses, your heavenly Father will also forgive you. But if ye forgive not men their trespasses, neither will your Father forgive your trespasses," Matt. vi. 14. He that is cruel to another cannot expect mercy, but in every prayer to God, indicts himself, and virtually pronounces his own condemnation.

(4.) The gospel enjoins contentment in every state, which is our great duty and felicity, mainly influential upon our whole life to prevent both sin and misery. "Be content with such things as ye have, for he hath said, I will never leave thee, nor forsake thee," Heb. xiii. 5. It forbids all murmurings against providence, which is the seed of rebellion, and all anxious thoughts concerning things future; "Take no thought for the morrow," Matt. vi. 34.—We should not anticipate evils by our apprehensions and fears, they come fast enough; nor retain their afflicting memory to embitter our lives, they stay long enough; " Sufficient unto the day is the evil thereof." Our corrupt desires are vast and restless as the sea, and when contradicted, they betray us to discontent and disobedience. The gospel therefore retrenches all inordinate affections, and vehemently condemns covetousness, as a vice not to be named among saints but with abhorrence. It discovers to us most clearly, that temporal things are not the materials of our happiness; for the Son of God voluntarily denied himself the enjoyment of them. And as the highest stars are so much distant from an eclipse, as they are above the shadow of the earth; so the soul that in its esteem and desire is above the world, its brightness and joy cannot be darkened or eclipsed by any accidents there. The gospel forbids all vain sorrows, as well as vain pleasures; and distinguishes real godliness from an appearance, by contentment as its inseparable character; "Godliness with contentment is great gain," 1 Tim. vi. 6. When we are in the saddest circumstances, our Saviour commands us to " possess our souls in patience ;" to preserve a calm constitution of spirit, which no storms from without can discompose. For this end he assures us that nothing comes to pass without the knowledge and efficiency, or at least, permission of God; that the hairs of our head are numbered, and not one falls to the earth without his license. Now the serious belief of a wise, just, and powerful providence, that governs all things, hath a mighty efficacy to maintain a constant tranquillity and equal temper in the soul amidst the confusions of the world. God " worketh all things according to the counsel of his own will :" and if we could discover the immediate reasons of every providence, we cannot have more satisfaction than from this general principle, that is applicable to all as light to every colour, that what God doth is always best. This resolves all the doubts of the most entangled minds, and rectifies our false judgments. From hence a believer hath as true content in complying with God's will, as if God had complied with his, and is reconciled to every condition. Besides, the gospel assures us, that " all things work together for good to them that love God ;" for their spiritual good at present, by weakening their corruptions; for affliction is a kind of manage, by which the sensual part is exercised and made pliable to the motions of the Spirit : and by increasing their graces, the invaluable treasures of heaven. If the dearest objects of our affections, the most worthy of our love and grief, are taken away, it is for this reason, that God may have our love himself in its most intense and inflamed degree. And afflictions are in order to their everlasting good. Now the certain expectation of a blessed issue out of all troubles, is to the heart of a Christian as putting a rudder to a ship, which without it is exposed to the fury of the winds and in continual dangers, but by its guidance makes use of every wind to convey it to its port. Hope produces not only acquiescence, but joy, in the sharpest tribulations, Rom. xii. 12. For every true Christian being ordained to a glorious and supernatural blessedness hereafter, all things that befal him here below as means, are regulated and transformed into the nature of the end to which they carry him. Accordingly the apostle assures us, that " our light affliction which is but for a moment, worketh for us a far more exceeding and eternal weight of glory," 2 Cor. iv. 17. To consider this life as the passage to another that is as durable as eternity, and as blessed as the enjoyment of God can make it, that the present miseries have a final respect to future happiness, will change our opinion about them, and render them not only tolerable, but so far amiable as they are instrumental and preparatory for it. If the bloody, as well as the milky way, leads to God's throne, a Christian willingly walks in it. In short, a lively hope accompanies a Christian to his last expiring breath, till it is consummated in celestial fruition; so that death, the universal terror of mankind, is made desirable as an entrance into immortality, and the first day of our triumph.

Thus I have considered some particular precepts of Christ, which are of the greatest use for the government of our hearts and lives, and the reasons upon which they are grounded to make them effectual. Now to discover more fully the completeness of the evangelical rule, I will consider it with respect to the law of Moses, and the philosophy of the heathens.

CHAPTER XVII.

THE PERFECTION OF THE LAWS OF CHRIST.

The perfection of the laws of Christ will further appear, by comparing them with the precepts of Moses, and with the rules which the highest masters of morality in the school of nature have prescribed for the directing of our lives.

(1.) The gospel exceeds the Mosaical institution,

First; in ordaining a service that is pure, spiritual, and divine, consisting in the contemplation, love, and praise of God, such as holy angels perform above. The temple service was managed with pomp and external magnificence, suitable to the disposition of that people and the dispensation of the law. The church was then in its infant state, as Paul expresses it, and that age is more wrought on by sense than reason; for such is the subordination of our faculties, that the vegetative first acts, then the sensitive, then the rational, as the organs appointed for its use acquire perfection. The knowledge of the Jews was obscure and imperfect, and the external part of their religion was ordered in such a manner, that the senses were much affected.—Their lights, perfumes, music, and sacrifices, were the proper entertainments of their external faculties. Besides, being encompassed with nations whose service to their idols was full of ceremonies, to render the temptation ineffectual and take off from the efficacy of those allurements which might seduce them to the imitation of idolatry, God ordained his service to be performed with great splendour. Add further, the dispensation of the law was typical and mysterious, representing, by visible material objects, and their power to ravish the senses, spiritual things and their efficacy to work upon the soul. But our Redeemer hath rent the veil, and brought forth heavenly things into a full day and the clearest evidence. Whereas Moses was very exact in describing the numerous ceremonies of the Jewish religion, the quality of their sacrifices, the place, the persons by whom they must be prepared and presented to the Lord; we are now commanded to draw near to God " with clean hands and pure hearts," and that " men pray every where, lifting up holy hands, without wrath and doubting," 1 Tim. ii. 8.—Every place is a temple, and every Christian a priest, to offer up spiritual incense to God. The most of the Levitical ceremonies and ornaments are excluded from the Christian service, not only as unnecessary but inconsistent with its spirituality; as paint, they corrupt the native beauty of religion. The apostle tells us, that human eloquence was not used in the first preaching of the gospel, lest it should render the truth of it uncertain, and rob the cross of Christ of its glory in converting the world; for there might be some pretence to imagine, that it was not the supernatural virtue of the doctrine and the efficacy of its reasons, but the artifice of orators that overcame the spirits of men. So if the service of the gospel were made so pompous, the worshippers would be inclined to believe, that the external part was the most principal, and to content themselves in that without the aims and affections of the soul, which are the life of all our services. Besides, upon another account, outward pomp in religion is apter to quench than inflame devotion; for we are so compounded of flesh and spirit, that when the corporeal faculties are vehemently affected with their objects, it is very hard for the spiritual to act with equal vigour; there being such commerce between the fancy and the outward senses, that they are never exercised in the reception of their objects, but the imagination is drawn that way, and cannot present to the mind distinctly and with the calmness that is requisite, those things on which our thoughts should be fixed. But when those diverting objects are removed, the soul directly ascends to God, and looks on him as the searcher and judge of the heart, and worships him proportionably to his perfections. That this was the design of Christ, appears particularly in the institution of the sacraments, which he ordained in a merciful condescension to our present state; for there is a natural desire in us to have pledges of things promised; therefore he was pleased to add to the declaration of his will in the gospel, the sacraments, as confirming seals of his love, by which the application of his benefits is more special, and the representation more lively, than that which is merely by the word. But they are few in number, only baptism and the Lord's supper, simple in their nature and easy in their signification, most fit to relieve our infirmities and to raise our souls to heavenly things. Briefly, the service of the gospel is answerable to the excellent light of knowledge shed abroad in the hearts of Christians.

Secondly; our Redeemer hath abolished all obligation to the other rituals of Moses, to introduce that real righteousness which was signified by them. The "carnal commandments" given to the Jews, are called "statutes that were not good," Ezek. xx. 25; either in respect of their matter, not being perfective of the human nature;

or their effect, for they brought death to the disobedient, not life to the obedient; the most strict observation of them did not make the performers either better or happy. But Christians are "dead to these elements," that is, perfectly freed from subjection to them. "The kingdom of God" consists "not in meat or drink, but righteousness, and peace, and joy in the holy Ghost; for he that in these things serveth Christ, is acceptable to God, and approved of men," Rom. xiv. 17, 18. We are commanded "to purge out the old leaven of malice and wickedness," that sours and swells the mind, and "to keep the feast" with the "unleavened bread of sincerity and truth." We are obliged to preserve ourselves undefiled from the moral imperfections, the vices and passions, which were represented by the natural qualities of those creatures which were forbidden to the Jews, and to purify the heart, instead of the frequent washings under the law. But the gospel frees us from the intolerable yoke of the legal abstinences, observations, and disciplines, the amusements of low and servile spirits, wherewith they would compensate their defects in real holiness, and exchange the substance of religion for the shadow and colours of it. For this reason the apostle is severe against those who would join the fringes of Moses to the robe of Christ.

Thirdly; the indulgence of polygamy and divorce that was granted to the Jews, is taken away by Christ, and marriage restored to the purity of its first institution. The permission of these was by a political law, and the effect was temporal impunity: for God is to be considered not only in the relation of a Creator and universal Governor, that gave laws to regulate conscience, but in a special relation to the Jews, as their King by covenant. Besides his general right and dominion, he had a peculiar sovereignty over them. And as in a civil state a prudent governor permits a less evil for the prevention of a greater, without an approbation of it; so God was pleased in his wisdom to tolerate those things, in condescension to their carnal and perverse humours, "for the hardness of their hearts," lest worse inconvenience should follow, Matt. xix. 8. But our Saviour reduces marriage to the sanctity of its original, when man was formed according to the image of God's holiness. "He which made them at the beginning made them male and female: for this cause shall a man leave father and mother, and cleave to his wife, and they twain shall be one flesh. What therefore God hath joined together, let not man put asunder," Matt. xix. 4—6. From the unity of the person, that one male was made and one female, it follows that the superinducing of another into the marriage bed is against the first institution. And the union that is between them, not being civil only in a consent of wills, but natural by the joining of two bodies, something natural must intervene to dissolve it, viz., the adultery of one party. Excepting that case, our Saviour severely forbids putting the wife away and marrying another, as a violation of conjugal honour.

Fourthly; our Redeemer hath improved the obligations of the moral law, by a clearer discovery of the purity and extent of its precepts, and by a peculiar and powerful enforcement. In his sermon on the mount, he clears it from the darkening glosses of the Pharisees, who observed the letter of the law, but not the design of the Lawgiver. He declares that not only the gross act, but all things of the same alliance are forbidden; not only murder, but rash anger and vilifying words which wound the reputation; not only actual pollution, but the impurity of the eye, and the staining of the soul with unclean thoughts, are all comprised in the prohibition. He informs them that every man in calamity is their neighbour, and to be relieved; and commands them to love their deadliest enemies. Briefly, he tells the multitude, that "unless their righteousness exceed the righteousness of the Scribes and Pharisees," that is, the utmost that they thought themselves obliged to, "they should not enter into the kingdom of heaven." Besides, our Saviour hath superadded special enforcements to his precepts. The arguments to persuade Christians to be universally holy, from Christ's redeeming them for that great end, were not known either in the economy of nature or the law; for before our lapsed state, there was no need of a Redeemer, and he was not revealed during the legal dispensation:

his death was only shadowed forth in types, and foretold in such a manner as was obscure to the Jews. The gospel argues new reasons to increase our aversion to sin, which neither Adam nor Moses was acquainted with. So the apostle dehorts Christians from uncleanness, because their bodies are "members of Christ," and "temples of the Holy Ghost," and therefore should be inviolably consecrated to purity. If the utensils of the temple were so sacred, that the employing of them to a common use was revenged in a miraculous manner; how much sorer punishment shall be inflicted on those who defile themselves, after they are "sanctified by the blood of the covenant," Heb. x. 19. The gospel also recommends to us love to one another, in imitation of that admirable love which Christ expressed to us, and commands the highest obedience even unto death when God requires it, in conformity to our Redeemer's sufferings. These and many other motives are derived from a pure vein of Christianity, and exalt the moral law to a higher pitch, as to its obligations upon men, than in its first delivery by Moses.

(2.) The laws of Christ exceed the rules which the best masters of morality in the school of nature have prescribed for the government of our lives. It is true there are remaining principles of the moral law in the heart of man; some warm sparks are still left, which the philosophers laboured to enliven and cherish. Many excellent precepts of morality they delivered, either to calm the affections and lay the storms in our breasts, whereby most men are guilty and miserable, or to regulate the civil conversation with others. And since the coming of Christ, Prometheus-like, they brought their dead torches to the sun, and stole some light from the scriptures. Yet upon searching, we shall easily discover, that notwithstanding all their boasts to purge the soul from defilements contracted by union with the body, and to restore it to its primitive perfection, "they became vain in their thoughts, and their foolish heart was darkened." Although the vulgar heathens thought them to be guides in the safe way, yet they were companions with them in their wanderings; and truth instructs us, that "when the blind leads the blind, both fall into the ditch."

I will briefly show that their morals are defective and mixed with false rules: only premising three things; 1. that I shall not insist on their ignorance of our Redeemer, and their infidelity in respect of those evangelical mysteries that are discovered only by revelation, for that precisely considered, doth not make them guilty before God; but only take notice of their defects in natural religion, and moral duties, to which "the law written in the heart" obliges all mankind; 2. that virtue is not to be confounded with vice, although it is not assisted by special grace. Those who performed acts of civil justice, and kindness, and honour, were not so guilty as those who violated all the laws of nature and reason. Their heroic actions were praiseworthy among men, and God gave them a temporal reward; although not being enlivened by faith, and purified by love to God and a holy intention for his glory, they were dead works, unprofitable as to salvation. 3. Their highest rule, viz., to live according to nature, is imperfect and insufficient: for although nature in its original purity furnished us with perfect instructions, yet in its corrupt state it is not so enlightened and regular, as to direct us in our universal duty. It is as possible to find all the rules of architecture in the ruins of a building, as to find in the remaining principles of the natural law, full and sufficient directions for the whole duty of man, either as to the performing of good, or avoiding evil. "The mind is darkened" and defiled with error, that indisposes it for its office.

I will now proceed to show how insufficient philosophy is to direct us in our duty to God, ourselves, and others.

In respect to piety, which is the chiefest duty of the reasonable creature, philosophy is very defective, nay, in many things contrary to it:

First; by delivering unworthy notions and conceptions of the Deity. Not only the vulgar heathens "changed the truth of God into a lie," when they measured his incomprehensible perfections by the narrow compass of their imaginations, or when looking on him through the appearing disorders of the world, they thought him unjust and cruel; as the most beautiful face seems deformed and monstrous in a disturbed stream: but the most renowned philosophers dishonoured him by their base apprehensions: for the true notion of God signifies a being infinite, independent, the universal Creator, who preserves heaven and earth; the absolute director of all events; that his providence takes notice of all actions; that he is a liberal rewarder of those that seek him, and a just revenger of those that violate his laws: now all this was contradicted by them. Some asserted the world to be eternal; others that matter was; and in that denied him to be the first cause of all things. Some limited his being, confining him to one of the poles of heaven; others extended it only to the amplitude of the world. The Epicureans totally denied his governing providence, and made him an idle spectator of things below. They asserted that God was contented with his own majesty and glory; that whatever was without him, was neither in his thoughts nor care; as if to be employed in ordering the various accidents of the world were incompatible with his blessedness, and he needed their impiety to relieve him. Thus by confining his power who is infinite, they denied him in confessing him. Others allowed him to regard the great affairs of kingdoms and nations, to manage crowns and sceptres; but to stoop so low as to regard particular things, they judged as unbecoming the divine nature, as for the sun to descend from heaven to light a candle for a servant in the dark. They took the sceptre out of God's hand, and set up a foolish and blind power to dispose of all mutable things. Seneca himself represents fortune as not discerning the worthy from the unworthy, and scattering its gifts without respect to virtue. Some made him a servant to nature, that he necessarily turned the spheres: others subjected him to an invincible destiny, that he could not do what he desired. Thus the wisest of the heathens dishonoured the Deity by their false imaginations, and instead of representing him with his proper attributes, drew a picture of themselves. Besides, their impious fancies had a pernicious influence upon the lives of men, especially the denial of his providence; for that took away the strongest restraint of corrupt nature, the fear of future judgment; for human laws do not punish secret crimes that are innumerable, nor all open, as those of persons in power, which are most hurtful; therefore they are a weak instrument to preserve innocence and virtue. Only the respect of God to whom every heart is manifest, every action a testimony, and every great person a subject, is of equal force to give check to sin in all, in the darkness of the night and the light of the day, in the works of the hand and the thoughts of the heart.

Secondly; Philosophy is very defective as to piety, in not enjoining the love of God. The first and great command in the law of nature (the order of the precepts being according to their dignity) is this, " Thou shalt love the Lord with all thy heart, soul, and strength." It is most reasonable that our love should first ascend to him, and in its full vigour; for our obligations to him are infinite, and all inferior objects are incomparably beneath him. Yet philosophers speak little or nothing of this, which is the principal part of natural religion. Aristotle, who was so clear-sighted in other things, when he discourses of God, is not only affectedly obscure to conceal his ignorance, as the fish which troubles the water, for fear of being catched; but it is on the occasion of speculative sciences, as in his physics, when he considers him as the first cause of all the motions in the world; or in his metaphysics, as the supreme Being, "the knowledge of whom," he saith, "is most noble in itself, but of no use to men." And in his morals, where he had reason to consider the Deity as an object most worthy of our love, respect, and obedience, in an infinite degree, he totally omits such a representation of him, although the love of God is that alone which gives price to all moral virtues. And from hence it is that philosophy is so defective as to rules for the preparing of men for an intimate and delightful communion with God, which is the effect of holy and perfect love, and the supreme happiness of the reasonable nature. If in the Platonic philosophy there are some things directing to it, yet they are but frigidly expressed, and so obscurely, that like inscriptions in ancient medals or marbles which are defaced, they are hardly legible. This is the singular character of the gospel, that distinguishes it from all human institutions—it represents the infinite amiableness of God and his goodness to us, to excite our affections to him in a superlative manner: it commands us to "follow him as dear children," and presses us to seek for those dispositions which may qualify us for the enjoyment of him in a way of friendship and love.

Thirdly; the best philosophers laid down this servile and pernicious maxim, that a wise man should always conform to the religion of his country. Socrates, who acknowledged one supreme God, yet, according to the counsel of the oracle that directed all to sacrifice according to the law of the city, advised his friends to comply with the common idolatry, without any difference in the outward worship of him and creatures; and those who did otherwise, he branded as superstitious and vain. And his practice was accordingly; for he frequented the temples, assisted at the sacrifices, which he declares before his judges, to purge himself from the crime of which he was accused. Seneca, speaking of the heathen worship, acknowledges it was unreasonable, and only the multitude of fools rendered it excusable; yet he would have a philosopher to conform to those customs, in obedience to the law, not as pleasing to the gods. Thus they made religion a dependence on the state. They performed the rites of heathenish superstition, that were either filthy, fantastical, or cruel, such as the devil, the master of those ceremonies, ordained. They became less than men, by worshipping the most vile and despicable creatures, and sunk themselves, by the most execrable idolatry, beneath the powers of darkness to whom they offered sacrifice. Now this philosophical principle is the most palpable violation of the law of nature; for that instructs us that God is the only object of religion, and that we are to obey him without exception from any inferior power. Here it was conscience to disobey the law, and a most worthy cause, wherein they should have manifested that generous contempt of death they so much boasted of. But they detained the truth in unrighteousness, and although "they knew God, they glorified him not as God, but changed the glory of the incorruptible God, into an image made like to corruptible man, and to birds, and beasts, and creeping things;" a sin of so provoking a nature, that God gave them up to the vilest lusts, carnal impurity being a just punishment of spiritual, Rom. i. 21, 24.

Fourthly; they arrogated to themselves the sole praise of their virtues and happiness. This impiety is most visible in the writings of the stoics, the Pharisees in philosophy. They were so far from depending on God for light and grace in the conduct of their lives, and from praying him to make them virtuous, that they opposed nothing with more pride and contempt. They thought that wisdom would lose its value and lustre, that nothing were in it worthy of admiration, if it came from above, and depended upon the grace of another. They acknowledged that the natural life, that riches, honours, and other inferior things, common to the worst, were the gifts of God; but asserted that wisdom and virtue, the special perfections of the human nature, were the effects of their own industry. Impious folly, to believe that we owe the greatest benefits to ourselves, and the lesser only to God! Thus they robbed him of the honour of his most precious gifts. So strongly did the poison of the old serpent, breathed forth in those words, " Ye shall be as God," that infected the first man, still work in his posterity. Were they angels in perfection, yet the proud reflecting on their excellencies would instantly turn them into devils. And as they boasted of virtue, so of happiness, as entirely depending on themselves. They ascribe to their wise man an absolute empire over all things; they raise him above the clouds, whatever may disquiet or disorder; they exempt him from all passions, and make him ever equal to himself; that he is never surprised with accidents; that it is not in the power of pains or troubles to draw a sigh or tear from him; that he despises all that the world can give or take, and is contented with pure and naked virtue: in short, they put the crown upon his head, by attributing all to the power of his own spirit. Thus they contradicted the rights of heaven. Their impiety was so bold, that they put no difference between God and their wise person, but this, that God was an immortal wise person, and a wise man was a mortal God. Nay, that he had this advantage, (since it is great art to comprise many things in a little space,) to enjoy as much happiness in an age, as Jupiter in his eternity. And, which is the highest excess of pride and blasphemy, they preferred the wretched imperfect virtue and happiness of their wise man, before the infinite and unchangeable purity and felicity of God himself; "For God," they said, "is wise and happy by the privilege of his nature; whereas a philosopher is so by the discourse of reason, and the choice of his will, notwithstanding the resistance of his passions, and the difficulties he encounters in the world." Thus to raise themselves above the throne of God, since the rebellious angels, none have ever attempted besides the Stoics. It is no wonder that they were the most early opposers of the gospel; for how could they acknowledge God in his state of abasement and humility, who exalted their virtuous man above him in his majesty and glory? Yet this is the sect that was most renowned among the heathens.

Fifthly; philosophy is very defective in not propounding the glory of God as the end to which all our actions should finally refer. This should have the first and chief place in that practical science; for every action receiving its specification and value from the end, that which is supreme and common to all actions, must be fixed before we come to the particular and subordinate; and that is the glory of God. Now the design of philosophers in their precepts, was either, 1. to use virtue as the means to obtain reputation and honour in the world. This was evident in their books and actions. They were sick of self-love, and did many things to satisfy the eye. They led their lives as in a scene, where one person is within, and another is represented without, by an artificial imitation of what is true. They were swelled with presumption, having little merit, and a great deal of vanity. Now this respect to the opinion of others corrupts the intention, and vitiates the action. It is not sincere virtue, but a superficial appearance that is regarded; for it is sufficient to that purpose to seem to be virtuous without being so. As a proud person would rather wear counterfeit pearls, that are esteemed right, than right which are esteemed counterfeit; so one that is vainglorious, prefers the reputation of being virtuous, before real virtue. From hence we may discover that many of their most specious actions were disguised sins; their virtues were as false as their deities. Upon this account St. Austin, Lib. 4, cont. Jul. c. 3, condemns the heroical actions of the Romans as vicious; "*Virtute civili, non vera, sed verisimili, humanæ gloriæ servierunt.*" Pride had a principal part in them.—Or, 2. the end of philosophy was to prevent the mischiefs which licentiousness and disorders might bring upon men from without, or to preserve inward peace, by suppressing the turbulent passions arising from lust or rage, that discompose the mind. This was the pretended design of Epicurus, to whom virtue was amiable only as the instrument of pleasure.—Or, 3. the height of philosophy was to propound the beauty of virtue, and its charming aspect, as the most worthy motive to draw the affections. Now supposing that some of the heathens, (although very few,) by discovering the internal beauty of virtue, had a love to it, and performed some things without any private respect, but for the rectitude of the action, and the inward satisfaction that springs from it, yet they were still defective; for virtue is but a ray of the Deity, and our duty is not complete, unless it be referred to his glory, who is the principle and pattern of it. In short, the great Creator made man for himself, and it is most just that as his favour is our sovereign happiness, so his glory should be our supreme end, without which nothing is regular and truly beautiful.

By these several instances it appears how insufficient philosophy is to direct us in our principal duty, that respects God.

Philosophy was defective also in its directions about moral duties that respect ourselves or others.

Philosophers were not sensible of the first inclinations to sin. They allow the disorder of the sensitive appetite as innocent, till it passes to the supreme part of the soul, and induces it to deliberate or resolve upon moral actions; for they were ignorant of that original and intimate pollution that cleaves to the human nature; and because our faculties are natural, they thought the first motions to forbidden objects, that are universal in the best as well as worst, to be natural desires, not the irregularities of lust. Accordingly all their precepts reach no farther than the counsels of the heart; but the desires and motions of the lower faculties, though very culpable, are left by them indifferent. So that it is evident that many defilements and stains are in their purgative virtues.

The Stoics not being able to reconcile the passions with reason, wholly renounced them. Their philosophy is like the river in Thrace,

> ———" Quod potum saxea reddit
> Viscera, quod tactis inducit marmora rebus." OVID.

For by a fiction of fancy they turn their virtuous person into a statue, that feels neither the inclinations of love nor the aversions of hatred ; that is not touched with joy or sorrow; that is exempt from fears and hopes. The tender and melting affections of nature towards the misery of others, they entirely extinguish as unbecoming perfect virtue. They attribute wisdom to none, but him whom they rob of humanity. Now, as it is the ordinary effect of folly to run into one extreme by avoiding another, so it is most visibly here ; for the affections are not like poisonous plants to be eradicated, but as wild, to be cultivated. They were at first set in the fresh soil of man's nature by the hand of God ; and the scripture describes the divine perfections, and the actions proceeding from them, by terms borrowed from human affections, which proves them to be innocent in their own nature. Plutarch observes when Lycurgus commanded to cut up all the vines in Sparta to prevent drunkenness, he should rather have made fountains by them to allay the heat of the wines, and make them beneficial : so true wisdom prescribes how to moderate and temper the affections, not to destroy them. It is true, they are now sinfully inclined, yet being removed from carnal to spiritual objects, they are excellently serviceable. As reason is to guide the affections, so they are to excite reason, whose operations would be languid without them. The natures that are purely spiritual, as the angels have an understanding so clear, as suddenly to discover in objects their qualities, and to feel their efficacy; but man is compounded of two natures, and the matter of his body obscures the light of his mind, that he cannot make such a full discovery of good or evil at the first view, as may be requisite to quicken his pursuit of the one and flight from the other. Now, the affections awaken the vigour of the mind to make an earnest application to its object. They are as the winds, which although sometimes tempestuous, yet are necessary to convey the ship to the port. So that it is contumelious to the Creator, and injurious to the human nature, to take them away as absolutely vicious. The Lord Jesus, who was pure and perfect, expressed all human affections according to the quality of the objects presented to him; and his law requires us not to mortify, but to purify, consecrate, and employ them for spiritual and honourable uses.

Philosophy is ineffectual by all its rules to form the soul to true patience and contentment under sufferings. Now, considering the variety and greatness of the changes and calamities to which the present life is obnoxious, there is no virtue more necessary. And if we look into the world before Christianity had reformed the thoughts and language of men, we shall discover their miserable errors upon the account of the seeming confusion in human affairs, the unequal distribution of temporal goods and evils here below. If the heathens saw injustice triumph over innocence, and crimes worthy of the severest punishment crowned with prosperity; if a young man died, who in their esteem deserved to live for ever, and a vicious person lived an age, who was unworthy to be born: they complained that the world was not governed according to righteousness, but rash fortune or blind fate ruled all. As the Pharisee in the gospel, seeing the woman that had been a notorious sinner, so kindly received by Christ, said within himself, "If this man were a prophet, he would know who it is that touches him;" so they concluded, if there were a providence that did see and take care of sublunary things, that did not only permit but dispose of all affairs, it would make a visible distinction between the virtuous and the wicked.

It is true, God did not leave the Gentiles without "a witness of himself;" for sometimes the reasons of his providence, in the great changes of the world, were so conspicuous, that they might discover an eye in the sceptre, that his goverement was managed with infinite wisdom. Other providences were veiled and mysterious; but the sight of those that were clear, should have induced them to believe the justice and wisdom of those they could not comprehend; as Socrates having read a book of Heraclitus, a great philosopher but studiously obscure, and his judgment being demanded concerning it, said, that what he understood was very rational, and he thought what he did not understand was so. But they did not wisely consider things. The present sense of troubles tempted them, either to deny providence or accuse it. Every day some unhappy wretch or other reproached their gods for the disasters he suffered. Now the end of philosophy was to redress these evils, to make an afflicted to be a contented state. The philosophers speak much of the power of their precepts to establish the soul in the instability of worldly things, to put it into an impregnable fortress by its situation above the most terrible accidents. They boasted in a poetical bravery, of their victories over fortune, that they despised its flattery in a calm, and its fury in a storm, and in every place erect trophies to virtue triumphing over it. These are great words and sound high, but are empty of substance and reality. Upon trial we shall find that all their armour, though polished and shining, yet is not of proof against sharp afflictions.

The arguments they used for comfort are taken 1. From necessity; that we are born to sufferings; the laws of humanity, which are unchangeable, subject us to them. But this consideration is not only ineffectual to cause true contentment, but produces the contrary effect; as the strength of Egypt is described to be like a reed that will pierce the hand instead of supporting it. Thus Solon, extremely lamenting the death of his son, and being asked why he shed so many barren tears that could not make his son spring out of the dust, replied, "For this reason I weep, because my weeping can do me no good." Our desires after freedom from miseries are inviolable; so that every evil, the more fatal and inevitable it is, the more it afflicts us. If there be no way of escape, the spirit is overcome by impatience or despair. 2. From reflection upon the miseries that befall others. But this kind of consolation is vicious in its cause proceeding from secret envy and uncharitableness. There is little difference between him that regards another's misery to lessen his own, and those who take pleasure in others' afflictions. And it administers no real comfort; if a thousand drink of the waters of Marah, they are not less bitter. 3. Others sought for ease under sufferings, by remembering the pleasures that were formerly enjoyed. But this inflames rather than allays the distemper; for as things are more clearly known, so more sensibly felt, by comparison. He that is tormented with the gout, cannot relieve his misery, by remembering the pleasant wine he drank before his fit. 4. The Stoics' universal cure of afflictions was, to change their opinion of them, and esteem them not real evils. Thus Posidonius, so much commended by Tully, who for many years, was under torturing diseases, and survived a continual death, being visited by Pompey at Rhodes, entertained him with a philosophical discourse; and when his pains were most acute, he said, "*Nihil agis, dolor, quanquam sis molestus; nunquam te esse confitebor malum.*" "In vain dost thou assault me, pain; though thou art troublesome, thou shalt never force me to confess thou art evil." But the folly of this boasting is visible; for though he might appear with a cheerful countenance in the paroxysm of his disease to commend his philosophy, like a mountebank that swallows poison to put off his drugs, yet the reality of his grief was evident; his sense was overcome, though his tongue remained a Stoic. If words could charm the senses not to feel pain, or compose the mind not to resent afflictions, it were a relief to give mollifying titles to them; but since it is not fancy that makes them stinging, but their contrariety to nature, it is no relief to represent them otherwise than they are. All those subtle notions vanish, when sensible impressions confute them. 5. Others composed themselves by considering the benefit of patience. Discontent puts an edge on troubles; to kick against the pricks, exasperates the pain; to be restless and turmoiling, increases the fever. But this is not properly a consolation; for although a calm and quiet submission prevents those new degrees of trouble, which by fretting and vexing we bring upon ourselves, yet it doth not remove the evil, which may be very afflicting and grievous in its own nature; so that without other considerations to support the mind, it will sink under it.

And as these, so many other arguments they used to fortify the spirit against sufferings, are like a hedge which at a distance seems to be a safe retreat from gun-shot, but those who retire to it, find it a weak defence. This appears by the carriage of the best instructed heathens in their calamities; professing themselves to be wise in their speculations, they became fools in practice, and were confounded with all their philosophy, when they should have made use of it. Some killed themselves from the apprehension of sufferings: their death was not the effect of courage, but of cowardice, the remedy of their fear. Others impatient of disappointment in their great designs, refused to live. I will instance in two of the most eminent among them, Cato and Brutus. They were both philosophers of the manly sect; and virtue never appeared with a brighter lustre among the heathens, than when joined with a stoical resolution. And they were not imperfect proficients, but masters in philosophy. Seneca employs all the ornaments of his eloquence to make Cato's eulogy: he represents him as the consummate exemplar of wisdom, as one that realized the sublime idea of virtue described in their writings. And Brutus was esteemed equal to Cato. Yet these, with all the power of their philosophy, were not able to bear the shock of adversity. Like raw fencers, one thrust put them into such disorder, that they forgot all their instructions in the place of trial; for being unsuccessful in their endeavours to restore Rome to its liberty, overcome with discontent and despair, they laid violent hands upon themselves. Cato being prevented in his first attempt, afterwards tore open his wounds with fierceness and rage; and Brutus, ready to plunge the sword into his breast, complained that virtue was but a vain name. So insufficient are the best precepts of mere natural reason to relieve us in distress. As torrents that are dried up in the heat of summer when there is the most need of them, so all comforts fail in extremity, that are not derived from the fountain of life.

I will only add how ineffectual philosophy is to support us in a dying hour. The fear of death is a passion so strong, that by it men are kept in bondage all their days. It is an enemy that threatens none whom it doth not strike, and there is none but it threatens. Certainly that spectre which Cæsar had not courage to look in the face, is very affrighting. Alexander himself, that so often despised it in the field, when passion that transported him cast a veil over his eyes; yet when he was struck with a mortal disease in Babylon, and had death in his view, his palace was filled with priests and diviners, and no superstition was so sottish, but he used it to preserve himself. And although the philosophers seemed to contemn death, yet the great preparations they made to encounter it, argue a secret fear in their breasts.

Many discourses, reasonings, and arguments are employed to sweeten that cruel necessity, but they are all ineffectual:—1. that is the condition of our nature; to be a man and immortal, are inconsistent. But this consolation afflicts to extremity. If there were any means to escape, the soul might take courage. He is doubly miserable, whose misery is without remedy. 2. That it puts a period to all temporal evils. But as this is of no force with those who are prosperous, and never felt those miseries which make life intolerable, so it cannot rationally relieve any that have not good hopes of felicity after death. The heathens discovered not the sting of death, as it is the wages of sin, and consigns the guilty to eternal death; so that they built upon a false foundation as if it were the cure of all evils. 3. They encouraged themselves from their ignorance of the consequences of death, whether it only changed their place, or extinguished their persons. Socrates, who died with a seeming indifference, gave this account of it, that he did not know whether death was good or evil. But this is not fortitude, but folly: as Aristotle observes, that readiness to encounter dangers arising from ignorance, is not true valour, but a brutish boldness. What madness is it then for one that enters upon an eternal state, not knowing whether it shall be happy or miserable, to be unaffected with that dreadful uncertainty?

But now the gospel furnishes us with real remedies against all the evils of our present state. It is the true paradise wherein the tree of life is planted, whose "leaves are for the healing of the nations." We are assured that God disposes all things, with the wisdom and love of a father; and that his providence is most admirable and worthy of praise in those things wherein they who are only led by sense, doubt whether it be at all; for as it is the first point of prudence to keep off evils, so the second and more excellent is, to make them beneficial. Christians "are more than conquerors through Christ that loves them." They are always in an ascending state; and believing, rejoice with an unspeakable and glorified joy. Death itself is not only disarmed, but made subservient to their everlasting good. Briefly, Christian patience endures all things as well as charity, because it expects a blessed issue. It draws from present miseries the assurance of future happiness. A believer while he possesses nothing but the cross, sees by faith the crown of the eternal kingdom hanging over his head; and the "lively hope" of it makes him not only patient, but thankful and joyful. This sweetens the loss of all temporal goods, and the presence of all temporal evils. Paul in his chains was infinitely more contented than Cæsar or Seneca, than all the princes and philosophers in the world.

I will conclude this argument by a short reflection on the immoral maxims of several sects of philosophers. The Cynics assert that all natural actions may be done in the face of the sun; that it is worthy of a philosopher to do those things in the presence of all, which would make impudence itself to blush—a maxim contrary to all the rules of decency, and corruptive of good manners; for as the despising of virtue produces the slighting of reputation, so the contempt of reputation causes the neglect of virtue. Yet the Stoics with all their gravity were not far from this advice. Besides, among other unreasonable paradoxes, they assert all sins are equal; that the killing a bird is of the same guilt with murdering a parent—a principle that breaks the restraints of fear and shame, and opens a passage to all licentiousness. They commended self-murder in several cases; which unnatural fury is culpable in many respects, of rebellion against God, injustice to others, and cruelty to one's self. Zeno, the founder of the sect, practised his own doctrine; for falling to the ground, he interpreted it to be a summons to appear in another world, and strangled himself. Aristotle allows the appetite of revenging injuries to be as natural as the inclination to gratitude, judging according to the common rule, that one contrary is the measure of another. Nay, he condemns the putting up with an injury as degenerous and servile. He makes indignation at the prosperity of unworthy men, a virtue; and to prove it, tells us the Grecians attributed it to their gods, as a passion becoming the excellency of their natures. But if we consider, the Supreme Disposer of all things may do what he pleases with his own, that he is infinitely wise, and in the next world will dispense eternal recompenses, there is not the least cause of irritation for that seeming disorder. He also allows pride to be a noble temper that proceeds from a sublime spirit. He represents his hero by this among other characters, that he is displeased with those who mention to him the benefits he hath received, which make him inferior to those that gave them; as if humility and gratitude were qualities contrary to magnanimity. He condemns envy as a vice that would bring down others to our meanness, but commends emulation, which urges to ascend to the height of them that are above us. But this is no real virtue, for it doth not excite us by the worth of moral good, but from the vain desire of equality or pre-eminence. And Plato himself, though styled divine, yet delivers many things that are destructive of moral honesty. He dissolves the most sacred band of human society, ordaining in his commonwealth a community of wives. He allows an honest man to lie on some occasions; whereas the rule is eternal, We must not do evil, that good may come thereby. In short, a considering eye will discover many spots, as well as beauties, in their most admired institutions. They commend those things as virtues which are vices, and leave out those virtues which are necessary for the perfection of our nature; and the virtues they commend, are defective in those qualities that are requisite to make them sincere. If philosophy were incarnate, and had expressed the purity and efficacy of all its precepts in real actions, yet it had abundantly fallen short of that supernatural, angelical, divine holiness, which the gospel requires. Till the wisdom of God removed his chair from heaven to earth to instruct the world, not only the depravation of the lower faculties, but the darkness of the human understanding, hindered men from performing their universal duty. The gospel alone brings light to the mind, peace to the conscience, purity to the affections, and rectitude to the life.

CHAPTER XVIII.

THE EXAMPLE OF CHRIST, AND THE GIFT OF THE HOLY SPIRIT.

THE second means by which our Redeemer restores us to holiness, is by exhibiting a complete pattern of it in his life upon earth.

For the discovery how influential this is upon us, we must consider, that of all the most noble works, the principal cause is an exact pattern in the mind of the agent which he endeavours to imitate; and examples are of the same nature. He that desires to excel in painting or sculpture, must view the most accomplished pieces of those arts. Thus in morality, the consideration of eminent actions performed by others, is of admirable efficacy to raise us to perfection.

That examples have a peculiar power above the naked precept, to dispose us to the practice of holiness, appears by considering,—1. that they most clearly express to us the nature of our duties in their subjects and sensible effects General precepts form abstract ideas of virtue, but in examples virtues are made visible in all their circumstances.—2. Precepts instruct us what things are our duty, but examples assure us that they are possible. They resemble a clear stream wherein we may not only discover our spots, but wash them off. When we see men like ourselves, who are united to frail flesh and in the same condition with us, to command their passions, to overcome the most glorious and glittering temptations, we are encouraged in our spiritual warfare.—3. Examples, by a secret and lively incentive, urge us to imitation. The Romans kept in their houses the pictures of their progenitors, to heighten their spirits, and provoke them to follow the precedents set before them. We are touched in another manner by the visible practice of saints, which reproaches our defects and obliges us to the same care and zeal, than by laws though holy and good.

Now the example of Christ is most proper to form us to holiness, it being absolutely perfect, and accommodated to our present state.

(1.) It is absolutely perfect. There is no example of a mere man, that is to be followed without limitation. "Be ye followers of me, as I am of Christ," saith the great apostle. Nay, if the exellencies of all good men were united into one, yet we might not securely follow him in all things; for his remaining defects might be so disguised by the virtues to which they are joined, that we should err in our imitation. But the life of Christ was as the purest gold, without any alloy or baser metal. His conversation was a living law. He did "no sin, neither was any guile found in his mouth." He was "holy, harmless, undefiled, separate from sinners," Heb. vii. 26. He united the efficacy of example with the direction of precepts; his actions always answered his words. Christianity, the purest institution in the world, is only a conformity to his pattern. The universal command of the gospel, that comprises all our duties, is, "to walk as Christ walked."

(2.) His example is most accommodated to our present state. There must be some proportion between the model, and the copy that is to be drawn by it. Now the divine nature is the supreme rule of moral perfections. We are commanded to be holy, "as God is holy." But such is the obscurity of our minds, and the weakness of our natures, that the pattern was too high and glorious to be expressed by us. We had not strength to ascend to him, but he had goodness to descend to us; and in this present state to set before us a pattern more fitted to our capacity. Although light is the proper object of sight, yet the radiancy and immense light of the sun in the meridian is invisible to our sight; we more easily discover the reflection of it in some opaque body; so the divine attributes are sweetened in the Son of God incarnate, and being united with the graces proper for the human nature, are more perceptible to our minds and more imitable by us. This was one great design of his coming into the world, to set before us in doing and suffering, not a mere spectacle for our wonder, but a copy to be transcribed in our hearts and lives. He therefore chose such a tenor of life as every one might imitate. His supreme virtue expressed itself in such a temperate course of actions, that as Abimelech said to his followers, Judges ix. 48, "What ye have seen me do, make haste and do as I have done;" so our true Abimelech, our Father and Sovereign calls upon us to imitate him. The first effect of predestination is to conform us to the image of the Son, who "was for this end made the first born among many brethren." He assumed the human nature, that he might partake of the divine, not only by his merit, but example.

This will appear more fully by considering, there are some virtues necessary to our condition as creatures, or with respect to our state of trial here below, which the Deity is not capable of; and those most eminently appear in the life of Christ. I will instance in three, which are the elements of Christian perfection—his humility in despising all the honour of the world, his obedience in sacrificing his will entirely to God's, and his charity in procuring the salvation of men by his sufferings: and in all these he denied to his human nature the privilege due to it by its union with the eternal Word.

Humility, in strictness, hath no place in God. He requires the tribute of glory from all his creatures. And the Son of God had a right to divine honour upon his first appearance here below. Yet he was born in a stable, and made subject to our common imperfections. Although he was ordained to convert the world by his doctrine and miracles, yet for the tenth part of his time, he lived concealed and silent, being subject to his mother and reputed father, in the servile work of a carpenter. And after his solemn investiture into his office by a voice from heaven, yet he was despised and contemned. He refused to be a king, and stooped so low as to wash his disciples' feet. All this he did to instruct us to be "meek and lowly," to correct our pride, the most intimate and radicated corruption of nature, Matt. xi. 29. For as those diseases are most incurable, which draw nourishment from that food which is taken for the support of life; so pride, that turns virtuous actions which are the matter of praise, into its nourishment, is most difficultly overcome. But the example of the Son of God, in whom there is a union of all divine and human perfections, debasing himself to the form of a servant, is sufficient, if duly considered, to make us walk humbly.

Obedience is a virtue that becomes an inferior, either a servant or subject, who is justly under the power of others, and must be complying with their will; so that it is very distant from God, who hath none superior to him in dominion or wisdom, but his will is the rule of goodness to his own and others' actions. Now the Son of God became man, and was universally obedient to the law of his Father. And his obedience had all the ingredients that might commend it to our imitation. The value of obedience arises upon three accounts: 1. the dignity of the person that obeys; it is more meritorious in an honourable than in a mean person: 2. from the difficulty of the command, it being no great victory over the appetite in obedience, "*ubi diligitur quod debetur*," where the instance is agreeable to our affections:

3. from the entireness of the will in obeying; for to perform a commanded action against our consent, is only to be subject in the meaner part of man, the body, and to resist in the superior, which is the mind. Now, in all these respects, the obedience of Christ was perfect. In the dignity of the person obeying, it exceeded the obedience of all the angels, as much as the divine person exceeded all created. The difficulty of the command is greater than ever was put upon servant or subject; " he was obedient to the death of the cross," that is, death with dishonour and torment, the evils that are most contrary to the human nature and appetite. And the completeness of his will in obeying, is most evident; for if Christ had desired deliverance from his persecutors, he had certainly obtained it. He tells his disciples, that upon his request his Father would send twelve legions of angels for his rescue. But he resigned the whole power of his will to his Father's; "Not my will, but thine be done," was his voice at his private passion in the garden. He submitted the act and exercise of his will; "Not what I will, but what thou wilt," he saith in another evangelist. He yielded not only the faculty and exercise of his will to do what God enjoined, but in that manner which was pleasing to him; "Not as I will, but as thou wilt," he expresses in the words of a third. Now, what is there in heaven or earth that can move our wills to entire obedience, if this marvellous pattern doth not affect us? " Let the same mind be in you that was in Christ," saith the apostle. How glorious is it to do what he did, and what a reproach to decline what he suffered, who had the holiness of God to give excellency to the action, and the infirmity of man to endure the sharpness of the passion!

Love to mankind is expressed by our Saviour in a peculiar manner; for although God is infinitely good to us, yet he doth not prefer the happiness of man before his own blessedness. The salvation of the whole world were not to be purchased with the least diminution of the divine felicity. But the Son of God suffered the extremest evil to procure the most sovereign good for us, who were in rebellion against his laws and empire.

Briefly, the life of Christ contains all our duties towards God and man expressed in the most perfect manner, or motives to perform them. We may clearly see in his deportment, innocent wisdom, prudent simplicity, compassionate zeal, perfect patience, the courage of faith, the joy of hope, the tenderness and care of love, incomparable meekness, modesty, humility, and purity. He spent the night in communion with God, and the day in charity to men. He perfectly hated sin, and equally loved souls. The nearest and readiest way to perfection is a serious regard to his precedent; for the causes of all sin are either the desire of what he despised, or the fear of what he suffered. He voluntarily deprived himself of riches, honours, pleasures, to render them contemptible: and endured outrages of all sorts, the " contradiction of sinners," and the sharpest sufferings, to make them tolerable. He ascended Mount Calvary to his cross, before he ascended from Mount Olivet to his throne: he was naked before he was clothed with a robe of light, and crowned with thorns before with glory. And thus he powerfully teaches us to follow his steps, " who suffered for us." If a physician of great esteem, in a disease, takes a bitter potion, it would persuade those who are in the same danger, to use the same remedy. Since the Son of God, to purchase our happiness, denied himself the enjoyment of worldly delights, and endured the worst of temporal evils, nothing can be more effectual to convince us, that the pleasures of the world are not considerable as to our last end, and that present afflictions are so far from being inconsistent with our supreme blessedness, that they prepare us for it.

In short, his excellent example not only enlightens our minds to discover our duty, but enables and excites us to perform it. As the eye in beholding visible objects, receives their image, so by contemplating the graces that are conspicuous in our Redeemer, we derive a similitude from them. "We all," saith the apostle, "with open face beholding as in a glass the glory of the Lord," that is, by viewing in the gospel the life of Christ which was glorious in holiness, "are changed into the same image, from glory to glory, even as by the Spirit of the Lord;"

that is, gradually fashioned in grace according to his likeness, 2 Cor. iii. 18.

And what can more powerfully move and persuade us to holiness, than to consider the precedent that Christ hath set before us? for how honourable is it to be like the Son of God! By conformity to Christ we partake of the divine perfections. The King of heaven will acknowledge us for his children, when we bear the resemblance of our elder brother. Besides the motive of honour, love doth strongly incline to follow holiness in imitation of our Redeemer. This is one difference between knowledge and love—the understanding draws the object to itself, and transforms it into its own likeness; thus material objects have an immaterial existence in the mind when it contemplates them: but love goes forth to the object loved; the soul is more where it loves than where it lives; that is, there is more of its intellectual presence, its thoughts and desires; and it always effects a resemblance to it. Thus love humbled God, and made him like to us in nature; and love exalts man, by making him like to God in holiness, for it excites us to imitate and express in our actions the virtues of him " who hath called us to his kingdom and glory."

3. In order to the restoring of holiness to lapsed man, the Lord Christ purchased and conveys the Spirit to them.

A state of sin includes a total deprivation of holiness, and an active contrariety against it. The sinner is dead as to the spiritual life, and as unable to revive himself, as a carcase is to break the gates of death and return to the light of the world; but he lives to the sensual life, and expresses a constant opposition to the law of God. He is without strength as to his duty, not able to conceive one holy thought, or to excite a sincere and ardent desire towards divine things; but hath strong inclinations of will and great power for that which is evil. Now to restore life to the dead soul, and to conquer the living enmity that is in it against holiness, no less than the divine power was requisite. And the effecting of this is peculiarly attributed to the Spirit. Our Saviour tells Nicodemus, " Except a man be born of water and of the Spirit, he cannot enter into the kingdom of God," John iii. 5. And the apostle saith, that "according to his mercy he saves us, by the washing of regeneration, and the renewing of the Holy Ghost," Tit. iii. 5. As in the creation, where all the persons concurred, it was the motion of the Spirit that conveyed the life of nature; so in the renovation of the world, where they all co-operate, it is the powerful working of the Spirit that produces the life of grace. He visits us in the grave, and inspires the breath and flame of heaven to animate and warm our dead hearts. It was requisite not only that the Word should take flesh, but that flesh should receive the Spirit to quicken and enable it to perform the acts of divine life. It is for this reason the third person is frequently styled in scripture "the Holy Spirit." That title hath not an immediate respect to his nature, but to the operations which are assigned to him in the admirable economy of our redemption. It is not upon the account of his essential and eternal purity, which is common to all the persons, but in regard of his office to infuse holiness into the depraved soul, and renew the divine image, that he is so called.

Now Jesus Christ purchased the Spirit by his humiliation and sufferings, and conveys him to us in his exaltation and glory.

(1.) He purchased the Spirit by his sufferings; for since man fell from his original innocence, he is justly deprived of special grace, that is necessary to heal and recover him. And till by a perfect sacrifice divine justice was appeased, (that had shut the treasure of heaven,) and the forfeiture taken off, he could not obtain the eternal riches. God must be reconciled before he will bestow the Holy Spirit, a gift so great and so precious, the earnest of his peculiar love and special favour to us. Therefore our Saviour tells his disciples, who were extremely afflicted for his departure from them, that it was expedient he should go away, for otherwise the Spirit would not come, whose office was to convince and convert the world, John xvi. 7. The departure of Christ implied his death and ascension, both which were requisite in order to the sending of him. If the blood of

Christ had not been shed on the cross, the Spirit had not been poured forth from heaven. The effusion of the one was the cause of the effusion of the other. The rock that refreshed the Israelites in the desert, did not pour forth its miraculous waters, till it was struck by the rod of Moses; to instruct us, that Christ, our spiritual Rock, must be struck with the curse of the law, the mystical rod of Moses, to communicate the waters of life to us, that is, the Spirit, who is represented in scripture under that element.

(2.) Our Redeemer conferred the Spirit after his glorious exaltation. "When he ascended up on high, he led captivity captive, and gave gifts unto men," Ephes. iv. 8. After his triumph over principalities and powers, he dispensed his bounty in this rich donative; for the Holy Spirit was first given to Christ, as the reward of his excellent obedience in dying, that was infinitely pleasing to God, to be communicated from him to men. And he received the Spirit in the quality of Mediator upon his entrance into heaven. The Psalmist declares this prophetically: "Thou hast ascended on high; thou hast led captivity captive; thou hast received gifts for men, yea, for the rebellious also, that the Lord God might dwell among them," Psalm lxviii. 18. He acquired a right to those treasures by dying, but he takes possession of them after his ascension. Now he is crowned, he holds forth the sceptre of his royalty. Therefore it is said, that when Christ was upon the earth, "the Holy Ghost was not given, because that Jesus was not yet glorified," John vii. 39.

If it be objected, that believers before the ascension of Christ were partakers of the Spirit, the answer is clear; 1. it was upon Christ's interposing in the beginning as Mediator, and with respect to his future death and ascension, that the Spirit was given to them. 2. The degrees of communicating the Spirit before and after the ascension of Christ, are very different. Whether we consider "the gifts of the Spirit," those extraordinary abilities with which the apostles were endued, or the "fruits of the Spirit," the sanctifying graces that are bestowed on believers, the measure of them far exceeds whatever was conveyed before. The Spirit descended as in a dew upon the Jewish nation, but it is now poured forth in showers "upon all flesh." Now, in the style of scripture, things are said to be, when apparently and eminently they discover their being; so that comparatively to the power and virtue of the Spirit discovered in the church since the glorification of Christ, he was not given before. All the former manifestations are obscured by the excess and excellency of the latter.

And not only the decree of God, which is sufficient to connect those things that have no natural dependence, but there are special reasons for the order of this dispensation; for the great end of the Spirit's coming was to reveal fully to the world the way of salvation, to discover the unsearchable riches of grace, to assure men of happiness after this life, that they might be reduced from a state of rebellion to obedience, and their affections be refined and purified from all earthliness, and made angelical and heavenly. Now the principal demonstrations which he used to persuade men of these things, are the death and resurrection of Christ, without which these mysteries had been under a cloud. That the instruction therefore of the Spirit might be clear and effectual, it was necessary Christ should suffer and enter into heaven, and accomplish those things he was to teach.

And from hence we may observe, that the sanctifying grace of the Spirit is the inseparable concomitant of the evangelical mercy. The gospel and the Spirit are the wings by which the Sun of righteousness brings healing and life to the world, Mal. iv. 2. The supernatural declaration of justice in the law from Mount Sinai, was not accompanied with the efficacy of grace; therefore, it is called "the ministration of death," 2 Cor. iii. 7. It conveyed no spiritual strength as delivered by the hands of Moses, considering him precisely in the quality of the legal Mediator, but threatened a curse to the breakers of it. All the promises of mercy scattered in the books of Moses belong to the covenant of grace. The gospel is called the "law of the Spirit of life," and "the ministration of the Spirit;" that is, the Spirit of holiness and comfort, from whom true and eternal life proceeds,

is communicated solely by it. The natural discovery of
the divine goodness in the works of creation and providence, is without the renewing power of the Spirit.
There is a correspondence between the external revelation of mercy, and the internal grace of the Spirit
in their original: as the one is supernatural, so is the
other.

Not that but the heathens had some fainter beams of
the Sun of righteousness, for he enlightens " every man
that cometh into the world;" and some lower operations
of the Spirit, whereby they were reduced from intemperance, incontinency, and other gross vices, to the practice
of several virtues that respect the civil life. And of this
we have an eminent instance recorded by Diogenes Laer-
tius; that Polemo half-drunk, crowned with roses, and in
the dress of a harlot rather than that of a man, coming
into the school of the severe Zenocrates, hearing him discourse of temperance, was so perfectly changed, as by a
charm, that casting away the garland from his head and
the lascivious ornaments that were about him, and, which
was more considerable, his vicious habits from his soul,
he that entered a reveller, came forth a philosopher, so
corrected and composed in his manners, that he was called the Doric tone, which of all others was the most
solemn and majestical in the music of those times. Now,
this alteration was wrought by the force of natural reason,
which prevailed on him to renounce those sensual and
base lusts that were inconsistent with the honour and
peace of a man in this present life; but still he was exceedingly distant from the purity of a true saint, who partakes "of the divine nature," and is inclined in all his
motions to God. "All the precepts of morality," to use
the similitude of Plutarch, " are like strong perfumes that
sometimes revive those that are in a swoon by the falling-
sickness, but never heal them:" so they may recover
those that are debauched, from the outward practice of
those ignoble vices which violate natural conscience, but
they cannot rectify and cure the corrupt nature. The
highest philosophical change was only from those vices
which were scandalous in the view of men, but consisted
with those which were, though more subtle, yet not less

sinful, and discernible by the pure eye of God. It was from one kind of sin to another, from sensual to spiritual, 'Satan casting out Satan," or from higher to lower degrees of sin; but not from sin to holiness. And although the same good works, as to the external substance, were performed by the heathens as by Christians, yet they vastly differ in their principle and end. A brute performs all the acts of sense that a man doth, but it is merely from the sensitive soul, that is of a lower order than that which animates a man; so in the heathen, it was only the human spirit excited by secular and private interests, self-love, servile fear, that performed moral actions. But the Holy Spirit (who infuses grace, that is, as it were, a second soul, to elevate that which before quickened the body) is the true principle of Christian virtues. This sanctifying Spirit, who transforms us into the divine nature, and makes an entire and thorough change in the heart and conversation, they did not receive in the way of nature. Of this we have a convincing proof in the example of the best masters of morality, who by their discourses or writings, raised it to the point of its perfection. Socrates, the father of philosophy, to whom this honour is ascribed among the Grecians, that he first made wisdom descend from heaven to earth, because he left the study of astronomy, in which the philosophers before him were most conversant, and applied himself to that which is useful for the government of life and reformation of manners; he that is propounded by the Gentiles as an unparalleled pattern, as one that discovered to what degree of excellency virtue might raise the human spirit, yet was guilty of great immorality and impiety. Those who pretended to have known the retirements of his life, accused him of impure commerce with Alcibiades. He betrayed the chastity of his wife by giving her to his friend. Plato and Xenophon, his admirers, declare his compliance with the common idolatry, which is justly aggravated by St. Austin, being against the convictions of his conscience; for although in private discourse with his friends he acknowledged but one God, and considered the sun and moon only as the works and instruments of the divine power, and in the rank of other creatures, yet in his apology before his judges, to prevent the fatal sentence, he charged his enemies to be guilty of impudent falsehood, who accused him that he did not believe the gods, since he believed, as all other men, that the sun and moon were gods. And during the time of his imprisonment, he never addressed one prayer to God for the pardon of his sins, for he had so high an opinion of his own virtues, that he was insensible of his vices; and dying, he commanded a cock to be offered to Æsculapius, that is, to the devil under the disguise of that famous physician. To Socrates I shall add Seneca. Never any, excepting the sacred writers, and those who are instructed by them, hath written more excellently. He describes virtue as if the living original were in his breast; but how dull a copy was drawn in his life! There is as great a difference between the expression of it by his pen and his actions, as between the lively picture of a face by a rare pencil, and the rude draught of it with a coal. What a villanous part did he act in exciting Nero to murder his mother, and afterwards in writing an apology for it, employing the colours of his rhetoric to cover one of the foulest blots which hath appeared in the succession of all ages! His philosophy was not a powerful antidote against the contagion of the court, (Tacit. lib. 15.) What just excuse can there be of his cruelty to his wife, in cutting her veins that she might die with him, from a vain-glorious desire to eternize their reputation? And whereas among the whole chorus of virtues, he in a special manner exalts magnanimity in the contempt of earthly things, and determines that the necessities of nature are the just measures of riches and delights and all other things which the irregular appetites of men pursue, so that one would think him an angel in flesh, conversing below to instruct the world how to be happy; yet the historians of those times tax him for insatiable avarice, that in a little time by unworthy arts he raked up an incredible sum of money. Supposing it a calumny that he forged many wills to seize upon the estates belonging to others, what excuse can there be for his excessive usury, his forcing the Britons to borrow a million of sesterces, and calling for it in, so much to their prejudice, as was likely to have caused their rebellion? What for his sumptuous palaces, and gardens of pleasure, exceeding the luxury of Nero; and all those possessed by a man who had no son to inherit, a philosopher, a Stoic, the great commender of blessed poverty? All the apology he makes, is, that a wise man, that is himself, "*non amat divitias sed mavult, non in animum illas sed in domum inducit, non respicit possessas sed continet;*" agreeing with Aristippus, a philosophizing animal, who being reproved for his entanglement in brutish love with a famous harlot, replied, "I possess her, not she me." The only difference is in the matter of their affections; the one was riches the other pleasure. By these instances we may judge of the rest of the philosophers. Although a vein of gold appear in their writings, yet their lives were full of dross. The best of them are charged to have practised vice with those, to whom they commended the precepts of virtue. The foulest actions were approved by some, and the most excellent condemned by others, that pretended to philosophical perfection. Unnatural lust was allowed as indifferent by Zeno and Chrysippus: and the noblest love in giving life itself for the glory of God in martyrdom, is censured by Epictetus and Antoninus, as the effect of foolish and incurable melancholy in Christians, who were disgusted with the world and devoted themselves to death.

The Spirit of holiness, who forms the powerful and lasting habits of true virtue in the soul, that effectually inclines, from the love of God, and, with an intention for his glory, to obey his will, as it was purchased by Jesus Christ, so is peculiar to the dispensation of the gospel that reveals him. The doctrine of it is not delivered with so much pomp, but with infinitely more efficacy than the most eloquent instructions of philosophers. One plain sermon that represents Christ as crucified before our eyes to obtain pardon of sin for us, inflames the soul with a more ardent love to God and vehement hatred of sin, than all their elegant and sublime discourses. There is the same difference between their morals and the evangelical institution, as between two nurses: the one is adorned and looks lovely to the eye, but wants milk to nourish the infant in her arms; the other is not so amiable in appearance, but hath a living spring of milk to nourish her child. Philosophy hath the advantage of artificial beauty, but cannot supply the nourishment that is necessary to maintain the spiritual life; but the gospel affords the sincere rational milk to the soul, that "it may grow thereby." It is therefore called the "word of life," a title that distinguishes it from the law, and all human institutions.

4. Jesus Christ hath presented the strongest inducements and motives to persuade us to holiness. The way which he takes to save us, is not by a mere act of power to raise us above ourselves; but he deals with us conveniently to our frame, in making use of our affections to bring us to himself. And whereas there are three affections that have a mighty power over the reasonable, and are the inward springs of human actions, viz. fear, hope, and love; he hath propounded such objects to them, which, being duly considered, are infinitely more efficacious than any thing that may divert us from our duty. The great temptations to sin are from the terrors or delights of sense, and to overcome these, he hath brought to our assistance "the powers of the world to come;" that is, hath revealed the dreadful preparations for the punishment of the wicked, and the glorious rewards that attend the godly in their future state.

Now, to discover the efficacy of these objects for persuading men to be holy, I will consider their greatness, as it is described in the gospel, and their truth and reality, of which our Saviour hath given us convincing evidence and assurance.

(1.) To excite our fear, he threatens torments extreme and eternal. These are set forth by such representations, as may impress the quickest sense of them upon man; for the imagination depends on sensible experience, and is strongly affected with those things that are terrible to our outward faculties. Now hell is described by "a worm" gnawing the most tender parts, that are most capable of pain, to signify the furious reflections of the guilty soul, the sting of the enraged conscience, the torment of those perfect passions that continually vex the damned. And it is set forth by "fire and brimstone," that is most fierce to sense; the serious consideration of which is enough to cause terror and amazement in all that are liable to it. And if the sole apprehension be intolerable, how much more will be the "dwelling with devouring fire, and everlasting burning!" It is called the "blackness of darkness," to signify the complete horror of that state. The fire hath force to burn only, not to give any light to mitigate the obscurity. It is called the "second death," in comparison of which that of the body is but the shadow of death. Nothing of life remains but the sense of misery, and that will be as strong for ever as at the first entrance into it. This infinitely increases the torment, that it shall never end. The suffering soul knows it shall be eternal, and as such it is felt and afflicts. The fire that devours, shall never say "It is enough;" that sad night shall never have a morning; that horrible tempest never any calm. The damned have no breathing of rest in their extreme pains, no shadow of hope to refresh them in their intolerable heat, but are under torment "day and night, for ever and ever," Rev. xx. 10.

Now what can be more powerful to restrain men from sin than the terrors of the Lord? If the desires of carnal and momentary pleasures are impetuous and urgent, what can be more effectual to give check to them, than the consideration that they are attended with a painful eternity; that within a little while nothing will remain of the most pleasant lusts but the worm and the fire? Thus one extreme is cured by another. Or, if the fear of men, who can inflict but outward evils and death on the body, at any time resists the performance of our duty, what is more proper to lessen the impression, than to remember how dreadful a thing it is to fall into the revenging "hands of the living God," who lives for ever, and can punish for ever? Thus our Saviour fortified his disciples against persecution. "I say unto you, my friends, be not afraid of them that kill the body, and after that have no more that they can do; but I will forewarn you whom you shall fear: fear Him which after he hath killed, hath power to cast into hell; yea, I say unto you, fear him," Luke xii. 4, 5. Eternal damnation is infinitely more fearful than temporal death. As the rod of Moses devoured the rods of the magicians, so the fear of hell overcomes the fear of death, and all the torments which end with this life.

I shall add further, to show how fit an argument this is to work on mankind, that usually the fear of evil more deeply affects than the hope of good. When the imagination is violently struck with an object, it hath a mighty force to turn the mind and will itself; therefore laws are secured by punishments, not by rewards. Indeed the fear of hell at first disposes us for the love of heaven; to escape the one, we fly to the other. As the virtue of the loadstone is increased by arming it with iron, which, although it hath no attractive power in itself, yet by conjunction it makes the other more forcible; so the promise of heaven makes a stronger impression upon us, by the threatening of hell to all that despise it. Were it not for the torments of hell, (which are more easily conceived by us whilst we are clothed with flesh, than celestial joys, and therefore more strongly affect us,) heaven would be neglected, and be as empty of saints as it is full of glory. To awaken us out of the deep lethargy of sensual lusts, the most pleasant music is ineffectual; nothing less is requisite than cutting and scarifying.

And not only those that begin and first enter in the ways of godliness, but those who are advanced in Christianity have need of this bridle; for there are some temptations wherein the flesh assaults the spirit with that violence, that love itself is obliged to call in fear to its assistance, as being more proper to repress its inordinate motions. It is only in heaven that perfect love will consume all concupiscence, and cast out fear of judgment; but whilst we are encompassed with temptations, we must not think, under the pretext of a more raised spirituality, that the fear of hell is either unbecoming or unnecessary. It is not unworthy a child of God to employ all the motives of the gospel. We are commanded to "work out our own salvation with fear and trembling," Phil. ii. 12.

But the opening of hell to our view is not sufficient

alone to make us holy; for the strongest terrors, although they restrain from the outward forbidden act, yet do not change the heart; according to that of St. Austin, "*Inaniter se victorem putat esse peccati, qui pœnæ timore non peccat; quia etsi non impletur foris negotium malæ cupiditatis, ipsa tamen cupiditas intus est hostis;*" that is, the fear of punishment can never make us truly victorious over sin, because although we do not actually accomplish the desires of the corrupt will, yet the corrupt will is still an enemy that lives within, and is destroyed only by the love of holiness, which allures us by the excellent reward that is promised to it. Besides, fear is a violent passion to which nature is repugnant, so that although its power is great, yet not constant. How strong soever the force is by which a stone is thrown upwards, yet the impression is weakened by degrees, and overcome by the natural weight of the stone whereby it falls to the centre: so the human nature resists fear, and lessens its impetuousness so far, that frequently it returns to sensual lusts. Therefore that the law of the spirit may be perfect and stable, it must be confirmed by the hopes of heaven. As the natural, so the spiritual life must be nourished by grateful food; it is not preserved with aloes or wormwood.

(2.) For this reason our Saviour, to encourage and raise our hopes, offers to us a reward infinitely valuable; for as God is infinite, such is the happiness he bestows on his favourites. It is described to us in scripture under the most enamouring representations, as a state of peace and love, of joy and glory.

The Prince of Peace reigns in the holy Jerusalem that is above, and preserves an everlasting serenity and calmness. The mutinous spirits that rebelled were presently chased from thence into this lower region, where they brought trouble and disorder. "He maketh peace in his high places," Job xxv. 2. The peace of heaven is like the crystal sea before the throne of the Lamb, which no unquiet agitation ever troubles or disturbs, Rev. iv. 6.

An inviolable love unites all his subjects; no division or jealousy discomposes their concord. They enjoy without envy; for infinite blessedness is not diminished by the number of possessors. The inheritance in light is communicated to all. Although the angels are distinguished by their several orders and ministrations, as seraphim and cherubim, thrones and powers, yet a chain of holy love binds all their affections together. And though the saints shine with different degrees of glory, yet, as in a chorus of music the different voices make one entire harmony, so love that ever continues, unites their wills in a delightful harmonious agreement. The millions of celestial inhabitants compose but one society, love mixing in one mass of light and glory all their understandings and wills.

And since all true joy and sweetness spring from love, it is impossible but they must feel unspeakable complacency in the reciprocal exercise of so holy and pure an affection. But their joy arises principally from the possession of God himself, by the clearest knowledge and purest love of his excellencies; they "see him as he is," 1 John iii. 2. Sight is the most spiritual and noble sense, that gives the most distinct and evident discovery of its objects. The soul in its exalted state "sees the King in his beauty," all the perfections of that infinitely glorious and blessed nature in their brightness and purity. And this sight causes the most ardent love, by which there is an intimate and vital union between the soul and its happiness; and from hence springs perfect delight; "In thy presence is fulness of joy," Psalm xvi. 11. It expels all evil that would embitter and lessen our felicity. And this is an admirable privilege for the human nature, that is so sensible of trouble. All complaints and cries, all sighings and sorrows, are for ever banished from heaven. If the light of the sun be so pleasant, that every morning revives the world, and renders it new to us, which was buried in the darkness of the night, how infinitely pleasant will the light of glory be, that discovers the absolute and universal excellencies of the Deity, the beauty of his holiness, the perfection of his wisdom, the greatness of his power, and the riches of his mercy! How inexpressibly great is the happiness that proceeds from the illumination of a purified soul, when such is the amiableness of God, that his infinite and eternal felicity arises from the fruition of himself! The joy of heaven is so full and satisfying, that a thousand years there are but as one day. Inferior earthly goods presently lose the flower of novelty, and languish in our enjoyment of them; variety is necessary to put an edge upon our appetites, and quicken our delights; because they are imperfect, and fall short of our expectations; but the object of our blessedness is infinitely great, and produces the same pure and perfect joy for ever. After the longest fruition it never cloys or satiates, but is as fresh and new as at the first moment.

And that which is the peculiar pleasure of the redeemed, is, that they shall be with Christ, and see his glory, John xvii. 24. What a marvellous joy will fill our hearts, to see our blessed Saviour, who suffered so much for us on earth, to reign in heaven! Here he was in his enemies' hands; there he hath them under his feet. Here he was in the "form of a servant;" there he appears in "the form of God," adorned with all the marks of majesty. Here he was under the cloud of his Father's displeasure; there he appears as the "brightness of his glory." Here he was ignominiously crucified; there he is crowned with immortal honour. Now considering the ardent affections which the saints have to their Redeemer, the contemplation of him in this glorious state must infinitely ravish their hearts; especially if we consider that the exaltation of Christ is theirs. The members triumph when the head is crowned. His excellent glory reflects a lustre upon them, and by the sight of it they are changed into his likeness. If the imperfect and dim sight of his divine virtues in the gospel, hath a power to change believers into his "image from glory to glory," how much more the vision of his unveiled face! Our graces here are but as the rude draught and first colours of the divine image, that shall then be in its perfection. "We know that when he appears, we shall be like him, for we shall see him as he is," 1 John iii. 2. The similitude between the saints above and Christ, is so exact, that if one should enter into the kingdom of heaven, and were not directed by the light of that place, he would be apt to think every glorified saint he meets to be more than a creature. John, the beloved of Christ, and as clear sighted as any of the apostles, mistook an angel for God; and would have adored him, although he did not appear in his full glory. The kingdoms of the world, with all their splendour, are no more in comparison to it, than a dead spark to the sun in its brightness. The very bodies of the saints shall be raised from the grave, and beautified with eternal ornaments; they shall be companions with the angels, and conformed to the glorious body of Christ.

Briefly, in the present state we are not capable of receiving the full knowledge of heaven. What we understand is infinitely desirable, but the most glorious part is still undiscovered. The apostle tells us, " Eye hath not seen, nor ear heard, neither have entered into the heart of man, the things which God hath prepared for them that love him," 1 Cor. ii. 9. All that is beautiful or sweet here, is but a shadow of that glory, a drop of that vast ocean of delights; for all that is desirable in the creatures, and is dispersed among them, is united in God as the original in an infinite and indeficient manner, with all the prerogatives that the creatures have not. Celestial blessedness as much exceeds our most raised thoughts, as God is more glorious in himself than in any representations made of him by the shadows of our earthly imaginations. There is a greater disproportion between the condition of a saint on earth and in heaven, than between the life of an infant in the womb, and of the same person when advanced to the throne, and attended with the nobility of a nation. John declares, " Now are we the sons of God, and it doth not yet appear what we shall be," 1 John iii. 2. Who knows the full signification of " being heirs of God, and joint heirs with Christ," of partaking in that glorious reward which is given to him for his great services to the crown of heaven? Who can tell the weight, the number, and measure of that blessedness? " To him that overcometh," saith our Redeemer, " will I grant to sit down with me in my throne, even as I also overcame, and am set down with my Father in his throne," Rev. iii. 21. We have reason to break forth in the language of the Psalmist, "How great is thy goodness which thou hast laid up for them that fear thee!" and supply the defects of our understanding with a holy admiration, that is the only measure of those things that are above our measure, Psalm xxxi. 19.

Besides, the reward as in excellency it is divine, so in duration is perpetual. Heaven is an inheritance as safe as great. Here we are subject to time, that carries us and all our goods down its swift stream; but there eternity, that is fixed and unchangeable, embraces us in its bosom. We shall be secure and at rest, for no person shall take away our crown; we "shall reign for ever and ever," Rev. xxii. 5. At God's "right hand are pleasures for evermore," that can never abate or end, Psalm xvi. 11. As his liberal hand bestows, so his powerful hand preserves our happiness. The blessed shall sing everlasting hymns of glory and songs of thanksgiving to the great Creator, Redeemer, and Sanctifier, who hath prepared and purchased that felicity for them, and hath brought them to the secure possession of it.

Now can there be a more powerful motive to obedience, than infinite and eternal blessedness? What can pretend to our affections in competition with it? Carnal pleasures gratify only our viler part, the body, in its vilest state; but the joys of heaven are spiritual and sublime, and proportioned to our noblest and most capacious faculties. Earthly delights cannot satisfy our senses, but "the peace of God passeth understanding." One hour's enjoyment of it is better than an eternity spent in the pleasures of sin. What inexcusable madness is it to prefer painted trifles before that inestimable treasure! Who can truly believe there is such an excellent glory, but he must love it, and vigorously endeavour to obtain it? Who would not go to the celestial Canaan, though the way lies through a wilderness where no flower or fruit grows? All temporal evils are not only to be endured, but cheerfully embraced in order to the possessing of it. The apostle tells us, "I reckon that the sufferings of this present time, are not worthy to be compared with the glory which shall be revealed in us,"

Rom. viii. 18. And he was the most fit person to make the comparison, having made trial of both states; for he was a man of sorrows, that had passed through afflictions of all kinds, and he was ravished up to paradise, where he heard those things that exceed all expressions of human words. Now after a serious estimate, he declares that the eternal weight of glory, infinitely outbalances the light and momentary troubles of this life, 2 Cor. iv. 17.

Thus from what has been said concerning the greatness of the recompenses hereafter, we may understand how powerful they are to deter men from sin, and to allure them to holiness.

That these objects may be effectual, our Saviour hath clearly revealed them, and given us convincing evidence and assurance of their reality. The heathens had only some glimmerings and suspicions of a future state. They were under doubts concerning the nature of the soul, whether mortal or incorruptible, wavering between the assent and denial, and inclining to this or that part, as sense persuaded them to believe themselves only as brutes, or reason to acknowledge themselves men. Socrates, before his judges, speaks as one that desired immortality; and in his last discourse to his friends, he endeavours to persuade them, but could not conquer his own doubts nor assure himself. All his discourses end in conjectures and uncertain guesses. Besides, the hell which they fancied, was made up of such ridiculous and senseless terrors, that could affect children only, who were not arrived to the perfect use of reason. And their apprehensions of happiness in the next life were so extravagant, that what the philosopher said in general of hope, that it is the dream of waking men, is more justly applicable to the hope of the heathens in respect of the future reward. For as the illusions of a dream have many times a real subject, but environed with so many fantastic imaginations as spoil all the proportions of it, so their opinion had a foundation in truth, but was mixed with many errors inconsistent with perfect felicity; and as the pleasure of a dream is slight and vanishing, so their uncertain expectation of felicity did but lightly touch their spirits. Briefly, they had no true knowledge, no firm belief of eternal blessedness in the vision of God, nor of the endless torments in hell; and wanting those great principles from whence the rules and power to live in a holy manner are derived, they fell short of that purity which is a necessary qualification to prepare men for heaven. They were in a confused labyrinth, without true light or guide, entangled with miserable errors; and stumbled every step whilst they sought after happiness. But the Lord Christ hath instructed the world concerning those invisible, future recompenses. He hath expressly threatened, whatever is to be feared by man as a rational or sensible creature, the worm that never dies, and the fire that shall never be quenched, in case of disobedience; and he hath promised whatever is to be hoped for, in case of obedience. "The wrath of God is revealed from heaven," in the gospel, "against all ungodliness, and unrighteousness of men;" and our Saviour hath brought "life and immortality to light," Rom. i. 18; 2 Tim. i. 10. He hath declared the nature and quality of eternal life; that it consists in the most perfect acts of our raised and most receptive faculties upon the most excellent objects; that it contains perfect holiness and pure felicity, being for ever distant from the infirmities and defilements of our mortal state. He hath revealed both the quality, and the extent of it, relating to the body as well as the soul; whereas the philosophers of several sects, the Academics, Stoics, Epicureans, labouring with all the force of their understanding, formed a felicity according to their fancies, which was either wholly sensual, or else but for half of man; for of the resurrection, and consequently the immortality of the body, not the least notice for many ages ever arrived to them. Our Saviour, who alone had " the words of eternal life," hath promised a happiness that respects entire man: the soul and the body which are his essential parts, shall be united and endued with all the glorious qualities becoming the sons of God. And of all this he hath given to the world the highest assurance, for he verified his doctrine by his own example, rising from the grave, and appearing to his apostles, crowned with immortality, and visibly ascending before them to heaven. Since there is no greater paradox to reason than the resurrection, which seemed utterly incredible to men, and not to be the object of a rational desire, God by raising him from the grave, hath given the most convincing argument that our Redeemer was sent from him, to acquaint the world with the future state. Thus the apostle speaks to the Athenians; "The times of this ignorance God winked at, but now commandeth all men every where to repent; because he hath appointed a day, in the which he will judge the world in righteousness, by that man whom he hath ordained, whereof he hath given assurance unto all men, in that he hath raised him from the dead," Acts xvii. 30. Jesus Christ who was attested from heaven to be the Son of God by that great and powerful act, declared the recompenses that shall attend men after death; therefore a full and perfect assent is due to his testimony. Hell, with all its dread and terror, is not a picture drawn by fancy to affright the world, but is revealed by him whose words shall remain when heaven and earth shall pass away. The heavenly glories are not the visions of a contemplative person, that have no existence, but are great realities promised by him, who, as he died to purchase, so he rose to witness the truth of them. And to bring these great things, that are separate and distant from this present state, nearer to us, he sometimes causes hell to rise up from beneath, aud flash in the face of secure sinners, that they may break off their sins by repentance; and sometimes he opens heaven from above, the paradise of true delights, and sends down " of the precious fruits of the sun, of the precious things of the lasting hills," that by the sight of their beauty and the taste of their sweetness, we may for ever abhor the pleasures of sin. By the frequent and sensible experience of the truth of the gospel in its threatenings and promises, innumerable persons have been converted from sin to holiness, from heaven to earth, from vanity to eternity.

Love is a prevalent affection, stronger than death; and kindness is the greatest endearment of love. Now, the Lord Jesus expressed such admirable love to us, that, being duly considered, it cannot but inspire us with love to him again, and with a grateful desire to please him in all things. He descended from heaven to earth, and delivered himself to a shameful death, "that he might redeem us from all iniquity, and purify unto himself a peculiar people zealous of good works," Tit. ii. 14. And what argument is more powerful to cause in us a serious hatred of sin, than the consideration of what Christ hath suffered to free us from the punishment and power of it? If a man for his crimes were condemned to the galleys, and a friend of his who had been extremely injured by him, should ransom him by a great sum; when the guilty person is restored to liberty, will he not blush for shame at the memory of what he hath done? but how much more if his friend would suffer for him the pains and infamy of his slavery? If any spark of humanity remain in him, can he ever delight himself in those actions, which made such a benefit necessary to him? Now, we "were not redeemed with corruptible things, as silver and gold, from our vain conversation," the most sordid and deplorable captivity, " but with the precious blood of Christ, as of a lamb without blemish and without spot," 1 Pet. i. 18, 19. And is it possible for a Christian to live in those sins for which Christ died? Will not love cause an humble fear lest he should frustrate the great design, and make void the most blessed effect of his terrible sufferings? Why did he redeem us with so excellent a price from our cruel bondage, but to restore us to his free service? Why did he vindicate us from the power of the usurper to whom we were captives, but to make us subjects of our natural Prince? Why did he purify us with his most precious blood from our deadly defilements, but that we might be entirely consecrated to his glory, and be fervent in good works? What can work upon an ingenuous person more than a sense of kindness? What can oblige more strongly to duty, than gratitude? What more powerful attractive to obedience, than love? This pure love confirms the glorified saints for ever in holiness; for they are not holy to obtain heaven, because they are possessed of it; nor to preserve their blessedness, because they are past all hazard of losing it; but from the most lively and permanent sense of their obligations, because they have obtained that incomparable felicity by a gift never to be reversed, and by a mercy transcendently great. And the same love to God that is in the saints above in the highest degree of perfection, and makes them for ever glorify him, will proportionably to our state in this life cause us to observe his commands with delight and constancy. A true Christian is moved by fear, more by hope, most by love

CHAPTER XIX.

PRACTICAL INFERENCES.

From hence we may discover the perfection and completeness of the redemption that our Saviour purchased for us. He fully repairs what was ruined by the fall. He was called Jesus, because he should save his people from their sins, Matt. i. 21. He reconciles them to God, and redeems them from "their vain conversation." He " came by water and blood," to signify the accomplishment of what was represented by the ceremonial purification, and the blood of the sacrifices. Satisfaction and sanctification are found in him. And this was not a needless compassion, but absolutely requisite in order to our felicity. Man, in his guilty corrupt state, may be compared to a condemned malefactor, infected with noisome and painful wounds and diseases, and wanting the grace of the prince to pardon him, and sovereign remedies to heal him. Supposing the sentence were reversed, yet he cannot enjoy his life till he is restored to health. Thus the sinner is under the condemnation of the law, and under many spiritual, powerful distempers, that make him truly miserable. His irregular passions are so many sorts of diseases, not only contrary to health, but to one another, that continually torment him. He feels all the effects of sickness. He is inflamed by his lusts and made restless, being without power to accomplish or to restrain them. All his faculties are disabled for the spiritual life, that is only worthy of his nature, and whose operations are mixed with sincere and lasting pleasure. Sin, as it is the disease, so it is the wound of the soul, and attended with all the evils of those that are most terrible. "The whole head is sick, and the whole heart faint; from the sole of the foot to the head, there is no soundness in it, but wounds, and bruises, and putrefying sores," Isa. i. 5. Now our Redeemer, as he hath obtained a full remission of our sins, so he restores holiness to us, the true health and vigour of the soul. He hath made a plaster of his living flesh mixed with his tears and blood, those divine and powerful ingredients, to heal our wounds. By the Holy Spirit it is applied to us, that we may partake of its virtue and influence. His most precious sacrifice purifies the conscience "from dead works," that we may serve the living God. Without this the bare exemption from punishment were not sufficient to make us happy; for although the guilty conscience were secure from wrath to come, yet those fierce unruly passions, the generation of vipers that lodge in the breast of the sinner, would cause a real domestic hell. Till these are mortified, there can be no ease nor rest. Besides, sin is the true dishonour of man's nature, that degrades him from his excellency, and changes him into a beast or a devil; so that to have a license to wallow in the mire, to live in the practice of sin that stains and vilifies him, were a miserable privilege. The scripture therefore represents the curing of our corrupt inclinations, and the cleansing of us from our pollutions, to be the eminent effect and blessed work of saving mercy. Accordingly Peter tells the Jews, "God having raised up his Son Jesus, sent him to bless you, in turning away every one of you from his iniquities," Acts iii. 26; that is, Christ in his glorified state gives the Spirit of holiness to work a sincere thorough change in men, from all presumptuous reigning sins, to universal holiness. Invaluable benefit, that equals if not excels our justification! for as the evil of sin in its own nature is worse than the evil of punishment, so the freeing of us from its dominion is a greater blessing than mere impunity. The Son of God for a time was made subject to our miseries, not to our sins.

He divested himself of his glory, not of his holiness. And the apostle in the ecstasy of his affection desired to be made unhappy for the salvation of the Jews, not to be unholy. Besides, the end is more noble than the means; now Jesus Christ purchased our pardon, that we might be restored to our forfeited holiness. He ransomed us by his death, that he might bless us by his resurrection. He "gave himself for us that he might redeem us from all iniquity, and purify unto himself a peculiar people, zealous of good works," Tit. ii. 14. Sanctification is the last end of all he did and suffered for us.

Holiness is the chiefest excellency of man, his highest advantage above inferior beings. It is the supreme beauty of the soul, the resemblance of angels, the image of God himself. In this the perfection of the reasonable nature truly consists, and glory naturally results from it. As a diamond, when its earthy and colourless parts are taken away, shines forth in its lustre; so when the soul is freed from its impurities and all terrene affections, it will appear with a divine brightness. The church shall then be glorious, when cleansed from every spot, and made complete in holiness. To this I will only add, that without holiness we cannot see God; that is, delightfully enjoy him. Suppose the law were dispensed with, that forbids any unclean person to enter into the " holy Jerusalem," the place cannot make him happy; for happiness consists in the fruition of an object that is suitable and satisfying to our desires. The holy God cannot be our felicity without our partaking of his nature. Imputed righteousness frees us from hell, inherent makes us fit for heaven. The sum is—Jesus Christ, that he might be a perfect Saviour sanctifies all whom he justifies; for otherwise we could not be totally exempted from suffering evil, nor capable of enjoying the supreme good; we could not be happy here nor hereafter.

II. From hence it appears, that saving grace gives no encouragement to the practice of sin; for the principal aim of our Redeemer's love in dying for us, was "to sanctify and cleanse us, by the washing of water and the word." And accordingly all the promises of pardon and salvation are conditional. The holy mercy of the gospel offers forgiveness only to penitent believers that return from sin to obedience. We are commanded to "repent and be converted, that our sins may be blotted out," in the times of refreshment from the presence of the Lord, Acts iii. 19. And heaven is the reward of persevering obedience; "To them who by patient continuance in well-doing, seek for glory, and honour, and immortality, eternal life," Rom. ii. 7. There cannot be the least ground of a rational just hope in any person without holiness; " Every man that hath this hope in him, purifieth himself even as he is pure," 1 John iii. 3. By which it appears, that the genuine and proper use we are to make of "the exceeding great and precious promises," is, "that by them we may be partakers of the divine nature," and escape "the pollution that is in the world through lust," 2 Pet. i. 4. Yet the corrupt hearts of men are so strongly inclined to their lusts, that they "turn the grace of God into wantonness," and make an advantage of mercy to assist their security; presuming to sin with less fear and more license, upon the account of the glorious revelation of it by our Redeemer. The most live as if they might be saved without being saints, and enjoy the paradise of the flesh here, and not be excluded from that of the spirit hereafter. But grace doth not in the least degree authorize and favour their lusts, nor relax the sinews of obedience; it is perfectly innocent of their unnatural abuse of it. The poison is not in the flower, but the spider. Therefore the apostle propounds it with indignation, "Shall we continue in sin, that grace may abound? God forbid," Rom. vi. 1. He uses this form of speech to express an extreme abhorrence of a thing that is either impious and dishonourable to God, or pernicious and destructive to men; as when he puts the question, "Is God unrighteous who taketh vengeance? God forbid," Rom. iii. 5, 6; and, "Is there unrighteousness with God? God forbid," Rom. ix. 14. He rejects the mention of it with infinite aversion.

Indeed, what greater disparagement can there be of the divine purity, than to indulge ourselves in sin upon confidence of an easy forgiveness, as if the Son of God had been consecrated by such terrible sufferings, to purchase and prepare a pardon for those who sin securely? What an inexpressible indignity is it to make a monstrous alliance between Christ and Belial!

And this abuse of grace is pernicious to men. If the antidote be turned into poison, and the remedy cherish the disease, the case is desperate. The apostle tells us, those that do evil that good may come thereby, their damnation is just. Suppose a presuming sinner were assured, that after he had gratified his carnal vile desires, he should repent and be pardoned; yet it were an unreasonable defect of self-love to do so. What Israelite was so fool-hardy as to provoke a fiery serpent to bite him, though he knew he should be healed by the brazen serpent? But it is a degree beyond madness for a man to live in a course of sin upon the hopes of salvation, making the mercy of God to be his bondage, as if he could not be happy without them. An unrenewed sinner may be the object of God's compassion, but while he remains so, he is incapable of communion with him here, much more hereafter. Under the law, the lepers were excluded the camp of Israel, where the presence of God was in a special manner; much more shall those who are covered with moral pollutions, be kept out from the habitation of his holiness. It is a mortal delusion for any to pretend that electing mercy will bring them to glory, or that the all-sufficient sacrifice of Christ will atone God's displeasure towards them, although they indulge themselves in a course of sin. The book of life is secret; only "the Lamb," with whose blood the names of the elect are written there, "can open the seals of it;" but the gospel, that is a lower book of life, tells us the qualifications of those who are vessels of mercy; they are by grace prepared for glory; and that there can be no benefit by the death of Christ without conformity to his life. Those who abuse mercy now, shall have justice for ever.

III. From hence we may discover the peculiar excellency of the Christian religion above all other institutions; and that in respect of its design and effect.

1. The whole design of the gospel is expressed in the words of Christ from heaven to Paul, when he sent him

to the Gentiles, "to open their eyes, and to turn them from darkness to light, and from the power of Satan to God; that they may receive forgiveness of sins, and inheritance among them which are sanctified by faith" in Christ, Acts xxvi. 18. One great end of it is to take away all the filthiness and malignity wherewith sin hath infected the world, and to cause in men a real conformity to God's holiness, according to their capacity. As the reward it promises is not an earthly happiness, such as we enjoy here, but celestial; so the holiness it requires, is not an ordinary natural perfection, which men honour with the title of virtue, but an angelical divine quality that sanctifies us in the spirit, soul, and body; that cleanses the thoughts and affections, and expresses itself in a course of universal obedience to God's will. Indeed, there are other things that commend the gospel to any, that with judgment compare it with other religions; as the height of its mysteries, which are so sacred and venerable, that upon the discovery they affect with reverence and admiration; whereas the religion of the Gentiles was built on follies and fables. Their most solemn mysteries, to which they were admitted after so long a circuit of ceremonies and great preparations, contained nothing but a prodigious mixture of vanity and impiety, worthy to be concealed in everlasting darkness. Besides, the confirmation of the gospel by miracles doth authorize it above all human institutions. And the glorious eternal reward of it infinitely exceeds whatever is propounded by them. But that which gives it the most visible pre-eminence, is, that it is "a doctrine which is according to godliness," 1 Tim. vi. 3. The end is the character of its nature. The whole contexture and harmony of its doctrines, precepts, promises, threatenings, is for the exaltation of godliness. The objects of faith revealed are not merely speculative, to be conceived and believed only as true, or to be gazed on in an ecstasy of wonder, but "are mysteries of godliness," that have a powerful influence upon practice. The design of God in the publication of them, is not only to enlighten the mind, but to warm the heart and purify the affections. God discovers his nature that we may imitate him and his works, that we may glorify him. All the precepts of the gospel are to embrace Christ by a lively faith; to seek for righteousness and holiness in him; to live godly, righteously, and soberly in this present world. When our Saviour was on the earth, the end of his sermons, as appears in the gospel, was to regulate the lives of men, to correct their vicious passions, rather than to explicate the greatest mysteries. Other religions oblige their disciples either to some external actions that have no moral worth in them, so that is impossible for any one that is guided by reason to be taken with such vanities; or they require things incommodious and burdensome. The priests of Baal cut themselves. And among the Chinese, though in great reputation for wisdom, their penitents expose themselves half naked to the injuries of the sharpest weather, with a double cruelty and pleasure of the devil, who makes them freeze here, and expects they should burn for ever hereafter. It is not the most strict observance of serious trifles, nor submitting to rigorous austerities, that ennobles human nature, and commends us to God. The most zealous performers of things indifferent, and that chastise themselves with a bloody discipline, labour for nothing, and may pass to hell through purgatory. But the religion of Christ reforms the understanding and will, and all the actions depending on them. It chases away error, and vice, and hatred, and sheds abroad light and love, purity and peace; and forms on earth a lively representation of that pure society that is in heaven. The end of it is to render men like the angels in holiness, that they may be so in blessedness. This will render it amiable to all that consider it without passion. And it is worthy of observation, that although many heathens and heretics have contradicted other parts of the Christian religion, yet none have dared openly to condemn the moral part of it.

2. The effect of the gospel hath been answerable to the design. One main difference between the old and the new law is, that the old gave the knowledge of rules without power to observe them; the new that is attended with the grace of Christ, enables us by a holy love to perform that which the other made men only to under-

stand. Of this we have the most sensible evidence in the primitive church, that was produced by the first beams of the Sun of righteousness, and had received the first fruits of the Spirit. What is more wonderful and worthy of God, than that perfect love which made all the first believers to have one heart and one soul? What greater contempt of the world can be imagined, than the voluntary parting with all their goods, in consecrating them to God for the relief of the poor? And the churches of the Gentiles, while the blood of Christ was warm, and his actions fresh in the memories of men, were exemplary in holiness. They were "as stars shining in a perverse generation." There was such a brightness in their conversations, that it pierced through the darkness of paganism, and made a visible difference between them and all others. Their words and actions were so full of zeal for the glory of God, of chastity, temperance, justice, charity, that the heathens from the holiness of their lives concluded the holiness of their law, and that the doctrine that produced such fruits could not be evil. The first light that discovered the truth of the Christian faith to many, was from the graces and virtues that appeared in the faithful. The purity of their lives, their courage in death, were as powerful to convert the world, as their sermons, disputations, and miracles. And those who were under such strong prejudices that they would not examine the doctrine of the gospel, yet could not but admire the integrity and innocency that was visible in the conversation of Christians. They esteemed their persons from the good qualities that were visible in them, when they hated the Christian name for the concealed evil they unreasonably suspected to be under it. This Tertullian excellently represents in his apology: "The most part are so prejudiced against the name, and are possessed with such a blind hatred to it, that they make it a matter of reproach even to those whom they otherwise esteemed. 'Caius,' they say, 'is a good man; he hath no fault but that he is a Christian.'" Thus the excellent holiness of the professors of the gospel forced a veneration from their enemies. But we are fallen from heaven, and mixed with the dust.

Our conversation hath nothing singular in holiness to distinguish us from the world. The same corrupt passions reign in professors of Christianity, as in those who are strangers to the sacred covenant. If we compare ourselves with the primitive church, we must confess our unworthiness to be called their successors. Seventeen hundred years are run out since the Son of God came down to sanctify and save the world, which are so many degrees, whereby we are descended from the first perfection. We are more distant from them in holiness than in time. So universal and great is the corruption, that it is almost as difficult to revive the dying faith of Christians, and to reform their lives according to the purity of their profession, as the conversion of the world was from heathenism to Christianity.

It is true, in every age there are some examples of the virtue of the gospel, that reflect an honour upon it. And this last age, which we may call the winter of the world, in which the Holy Spirit hath foretold, "that the love of many shall grow cold," by a marvellous antiperistasis, hath inflamed the hearts of some excellent saints towards God and religion. But the great number of the wicked and the progress of sin in their lives, there is no measure of tears sufficient to lament.

It remains for me to press Christians to walk " as becometh the gospel of Christ," answerably to the holiness and purity of that divine institution, and to those great and strict obligations it lays upon us. The gospel requires an entire holiness in all our faculties, an equal respect to all our duties: we are commanded to cleanse ourselves from all pollutions of flesh and spirit, to be "holy in all manner of conversation." We are enjoined to be " perfecting holiness in the fear of God ;" to be holy, " as he that hath called us is holy." A certain measure of faith, and love, and obedience, a mediocrity in virtue, we must not content ourselves with. It is not a counsel of perfection given to some Christians only of a peculiar order and elevation; but the command of a law that without exception binds all. "Be ye perfect, even as your Father which is in heaven is perfect," Matt. v. 48. The gospel gives no dispensation to any person, nor in any duty. The doctrine that asserts there are some excellent works to which the lower sort of Christians is not obliged, is equally pernicious, both to those who do them by presumption, as if they were not due, and were therefore meritorious; and to those who neglect them, by a blind security, as if they might be saved without striving to reach the highest degrees of obedience. It is a weak pretence, that because the consummate measure of sanctification can be attained only in the next life, therefore we should not endeavour after it here; for by sincere and constant endeavours we make nearer approaches to it; and according to the degrees of our progress, such are those of our joy. As nature hath prescribed to all heavy bodies their going to the centre, and although none come to it, and many are at a great distance from it, yet the ordination of nature is not in vain; because by virtue of it every heavy body is always tending thither in motion or inclination: so although we cannot reach to complete holiness in this imperfect state, yet it is not in vain that the gospel prescribes it, and infuses into Christians those dispositions whereby they are gradually carried to the full accomplishment of it. Not to arrive to perfection is the weakness of the flesh, not to aspire after it is the fault of the spirit.

To excite us, it will be of moment to consider the great obligations that the gospel lays upon Christians to be holy, 1 John iii. 1. By that covenant the holy God is pleased to take them into the relation of his children. And as the nature of sanctification, so the motives of it are contained in that title; for so near an alliance obliges them to a faithful observation of his commands, and to imitate him with the greatest care, that the vein of his Spirit, and the marks of his blood may appear in all their actions. "Whosoever is born of God, doth not commit sin," 1 John iii. 9. The allowed practice of it is inconsistent with the quality of a son of God; it is contrary to the grace of his divine birth. Nay, the omission of good, as well as the commission of evil, is inconsistent with that relation. It is for this reason, that holiness is so much the character of a true Christian, that to be a Christian and a saint are the same thing in the writings of the apostles. That venerable title obliges him to a higher practice of virtue, than ever the pagans imagined. He is far behind them, if he do not surpass them; and if he is surpassed by them, he will be clothed with shame. Besides, our Redeemer who hath a right to us by so many titles, by his divine and human nature, by his life and death, by his glory and sufferings, as he strictly commands us to be holy, so he hath joined example to his authority, that we may walk as he walked, and be as he was in the world. Paul makes use of this consideration, to restrain the disciples of Christ from all sin, and to persuade them to universal holiness. After he had mentioned the disorders of the Gentiles, to deter the Ephesians from the like, he tells them, "But ye have not so learned Christ;" that is, his rule and practice instructed them otherwise. And when he commands the Romans to "walk honestly as in the day, not in rioting and drunkenness, not in chambering and wantonness, not in strife and envying;" he opposes to all these vices the pattern that Christ set before us: "But put ye on the Lord Jesus Christ," Rom. xiii. 13, 14. The expression intimates the duty, that as the garment is commensurate to the body, so we are to imitate all the parts of his holy conversation.

It is no wonder that the heathens gratified the inclinations of lust or rage, when their gods were represented acting in such a manner as to authorize their vices. "*Semina pene omnium scelerum, a diis suis peccantium turba collegit,*" as Julius Firmicus justly reproaches them. There was no villany how notorious soever, but had some deity for its protector. They found in heaven a justification of all their crimes, and became vicious by imitation. For it is very congruous for men to follow those whom they esteem to be perfect, and to whom they think themselves accountable. If they attribute to their supreme God, the Judge of the world, vices as virtues, what virtues will there be to reward, or vices to punish, in men? But for those that name the name of Christ to continue in iniquity, is the most unbecoming thing in the world; for they live in the perfect contradiction of their profession. An unholy Christian is a real apostate from Christ, that retracts by his wickedness the dedication that was made of him in his baptism. Although he doth not abjure our Saviour in words, he denies him in his works. A proud person renounces the Saviour's humility, the revengeful his mercy, the lukewarm his zeal, the unclean his purity, the covetous his bounty and compassion, the hypocrite his sincerity. And can there be any thing more indecent and absurd, than to pretend the relation and respect of disciples to such a holy Master, and yet by disobedience to deny him? When the bloody spectacles of the gladiators were first brought to Athens, a wise man cried out to the masters of the prizes, that they should remove the statue and altar of mercy out of the city, there being such an incongruity between the goddess they pretended to worship, and that cruel sacrifice of men for the sport of the people. It were more suitable for those who are not afraid to violate the most holy laws, and to contradict the pattern of Christ, to leave their profession, and to take some other more complying with their lusts. It is not the title of a Christian, that sanctifies those who pollute and defame it. It is not wearing the livery of Christ, that can honour those who stain it by their filthiness: but it is an aggravation of their guilt. It is an inconceivable indignity to our Saviour, and revives the old calumnies of the heathens, as if the gospel were a sanctuary for criminals, when those that call him Lord, do not what he commands them. "I know," saith Christ, "the blasphemy of them that say, they are Jews, and are not, but are the synagogue of Satan," Rev. ii. 9. Those that own the profession of Christianity, and live in unchristian practices, are baptized pagans, and in effect revile our blessed Redeemer, as if he had proclaimed a licentious impunity for sinners. Such wretches may deceive themselves with a pretence they believe in Christ, and that visibly they declare their dependence on him; but this pretence will be as unprofitable as it is vain; it is not the calling of him Lord, that will give them admission into the kingdom of heaven, Matt. vii. 21. The naked name of a Christian cannot protect them from the wrath of God. Tertullian smartly upbraids some in his time, who were careless of the dignity and purity of the

Christian profession in their lives, imagining that they might reverence God in their hearts without regarding him in their actions; that they might " *salvo metu et fide peccare,*" sin without losing their fear of God and their faith. To refute this gross contradiction, he propounds it in a sensible example : " *Hoc est, salva castitate matrimonium violare ; salva pietate parenti venenum temperare ,*" this is the same thing as to violate the fidelity of marriage without the wounding of chastity, or to poison a parent without failing in the duty that is owing to them. And to express his indignation, he tells them, " *Sic ergo et ipsi salva venia in gehennam detruduntur, dum salvo metu peccant :*" let them expect that God will cast them into hell, without prejudice to their pardon, as they pretend to sin without prejudice to the respect they bear him.

To sum up all, Jesus Christ, as by his doctrine and life he clearly discovered our duty, so he offers to us the aid of his Spirit for our assistance, by which the commands of the gospel are not only possible but easy: and to enforce our obligations, he hath threatened such vengeance to the rebellious, and promised such a reward to those that obey the gospel, that it is impossible we should not be deeply affected with them, if we seriously believe them : and he hath given such an evidence of their truth, that it is impossible we should not believe them, unless " the god of this world has blinded our minds." It is matter therefore of just astonishment, that Christians should not express the efficacy of the gospel in their actions. How can a reasonable creature believe that eternal damnation shall be the punishment of sin, and yet live in the wilful practice of it? The historian speaking of mushrooms that sometimes proved deadly to whole families, asks with wonder, " What pleasure could allure them to eat such doubtful meat?" yet they may be so corrected as to become innocent. But when it is certain that the pleasures of sin are mortal, can any one be tempted by those attractives to venture on that which will undoubtedly bring death to the soul? Let sense itself be judge, and make the comparison between whatsoever the present life can afford for delight in sin, and what the future death will bring to torment it. Let the flesh see into what torments all its delights shall be changed, and with what other fire than of impure lust it shall burn for ever.

Besides, we are encouraged to our duty with the assurance of a happiness so excellent, that not only the enjoyment of it in the next world, but the just expectation of it here makes us truly blessed. If the reward were small or the promise uncertain, there might be some pretence for our not performing the conditions to obtain it; but when the one is infinitely great, and the other as true as the God of truth, what more powerful motive can be conceived to make us holy? It is the apostle's chosen argument, that we should " walk worthy of him who hath called us to his kingdom and glory." The heathens were in a great measure strangers to the secrets of another world : they had but a shadow of probability; we have the light of truth brought down from heaven by the Son of God, that reveals to us a blessedness that deserves our most ardent active affections. But if men are not wrought on by natural reason nor divine faith; if neither the terrors of the Lord, nor the blessed hope can persuade them from sin to holiness, their condition is irrecoverable. In this the rules of natural and spiritual healing agree, Hippocrat. Sect. 7. Aphor. ult. Where neither corrosives nor lenitives are successful, we must use the knife; if cutting off is unprofitable, we must sear the part; if the fire is ineffectual, the ulcer is incurable. If the threatening of hell-fire through unbelief and carelessness is not feared, and hath no efficacy to correct and change sinners, what remains but to make a presage of eternal death, that will unavoidably and speedily seize on them ? And if so clear a discovery of the heavenly glory doth not produce in men a living faith that works by love, and a lively hope that purifies the heart and conversation, what can be concluded, but that they are wholly sensual and senseless, and shall be for ever deprived of that blessedness they now despise and neglect.

CHAPTER XX.

THE POWER OF GOD IN REDEMPTION.

The divine power is admirably glorified in the creation of the world, not only in regard of the greatness of the effect, that comprehends the heavens and earth and all things in them, but in regard of the marvellous way of its production; for he made the great universe without the concurrence of any material cause, from nothing. For this reason the raising of this glorious fabric is produced as the distinctive character of the Deity from the troop of false gods. The Psalmist declares, " The Lord is to be feared above all gods; for all the gods of the nations are idols, but the Lord made the heavens," Psalm xcvi. 4, 5. And as he began the creation by proceeding from nothing to real existence, so in forming the other parts, he drew them from infirm and indisposed matter, as from a second nothing; that all his creatures might bear the real testimonies of infinite power. Thus he commanded light to arise out of darkness, and sensible creatures from an insensible element. He created man, the accomplishment of all his works, from the lowest and grossest element, the earth.

Now although at the first view we might conceive that the visible world is the greatest miracle that ever God performed, yet upon serious reflection we shall discover, that the works of grace are as wonderful as the works of nature, and that the power of God is as evidently expressed in our redemption, as in the creation.

For the fuller understanding of this, I will consider some of the principal effects of the divine power in order to our blessed recovery.

I. The incarnation of the Son of God, in accomplishing whereof such power was exercised, as no limited understanding is able to comprehend. " The word was made flesh," John i. 14. This signifies the real union between the human nature and the divine in our Redeemer. Before his incarnation he appeared in a human form to the patriarchs, and in the flaming bush to Moses; but it is never said with respect to those apparitions, that the word was made flame or man. But when he came into the world to save us, he assumed the complete nature of man into a hypostatical union with himself. That admirable person possesses the titles, qualities, and natures of God and man. In that ineffable union, each of the natures preserves its proper form, with all the necessary consequences proceeding from it. The human nature is joined to the eternal Word, but not changed into its divinity: it is not infinite and impassible. The Deity is united to flesh, but not transformed into its nature; it is not finite and passible. Though there is a distinction, yet no separation; there are two natures, but one sole Jesus. In the same subsistence the Creator and the creature are miraculously allied. Now this is a work fully responsible to Omnipotence, and expresses whatever is signified by that title. The apostle mentions it with an attribute of excellency; "Without controversy, great is the mystery of godliness; God was manifest in the flesh," 1 Tim. iii. 16. It is as sublime, as holy. In this the divine power appears in its magnificence, and in some respects more gloriously than in the creation; for there is incomparably a greater disparity between the majesty, greatness, and infiniteness of God, and the meanness of man, than between the whole world and nothing. The degrees of disparity between the world and nothing are not actually infinite, but between the most excellent creature and the glorious Creator, they are absolutely infinite. From hence it is, that that which in other things resolves our doubts, here increases the wonder, and in appearance makes it more incredible. "Ye do err," saith Christ to the Sadducees, who denied the resurrection, "not knowing the power of God." But the more raised thoughts we have of his immense power, the more unlikely his conjunction with a nature so far beneath him will seem to be.

II. The divine power was magnified in our Redeemer's supernatural conception. It was requisite his body should be miraculously formed of the substance of a woman by the operation of the Holy Ghost, not only in respect of its singular dignity, and that he might be the pattern of our regeneration that is performed by the efficacy of the Spirit not of the flesh, but in respect of his office; for undertaking to reconcile God by the expiation of our sin, he must be allied to us, and absolutely pure from the stain of sin. Heaven and earth concurred to form that divine man the King of both, the earth furnishing matter, and heaven the principle of his conception. Accordingly the angel told Mary, who questioned how she could be a mother not having known a man, "The Holy Ghost shall come upon thee, and the power of the Highest shall overshadow thee; therefore also that holy thing which shall be born of thee, shall be called the Son of God," Luke i. 35. This was foretold many ages as an admirable effect of God's power. When Judah was oppressed by two potent kings, and despaired of an escape, to raise their drooping spirits, the prophet tells them, the Lord himself would give them a sign of their future deliverance; "Behold, a virgin shall conceive and bear a son, and shall call his name Emmanuel," Isa. vii. 14. The argument is from the greater to the less; for it is apparently more difficult that a virgin, without injury or blemish to her purity and integrity, should conceive and bring forth Emmanuel, than the defeating of human forces how great soever. If God will accomplish that stupendous, unheard of wonder, much more would he rescue his people from the fury of their adversaries.

III. The divine power was eminently declared in the miracles our Saviour wrought during the time of his public ministry to verify his divine mission, that he was the great prophet sent from God to instruct men in the way of life.

In discoursing of this, I will briefly show, that miracles were a convincing proof of his celestial calling, and that the performance of them was necessary in order to the conviction of the world, and consider particularly those he wrought.

A miracle is an extraordinary operation of God in nature, either in stopping its course, or in producing some effects that are above its laws and power ; so that when he is pleased to work any, they are his seal to authorize the person and doctrine to which they are annexed. By them faith is made visible ; the unbeliever is convinced by his senses, the only witnesses above reproach in his account. From hence Nicodemus addresses himself to Christ, " Rabbi, we know that thou art a teacher come from God ; for no man can do those miracles that thou doest, except God be with him ;" John iii. 2. That is, no inferior agent can perform them, without the special assistance of the divine power ; and it is not to be supposed that God will lend his omnipotency to the devil to work a real miracle, to confirm a falsity ; and thereby necessarily induce men into error in a matter of infinite moment : for such is the doctrine of salvation that Christ preached.

The working of miracles was necessary to convince the world that Jesus Christ was sent from God, whether we consider the Jews or the Gentiles.

It was necessary to convince the Jews upon a double account ;—because the performance of them was one of the characters of the promised Messiah. For this reason when two of John's disciples came to inquire whether he were the expected prophet, he returns this answer to the question ; " Go and show John those things which ye do hear and see, the blind receive their sight, and the lame walk, the lepers are cleansed, and the deaf hear, the dead are raised up, and the poor have the gospel preached to them," Matt. xi. 4, 5. Thus he described his office, and verified the commission he had from God, by representing his miracles in the words of the prophecy, Isa. xxxv. 5—9.—Our Saviour came to alter the religion of the Jews, that had been confirmed by many illustrious miracles ; therefore to assure them that he was authorized from heaven, he wrought such and so many, that for their greatness, clearness, and number, exceeded all that were done before his coming. Our Saviour tells the Jews, "If I had not done among them the works which none other man did, they had not had sin :" that is, in rejecting him ; for if he had exercised only a power like unto that of Moses and the prophets, in his miraculous actions, they had been obliged to have honoured him as one of their rank, but not to have attributed an incomparable dignity to him, John xv. 24. But he did those which neither Moses nor the prophets had performed ; and in those that had been done, Christ excelled them in the manner of doing them. This the Jews could not contradict, and from hence, their infidelity was made culpable.

Miracles were necessary to convince the Gentiles;— for the gospel forbids the various religions among them, and commands all to worship God alone in Christ Jesus; so that without a sensible demonstration, that that was the way wherein he would be served, their prejudices had been invincible. The gospel propounds threatenings and promises that regard a future state, where no living eye can see their effects; so that without an extraordinary confirmation it was not likely that men should yield a firm assent to them. If it be said, our Saviour did his miracles only in Judea, where very few of the Gentiles saw his person or works; I answer, his miracles were primarily designed for the conviction of the Jews, and in a secondary intention, to disarm infidelity among the Gentiles. Therefore the testimony of thèm was conveyed by those who were eye-witnesses and most worthy of credit, and who did many great wonders in the name of Christ, to verify the report of his famous miracles, and declare his power and divinity. Of this more afterwards.

Now I will briefly consider the miracles wrought by Christ, that were the certain signs of God's favouring him, and made his commission authentic. Before his coming, the hand of the synagogue was dried up, and impotent to produce miracles. The Holy Spirit was withdrawn, and for the space of four hundred years, no prophet nor worker of wonders appeared. John the Baptist, though the angel deputed to signify the coming of Christ, yet did no miracles. But our Saviour was invested with power from above, and performed many.

Their quality and number are considerable.

1. Their quality. They were not mere signs, as the

conversion of Moses' rod into a serpent; nor destructive and punishing, as the wonders in Egypt; but advantageous and beneficial to men, the equal demonstations of his mercy and power.

He cured diseases that were absolutely desperate, without means, by his omnipotent will, as the son of the nobleman who was sick at Capernaum, when himself was at Cana in Galilee; or by such visible means, that the spectators might be fully convinced, that it was not the external application, but his sole virtue and divine power that produced the effect. Thus by anointing with clay and spittle the eyes of him that was born blind, who never had any natural possibility of seeing, he wrought an unparallelled cure: " Since the world began was it not heard that any man opened the eyes of one that was born blind," John ix. 32. Therefore he that was healed, inferred from that, as a most pregnant proof, that our Saviour was from God.

He raised the dead. This effect exceeds the power not only of men, but of the angels. It is true that one angel destroyed in a night a hundred four-score and five thousand of the Assyrian army; but it is as true, that all the angels together cannot raise from the dead one man. It is wholly the work of the Lord of nature, who holds the keys of life and death in his hands. It is only his light can dispel the darkness, his voice can break the silence of the grave. And it is observable, that our Saviour who sometimes concealed his miraculous works and forbade the publishing of them, yet performed this kind before many witnesses, that they might publish and verify it, as being most conclusive of his mission from God. He raised to life the ruler's daughter, to the astonishment of all that were present to attend her funeral, Mark v. 42. The widow's son of Nain was carried without the gates of the city to his grave; Jesus stops the sad train, and restores life to the young man, and to his mother something more dear than her life, Luke vii. 15. And the more signally to triumph over death, he pursued it to its fort, the obscurity of the grave. Lazarus was buried four days, his carcase was corrupted; Jesus calls him from the bottom of his tomb with that powerful voice that created the world; the dead answers, and comes forth to the amazement of all that saw the glory of God so clearly manifested, John xi. 44. The evangelist reports, that the people afterwards were as desirous to see Lazarus as Jesus.

Add to these his casting out of devils. Before the fall, the unclean spirit was incorporated with the serpent, but now with man himself. He seizes on the external organs and internal faculties, and rules him at his pleasure. In the time of Christ great numbers were possessed; for the devil perceiving the ruin of his kingdom approaching, would extend the limits of it here, and by the perfect possessing of sinners, begin their torments, which is one act of his principality. The case of those persons was most compassionable; for in that close fight the soul was disarmed of its defensive weapons, being hindered in a great measure of the free use of its faculties. Whereas in other temptations he works by outward objects at a distance, here he makes a violent assault on both parts. It is the true anticipation of hell; for the possessed person is not exempted from suffering, the privilege of death; nor enjoys the free power of doing, the effect of life. Now the rejecting of this enemy was above the force of any human means; no material applications had power over immaterial spirits. But our Saviour by a word commanded them forth of their garrisons: and the evangelists observe that the sight of it affected the people in an extraordinary manner above what his other miracles did. It is said, "They were all amazed, insomuch that they questioned among themselves, saying, What thing is this? what new doctrine is this? For with authority commandeth he even the unclean spirits, and they do obey him," Mark i. 27—29. His empire over evil spirits was more admired than over diseases, or death itself. Those who were insensible of his former miracles, received impression from this: "They were all amazed at the mighty power of God," confessing that "it was never so seen in Israel," Luke ix. 43; Matt. ix. 33. And another time they said, "Is not this the Son of David?" that is, the Messiah, Matt. xii. 23. The Pharisees, his obstinate enemies, were more troubled about this, than any other action; and to elude the present conviction that he came from God, ascribed it to a secret compact with Beelzebub; as if there were a collusion between the evil spirits; a lesser devil retired that the prince might reign. But so great was the evidence of the Spirit of God in that act of jurisdiction over the devils, that our Saviour charges them with unpardonable guilt for their wilful denying of it.

2. Their number. The number of his miracles was so great, that John saith, if all were written, "the world could not contain the books." We may in part conjecture how numerous they were, by taking notice how many he performed in one day. He dined with Matthew at Capernaum; whilst he was there, Jairus entreats him to go to his daughter newly dead: as he went, the woman with the bloody issue touched the hem of his garment, and was healed; he raised the dead maid; in his returning he healed two blind men, and immediately after cast out the devil from one that was dumb, Matt. ix. And in all these miraculous operations the glory of God's power was clearly manifested.

IV. The divine power admirably appeared in making the death of Christ victorious over all our spiritual enemies.

Now to show what an eminent degree of power was exercised in the effecting of this, we must consider, that after Satan was cast out of heaven for his rebellion, he set up a throne on the earth, and usurped an absolute empire over mankind. His power was great, and his malice was equal to his power. The apostle represents him with his black army, under the titles of "principalities and powers, the rulers of the darkness of this world, spiritual wickedness in high places," as in respect of the order among them, so in respect of the dominion they exercised in the world," Ephes. vi. 12. His principality hath two parts,—to tempt men powerfully to sin, and to execute the wrath of God upon them. He works effectually "in the children of disobedience." He fires their lusts, and by the thick ascending smoke darkens their minds, and hurries them to do the vilest actions. "And he hath the power of death," to torment sinners; God justly permitting him to exercise his cruelty upon those who comply with his temptations. Now in the time of Christ, seeing many ravished out of his hands and translated into the kingdom of God, he grew jealous of his state, and by his instruments brought him to a cruel and shameful death. He then in appearance obtained a complete conquest, but in truth was absolutely overcome. And from hence the glorious power of Christ is most clearly manifested. As he that will take the height of a mountain must descend to the lowest part of the valley, where fixing his instrument, he may discover the distance from the foot to the top of it; so we must descend to the lowest degree of our Saviour's abasement, to understand the height of his exaltation. By death he overcame him "that had the power of death, that is, the devil," Heb. ii. 14; for his cruel empire was founded in man's sin; his greatness was built on our ruins. All the penal evils he brings on mankind are upon the account of our disobedience, and his mighty power in temptations is from inward corruption: otherwise he might surround, but could not surprise us. Now the Lord Christ by his death hath taken away the guilt and power of sin; the guilt, in enduring the curse of the law, and thereby satisfying eternal justice, which all the creatures in heaven and earth could not do; and the power of it, by crucifying "our old man with him, that the body of sin might be destroyed, that henceforth we should not serve sin," Rom. vi. 6. By the cross of Christ the world is crucified to us; and we are crucified to the world, Gal. vi. 14. By it we are vindicated from the power of Satan, "into the glorious liberty of the sons of God." For this reason our Saviour, a little before his passion, said, "Now shall the prince of this world be cast out." By the cross he "spoiled principalities and powers, and made a show of them openly, triumphing over them in it," to their extreme confusion, in the view of heaven and earth, Col. ii. 15. Although the resurrection and ascension of Christ are the proper acts of his triumph, yet his death is the sole cause and original of it. The nails and spear that pierced his body were his omnipotent arms, and the cross, the instrument of his sufferings, was the trophy of his victory. All our triumphant palms are gathered from that tree. It is there our Saviour bruised the head of the old serpent, and renewed his ancient victory over him.

And from hence it was, that upon the first preaching of Christ crucified, oracles were struck dumb and put to eternal silence; invisible powers were forced to do him visible honour. As the rising sun causes the night-birds to retire, so his name chased the rout of deities into darkness. They continue to be our enemies, but not our lords. Now where did the divine power ever appear more glorious than in our crucified Saviour? He hath done greater things suffering as man, than acting as God. The works of creation and providence are not equal to the effects of his death. In the creation a corruptible world was produced from nothing, which as it had no disposition, so no contrariety to receive the form the Creator gave it; but the new world of grace that is immortal, was formed out of rebellious matter. The most eminent work of providence was the drowning of the Egyptians in the Red Sea; but the spiritual Pharaoh and all his hosts were drowned in his blood. In short, the cross hath opened heaven to us, and wrought a miraculous change on the earth. But this I shall more particularly consider under another head of discourse.

V. The divine power was eminently magnified in Christ's resurrection from the grave. This was foretold concerning the Messiah, by the prophet David speaking in the type; "My flesh shall rest in hope; for thou wilt not leave my soul in hell, neither wilt thou suffer thy Holy One to see corruption," Psalm xvi. 9, 10. As it was ordained by God's counsel, so it was executed by his power. This is decisive, that he is the Messiah. His other miracles were performed by the prophets, but this was singular, and done only by the God of the prophets.

The reasons of it prove, that it was equally necessary for his glory and our salvation. The quality of his person required it; for he was a heavenly man without guilt, therefore immortal by the original constitution of his nature. Death, that is the wages of sin, had no power over him. He was subject to it, not by the law of his conception, but the dispensation of his love : not to satisfy nature, but purchase our salvation : therefore the eternal law that annexes immortality to innocence, would not suffer that he should remain in the state of death. The nature of his office made it necessary. As the economy of our redemption required that he should descend from heaven, the seat of his glory, that by dying he might expiate our sins ; so after his lying in the grave so long as to attest the reality of his death, it was necessary he should rise again in order to his dispensing the glorious benefits he had purchased. The apostle tells the Corinthians, " If Christ be not risen, then is our preaching in vain, and your faith is also in vain," 1 Cor. xv. 14. For the faith of Christians hath a threefold reference ;—to the person of Christ, that he is the Son of God ;—to his death, that it is an all-sufficient sacrifice for sin ;—to his promise, that he will raise believers at the last day. Now the resurrection of Christ is the foundation of faith in respect of all these.

1. He was declared " to be the Son of God with power, according to the spirit of holiness, by the resurrection from the dead," Rom. i. 4. He was the Son of God from eternity as the Word, and from the first moment of his incarnation as God-man ; but the honour of this relation was much eclipsed in his poor life and ignominious death. And although his darkest night was enlightened with some discoveries of his Deity, yet they were transient and soon vanished. But in his resurrection God did publicly own him in the face of the world ; therefore he is represented testifying from heaven, " Thou art my Son ; this day have I begotten thee ;" according to the phrase of scripture, then things are said to be, when they conspicuously appear, Acts xiii. 33. All the miraculous proofs by which God acknowledged him for his Son during his life, had been ineffectual without this. If he had remained in the grave, it had been reasonable to believe him an ordinary person, and that his death had been the punishment of his presumption ; but his resurrection was the most illustrious and convincing evidence, that he was what he declared himself to be ; for it is not conceiva-

ble that God should put forth an almighty power to raise him, and thereby authorize his usurpation, if by robbery he had assumed that glorious title. He is therefore said to be "justified by the Spirit" which raised him, from all the accusations of his enemies, who charged him with blasphemy for making himself equal with God. Upon the evidence of it, Thomas adored him as his Lord and God.

2. His resurrection is the most pregnant proof of the all-sufficiency of his satisfaction. This was special in the death of Christ, that the curse of the law accompanied it, and seemed like an infinite weight to lie on his grave. But in rising again, the value and virtue of his sufferings was fully declared. Therefore the apostle tells us, that " he was delivered for our offences, and raised again for our justification," Rom. iv. 25. Although his death was sufficient to merit our pardon, yet since believers alone actually partake of the benefit, and none could believe, if he had not risen from the grave, it is clear his death had been ineffectual without it.

3. Our faith in his promises to give life and glory to his servants, is built on his resurrection; for how could we believe him to be the author of life, who remained under the power of death? How could he who finally perished, quicken and glorify us? If he had been confined to the grave, all our hopes had been buried with him. But his resurrection is the cause, pattern, and argument of ours. He did not only raise our body from the grave, but his church with him. Now the effecting of this is attributed to the divine power, with a note of eminency; "Christ was raised by the glory of the Father," Rom. vi. 4; that is, by his power, which in that act was manifested in its full splendour; for what is stronger than death, and more inexorable than the grave? Omnipotency alone can break its gates, and loose its bands.

CHAPTER XXI.

THE POWER OF GOD IN REDEMPTION.

VI. The divine power was glorified in the conversion of the world to Christianity.

The apostle tells us, " that Christ crucified was to the Jews a stumbling-block, and to the Gentiles foolishness." The Jews expected the Messiah to deliver them from temporal servitude and establish a universal empire, either by the force of arms, or by the terror of signs and prodigies, as Moses did against the Egyptians. But when instead of power, they saw nothing but weakness, and instead of a glorious triumph, a disgraceful punishment, they despised his person and rejected his doctrine. But notwithstanding this imaginary infirmity in Christ crucified, yet " to those that are called" according to the divine purpose, he was the most excellent " power of God ;" it being more glorious to subdue the world to the faith and obedience of a crucified person, than if he had appeared with all the powers of heaven, and princes of the earth as his attendants. For this reason the apostle declares, he was " not ashamed of the gospel of Christ," it being " the power of God to salvation to every one that believeth, to the Jew first, and also to the Greek," Rom. i. 16. And he prays for the Ephesians, that " the eyes of their understandings being enlightened, they might know what is the exceeding greatness of his power to us-ward who believe, according to the working of his mighty power which he wrought in Christ, when he raised him from the dead, and set him at his own right hand in the heavenly places," Ephes. i. 18—20. He uses various and lofty expressions, as if one had been insufficient to signify the extent and efficacy of that power which produced the faith of Christ in the heathens. And if we duly consider things, it will appear, that the terms of the apostle are not too strong and hyperbolical, but just and equal to the degree of power requisite for the accomplishment of tha great work.

For the understanding of this, I will consider three things;

1. The numerous and great difficulties that obstructed the receiving of the gospel.

2. The quality of the means by which it was conveyed and became successful.

3. The eminent, sudden, universal, and lasting change made by it in the world.

1. The numerous and great difficulties that obstructed the receiving of the gospel. This will appear by representing the state and disposition of the world at that time when it was first preached.

(1.) Ignorance was universal: a deep thick darkness covered the face of the earth. And the consequences of that gross palpable ignorance, were execrable idolatry, and the most notorious depravation of manners.

First; execrable idolatry; for as in the night, spectres walk; so in the times of ignorance, the prince of darkness made his progress in the earth. He reigned in the hearts of men and in the places of their devotion. The whole world was filled with idols of several forms and mysteries, some amiable, others terrible, according to the humour of superstition. For many ages Satan had kept peaceable possession of his empire: for the ignorant world did not understand its misery, but willingly paid that honour to the cruel usurper, that was only due to the lawful Sovereign.

They were confirmed in their idolatry by several things.—They were trained up in it from their infant state. Now the first persuasions of the mind though grossly false, and ill habits, do strangely captivate, and are with difficulty removed; because the concurrence of those faculties is requisite, which are under the power of error and vice. No tyrant is so exactly obeyed as custom, especially in things esteemed sacred; for the conceit that the service is pleasing to the Deity, renders men incapable to believe any thing that contradicts it. It was as hard to make the Gentiles forsake the religion they received from their birth, and to lose the impressions made in their tender age, as to make the Africans change their skin and become fair, and the Europeans to turn black; for the tincture which the religion practised in each country conveys to the souls of men, is as deep and lasting, as that which the sun impresses upon their bodies, according to the diversity of its aspects.—The pagan religion was derived through a long succession from their progenitors. Antiquity brings I know not what respect to things, but it is specially venerable in matters of religion. Therefore the heathens accused the Christian religion of novelty, and urged nothing more plausibly than the argument of immemorial prescription for their superstition. They would not consider whether it were just and reasonable, but with a blind deference yielded up themselves to the authority of the ancients. They resolved not to condemn their parents and friends, that had gone before them in the road of damnation, but chose to die in their idolatry. So hard is it to resist the current of the world, and to rescue ourselves from the bondage of popular errors.—The pomp of the pagan worship was very pleasing to the flesh. The magnificence of their temples, adorned with the trophies of superstition, their mysterious ceremonies, their music, their processions, their images and altars, their sacrifices and purifications, and the rest of the equipage of a carnal religion, drew their respects, and strongly affected their minds through their senses; whereas the religion of the gospel is spiritual and serious, holy and pure, and hath nothing to move the carnal part. Now how difficult was it to overcome paganism when fortified by antiquity, universality, and so agreeable to sense! How hard was it to free men from the double tyranny of custom from without, and blind affections from within.

Secondly; the depravation of manners was such in the heathen world, that if the unclean spirits had been incarnate, and taken their residence among men, they could not have acted worse villanies. The whole earth was covered with abominations, as Egypt with the frogs that poisoned the whole climate. We may see a picture of their conversation in the first to the Romans. And it could be no otherwise; for as the apostle saith, "those who are drunk, are drunk in the night," so when the mind is darkened with ignorance and error, the affections are corrupted, and men give up themselves to the " unfruitful works of darkness." Unnatural crimes were committed even among the Grecians and Romans, with that liberty, as if no spark of common reason had remained in them. The most filthy lusts had lost the fear and shame that naturally attends them. They esteemed those things to be the means to obtain happiness, that were the causes of the contrary. They placed their sovereign good in extreme evil, that is, sinful pleasures. They were encouraged to " work all uncleanness with greediness," not only upon the account of present impunity, for their laws left almost all vices indifferent but what disturbed the tranquillity of the state; and not only by the multitude of examples, so that vices by their commonness had lost their names, and were styled virtues; nay, it was a crime to appear innocent among the guilty; but principally because they thought themselves secure as to a future state; for either they wholly disbelieved it, and it is congruous that those who think to die like beasts, should live like beasts; or else, by attributing to their deities those passions and vices that so powerfully reigned in themselves, they were strongly persuaded no punishment would be inflicted; for how could the gods make them sacrifices to their justice, who were companions with them in their crimes, or revenge the imitation of their own actions? This was to cast down the banks, and to let the torrent of corrupt nature break forth in all its fury; as St. Austin observes of Homer, the father of poetical fictions, that representing the murders, thefts, and adulteries of their gods, he made those sins divine properties, and effectually commended them to the heathens; " *Quisquis ea fecisset, non homines perditos sed cœlestes deos videbatur imitatus.*" And he gives an instance of this from a comedy of Terence, where a vicious young man is introduced, reporting how he animated himself to satisfy his brutish lust, as having no less a deity than Jupiter for his master and model. In short, the theology of the Pagans inflamed them to the bold commission of every pleasant sin. The history of their gods was so interspersed with the most infamous impurities, that at the first reading, "*verterunt pupillas virgines in meretrices;*" they lost the virginity of their eyes, then of their souls, and then of their bodies. Now the gospel is a holy discipline that forbids all excesses, that enjoins universal purity and chastity; so that when it was first preached to the heathens, they thought it impossible to be obeyed, unless men were angels without bodies, or statues without souls.

(2.) I shall add further, that the aversion of the heathens to Christianity was much strengthened by those, who were in veneration among them and vehemently opposed it. And these were the philosophers greatly esteemed for wisdom, their priests that had dominion over their consciences, and their princes that had power over their states and lives.

First; philosophers vehemently opposed the receiving of the gospel. At the first view it may be just matter of wonder that they should be enemies to it, whether we consider the object of faith, or the rules of life laid down in it. The objects of faith were new and noble, of infinite beauty and profit, and most worthy of a rational contemplation to be exercised upon them. Now that the philosophers who were so diligent to improve their minds, who received with complacency truths of a lower descent and of infinitely less importance, should reject evangelical truths, sublime in their nature, saving in their efficacy, and revealed from heaven, what account can be given of it? Tertullian reproaches them, with reason, that the Christian faith was the only thing, which curiosity did not tempt them to search into; "*Hic solum curiositas humana torpescit.*" Besides, whereas the gospel is a plain and perfect institution for the government of life, wholly conversant about the souls of men, and assures a blessedness infinitely more excellent than was ever thought of by them, it might have been expected that those who in regard to morality seemed most to approach to it, and whose professed design was to search after happiness, should have readily entertained and used their best endeavours to have drawn others to embrace it. But if we consider things aright, our wonder will vanish; for their knowledge and morality, which in themselves were preparatives, yet accidentally hindered their submission to the gospel, and caused the most potent prejudices against it; and that upon a double account, 1. of pride 2. of satisfaction in their own way.

1. Pride was their universal disease. They had a liberal esteem of themselves as raised above the common rank of men, and were lovers of glory more than of wisdom. And because philosophy had instructed them in some truths, they believed its false as well as true dictates, and concluded all things impossible that did not concur with their old tenets. They admitted no higher principle than natural reason, and utterly rejected divine revelation; which was as unreasonable as if one that never saw but the light of a candle, should contend that there was no other light in the world. Now a person that doth not believe divine revelation, is wholly unqualified to judge of supernatural mysteries; for till the authority of the revealer is submitted to, he cannot truly consider their cause and their end. Besides, they looked on it as a reproach, that any secret should be revealed to others and not to them. It seemed to darken their glory, that any school should be more knowing than theirs. Therefore they chose to be instructors of error, rather than disciples to the truth. And further, they thought their honour concerned to defend the principles they had once espoused. From hence arose the great contentions among themselves, accompanied with invectives and satires, being very jealous for their opinions, and passionate for the interest of their sects. Now the gospel was in some things contrary to all of them, so that being imperious and impatient of contradiction and touched in their tenderest part, no wonder they were so violent against it. They were unwilling to receive a doctrine that discovered their errors, and lessened their esteem. Our Saviour asks the Jews, " How can ye believe which receive honour one of another, and seek not the honour that cometh from God only?" John v. 44. He propounds it as an impossible thing. The gospel would strip them of all their pretended excellencies, and divest them of many vain conceptions adorned with so much art, and commanded

as its first article, they should humbly resign their understandings to divine revelation; this they looked on as a submission unworthy of their refined, strong spirits. They had satisfaction in their own imperfect virtues. Because they did some things to recover the human nature from its degenerate state, they were more confirmed in their infidelity than the grossest idolaters and the most vicious persons; for the more probable arguments they had to obtain happiness in their own way, the more obstinately they refused any other. They thought there was no need of supernatural revelation to direct, nor of supernatural grace to assist them; but without the intercession of a Saviour and the power of the Holy Spirit, they had self-sufficiency to obtain perfection and felicity. Like foolish chemists that have melted away a great part of their estates in vain, and little remaining to support their wretched lives, yet in expectation of the great elixir, create in their fancies treasures of gold, t enrich themselves, so the philosophers, who wasted their time and spirits in searching after happiness to little purpose, although the best of their principles and the height of their virtue were insufficient to support them under any pressing afflictions, yet had vain hopes of obtaining perfect tranquillity and content by them. Now the gospel commanding an entire renouncing of ourselves, to embrace the sole goodness and will of God, it was hard for those who were so full of pride and vanity to relish a doctrine so contrary to them. In truth, whatever the philosophers pretended concerning the incredibility that the Son of God should suffer death, yet it was not so much the cross to which Christ was nailed by his enemies that made them reject the gospel, as the other cross to which Jesus would fasten them, that is, the strict and holy discipline to which he commands them to submit; a discipline that condemns their vain boasting of wisdom and virtue, that mortifies sensual pleasures, which many of the philosophers indulged themselves in, notwithstanding all their discourses of the purgative and illuminative life. And that this was the real cause of their rejecting a crucified Saviour, is evident, for they knew that sufferings of the worst kind are not always infamous, but must be esteemed according to the quality of their causes and ends. Those who for public good generously expose themselves to disgrace and misery, are honoured for their heroic courage as patriots of the noblest strain. And it is not unusual for persons of extraordinary wisdom and virtue to suffer in the world. Their presence and example upbraid the vicious, and wound their spirits, as a great light does distempered and sore eyes. And some of them acknowledged the wisdom of providence in permitting this for an excellent end, that virtue tried in the fire might be more resplendent. Plato, an eminent philosopher, describes a man truly just, by this proof of his integrity, that he shall suffer the loss of estate and honour; be scourged, racked, bound, and have his eyes plucked out, and after the enduring of all miseries, at last be crucified. Socrates, so admired by them, was so disguised by the malice of his enemies, that he was condemned to die by poison; yet this was so far from obscuring his reputation, that his suffering death was esteemed the most noble effect of his courage, and the most excellent proof of his virtue. Why then should they make a contrary judgment of our Redeemer's sufferings, whose innocence was perfect, and whose patience was so holy and divine, that in the midst of his torments he prayed for his murderers? No reason can be justly alleged, but some darling lust, spiritual or fleshly, which they were resolved to cherish. The light that comes from above illuminates the humble and dazzles the proud. The presumption of their own knowledge, was the cause of their prodigious stupidity. Simple ignorance is not so dangerous as error: a false light that deceives and leads to precipices is worse than darkness. We find therefore that none were fiercer enemies to the gospel than the philosophers.

The sacred story tells us, that when the apostle preached at Athens, that was as much the seat of superstition as of sciences, the Epicureans and Stoics, though most opposite in their principles, yet conspired to encounter him. They entertained him with scorn; "What will this babbler say?" and his success was but small there. He that fished with a net in other places, and brought great numbers to baptism, did there only with an angle, and caught but one or two souls. And in the progress of the gospel they persisted in their opposition. The most grave and virtuous among them censured the martyrs as fool-hardy in their generous sufferings for the name of Jesus Christ. Antoninus accused the Christians of obstinacy in their readiness to endure torments. Arrianus represents their courage as proceeding from a customary contempt of death, which he opposes to judgment and reason. Crescens, the Cynic, was the persecutor of Justin Martyr. In all ages the gospel felt the sharp points of their malicious wits. They despised it as an ill-contrived fable, as the entertainment of small understandings; and faith, as the "*praesidium*" of the weak and illiterate, who were incapable of consideration. Now when those who were in highest reputation for their morality and learning, discountenanced Christianity, it was a strong argument to move the vulgar heathens to judge of it as a mere delusion. In our Saviour's time it was urged as a sufficient reason against the receiving of him as sent from God, because none of the pharisees, the most learned and most likely to understand the prophecies concerning the Messiah, believed on him. John vii. 48.

Secondly; the heathen priests vehemently obstructed the reception of the gospel; for their interest was specially concerned upon the account of their reputation and gain. With great art they had kept the people in ignorance for a long time. They persuaded them that their idolatrous ceremonies, sacrifices, and festivals made the gods favourable, and were the supreme causes of their prosperity; and that ill success in war, public disasters, and great contagions were sent for the neglect of their service. From this fountain all superstition was derived. Now if the doctrine of Christ, that strictly forbids the worship of idols, were received, who would attend to their old lies? who would purchase their deceitful promises? who would maintain them with prodigal donatives? who would esteem them divine men? They must lose their honour and support, and for their fables be the scorn of the multitude. It is no wonder then that their passions should be edged, and their endeavours furious in opposing the truth. And since the people had a reverend regard for their office, and a high opinion of their wisdom, authority, and sanctity, they readily joined with them in their opposition.

Thirdly; princes, who were adored by the people, thought themselves obliged to prevent the introduction of a new religion, lest their empire should be in hazard, or the majesty and greatness of it lessened ; for religion being the true foundation of public peace, every change in it is suspected as dangerous, and likely to bring some eminent alteration in the state. Paul was accused for teaching customs which were not lawful for them to observe, being Romans, Acts xvi. 21. And in after-times, Christians were condemned as seditious and mutinous, and their assemblies as riotous and unlawful. And it is observable, that there never was a less favourable constitution of time, than when the gospel was first preached; for Tiberius was extremely cruel and extremely jealous of all novelty that might disturb his repose. And Nero, the bloodiest tyrant that ever sat on the Roman throne, endeavoured to strangle Christianity in the cradle.

Besides, the doctrine of Christ was not only new and strange, but severe ; for it gives no dispensation for persons of the highest rank from universal duty. It is the law of God to whom all are equally subject and must be equally obedient. It gives rules without exception, to the court as well as the cottage ; to those clothed in purple, and those in sackcloth ; it condemns the greatest for delinquents and guilty of eternal death, if they do not abandon those pleasures to which corrupt nature and many strong temptations violently incline them. Now the heathen princes who were prosperous and vicious, could not relish a doctrine that retrenched their exorbitant desires, and strictly forbade their unconfined enjoyment of sensual delights, which they esteemed the prerogatives annexed to their supreme dignity ; and the minds of subjects are tainted with dependence on the powerful.

From what hath been discoursed, we may judge how great resistance the gospel met with in its first publication; for all things that can make an enterprise impossible, were united together against it. Wisdom and power, the pleasures of sin, and zeal for religion; the understandings and wills of men were combined in opposition to its progress. The learned and ignorant, magistrates and people, men and devils joined to suppress it. Hell was in a commotion and the prince of darkness in arms, not to suffer the crowns of so many kingdoms to fall from his head, which for so many ages he had kept. He was enraged to lose the homage and service, especially of the more knowing nations, as the Grecians and Romans; who, by how much the more capable of truth, with so much the more art, to the dishonour of God, for a long time had been kept under his deceit.

2. If we consider the means by which the gospel was conveyed, it will be more evident that omnipotence alone made it successful. When Christ came from heaven to convert the world, it had been according to the law of reason more suitable to his purpose to have been born at Rome, the seat of the empire, wherein the confluence of all nations met, than in an obscure corner. So when the apostles were first sent forth to propagate the gospel, human prudence would judge, that they should have been assisted either with authority and power, or with learning and eloquence, to compel or persuade to a submission to it. But if there had been any proportion between the quality of the instruments and the effects produced, the gospel had been esteemed a doctrine purely human. The immediate agents had been entitled to all the honour by the suffrage of the senses, and their proper sufficiency would have obscured the virtue of Christ that wrought in them. Therefore God chose " the weak things of the world, to confound the mighty; and base things of the world, and things which are despised hath God chosen; yea, and things which are not, to bring to nought things that are," that his glorious power may be fully manifested, 1 Cor. i. 27, 28. Christianity, like its author, sprang " as a root out of a dry ground," and grew into a fair and strong tree, not by human planting and watering, but by the miraculous influences of heaven.

The persons employed were a few fishermen, with a publican and a tent-maker, without authority and power to force men to obedience, and without the charms of eloquence to insinuate the belief of the doctrines they delivered. And with these disadvantages they could never have conceived a thought, much less had courage to attempt the great impossibility of converting the whole world to Christ, and subjecting the heads of princes, and the learned and wise, to the foot of a crucified person, without the divine assistance.

(1.) They were without authority and power. Other religions were established in several nations, by persons of the greatest eminency and credit among them; that of the Persians by Zoroaster, that of the Egyptians by Hermes, that of the Grecians by Orpheus, that of the Romans by Numa, all kings, or of great reputation for their wisdom and virtue; and they were received without contradiction; for being correspondent to the corrupt inclinations of men, it was not strange that the princes had either capacity to invent them, or power to plant them. And in later times Mahomet opened a way for his religion by his sword, and advanced it by conquest. Now it is no wonder that a religion so pleasing to the lower appetites, that gives license to all corrupt affections in the present life, and promises a sensual paradise suitable to beasts in the future, should be embraced by those who were subject to his arms. But the apostles were meanly born and educated, without credit and reputation, destitute of all human strength, and had only a crucified person for their leader. Christianity was exposed naked, in the day of its birth, without any shelter from secular powers.

(2.) They had not the advantage of art and eloquence to commend their religion. There is a kind of charm in rhetoric, that makes things appear otherwise than they are: the best cause it ruins, the worst it confirms. Truth, though in itself invincible, yet by it seems to be overcome, and error obtains a false triumph. We have a visible proof of this in the writings of Celsus, Symmachus, Cæcilius, and others, for paganism against Christianity. What a vast difference is there between the lies and filthiness of the one, and the truth and sanctity of the other! Yet with what admirable address did they manage that infamous subject! Although it seemed incapable of any defence, yet they gave such colours to it, by the beauty of their expressions and their apparent reasons, that it seemed plausible; and Christianity, notwithstanding its brightness and purity, was made odious to the people. But the apostles were most of them wholly unlearned. Paul himself acknowledges, that he was weak in presence, and "his speech was not with enticing words of man's wisdom," 2 Cor. ii. 4. A crucified Christ was all their rhetoric. Now these impotent, despicable persons were employed to subdue the world to the cross of Christ; and in that season, when the Roman empire was at its height, when the most rigorous severities were used against all innovations, when philosophy and eloquence were in their flower and vigour; so that truth, unless adorned with the dress and artifice of falsehood, was despised, and a message from God himself, unless eloquently conveyed, had no force to persuade. Therefore the apostles debased themselves in the sense of their own weakness; "We have this treasure in earthen vessels, that the excellency of the power may be of God, and not of us," 2 Cor. iv. 7. It was from distrust of themselves, their true confidence in God proceeded. They were only so far powerful as he enabled them; like instruments in which there is not virtue sufficient for the carving of a statue, if they do not receive it impressed from the artificer that uses them. Briefly, as God, the author of wonders, uses that which is weak in nature, to conquer the most rebellious parts of it; he makes the weak sand a more powerful bridle to the impetuous element of waters, than the strongest banks raised by the industry of men, and composed of the most solid materials; so he was pleased, by a few artless, impotent persons, to confound the wisdom, and overcome the power of the world.

3. The great, sudden, and lasting change that was made in the world, by the preaching of the gospel, is a certain argument of the divine power that animated those

mean appearances, and that no instrument is weak in God's hands.

(1.) The greatness of the change is such, that it was only possible to divine power. It is a great miracle to render sight to the blind, but it is more miraculous to enlighten the dark mind, to see the truth and beauty of supernatural mysteries, when they are disguised under reproach and sad representations, and effectually to believe them, especially when the inferior appetite is so contrary to faith. It is a prodigy to raise the dead, but it is more admirable to sanctify an habituated sinner; for in comparing the quality of those miracles, that is the greatest, in the performing whereof God is discovered to be the absolute Lord of the greater nature; now the intellectual nature is superior to the corporeal. Besides, there is no contradiction from a dead body against the divine power in raising it; on the contrary, if any sense were remaining, it would ardently desire to be restored to the full enjoyment of life; but corrupt nature is most opposite to renewing grace. And in this sense our Saviour's promise to the disciples was principally accomplished; "Verily I say unto you, he that believeth on me, the works that I do shall he do also, and greater works than these shall he do, because I go to the Father," John xiv. 12; for the strange conversion of the Gentiles by the preaching of the gospel, was the most divine and powerful work of our Saviour in glory, after his sending the Holy Ghost, and exceeded all the miraculous operations performed by him on the earth. The glorious light of truth scattered the thick and terrible darkness of ignorance and error, that was so universal. The gospel, in its power and the quality of its effects, was like those words, "Let there be light," which the eternal Word pronounced upon the confused chaos, and infused a soul and life into the world. The clear knowledge of God in his nature, and glorious works of creation and redemption, of the duty of man, of the future state, was communicated to the meanest understandings.

And in proportion to the light of faith, such was the measure of piety and holiness. Idolatry that had number, antiquity, authority on its side, was entirely abolished. The false deities were cast out of the temple, and the cross of Christ was planted in the hearts of men. The pure beams of the Sun of Righteousness quickly extinguished the fires of the devil's altars, and the real miracles performed by the divine power exposed his lying wonders to contempt. Accordingly the apostle tells the Thessalonians; "For they themselves show of us, what manner of entering in we had unto you, and how ye turned to God from idols, to serve the living and true God, and to wait for his Son from heaven, whom he raised from the dead, even Jesus which delivered us from the wrath to come," 1 Thess. i. 9. Innumerable from secret atheism and public gentilism were converted to acknowledge and accept of the Redeemer for their Lord. What could produce such a marvellous change in the world but an Almighty power? How seemingly impossible was it to bring so many who were proud in their natures, perverse in their customs, and indubitably assenting to their false religions, from such a distance as the worship of innumerable deities, to adore a crucified God! It was admirable that Alexander broke the Persian empire with an army of thirty thousand; but what is there comparable in that conquest to the acts of the apostles? How much less difficult is it for some nations to change their kings, than for all to change their gods! How far more easy is it to overcome the bodies of men, than subdue their souls! Upon the most exact inquiry, there will never be found in human nature any cause capable to produce such an effect, nor in the records of all ages any example like it.

Add to this, the excellent reformation in the hearts and lives of men. As their understandings, so their wills and affections, the sources of action, were miraculously altered. What the sages of the world could not effect in a few select persons, the gospel hath done in great numbers; nay, raised them above all their feigned ideas, above the highest pitch of their proud philosophy. Those strong and furious passions, which natural reason was as unable to restrain as a thread of silk is to govern a fierce beast, the gospel hath tamed and brought into order. It hath executed what philosophy durst never enterprise, despairing of success. The gospel overcame all those carnal reluctancies that seemed insuperable: it made the wise men of the world resign their reason to faith; it persuaded carnal men to mortify the flesh, the ambitious to despise secular honours, the voluptuous to renounce their pleasures, the covetous to distribute their goods to the poor, the injured and incensed to forgive their enemies; and all this for love to God, an affection unknown to all other laws and institutions. Wherever it came, it miraculously transformed pagans into Christians, which was as truly wonderful, as for the basilisk to part with its poison, for a wolf to be changed into a lamb, nay, for dogs, (such were the Gentiles in our Saviour's language,) to be changed into angels of light and purity. An eminent instance we have of its efficacy in the Corinthians, who in their heathen state were guilty of the vilest enormities: but after their receiving the gospel, the apostle testifies, they "were washed, sanctified and justified in the name of the Lord Jesus, and by the Spirit of our God," 1 Cor. vi. 10, 11. Justin Martyr tells Triphon that those who had been stained with all filthiness, and enslaved by charming imperious lusts, yet becoming Christians, they were purified and freed, and delighted in those virtues that were most contrary to their former vices. This alteration was so visible, that the lives of the first Christians were an apology for their faith. And it is strongly urged by Origen, Tertullian, Lactantius, and others, as a convincing proof of the divinity of the Christian doctrine, that it made the professors of it divine in their conversations. The creation of grace was like the creation of nature, when trees sprang up in an instant laden with fruits; so in the converted, all the blessed fruits of the spirit, "love, joy, peace, long-suffering, gentleness, goodness, faith, meekness, temperance," abounded. This testimony even a pagan persecutor gives the common sort of Christians, that they assembled to sing hymns to Christ; that they obliged themselves solemnly to injure no person, to deceive none, to preserve faithfully what was committed to them, to be always true.

And as, in obedience to the gospel, they gave a divorce to all the sinful delights of sense, so, which was incomparably more difficult, they embraced those things which nature doth most abhor. No religion ever exposed its followers to such sufferings, nor inspired them with such resolution to sustain them. All other religions were productions of the flesh, and being allied together, if any time jealousy caused a discord between them, yet an open persecution was unusual. But when Christianity first appeared, they all turned their hatred and violence against it, as a foreigner of a different extraction. How many living martyrs were exiles for the faith, and deprived of all human consolation! yet they esteemed themselves more blessed in their miseries, than others in their pleasures. How many thousands were put to death for the honour of our Redeemer! yet the least thing is the number, in comparison of the manner of their sufferings. If they had suffered a mild martyrdom, an easy and sudden death, wherein the combat and victory had been finished at a blow, their love and courage had not been so admirable; but they endured torments so various and terrible, that had they not been practised upon them by their enemies, it were incredible that ever malice should be so ingenious to invent, or cruelty so hardened to inflict them. If all the furies of hell had come forth to suggest new tortures, they could not have devised worse. Neither was their mere suffering such torments so astonishing, as their readiness to encounter them, and their behaviour under them. They maintained their faith in the presence of the most formidable princes. Some, who might by favour, were afraid to escape the common persecution, esteeming no death precious but martyrdom. They contended earnestly to suffer, and envied others the honourable ignominy and happy torments that were endured for their beloved Redeemer. We have an instance of their courage in Tiburtius, who thus spake to his judges: "Bind me to racks and wheels, condemn me, banish me, load me with chains, burn me, tear me, omit no kind of torment. If you banish me, the smallest corner of the earth shall be to me as the whole world, because I shall find my God there; if you kill me, by the same act you will give me the happy liberty I sigh after, and deliver me from a prison on earth to reign in heaven; if you condemn me to the fire, I have quenched other flames in resisting concupiscence. Ordain what torment you please, it shall not trouble me, since my heart is filled with love to suffer and desire it." They were thankful to those who condemned them, and regarded their executioners with the same eye, as Peter did the angel that brake off his fetters to restore him to freedom : they cheerfully received them, as those who brought the keys of paradise in the same hands wherewith they brought their swords. They entered into the fire with joy, and were not only patient but triumphant in their sufferings ; as if they had been glorified in their souls, and impassible to the sufferings of their bodies. "I have seen," saith Eusebius, "the executioners tired with tormenting them, lie down panting and breathing, and others not less fierce, but more fresh, succeed in their cruel service ; but I never saw the martyrs weary of sufferings, nor heard them desire a truce, much less deliverance from them." If the judges were softened with their blood, and by the force of nature were compelled to be compassionate, so as to offer them a release if they would but feign to deny Christ; they were filled with indignation, esteeming it the worst injury, that the persecutors expected they would be guilty of but the shadow of infidelity to their dear Saviour. They were ambitious of the longest and most terrible sufferings for his sake, to be martyrs in every member. They sang the praises of Christ (their tongues being harmonious with the affections of their hearts) in the flames; they preached him from the crosses ; they rejoiced in him as their only good, in the midst of devouring beasts. Briefly, they preserved an inviolable faith to him, notwithstanding the most furious batteries against them. The barbarous enemy might tear their hearts from their breasts, but never Christ from their hearts, to whom they were inseparably united by love, stronger than the most cruel death.

Now what less than the divine power could support them under those torments, which it is almost incredible that bodies made of flesh could endure ? I will not dispute whether it exceeds all natural force to suffer such a vicious affection of pride or obstinacy; but the frequency of it exceeds all natural possibility. It was not impossible for Mucius Scævola, one of the Romans, being transported with indignation for missing his design, to hold his right hand unmoved in the fire, (more grieved at the error than the burning of it,) to extinguish in the king, their enemy, all hopes of drawing from him the secret of his country by the force of torments; but though it were but the suffering of one part and for a short time, yet it was not possible that many thousands such should have been at Rome; for then that single example had not been so wonderful in all antiquity: but the noble army of martyrs who overcame in the most bloody battles, was numerous beyond account, and composed of all sorts of persons, of the aged and infirm, of tender youths, of delicate women, of the honourable and obscure; yet in that difference of ages, and sexes, and states, there appeared such an equality of virtue, that it was visible, the same heavenly Spirit inspired them all with courage, and by assuring them of eternal life, made them despise present death. Such heroical and frequent constancy must be ascribed to the "breast-plate of faith and love" of a celestial temper, wherewith the Almighty had armed them.

If it be said that some have died for a false religion, so that the extraordinary assistance of heaven was not necessary to encourage the Christian martyrs, the answer is clear, there is a vast difference between the number of the sufferers and manner of their sufferings. Some few, moved by vanity and melancholy, or compelled, have suffered for a false religion, that was authorized by the custom of their country for many ages; but innumerable Christians, animated by the example of their crucified king, freely sacrificed themselves for the testimony of the gospel upon the first revelation of it, before any human respects gave colour to it. In those who suffered for a false religion, were visible either fear or vain-glory, stubbornness or rage; but the Christians in their greatest sufferings expressed magnanimity without pride, constancy without fierceness, patience without stupidity, and such an admirable compassion for their enemies, as persuaded some of their tormentors to be companions with them in martyrdom.

(2.) The suddenness and universality of the change effected by the gospel, is a signal evidence of the divine power that attended it. The apostle declares the admirable progress of it "in all the world," during his time, Col. i. 6. In a few years with incredible swiftness it passed through Judea, Samaria, Syria, Greece, and all the parts of the known habitable world. Tacitus acknowledges that in the eleventh year of Nero, great numbers of Christians were at Rome, at a great distance from the place where the gospel was first preached. It appears from the writings of the primitive Christians, that in the second century after the death of Christ, the Roman empire was filled with Christian churches. The world was peopled with a new generation. Now what secret power produced that sudden and universal change? How came it to pass that the gospel, contrary to the order of new things, should be so readily received, and in those places where the most insuperable obstacles opposed it; in Corinth, the seat of luxury and voluptuousness; in Ephesus, where idolatry had its throne; in Rome itself, where honours, riches, pleasures, were adored? Moses with all his great miracles never conquered one nation to the true God; the pharisee "compassed sea and land to make one proselyte," but the gospel in a little time converted many nations from their opinions and manners wherein they had been instructed and educated, to those that were not only different, but contrary. The wonder in Isaiah was exceeded, that a nation was born in a day; for the world were renewed as it were in a moment. Such a quickening universal efficacy was joined with the preaching of the gospel, that the power of God was never more visibly manifested in any work. Therefore the apostle mentions it as one part of the great mystery of godliness, that Christ was "believed on in the world," 1 Tim. iii. 16. There is nothing but supernatural, as in the birth, so in the progress of Christianity.

(3.) The lasting change made by the gospel is the

effect of infinite power. Philosophy, though maintained by the successive force of the greatest wits, yet declined and came to nothing; but Christianity, attended only by its own authority, established its dominion, and raised an eternal empire of truth and holiness in the world. The reason of man cannot inspire into its productions a principle of life; only that power which conveys to man an immortal soul, can derive to its institutions a spirit to animate and preserve them. And this victorious permanent virtue of the gospel is more admirable in regard it prevailed without the assistance, and against the opposition of all. Nothing could effectually resist the sacred force of naked truth. The more it was oppressed, the more it prospered. It gained credit and disciples by contradiction and persecution; it was multiplied by the deaths of its followers. "The cloud of witnesses" dissolving in a shower of blood, made the church fruitful; for many spectators that saw the Christian faith so fiercely persecuted, from a desire to know the cause that made it so hateful, by searching for its supposed guilt, found its real innocence. And thus to discover the truth, the tempests it suffered were more serviceable than the calm it enjoyed. Although some persecutors have boasted of their utter abolishing the Christian name in all parts of the empire, yet those inscriptions are the proud monuments of their vanity, not victory. Tyrants are perished, but truth remains for ever. By which it is evident, that as the gospel had a higher principle than what is from below, so it was assisted with more than human power.

To sum up in short what hath been amplified; how gloriously was the arm of the Lord revealed in raising the world, that for four thousand years lay in wickedness! What less than a divine power could soften such an obstinate hardness, as long custom in sin brings? What could pluck up errors that had taken such deep root in the spirits of men and were naturalized to them, and plant a discipline so austere and thorny to sense? Who but the Almighty could cast out the devil from his empire so universally and long usurped, and withdraw his subjects that were captivated by the terror of laws and by the delights of the flesh? What invisible power made innumerable of the tender sex, who were not by temper courageous, nor by obstinacy inflexible, nay, who were so fearful that they could not see a drawn sword without affrightment, yet so resolute as to despise all the instruments of cruelty? What is more astonishing than to see a flock of sheep encounter and overcome an army of lions? "This was the Lord's doing," and it ought to be "marvellous in our eyes." Briefly, the making of a crucified person to reign in the midst of his enemies, and to give laws to the whole earth, is a victory worthy of the Lord of hosts. The conversion of the world to Christianity was the effect of infinite mercy and equal power.

VII. The divine power shall be gloriously manifested in the complete salvation of the church at the end of the world.

Jesus Christ as mediator is invested with sovereign "power in heaven and in earth;" and in that quality he shall exercise it, till our salvation is finished; "for he must reign till he hath put all enemies under his feet," 1 Cor. xv. 25. "But we see not yet all things put under him," Heb. ii. 8. Although those persons and things that never degenerated from their original, are entirely subject to him; the angels obey his will, universal nature is governed by his providence; the heavens, the earth, the waters, and all things produced from them, never resist the direction of his hand; yet there are others that fell from their integrity, and some things consequent to man's rebellion, which either oppose the power of Christ or are not yet actually subdued; and they are the enemies of our salvation, Satan, sin, and death. Now the perfect freedom of the church from all these, will be the last glorious act of Christ's regal office. And it is observable, the day of judgment is called the day of redemption, with respect to the final accomplishment of our felicity, that was purchased by the infinite price of his sufferings. The day of Christ's death was the day of redemption, as to our right and title; for then our ransom was fully paid, and it is by the immortal efficacy of his blood that we partake of the glorious liberty of the sons of God; but the actual enjoyment of it shall be at the last day. Therefore the perfection of all our spiritual privileges is referred to that time, when "death our last enemy" shall be overcome. The apostle saith, "And not only they, but ourselves also, which have the first fruits of the Spirit, even we ourselves groan within ourselves waiting for the adoption; to wit, the redemption of our body," Rom. viii. 23. During the present life, we are taken into God's family in the quality of his children; but the most solemn act of our adoption shall be at the last day. In this there is a similitude betwixt Christ and his members; for although he was the Son of God by his marvellous conception, and owned by him while he performed his ministry upon the earth, yet all the testimonies of God's favour to him were not comparable to the declaration of it in raising him from the grave; then in the face of heaven and earth, he said, "Thou art my Son, this day have I begotten thee." So in this life God acknowledges and treats us as his children; he clothes us with the righteousness of his Son, feeds us with his word, defends us from our spiritual enemies; but the most public declaration of his favour shall be in the next life, when all the "children of the resurrection" shall be born in a day. Add further, although the souls of believers immediately upon their separation are received into heaven, and during the sleep of death enjoy admirable visions of glory; yet their blessedness is imperfect, in comparison of that excellent degree which shall be enjoyed at the resurrection. As the Roman generals, after a complete conquest, first entered the city privately, and having obtained license of the senate, made their triumphant entry with all the magnificence and splendour becoming the greatness of their victories; so after a faithful Christian "hath fought the good fight," and is come off more than conqueror, he enters privately into the celestial city; but when the body is raised to immortality, he shall then, in the company and with the acclamations of the holy angels, have a glorious entry into it.

I will briefly consider why the bodies of the saints shall be raised, and how the divine power will be manifested in that last act.

1. (1.) The general reason is from God's justice. As

the economy of divine providence requires there must be a future state, when God shall sit upon a judicial throne to weigh the actions of all men, and render to every one according to their quality; so it is as necessary that the person be judged, and not one part alone. The law commands the entire man composed of essential parts, the soul and body; and it is obeyed or violated by both of them. Although the guilt or moral goodness of actions is chiefly attributed to the soul, because it is the principal of them, yet the actions are imputed to the whole man. The soul is the guide, the body the instrument; it is reasonable therefore that both should receive their recompense. We see the example of this in human justice, which is a copy of the divine. The whole man is punished or rewarded: The soul is punished with disgrace and infamy, the body with pains; the soul is rewarded with esteem and honour, the body with external marks of dignity. Thus the divine justice will render to every one according to the things done in the body, whether good or evil, 2 Cor. v. 10.

(2.) The special reason of the saints' resurrection is their union with Christ; for he is not only our Redeemer and Prince, but our second Adam; the same in grace, as the first was in nature. Now as from the first the soul was destroyed by sin, and the body by death; so the second restores them both to their primitive state, the one by grace, the other by a glorious resurrection. Accordingly the gospel saith, that " by man came death," and " by man came also the resurrection of the dead," 1 Cor. xv. 21. Christ removed the moral and natural impossibility of our glorious resurrection; the moral, by the infinite merit of his death, whereby divine justice is satisfied, that otherwise would not permit the guilty to be restored to eternal life; and the natural, by his rising from the grave to a glorious immortality; for his infinite power can do the same in all believers. It is observable, the apostle infers the resurrection of believers from that of Christ, not only as the cause, but the original example; for the members must be conformed to the head, the children to their father, the younger to the elder brother. Therefore he is called " the first fruits of them that slept," and " the first begotten of the dead," 1 Cor. xv; Rev. i. 5. In Christ's resurrection ours is so fully assured, that the event is infallible.

2. Now no less than infinite power is requisite to raise the bodies of the saints from the dust, and to transform them into the similitude of Christ's.

(1.) To raise them. Nothing is more astonishing to nature, than that the bodies which after so many ages in the perpetual circulation of the elements have passed into a thousand different forms, one part of them being resolved into water, another evaporated into air, another turned into dust, should be restored to their first state. What wisdom is requisite to separate the parts so mixed and confounded! what power to re-compose them! what virtue to reinspire them with new life! It may seem more difficult than to revive a dead body whose organs and matter is not changed, of which we have examples in the scriptures. When the Spirit of the Lord placed Ezekiel in the midst of a valley covered with bones, and caused him to consider attentively their number, which was very great, and their extreme dryness, he asked him whether these bones could live? upon which, as one divided and balanced between the seeming impossibility of the thing in itself, and the consideration of the divine power to which nothing is impossible, he answered, "Lord, thou knowest." Upon this God commanded him, to prophesy upon those bones, and to speak to them, as if they had been endued with sense and understanding: " O ye dry bones, hear the word of the Lord: thus saith the Lord God unto these bones, behold, I will cause breath to enter into you, and ye shall live. And I will lay sinews upon you, and will bring in flesh upon you, and cover you with skin, and put breath in you, and ye shall live, and ye shall know that I am the Lord," Ezek. xxxvii. 4—6. And immediately there was a general commotion among them; they joined together, the sinews and flesh came upon them, and the skin covered them; and upon a second prophecy they were all inspired with the breath of life, and stood up " an exceeding great army." Now whether this was really represented to his outward senses, or only by the efficacy of the Spirit to his imagination, no doubt so strange a spectacle vehemently affected him; as with joy in hope of the miraculous restoration of Israel, which that vision foretold, so with admiration of the divine power. But when the trumpet of the archangel shall sound the universal jubilee, and call forth the dead from all their receptacles, when the elements, as faithful depositaries, shall effectively restore what was committed to them, how admirable will the power of God appear!

(2.) No less than infinite power is able to change the raised bodies into the likeness of Christ's. The apostle speaks with an exaggeration of it: for " our conversation is in heaven, from whence also we look for the Saviour, the Lord Jesus Christ, who shall change our vile body, that it may be fashioned like unto his glorious body, according to the working whereby he is able even to subdue all things to himself," Phil. iii. 21. This resemblance will be only in the person of believers. All men shall rise to be judged, but not all to be transformed. There is a resurrection to death, as well as to life. Unhappy resurrection, which only serves to make the body the food of eternal death! But the saints who endeavour to be like to Christ in purity, shall then have a perfect conformity to him in glory and immortality. How glorious the body of Christ is, we may conjecture in part by what the apostle relates to Agrippa, " At mid-day, O king, I saw in the way a light from heaven, above the brightness of the sun, shining round about me;" which was no other but the light of the face of Christ that struck him with blindness, Acts xxvi. 13. One ray of this reflecting upon the first martyr Stephen in his sufferings, gave an angelical glory to his countenance. And John tells us, " When he appears, we shall be like him," 1 John iii. 2. He alludes to the rising of the sun, but with this difference—when the sun appears in the morning, the stars are made invisible; but the bodies of the saints shall be clothed with a sun-like lustre, and shine in the midst of Christ's glory. Omnipotency alone that subdues all things, can raise and refine them from their dross unto such an admirable brightness. The angels will be surprised with wonder to see millions of stars spring out of the dust. The Lord Jesus Christ will be admired in "all them that believe," 2 Thess. i. 10.

Their bodies shall be raised to a glorious immortality. In this the general resurrection is different from that which was particular, as of Lazarus. By the one, death was overcome and put to flight only for some time, for his second life was no more exempt from death than his first: but by the other, "death shall be swallowed up in victory," and lose its force for ever. Then shall our true Joshua be magnified in the sight of the whole world, and the glorious number of saints shall cast their crowns at his feet, and sing the triumphant song, "Thou hast redeemed us to God by thy blood," and rescued us by thy power from all our enemies, and "art worthy of honour, and glory, and blessing, for ever."

CHAPTER XXII.

PRACTICAL INFERENCE.

From what hath been discoursed concerning the extraordinary working of the divine power, we have a most convincing proof of the verity of the Christian religion; for since God hath by so many miraculous effects, the infallible indications of his favour to the person of Jesus Christ, justified his doctrine, no reasonable doubt can remain concerning it. Indeed the internal excellencies of it, which are visible to the purged eye of the soul, are clear marks of its divinity. The mystery of our redemption is made up of various parts, in the union of which such an evident wisdom appears, that the rational mind, unless enslaved by prejudice, must be ravished into a compliance. Even that which most offends sense, the meanness of our Saviour's condition in the world, and the miseries to which he was exposed, do so perfectly correspond with his great design to make men holy and heavenly, that it appears to be the effect of most wise counsel. His death on the cross is so much not unbecoming God, as an infinite love and unconceivable compassion are becoming him. And such a beauty of holiness shines in the moral part, as clearly proves God to be its author. It denounces war against all vices and commands every virtue. All that is excellent in human institutions it delivers with infinitely more authority and efficacy; and what natural reason did not reach to, it fully describes, in order to the glory of God and the happiness of man.

Now as God, the Author of nature, hath by tastes, and smells, and other sensible qualities, distinguished things wholesome from noxious, even to the lowest living creatures, so he hath much more distinguished objects that are saving from deadly, that is, the true religion from the false, by undoubted evidences, to any one who will exercise their spiritual senses, and sincerely desire to know and obey it. And that all the wise and holy embraced it in the face of the greatest discouragements, is an unanswerable argument that it is pleasing to God; for how is it possible that the good God should suffer those to fall into mortal error, who from an ardent affection to him despised whatever is terrible or amiable in the world? How is it possible he should deny the knowledge of himself to those, to whom he gave such a pure love to himself?

But the human nature, in its corrupted state, is contrary both to the doctrine of the gospel, that propounds supernatural verities hard to believe, and to the commands of it, that enjoin things hard to do. For this reason it was necessary that God by some external operations, the undeniable effects of his power, should discover to the world his approbation of it.

Now that Christ is the Son of God and Redeemer of the world, was miraculously declared from heaven by the whole divinity; "There are three that bear record in heaven, the Father, the Word, and the Holy Ghost; and these three are one," 1 John v. 7. The Father testified by a voice as loud as thunder at his baptism and transfiguration, "This is my beloved Son, in whom I am well pleased," Matt. iii. 17. The Son, by his glorious apparition to Paul, when he struck him to the earth with these words, "why persecutest thou me?" Acts ix. 4.

The light was so radiant, the voice so strong, the impression it made so deep and sensible, that he knew it came from God. And he manifested himself to John with that brightness, that he "fell at his feet as dead," till in compassion he revived him, and said, "I am he that liveth and was dead, and, behold, I am alive for evermore," Rev. i. 17, 18. And the Holy Spirit, by his miraculous descent in the shape of a dove upon him, and in fiery tongues upon the apostles, gave a visible testimony that Jesus Christ was sent from God to save the world.

I will particularly consider one effect of the divine power, the resurrection of Christ, this being the most important article of the gospel, and the demonstration of all the rest; for it is not conceivable that God would by his almighty power have raised him from the grave to a glorious life, (and it is impossible he should be otherwise,) if he had taken the name of the Son of God in vain, and arrogated to himself divine honour, and only pretended that he was sent from him. By the resurrection he was "declared to be the Son of God with power;" for that being the proof of his mission, justifies the truth of his doctrine, and particularly of the quality of God's Son which he always attributed to himself.

Now if infidelity object, that we who live in the present age have no sensible testimony that Christ is risen; and what assurance is there that the apostles who reported it were not deceivers or deceived? In answer to this, I will briefly show how valuable the testimony of the apostles is, and worthy of all acceptation; and that it was equally impossible they should be deceived, or intend to deceive?

His death is attested by his enemies. Tacitus, a pagan, relates that he suffered under Pontius Pilate; and the Jews to this day are so unhappy as to boast of their being the causes of his crucifixion, and call him by a name that is the mark of his punishment. But his resurrection they peremptorily deny. Now the apostles being sent to convert the world, were to lay this down as the foundation of their preaching, that Jesus Christ was raised from the dead, that all might yield faith and obedience to him. This was their special charge, as Peter declares; "Wherefore of these men which have companied with us all the time that the Lord Jesus went in and out among us, beginning from the baptism of John, unto that same day that he was taken up from us, must one be ordained to be a witness with us of his resurrection," Acts i. 21. They were to testify concerning his doctrine and life, his miracles and sufferings, but principally his resurrection. For this reason Paul, who was extraordinarily admitted into their order, had a miraculous sight of Christ from heaven to testify it to the world; "Last of all he was seen of me," 1 Cor. xv. 5.

Now for our full conviction it is necessary to consider the quality of the witnesses, and the nature of their testimony.

1. The witnesses were such, of whom there cannot be the least reasonable suspicion. In civil causes of the greatest moment, the testimony of the honourable and the rich is accounted valuable, because they are not easily corrupted: one of a low degree may from baseness of spirit, through cowardice and fear, be tempted to deny the truth; one in a poor condition may be so dazzled with the lustre of gold, when he considers the price of perjury, as to be induced to assert a falsehood. But who is more incorruptible, the noble that from a sense of honour abhors a lie, or those who by their divine birth and qualities did so detest it, that they would not tell a lie for the glory of God? Who is more worthy of credit, the rich whose riches sometimes excite their desires after more, or those who by a generous disdain despised all things? Besides, persons of known integrity, whom the different images of hopes and fears cannot probably incline to evil, are admitted to decide the weightiest causes; now the apostles were so innocent, sober, honest, and unblamable, in the whole tenor of their conversations, that their most malignant adversaries could never fasten an accusation upon them. Indeed if their carnal interests had been concerned, there might have been some coloured objections against their testimony; but if we duly consider things, it will appear utterly incredible that any deceit could be in it; for as all the actions of

reasonable men proceed from reason solid or apparent, so particularly imposture and fiction are never without some motive and design; for being contrary to nature there must intervene a foreign consideration for their contrivance.

Now the universal motives to invent fables are honour, riches, or pleasure. But none of these could possibly move the apostles to feign the resurrection of Christ. Not to insist on the meanness of their extraction and education, who had only seen boats and nets, and conversed with lakes and fishes, whereas ambition usually springs up in persons of high birth and breeding; it is evident that no respect to human praise excited them, since they attributed the doctrine of the gospel that should give them reputation in the world, to the Holy Spirit, and ascribed the glory of their miraculous actions entirely to the divine power, Acts iii. 12, 13. When the people of Lystra would have given divine honour to Paul, he disclaimed it with abhorrency: and presently after, those who would have adored him as a god, stoned him as a malefactor; he chose to be their sacrifice rather than their idol, Acts xiv. 19. Besides, how could they expect to be great or rich by declaring that one who came to such a tragical end in the face of the world, was raised to life, when the hands of the Jews were still bloody with the wounds of their Master, and their hearts so enraged against all that honoured his name, as to excommunicate them for execrable persons. It had been as extravagant to have designed the acquiring of reputation or riches by their preaching, as for one to throw himself into a flaming furnace to be cooled and refreshed. And that pleasure could not be their aim, is manifest; for they met with nothing but poverty and persecutions, with derision and disgrace, with hardships and all the effects of fury, which they willingly endured rather than cease from preaching, or deny what they had preached. Their unheard-of resolution to forsake their native country, and travel to all the known parts of the earth to convey the doctrine of Jesus Christ, is a strong demonstration that they believed it to be true and of infinite moment, most worthy of all the dangers to which they voluntarily exposed themselves. Never did ambition or avarice, the most active passions, cause men to be more diligent, than they were to communicate the knowledge of our Saviour to all nations. Now what greater assurance can we possibly receive that they were sincere in their report?

2. The nature of the testimony makes it very credible. It was matter of fact. If it had been some high speculation of universal things, abstracted from matter and above the cognizance of the senses, there might be some pretence to object, that the disciples, unexercised in sciences, were deceived by the subtilty of their Master: but it is a singular thing, of which the senses are the most faithful informers and competent judges.

It was an ocular testimony, which as it makes the strongest impression upon the spectator, so upon the belief of others. Thus John; "That which we have seen with our eyes, which we have looked upon, declare we unto you," 1 John i. 1. And that they were not deceived, we have great certainty; for Jesus had conversed a long time with them before his death, and their respect and love to him, and afterwards their compassion, had deeply engraved the lineaments of his visage in their memories; and he presented himself not many years, but three days after his absence, so that it was impossible they should have forgotten his countenance. He appeared to them not once or twice, but many times; and not suddenly as a flash of lightning that presently vanishes, but conversed with them familiarly for forty days.

And it is observable, the apostles themselves were not easily wrought on to believe this truth. When the testimony of the angels assured them that he was risen, they received it with doubting, wonder, and troubled joy, and were suspended between hopes and fears; and at his first appearance they were vehemently surprised. They saw him die on the cross three days before, and their memories were still filled with the frightful images of his sufferings; so that they were balanced between the present testimony of sense, and the fresh remembrance of what they had seen. Therefore he justified the truth of his resurrection to all their senses. He discoursed with them, made them feel his wounds, ate and drank with them; so that it was impossible they should be deceived unless willingly. Thus by the wise dispensation of God, their doubting hath confirmed our faith.

3. The uniformity of the testimony makes it valuable upon a double account;—first, as it secures us, there was no corruption in the witnesses; secondly, that it was no illusion.

(1.) That there was no corruption in the witnesses. The most prudent way to discover the falsity of a testimony, is to interrogate the witnesses severally, to see if there be any contradiction between them. But if they concur not only as to the substance but circumstances, their deposition is very credible. Now the apostles exactly agreed in their testimony, as appears by the several gospels, in which, although written in divers times and places, yet there is an admirable harmony, not only as to the fact itself, but the least particularities.

(2.) The agreement of so many proves it was no illusion that depended on fancy for its existence; for deceptions of the brain are not common to many at once as visible bodies are, but singular because of the variety of fancies. If he had only appeared to some persons separately, carnal reason, which is ingenious to deceive itself, might object that it was only the effect of a distempered fancy, and no real object of sense. But after he had shown himself to some of the disciples apart, and that holy company was met together, uniting the several sparks, to encourage their hopes of his resurrection, he came to them all together, and for many days conversed with them. Now who can believe that so many should be obstructed with melancholy for so long time, so as constantly to remain under the power of a delusion? Besides, he afterwards appeared to "five hundred" at once: and how could such a number of different ages, sexes, temperaments, be at the same time struck with the same imagination?

Add further, if a strong imagination had deceived them by melancholy, there would have been some discoveries of that humour in their actions; for it is impossible that the mind so indisposed, should for a long time act regularly. But in the whole course of their lives not the least extravagancy appears. Their zeal was tempered with prudence, their innocence was without folly, their conversation was becoming their great office. And of this we have unquestionable evidence; for otherwise so many persons of excellent wisdom had never been persuaded by them to embrace Christianity, neither had their enemies so furiously persecuted them; for it is beyond belief that they had so far extinguished the sentiments of humanity, as to treat the apostles as the most guilty criminals, whom they knew to be distracted, and therefore worthy of compassion rather than hatred.

But if it be objected, that it might be a phantasm, or solid body formed according to the likeness of Christ, that abused the apostles, and after some time withdrew itself; the vanity of the objection is very apparent, for such an effect could not be without the operation of a spiritual cause. Now the good angels cannot be guilty of falsehood, of which they had been in that representation, for he that appeared declared himself to be Jesus that suffered; neither would the evil use such an artifice. The old serpent was too wise to promote the belief of Christ's resurrection, which is the foundation of Christianity, an institution most holy, that would destroy his altars, discredit his oracles, bring glory to God and happiness to man, to both which he is eternally opposite. By all which it appears there was no deceit in the subject nor object.

4. They sealed it with their blood. This last proof confirms all the others. If a person of clear fame assert a thing, which he is ready to maintain with the loss of his life, there is no reason to doubt of the truth of his deposition. It is no wonder that Philostratus, a bold Grecian, to show his art, painted Apollonius Tyanæus as a demi-god, exempted from death, and clothed with immortality. But if he had been drawn from his study, where he dressed that idol of iniquity, to appear before the magistrates to give an account of the truth of his relation, he certainly would have renounced his pretended hero, rather than have given his life for a lie

Now the apostles endured the most cruel death, to confirm the truth of their testimony. And what could possibly induce them to it, if they had not been certain of his resurrection? Could love to their dead Master animate them to suffer for the honour of his name? This is inconceivable; for he promised that he would rise the third day, and ascend to heaven, and make them partakers of his glory; so that if he had lain in the rottenness of the grave, what charm, what stupidity was able to make them preserve so high a veneration for a deceiver?

Nothing could remain in them but the memory and indignation of his imposture. Now if it be the dictate of natural reason, that the concurrent testimony of two or three credible persons, not weakened by any exception, is sufficient to decide any cause of the greatest moment, that respects life, honour, and estate; how much more should the attestation of the apostles put this great truth beyond all doubt, since they parted with their lives, the most precious possession in this world, for it! and which is infinitely more, if deceivers, they would certainly be deprived of eternal life in the next!

In short, since the creation, never was a testimony so clear and authentic, the divine providence so ordering the circumstances, that the evidence should be above all suspicion. Neither did it ever happen, that any thing affirmed by so many and such worthy persons, was ever suspected, much less found to be false. It is the most unreasonable stiffness not to yield an entire assent to it; for there would be no secure foundation of determining innumerable weighty cases, if we should doubt of things reported by the most credible circumspect persons, since we can be certified by our own senses, but of a few objects.

5. I shall only add, that the apostles did many great miracles in the name of Christ, which was the strongest demonstration that he was raised to a glorious life. They were invested by the Spirit with the habits of various tongues. This kind of miracle was necessary for the universal preaching of the gospel; for how difficult and obstructive had it been to their work, if they must have returned to their infant state, to learn the signification of foreign languages, to pronounce the words in their ori-

ginal sound, and the accents proper to their country! Therefore the Holy Spirit, according to the promise of Christ, descended upon them, and became their master, and in a moment impressed on their memories the forms of discoursing, and on their tongues the manner of expressing them. Wherever the doctrine of Jesus was preached, " God bare them witness both with signs and wonders, and with divers miracles and gifts of the Holy Ghost, according to his own will," Heb. ii. 4. When Peter passed through the streets filled with persons diseased and half dead, he caused a universal resurrection, by touching them with his reviving shadow. They tamed serpents, and quenched the malignity of their poison; they commanded death to leave its prey, and life to return to its mansion that was not habitable for it. And that miraculous power continued in their successors so long as was requisite for the conviction of the world. Justin Martyr, Irenæus, Tertullian, Origen, Cyprian, mention divers miracles performed by Christians in those times. Tertullian offers to the emperor to whom he addressed his admirable apology, to compel the devils that possessed human bodies to confess themselves to be evil spirits, and thereby constrain the prince of darkness to enlighten his own slaves. And Cyprian assures the governor of Africa, that he would force the devils to come out of the bodies they tormented, lamenting their ejection. Now we cannot imagine they would so far discredit their doctrine and reputation, as to pretend to such a power unless they had it. In short, to deny the miracles wrought by the primitive Christians, were as great rashness, as to deny that Cæsar conquered Pompey, or that Titus succeeded Vespasian; for we have the concurrent testimony of the gravest and best men, of understanding and conscience, who were eye-witnesses; and which was not contradicted by those of the same age. Briefly, there are such clear characters of the divine hand to render the gospel authentic, that to deny it to be true, is to make God a liar.

The conclusion is this—we see how reasonable it is to give an entire assent to the truth of Christianity. The nature of the doctrine that is perfectly divine, declares its original. It is confirmed by supernatural testimonies. The doctrine distinguishes the miracles from false wonders, the illusions of Satan, and the miracles confirm the doctrine. What doubt can there be after the full deposition of the Spirit in raising Christ from the grave, in qualifying the apostles, who were rude and ignorant, with knowledge, zeal, courage, charity, and in all the graces requisite for their great enterprise, and in converting the world by their ministry and miracles? If we believe not so clear a revelation, our infidelity is desperate. When our Saviour was upon the earth, the meanness and poverty of his appearance lessened their crime, who did not acknowledge and honour him in the disguise of a servant; therefore they were capable of favour. Many of his bloody persecutors were converted and saved by the preaching of the apostles. But since the Holy Ghost hath convinced the world, by so strong a light, of sin, righteousness, and judgment, viz., that Jesus, whom the Jews most unworthily crucified, was the Son of God; that in dying he purchased the pardon of sin; since he is risen and received to glory, "that all power in heaven and earth is given to him," the effect of which is most visible, for spiritual wickednesses trembled at his name, were expelled from their dominions, and sent to their old prison to suffer the chains and flames due to them; to refuse his testimony, is a degree of obstinacy not far distant from the malice of the devils, and puts men without the reserves of pardoning mercy. And it is not a slight, superficial belief of this great truth, that is sufficient, but that which is powerful in making us universally obedient to our glorified Redeemer, who will distribute crowns to all his faithful servants. We cannot truly believe his resurrection without believing his doctrine, nor believe his doctrine without unfeigned desires after the eternal felicity it promises, nor desire that felicity without a sincere compliance to his commands in order to the obtaining of it. In short, it is infidelity approaching madness, not to believe the truth of the gospel; but it is madness of a higher kind and more prodigious, to pretend to believe it, and yet to live in disobedience to its precepts, in contempt of its promises and threatenings, as if it were a mere fable.

CHAPTER XXIII.

THE TRUTH OF GOD IN REDEMPTION.

THE original law given to man in paradise had a severe penalty annexed, that upon the first breach of it he should die. The end of the threatening was to preserve in him a constant reverence of the command. After his disobedience, the honour of the divine truth was concerned as to the inflicting of the punishment; for although the supreme Lawgiver hath power over the law to relax the punishment as to particular persons, yet having declared that according to that rule he would proceed in judgment with man, the perfection of his truth required, that sin should be punished in such a manner, that his righteousness and holiness might eminently appear, and the reasonable creature for ever fear to offend him. Now the God of truth hath by the death of his only Son so completely answered the ends of the legal threatening, that the glory of that attribute is broke forth like the sun through all the clouds that seemed to obscure it. " Mercy and truth are met together; righteousness and peace have kissed each other," Psalm lxxxv. 10. Of this I have so largely treated before, that I shall add nothing more concerning it.

There is a secondary respect wherein the truth of God is concerned, as to the accomplishing of our redemption by Jesus, which I will briefly explicate. God having decreed the sending of his Son in the quality of Mediator to purchase our salvation, was pleased by several promises to declare his merciful purpose, and by various types to show the design of that glorious work, before the exhibition of it. This was the effect of his supreme wisdom and goodness—to comply with the weakness of the church, when it was newly separated from the world; for, as a sudden strong light overpowers the eye that hath been long in the dark, so the full, bright revelation of the gospel had been above the capacity of the church, when it was first freed from a state of ignorance! Light mixed with shadows was proportionable to their sight. Therefore he was pleased by several representations and predictions to exercise the faith, entertain the hope, and excite the desires of his people before the accomplishment of our salvation by his Son—to render the belief of it easy and certain afterwards. Now, for the honour of his truth, he was engaged to make good his word; for although pure love and mercy is the original of all God's promises to man, yet his truth and fidelity are the reasons of his fulfilling them. Not that God is under the obligation of a law, but his own righteous name is the inviolable rule of his actions. Accordingly the apostle lays it as the foundation of our hopes, that "God who cannot lie," hath promised eternal life, Tit. i. 2. The divine decree alone concerning our salvation by Christ, is a sure foundation; for God is as unchangeable in his will, as his nature; in him there is "no variableness, neither shadow of turning," Jam. i. 17. But the promise determines the will of God to perform it upon another account; for it is not single inconstancy but falsehood, not to perform what is promised; from both which he is infinitely distant. Paul alleges this for the reason why the covenant of grace is unchangeable and of everlasting efficacy, in that the counsel of God was by his promise and oath confirmed, "that by two immutable things, in which it was impossible for God to lie, we might have strong consolation," Heb. vi. 18. For the promise gives a rightful claim to the creature, and the fulfilling of it is the justification of God's fidelity. In this sense it is said, "the law was given by Moses, but grace and truth came by Jesus Christ;" that is, the grace of the gospel is the substantial and complete accomplishment of the types and promises under the law.

I. I will not enter into the discussion of all the prophecies concerning the Messiah in the old testament, to show how they are verified in Jesus Christ; but briefly consider some special predictions that concern the time of the Messiah's coming, his person, and offices.

1. The prophecy of dying Jacob; " The sceptre shall not depart from Judah, nor a lawgiver from between his feet, until Shiloh come," Gen xlix. 10. By the sceptre and lawgiver are meant divers forms of government, the first being the mark of regal power; the other title respects those whose power succeeded that of their kings, in the person of Zerubbabel and his successors. Jacob prophetically declares two things, their establishment in Judah, and their continuance till the coming of Shiloh. This oracle doth not precisely respect the person of Judah, for he never ascended the throne, nor possessed the empire over his brethren; nor foretold his posterity as a tribe distinguished from the rest, although it had special advantage from that time; for the banner of Jadah led the camp in their march through the wilderness, Numb. ii. 3; that tribe had the first possession of the land of Canaan; these were the beginnings of its future glory. And from David to the captivity, that tribe possessed the kingdom; but the glory of his sceptre was lost in the person of Zedekiah; therefore the full meaning of the prophecy regards the people of Israel in the relation they had to the tribe of Judah, for that tribe alone returned entire from the captivity with some relics of Levi and Benjamin; so that the nation from that time was distinguished by the title of the Jews in relation to it; and the right to dispose of the sceptre was always in the tribe of Judah, for the Levites that ruled after the captivity received their power from them. " Till Shiloh come," that is, the Messiah, as the Chaldee paraphrase and the ancient Jewish interpreters expound; so that the intent of the oracle is, that after the establishment of the supreme power in the family of Judah, it should not pass into the hands of strangers, but as a certain presage and immediate forerunner of the coming of Shiloh. And this was fully accomplished; for in the captivity there was an interruption, rather than an extinction of their government; their return was promised at the time they were carried captives to Babylon. But at the coming of Christ, Judea was a province of the Roman empire;

Herod an Edomite, sat on the throne; and as the tribe of Judah in general, so the family of David in particular was in such a low state, that Joseph and Mary that were descended from him, were constrained to lodge in a stable at Bethlehem. And since the blessed Peace-maker hath appeared on the earth, the Jews have lost all authority: their civil and ecclesiastical state is utterly ruined, and they bear the visible marks of infamous servitude.

2. The second famous prediction is by an angel to Daniel, when he was lamenting the ruin of Jerusalem, who comforted him with an assurance that the city should be rebuilt; and farther told him, "that from the going forth of the commandment to restore and to build Jerusalem, unto the Messiah, the Prince, shall be seven weeks, and three-score and two weeks: the street shall be built again, and the wall even in troublous times. And after three-score and two weeks shall Messiah be cut off, but not for himself; and the people of the prince that shall come, shall destroy the city and sanctuary, and the end thereof shall be with a flood, and to the end of the war desolations are determined," Dan. ix. 25. The clear intent of the angel's message is, that within the space of seventy prophetical weeks, (that is, four hundred and ninety years, according to the exposition of the rabbins themselves) after the issuing forth of the order for the rebuilding Jerusalem, the Messiah should come, and be put to death for the sins of men, which was exactly fulfilled.

3. The time of the manifestation of the Messiah is evidently set down in Haggai, ii. 7—9; "I will shake all nations and the Desire of all nations shall come; and I will fill this house with glory, saith the Lord of hosts. The silver is mine, and the gold is mine, saith the Lord of hosts. The glory of this latter house shall be greater than that of the former, saith the Lord of hosts; and in this place will I give peace." The prophet to encourage the Jews in building the temple, assured them that it should have a surpassing glory by the presence of the Messiah, who is called the Desire of all nations; and being the Prince of peace, his coming is described by that blessed effect; "And in this place will I give peace, saith the Lord of hosts."

The second temple was much inferior to Solomon's, as in magnificence and external ornaments, so especially because defective in those excellencies that were peculiar to the first. They were the ark of the covenant, and the appearance of glory between the cherubim; the fire from heaven to consume the sacrifices, the urim and thummim, and the Holy Ghost who inspired the prophets. But when the Lord came to his temple, and performed many of his miracles there, this brought a glory to it infinitely exceeding that of the former; for what comparison is there between the shadowy presence of God between the cherubim, and his real presence in the human nature of Christ, in whom the fulness of the God-head dwelt bodily? How much inferior were the priests and prophets to him who came from heaven, and had the Spirit without measure, to reveal the counsel of God for the salvation of the world!

4. The particular circumstances foretold concerning the Messiah, are all verified in Jesus Christ. It was foretold that the Messiah should have a forerunner, to prepare his way by preaching the doctrine of repentance; that he should be born of a virgin, and of the family of David, and in the town of Bethlehem; that he should go into Egypt, and be called forth from thence by God; that his chief residence should be in Galilee, the region of Zebulun and Naphtali; that he should be poor and humble, and enter into Jerusalem on the foal of an ass; that he should perform great miracles in restoring the blind, the lame, the deaf and dumb; that he should suffer many afflictions, contempt, scorn, stripes, be spit on, scourged, betrayed by his familiar friend, sold for a sordid price; that he should be put to death; that his hands and feet should be bored, and his side pierced; that he should die between two thieves; that in his passion he should taste vinegar and gall; that his garments should be divided, and lots be cast for his coat; that he should be buried, and his body not see corruption, but rise again the third day; that he should ascend to heaven, and sit at the right hand of God: and all these predictions are exactly fulfilled in the Lord Christ.

5. The consequences of his coming are foretold:

(1.) That the Jews should reject him, because of the meanness of his appearance. They neither understood the greatness and majesty, nor the abasement of the Messiah described in their prophecies;—not his greatness, that the son of David was his Lord, that he was before Abraham who rejoiced to see his day; for they did not believe the eternity of his divine nature;—they did not understand his humiliation to death; therefore it was objected by them that " the Messiah remains for ever, and this person saith, he shall die." They fancied a carnal Messiah, shining with worldly pomp, accompanied with thundering legions, to deliver them from temporal servitude; so that when they saw him " without form and comeliness," and that no beauty was in him to make him desirable, they " hid their faces from him," they " despised and esteemed him not." Thus by their obstinate refusal of the Messiah, they really and visibly fulfilled the prophecies concerning him.

(2.) That the Levitical ceremonies and sacrifices should cease upon the death of the Messiah, and the Jewish nation be dissolved. Although the legal service was established with great solemnity, yet there was always a sufficient indication that it should not be perpetual. Moses, who delivered the law, told them, that God would raise up another prophet whom " they must hear." And David composed a psalm to be sung in the temple, containing the establishment of a priest, not according to the order of Levi but Melchizedec, who should bring in a worship spiritual and divine, Psalm cx. 3. And we see this accomplished: all the ceremonies were buried in his grave, and the sacrifices for above sixteen hundred years are ceased. Besides the destruction of the holy city and sanctuary, the Jews are scattered in all parts, and in their dreadful dispersion suffer the just punishment of their infidelity.

(3.) It was prophesied that in the time of the Messiah idols should be ruined, and idolaters converted to the knowledge of the true God; that he should be " a light to the Gentiles," and to him the gathering of the people should be. And this is so visibly accomplished in the conversion of the world to Christianity, that not one jot or tittle of God's word hath failed; so that besides the glory due to his power and mercy, we are obliged to honour him as the fountain of truth.

II. I will now make some short reflections upon the types of the law, to show how they are completed in Christ.

The Mosaic dispensation was so contrived as to bear a resemblance of the Messiah in all its parts. The law had "a shadow of good things to come," Heb. x. 1. "Christ is the end of the law," the substance of those shadows, Rom. x. 4. The main design of the epistle to the Hebrews is to show, that in the ancient tabernacle there were models of the heavenly things revealed in the gospel. The great number of types declare the variety of the divine wisdom, and the admirable fulness of Christ in whom they are verified.

Three sorts were instituted: 1. some were things without life, whose qualities and effects shadowed forth his virtues and benefits; 2. things endued with life and sense; 3. reasonable persons, that either in their offices, actions, or the memorable accidents that befell them, represented the Messiah.

1. Of the first sort, I will briefly consider the manna that miraculously fell from heaven, the rock that by its stream refreshed the Israelites in their journey to Canaan, and the brazen serpent: premising two things—that in comparing them with the truth, we are to observe the design of God, and not to seek for mysteries in every thing; as in pictures, some strokes of the pencil are for ornament only, others for signification:—besides, when superlative things are spoken of them, exceeding their nature and that cannot be applied to them without a violent figure, the full and entire truth is found only in Jesus Christ.

(1.) The manna was an eminent type of him. Accordingly the apostle declares of the Israelites, they "did all eat the same spiritual meat," not in the respect of its material, but symbolical nature, 1 Cor. x. 3.

The express analogy between manna and Christ, is visible in respect of its marvellous production. The Mosaical manna was not the fruit of the earth, procured by human industry, but formed by the divine power, and rained down upon them; therefore it is called " the corn of heaven," Psalm lxxviii. 24. This typified the celestial original of our Redeemer. He is the true bread from heaven, given by the Father, John vi. 32. He is called the gift of God eminently, being the richest and freest, without any merit or endeavour of men to procure it. And we may observe the truth infinitely exceeded the type; for manna descended only from the clouds, therefore our Saviour tells the Jews, "Moses gave you not that bread from heaven;" but He really came from heaven, where the great and glorious presence of God is manifested, and appeared under a visible form in the world. Manna was only styled the "bread of angels," to signify its excellency above common food;" but "the bread of God is he which cometh down from heaven."

Manna was dispensed to all the Israelites equally; not as the delicious fruits of the earth, that are the portion of a few, but as the light and influences of heavens, that are common to all. And herein it was a representation of Christ, who is offered to all without distinction of nations, to the Jews and Gentiles, to the Grecians and barbarians; and without the distinction of quality, to the honourable and mean, the rich and the poor, the learned and ignorant. And here we may observe the excellency of the spiritual manna above the mosaical; for that fed but one nation, but the bread of God gives life to the world; his infinite merit is sufficient for the salvation of all.

Manna was a delicious food; the taste of it is described to be like wafers mixed with honey, that have a pure, chaste sweetness. This typified the love of Christ shed abroad in the hearts of believers. Such an exalted ravishing pleasure proceeds from it, that the Psalmist breaks forth in an ecstasy, "Taste and see that the Lord is good," Psalm xxxiv. 9.

Manna was their only support in the wilderness, strengthening them to vanquish their enemies, and endure the hardships to which they were incident in their passage to Canaan. In this regard it was a lively image of Christ, who is our spiritual food while we are in the desert of the lower world, the place of our trial, exposed to dangers. By him alone we shall be finally victorious over the enemies of our salvation. And in this also the truth is infinitely above the type that prefigured it; for manna could preserve the natural life for a time only; as our Saviour tells the Jews, "Your fathers did eat manna in the wilderness, and are dead." But Jesus Christ is "the living bread that came down from heaven," and hath a supernatural virtue, to convey a life incomparably more noble, and answerable to the quality of his original. It is incorruptible, as heaven from whence he came. "If any man eat of this bread, he shall live for ever," John vi. 51. Death is so far from extinguishing, that it advances the spiritual life to its perfection.

(2.) The rock. The apostle testifies that the Israelites "drank of that spiritual rock that followed them, and that rock was Christ," 1 Cor. x. 4. That the miracle was mysterious, is evident from the circumstances related of it. When the Israelites were in great distress for water, the Lord said to Moses, "I will stand before thee there upon the rock in Horeb, and thou shalt smite the rock, and there shall come water out of it, that the people may drink," Exod. xvii. 6. If there had been no other design but the relieving of their necessity, that might have been supplied by rain from heaven; or if only to give a visible effect of the divine power, that had been discovered in causing new springs to rise from the earth, or the command of God had been sufficient to strike the rock; but he went to it to signify the respect it had to himself. He was the Son of God that spake to Moses, and conducted the people; for this reason he is styled the angel of God's presence, not with respect to his nature, but offices.

I will briefly observe the parallel between the rock and Christ.

A rock is the ordinary title of God in scripture to represent his unchangeable nature and infinite power, whereby he upholds the world; and in a special manner it resembles the Messiah. He is called "the stone which the builders refused, that was made the head of the corner," 1 Pet. ii. 7, 8. He is the rock upon which the church is built, and secured against the violence of hell,

Matt. xvi. 18. Now Israel was not supplied from the clouds or the valleys, but the rock, to show that the mystical rock, the Son of God only, can refresh the spiritual Israel with living water.

The quality of the rock hath a proper signification; for although it had in its veins a rich abundance of waters, yet to appearance nothing was more dry and hard. In this it was a figure of the spiritual rock. The effects have discovered in him unfathomable depths of righteousness, grace, and salvation; yet at the first view we had no hopes; for if we consider him as God, he is infinitely holy and just, encompassed with everlasting flames against sin; and how can we expect any cooling streams from him? If we consider him as a man, he is resembled to " a root out of a dry ground." The justice of the divine, and the infirmity of the human nature did not promise any comfort to us. But what cannot infinite love, united to infinite power perform? Divine goodness hath changed the laws of nature in our favour, and by an admirable act opened the rock to refresh us.

The rock was struck with the rod of Moses, a type of the law, before it sent forth its streams; thus our spiritual rock " was wounded for our transgressions, bruised for our iniquities," and then opened all his treasures to us. Being consecrated by suffering, he is " the Author of eternal salvation." In this respect the gospel propounds him for the object of saving faith; " I determined to know nothing among you but Jesus Christ, and him crucified." The sacraments, the seals of the new covenant, have a special reference to his death, the foundation of it.

The miraculous waters followed the Israelites in their journey, without which they had perished in the wilderness. This represents the indeficiency of the grace of Christ. A sovereign stream flows from him to satisfy all believers, John vii. 37. He tells us, " Whosoever drinketh of the water that I shall give him, shall never thirst; but the water that I shall give him, shall be in him a well of water, springing up into everlasting life," John iv. 14.

(3.) The brazen serpent sensibly expressed the manner of his death and the benefits derived from it. Therefore Jesus, being the minister of the circumcision, chose this figure for the instruction of the Jews; "As Moses lifted up the serpent in the wilderness, even so must the Son of man be lifted up; that whosoever believeth in him should not perish, but have eternal life," John iii. 14, 15. The sacred story relates, that the Israelites, by their rebellious murmuring, provoked God to send serpents among them, whose poison was so fiery and mortal, that it brought the most painful death. In this affliction they addressed themselves to the Father of mercies, who, moved by their repentance, commanded Moses to make a serpent of brass, and erect it on a pole in the view of the whole camp, that whosoever looked on it should be healed. By this account from scripture, we may clearly understand something of the greatest consequence was represented by it; for the only wise God ordains nothing without just reason. Why must a serpent of brass be elevated on a pole? could not the divine power recover them without it? Why must they look towards it? could not a healing virtue be conveyed to their wounds but through their eyes? All this had a direct reference to the mystery of Christ; for the biting of the Israelites by the fiery serpents, doth naturally represent the effects of sin, that torments the conscience, and inflames the soul with the apprehensions of future judgment. And the erecting of a brazen serpent upon a pole, that had the figure, not the poison, of those serpents, doth in a lively manner set forth the lifting up of Jesus Christ on the cross, who had the similitude only "of sinful flesh." The looking towards the brazen serpent is a fit resemblance of believing in Christ crucified for salvation. The sight of the eye was the only means to derive virtue from it, and the faith of the heart is the means by which the sovereign efficacy of our Redeemer is conveyed. "This is the will of him that sent me," saith our Saviour, "that every one which seeth the Son and believeth on him, may have everlasting life," John vi. 40. As in the camp of Israel, whoever looked towards the brazen serpent, whatever his wounds were or the weakness of his sight, had a present remedy; so how numerous and grievous soever our sins be, how infirm our faith, yet if we sincerely regard the Son of God suffering, he will preserve us from death. For this end he is presented in the gospel as crucified before the eyes of all persons.

2. Things endued with life and sense prefigured the Messiah.

I shall particularly consider the paschal lamb, an illustrious type of him. "Christ our passover is sacrificed for us," 1 Cor. v. 7. The whole scene, as it is laid down in the 12th of Exodus, shows an admirable agreement between them.

A lamb in respect of its natural innocency and meekness, that suffers without resistance, was a fit emblem of our Saviour, whose voice was not heard in the street, who did not break the bruised reed nor quench the smoking flax, Isaiah xlii. 3. "He was oppressed, and he was afflicted, yet he opened not his mouth: He is brought as a lamb to the slaughter, and as a sheep before her shearers is dumb, so he openeth not his mouth," Isa. liii. 7.

The lamb was to be without spot, to signify his absolute perfection. We are redeemed " with the precious blood of Christ, as a lamb without blemish and without spot," 1 Pet. i. 19.

The lamb was to be separated from the flock four days. The Lord Jesus was separated from men, and consecrated to be the sacrifice for the world, after three or four years spent in his ministerial office, preparing himself for that great work.

The paschal lamb was sacrificed and substituted in the place of the first-born. The Levitical priesthood not being instituted at their going forth from Egypt, every master of a family had a right to exercise it in his own house. Our Redeemer suffered in our stead, to propitiate God's justice towards us.

The blood was to be sprinkled upon the posts of the door, that death might not enter into their houses. That sacred ceremony was typical; for the sign itself had no resemblance of sparing, and certainly the angel could distinguish between the Israelites and the Egyptians without the bloody mark of God's favour: but it had a final respect to Christ. We are secured from destruction "by the blood of sprinkling."

They were to eat the whole flesh of the lamb, to signify our entire taking of Christ upon the terms of the gospel to be our Prince and Saviour. The effects attributed to the paschal lamb, viz., redemption from death and bondage, clearly represent the glorious benefits we enjoy by Jesus Christ. The destroying angel passed over their houses, and caused the Egyptians to restore them to full liberty. That which all the dreadful signs wrought by Moses could not do, was effected by the passover, that overcame the stubbornness of Pharaoh, and inspired the Israelites with courage to undertake their journey to the promised land. Thus we pass from death to life, and from bondage to the glorious liberty of the sons of God, by virtue of Christ's blood.

3. Reasonable persons represented our Saviour, either in their offices, or actions, or in the memorable accidents that befell them.

Joseph, the beloved of his father, sent by him to visit his brethren, by them unworthily sold to strangers, and thereby raised to be their Lord and Saviour, was a lively type of him.

Jonah three days and nights in the whale's belly, and miraculously restored, was a type of his lying in the grave, and resurrection.

Moses, in his prophetical, and David, in his kingly office, prefigured him.

The priestly office, being the foundation of the other two, and that upon which our salvation principally depends, was illustrated by two glorious types, Melchizedec and Aaron. The one the high-priest in ordinary, the other the priest of God by extraordinary designation. I will briefly touch upon the resemblance between Melchizedec and Christ.

Although sacrifices were offered from the beginning; yet he is the first to whom that title is given, as called to that office in a special manner. The divinity of Christ's person, the eternity of his office, and the infinite value of his oblation were shadowed forth by him. Melchizedec is introduced into the sacred story, as one descending from heaven and ascending thither, without any account of his birth or death. The silence of the scripture is mysterious; for the Spirit conducted holy men in their writings. The Levitical priests descended by natural generation from their predecessors, and had successors in their office, which was annexed to the race of Levi. But Melchizedec is represented without father and mother, without beginning and end of days, whose priesthood was permanent in himself, Heb. vii. 3; for things and persons have a double being, real in themselves and notional as they exist in the mind; so that no mention being made of his coming into the world, or leaving it, the silence of the scripture is equivalent to his continual duration. Now in this was an adumbration of Christ, who was the eternal Son of God, and really came from heaven to execute his office, and ascended thither. And although his oblation was finished on the earth and his intercession shall cease in heaven, yet the effects of it shall be eternal in his people, and the glory of it in himself.—The apostle observes another resemblance between the supreme quality of Melchizedec, king of Salem, and Jesus Christ. He was "king of righteousness and peace;" he governed his subjects in righteousness, and never stained those hands with human blood, that were employed in the sacred office of the priesthood. And by those glorious titles are signified the benefits our Saviour conveys to his people. He is the true "King of righteousness;" by which is not intended the righteousness that justifies before God, in which respect he is called "the Lord our righteousness," and is said "to have brought in everlasting righteousness," for that respects his priestly office; in that quality he acquired it: but that title signifies his giving most righteous laws for the government of the church, and his dispensing righteous rewards and punishments, eternal life and death, by which he preserves the majesty of his laws, and secures the obedience of his subjects. And he is "King of peace;" by which we are not to understand his temper and disposition; nor our peace with God, for reconciliation is grounded on his sacrifice; nor peace with conscience, the effect of the other; but that which depends on his royalty. As the King of peace, he keeps his subjects in a calm and quiet obedience; all their thoughts and passions are regulated by his will. The laws of secular kings are only exposed to the eyes, or proclaimed to the ears of their subjects; but his are engraven in their hearts. By the inward and almighty efficacy of his Spirit he inclines them to their universal duty; and will bring them to eternal peace in his glorious kingdom.

1. From hence we have an irrefragable argument of the truth and divinity of the gospel; for it is evident by comparing the ancient figures with the present truth, the copies with the original, the pictures with the life, that eternal wisdom contrived them; for no created understanding could frame so various representations of Christ, and all exactly agreeing with him, at such a distance before his appearance. And if we compare the predictions with the events, it is most clear that the divine knowledge alone could reveal them; for otherwise how was it possible, that the prophets so many ages before the coming of Christ should predict those things concerning him, that exceeded the foresight of all the angels of light? What intelligence could there be between Moses, and David, and Isaiah, that lived such a distance of time from one another, to deliver such things as meet in him as their centre? And these prophecies are conveyed to us by the Jews, the most obstinate enemies of Christianity, who, although they reverence the letter, yet abhor the accomplishment of them; so that there can be no possible suspicion that they are feigned, and of a later date than their titles declare. Their successive fulfilling is a perpetual miracle to justify the truth of our religion. Our Saviour used this method for the instruction of his disciples; "These are the words which I spake unto you, that all things must be fulfilled which were written in the law of Moses, and in the prophets, and in the psalms, concerning me," Luke xxiv. 44. As by dissecting a dead body we see the order and position of parts in the living, so by searching into the legal types, we may discover the truth of evangelical mysteries. Ac-

cordingly Paul framed a powerful demonstration from the scriptures, to prove that "Jesus was the Christ." In his writings he deciphers the riddles of the law, and removes the veil to discover the face of Christ engraven by the divine Artificer. Briefly, by showing the consent between the two testaments, he illustrates the old by the new, and confirms the new by the old. Now what religion is there in the world, whose mysteries were foretold by the oracles of God and figured by his institutions above two thousand years before it was exhibited; whose doctrine perfectly accords with the most ancient, venerable, and divine writings? Can that religion be any other than divine, which God did so expressly predict, and portray in such various manner, for the receiving whereof he made such early preparations in the world? Certainly without offering the greatest violence to our rational faculties, none can disbelieve it. He degrades himself from the dignity of being a man, that refuses to be a Christian.

2. From hence we may understand the excellent privileges of Christians, not only above the heathens, who by divine desertion were wholly strangers to the covenant of mercy, but above God's peculiar people. The Messiah was the expectation and desire of heaven and earth. Before his coming, the saints had some glimmerings of light, which made them inwardly languish after the blessed manifestation of it; but that was reserved for believers in the last ages of the world. That ancient promise, the morning-blush of the gospel-day, that the seed of the woman should break the head of the serpent, and the serpent bruise his heel, signified the bloody victory the Messiah should obtain over Satan; but how little of it was understood! One may as well from the sight of the root foretel the dimensions of a tree, the colour, figure, and taste of its fruit, as from that prediction have discovered all the parts of our Mediator's office, and the excellent benefits resulting from it. The incarnation, crucifixion, resurrection, and ascension of Christ, are in the types and prophecies of the old testament, as corporeal beings are in the darkness of the night; they

have a real existence, but no eye is so clear as to enlighten the obscurity. The most sharp-sighted seer might say, "I shall see him, but not now." The ministry of the law is compared to the light of a candle, that is, shadowy, and confined to a small place; that of the gospel is like the sun in its strength, that enlightens the world, 2 Pet. i. 19. The prophets who were nearer the coming of Christ, had clearer revelations, but did not bring perfect day; as some new stars appearing in the firmament, increase, but do not change the nature of the light. Isaiah, who is so exact in describing the circumstance of our Saviour's death, and his innocence, humility, and patience, that he seems to be an evangelist rather than a prophet; yet the Ethiopian proselyte, who certainly was a proficient in the Jewish religion, understood not of whom the prophet spake. We see what they were ignorant of; not that our sight is stronger, but our light is more clear. The doctrine of the Messiah saved them, but it was then seen at a distance, and under a veil of ceremonies after the Jewish fashion, that concealed its native beauty. The manifestation of it is more evident in the accomplishment, than while the object of future expectation. The passover had respect to their deliverance from Egypt that was past, and therefore easily apprehensible; but it was also a type of the Lamb of God, that was to take away the sins of the world; and in this relation not so clearly understood. Our sacraments have a relation to what is past, and excite the memory by a clear signification of his sufferings. The full discovery of these mysteries was reserved as an honour to our Saviour's coming. He expounded the silent types and speaking oracles by an actual accomplishment and real comment in his person, life, and death. He is the Sun of righteousness, and sheds abroad a light that excels that of all the prophets in brightness, as well as his person transcends theirs in dignity. And how should the evangelical light warm our hearts with thankfulness to God for this admirable privilege! The dim foresight of the Messiah two thousand years before his coming, put Abraham into an ecstacy of joy; how should the full revelation of him affect us! Many holy prophets and kings desired to see the things that we see. "They embraced" the promises; we have the blessed effects; they had the shadows; we have the light. They saw only the veiled face of Moses; "we all with open face as in a glass behold the glory of the Lord." Now what is our duty becoming this privilege, but to be "transformed into the same image from glory to glory, as by the Spirit of the Lord?" The life of every Christian should be a shining representation of the graces and virtues of Christ, that are so visible in the gospel. Their holiness and heavenliness, their hopes and joys, should as much exceed the graces and comforts of believers under the legal dispensation, as their knowledge is incomparably more clear and perfect.

3. To conclude; from the accomplishment of the ancient prophecies in the first coming of the Messiah, we may confirm our faith in those glorious promises that are to be fulfilled at his second; for it is the same divine goodness, the same fidelity, the same power still, upon which we are to build our hopes. And the consideration, that the perfection of our happiness is reserved till that time, should inflame our desires after it.

It was the character of believers of the old testament, they "waited for the consolation of Israel;" it is the description of the saints in the new, they love the appearance of Christ. If they longed for his coming in the flesh, though it was attended with all the circumstances of meanness and dishonour, the effects of our sins; with what ardent and impatient desires should we hasten his coming in glory, when he shall "appear the second time unto them that look for him, without sin, unto salvation!" Heb. ix. 28. Then he will put an end to all the disorders of the world, and begin the glorious state wherein holiness and righteousness shall be crowned and reign for ever. The Christian church joins in that ardent address to our Saviour, Isa. lxiv. 1, 2. And although the beauty and frame of this visible world shall be destroyed, yet that dreadful day shall be joyful to the saints; for then all the preparations of infinite wisdom and goodness, the things that "eye hath not seen, nor ear heard, neither have entered into the heart of man," shall be the everlasting portion of those who love God. "Come, Lord Jesus."

THE END.

www.ingramcontent.com/pod-product-compliance
Lightning Source LLC
Chambersburg PA
CBHW021758220426
43662CB00006B/112